P9-CMC-524

THE DEVIL'S MERCEDES

ALSO BY
ROBERT KLARA

The Hidden White House
FDR's Funeral Train

THE
DEVIL'S
MERCEDES

THE BIZARRE AND
DISTURBING ADVENTURES OF
HITLER'S LIMOUSINE IN AMERICA

ROBERT KLARA

THOMAS DUNNE BOOKS
ST. MARTIN'S PRESS
NEW YORK

THOMAS DUNNE BOOKS.
An imprint of St. Martin's Press.

THE DEVIL'S MERCEDES. Copyright © 2017 by Robert Klara. All rights reserved.
Printed in the United States of America. For information, address St. Martin's
Press, 175 Fifth Avenue, New York, N.Y. 10010.

www.thomasdunnebooks.com
www.stmartins.com

Designed by Steven Seighman

The Library of Congress Cataloging-in-Publication Data is available upon
request.

ISBN 978-1-250-06972-6 (hardcover)
ISBN 978-1-4668-7858-7 (e-book)

Our books may be purchased in bulk for promotional, educational, or business
use. Please contact your local bookseller or the Macmillan Corporate and
Premium Sales Department at 1-800-221-7945, extension 5442, or by e-mail at
MacmillanSpecialMarkets@macmillan.com.

First Edition: March 2017

10 9 8 7 6 5 4 3 2 1

For David, who liked this one

CONTENTS

THE DEVIL'S MERCEDES

1

THE STOCKHOLM DEAL

Though he'd read philosophy at Oxford, strung for *The New York Times*, and slipped into wartime Egypt as an emissary for the State Department, no experience in his thirty-six years could prepare Christopher Janus for what lay at the other end of an ordinary telephone call on a summer day.

It was June of 1948, and Janus was in his office at the Chicago Board of Trade building.[1] The magnificent art deco skyscraper dominated the Loop, stretching its gray limestone neck above the din of taxi horns and the haze of locomotive smoke from LaSalle Street Station. Janus was the managing director of Eximport Associates, a firm in the business—as its name suggested—of exporting and importing. Eximport's inventory was nothing especially fancy: "hardware, office equipment, household supplies, drugs, cosmetics, and other lines," its opening announcement in the *Chicago Tribune* had said.[2] But with the war over, Europe rebuilding, and American consumption surging by double digits, it was a good time to be buying and selling almost anything.

Eximport itself was only two years old, though its founder, a Turkish-born entrepreneur named Milton Baldji, had spent thirty years in international trade. In contrast, Baldji's junior partner was green. True, Christopher Janus had traveled the world and even once lunched with philosopher-poet George Santayana in Rome, but he had never run a business. This day Janus was on an international call patched all the way through to Stockholm. It was one of his first deals, and it wasn't going well.

A few weeks earlier, Janus had exported thirty-five thousand dollars' worth of machinery (auto parts, mainly, including a large shipment of ball bearings) to Sweden.[3] Bildels AB, the firm that had bought the parts, had agreed to pay Janus in dollars. Now that the note was due, however, it was clear that Bildels didn't have greenbacks, only Swedish kronor. In postwar Europe, that currency was unstable, and Janus wouldn't touch it. What to do? Janus's shipment had already left America, and he risked red ink if he didn't come up with something. That's when the buyer suggested a trade.

"What do you have?" Janus asked.

"An automobile," said the Swede.[4]

Janus considered. He *did* need a new car, and there was a long waiting list for them. Scrambling to retool its factory lines after years of armaments production, Detroit had only recently begun introducing new models. "I was tempted to accept the car for that reason alone," Janus admitted later.[5] Still, even a top-of-the-line convertible like a Cadillac Series 62, priced at three thousand four hundred dollars, didn't come close to the money Janus was on the hook for.

"I'm not interested in a car for thirty-five thousand dollars," Janus countered.

"It's not *just* a car," said the man on the phone, pausing. "It is Hitler's."[6]

Adolf Hitler's car. The man was not speaking of a Volkswagen. The automobile in question was a limousine, specifically, a custombuilt 1941 Mercedes-Benz Grosser 770K model W150 open touring car. It was twenty feet long, could carry eight passengers, and, with its 1¼-inch bulletproof windows and armor plating, tipped the scales at nearly five tons.

To this heady piece of information, the offer wholly out of left field, the young Chicago broker could say but one thing: He would call back.

That an automobile that had belonged to the most notorious and despised man of the twentieth century would end up as collateral in a ball-bearing deal out of Chicago was, if anything, the product of incredible odds. And yet, in his memoirs, Janus does not confess to a feeling of surprise in being offered Hitler's car. Perhaps it was merely because wheeler-dealers (and in time, Janus was to become a very good one of those) do not betray their emotions. Or maybe it was because Christopher Janus was accustomed to long odds already. It was, for instance, no small miracle in the first place that Janus was in Chicago with money in his pocket and a tailor-made suit on his back.

His family had come to the United States from Greece in 1910, settling in Montgomery, West Virginia, where his father had found a factory job. The Januses' relative stability lasted only until 1918, when another visitor from the old world, the Spanish flu, slipped in the door. Within weeks, Janus's father, sister, and younger brother were dead. The three surviving family members headed north in 1926, settling in Montclair, New Jersey. But without a bread-winner, it was clear they could not keep going. Janus's older brother struck out on his own. His mother returned to Greece. A now-teenage Janus had few prospects—until Dr. and Mrs. George Biggs, a well-connected local couple of considerable means, took an interest in the polite, dark-haired boy who could read Plato in the original Greek. The Biggses gave him a stipend, a place to stay, and pulled a few strings. By 1932, Christopher Janus was on his way to Harvard.

This Algeresque deliverance would later lead Janus to say that he'd lived life with an angel on his shoulder, one always on the lookout for the right opportunity to steer his way. Another stroke of luck had been meeting his wife, Beatrice, a beautiful heiress whose father, Jeffrey R. Short of the J. R. Short Milling Company, had set them up comfortably in Chicago.[7] Could Hitler's old Mercedes be still another opportunity? Janus had a feeling that it was. An idea had occurred to him during that difficult telephone call: What if he took the limousine and put it on a tour of the United States? Wouldn't Americans want to see the prized possession of the despot they'd just defeated?

"Hitler's car would be a great attraction to make money for charity," Janus later recounted—"and, incidentally, to get my investment back and even make a profit."[8] Surely he could sell the car for a tidy sum, especially once he'd succeeded in getting the newspapers to write about it. In the years just prior to his joining Eximport Associates, Janus had done stints as a daily reporter and later as a copywriter for the ad agency J. Walter Thompson. He understood the value of publicity and how to create it.

But the life-changing patronage of Dr. and Mrs. Biggs had also taught Janus something else: the value of knowing the right people and of soliciting their advice. Janus suspected that bringing such an ignoble automobile to the United States would be no small affair—though, on this spring day of 1948, he had no inkling of just how massive and messy an affair it would become. "I wanted to discuss the project with people who knew show business," he later recalled. And so right after he'd hung up the phone with the man from Stockholm, Christopher Janus called Spyros Skouras.

Though his name is largely forgotten now, in the late 1940s Spyros Skouras was one of the most influential tastemakers in the United States. Even those who didn't know his name had seen his work. Skouras was president of 20th Century–Fox, one of Hollywood's "Big Five" movie studios. He was rich, powerful, and, as Damon Runyon once put it, "a good man to have as a friend."[9]

That Janus even knew a mogul like Skouras was, once again, the work of his angel. After the Japanese attack on Pearl Harbor in 1941, Janus was one of millions of American men who made tracks for the nearest recruitment office. But the sight in Janus's left eye was poor, and the navy sent him away. Dejected, Janus cast about for other ways to help with the war effort. He found them in fund-raising work—first for the families of men off fighting in the navy, and next for Greece, whose citizens were literally starving under Nazi occupation. It was his work with the Greek War Relief Association that introduced Janus to influential business leaders of Mediterranean descent, among them Milton Baldji, with whom he would work at Eximport Associates, and Spyros Skouras, whose telephone number he now dialed.

An executive like Skouras could be anywhere in the world at a given moment, but he spent a great deal of time at Fox's New York headquarters at 444 West Fifty-sixth Street, which is where Janus most likely found him.[10] Fox's East Coast offices filled a redbrick edifice that loomed over the tenement blocks of Hell's Kitchen, a grimy neighborhood of gangsters and longshoremen, which was an unlikely backdrop for the varnished opulence of Skouras's corporate lair, itself bigger than most New York apartments. With his hair slicked back like Errol Flynn's and his face almost as handsome, the pinstriped potentate sat behind a desk the size of a piano, a slab of beige marble sunken into its cabinetry. Behind him, below a map of the world pinned with the location of every Fox satellite office, stretched a long credenza jammed with family photos and telephones.[11]

Spyros Panagiotis Skouras had fled Greece for America at seventeen with two brothers and empty pockets. Yet within four years, using pooled savings from their wages as hotel waiters in St. Louis, the young brothers—"the greatest family act since the Medicis," Skouras would later say—managed to buy their first theater.[12] By 1926, Spyros Skouras was the most formidable operator in the Midwest, with thirty-seven movie houses under his control. He took over theater operations for Warner Bros., then Paramount. The merger between Fox and Twentieth Century Pictures had been his enterprise and had made him into a magnate. Though Skouras still spoke with an accent thicker than a lobby carpet, he was renowned as a passionate and convincing orator. He was also tempestuous, mercurial, and capable of arguing conflicting viewpoints at the same time.[13] Callers to Skouras's third-floor office never knew what they were going to get when in audience with the "tiger of motion pictures," as journalist Jim Bishop would call him, but just like sitting in the front row of one of Skouras's old movie palaces, they could at least be assured of a good show.[14]

When Skouras picked up the phone, Christopher Janus— "Chreese," as Skouras pronounced his first name—explained his export deal gone bad and then posited his idea of accepting this Hitler car in lieu of American dollars. No sooner had Janus uttered Hitler's name than Skouras hit the roof.

"You must be out of your mind! Chreese, are you crazy?" Skouras shouted into the phone. "You want to get involved with that monster Hitler? What will people say? Do you want to ruin your reputation?"[15]

Scolding of this sort was a Skouras trademark. Just a few years later, playwright Arthur Miller—treated to a Skouras tirade in this very office—would observe how the movie executive "worked over many an actor and director with his persuasive mixture of real conviction, paternalism, and the normal show business terrors of bad publicity."[16]

And such tactics usually worked. But when Skouras realized his failure to sway his young friend, he downshifted to a more practical line of reasoning. "Who is going to pay to see Hitler's automobile?" Skouras challenged. "He is the worst person who ever lived."

Janus spoke up to agree: Hitler *was* the worst person who'd ever lived. But, Janus added, he wasn't taking up with Hitler (who'd been dead three years, in any case); he was only interested in his old car—and solely as a business venture.

Skouras couldn't get his arms around such a preposterous idea, and he didn't try. "Take the Swedish kronor and play roulette at Monte Carlo," he said. "Your chances of success are infinitely better." Then Janus heard the line go dead. Spyros Skouras had hung up.

The truth of the matter was that Janus's mind had been made up before he'd even called Spyros Skouras. "When we ask for advice from a friend," Janus later explained, "we often really want them to agree with us."[17] That Skouras didn't agree perhaps deprived Janus of some added assurance, but that was about all. The older man's warnings about the trouble the car would bring had been sensible, but Janus didn't seem to have heard those. He picked up the phone and called the man in Stockholm back.

Yes, he would take Hitler's car.

2

THE SCREWBALL
OF WINNETKA

Janus could have had the car transported to Illinois, but he was so eager to see it that he "went to New York personally from Chicago to receive it," he later said.[1] June 28 was a humid Monday, the bleary skies threatening rain. Well turned out in a striped necktie and lightweight summer suit, Janus found his way to Pier 97, where West Fifty-seventh Street ended in a splay of cobblestones in the shadow of the West Side Highway. Beyond the tall brick archway of the Swedish American Lines' headhouse, the 11,650-ton MS *Stockholm* pulled at her mooring ropes as she bobbed gently in the eddies. The white paint of the ship's 525-foot hull bore a striking contrast to the black iron shed of the pier, sticking out like a bony finger into the foul-smelling bilge of the Hudson.

Since the *Stockholm* could make only 19 knots, her crossing had been slow. Coupled with the time it had taken to load the car in Sweden, Janus had waited three long weeks for this moment, when his prize automobile would be hoisted from the ship's cavernous belly.

Janus looked around and realized that many of the men on the dock were not waiting for the ship's passengers but for him. "Word had gotten out that there was an American who had bought Hitler's car," he recalled, "and when I arrived at the 57th Street pier to pick it up, I was greeted by no fewer than 20 reporters and cameramen."[2] Janus suspected that someone at the Swedish American Line had tipped off the papers, but he was not upset. If publicity is what he wanted for his car, it might as well start now.

Possibly because so many reporters were present, Janus was invited to come up to the forecastle, where the whitewashed cargo cranes moved like giant insect legs above the chain lockers and acres of teak decking. The *Stockholm*'s forward hatchway lay open to the sun, hoisting cables disappearing into the inky darkness of the well below.

Janus watched as the drum winches began to turn. It took a long while for the derrick to pull the Mercedes all the way up, for the car had crossed the Atlantic at the bottom of the No. 1 cargo hold, far down on D deck and well below the waterline. No passengers were permitted this far forward in the vessel, only freight and crew. Hitler's limousine had crossed the ocean in the company of the postal workers and the kitchen boys, whose bunks lay on the other side of the bulkhead.[3]

The car's windshield appeared first, its thick greenish glass braced by heavy strips of chromed steel. Seconds later, a wedge-shaped grille rose into view, fronting a narrow hood that looked longer than a bowling alley. Slowly, the rest of the titanic limousine emerged from the hold, the hoisting ropes netted around the car's fat tires straining to lift the burden. The car was nothing less than a monster—seven feet wide, and nearly as long as the front of a tenement house. The 1941 Mercedes-Benz now floating in the humid harbor breeze weighed as much as an Asian elephant, as much as two thousand red bricks, as much as the clock mechanism for Big Ben.

Even as it dangled in space, the phaeton looked like it was lunging forward, its bulbous fenders slipping over the tires like panther

9

paws, the fat chrome exhaust hoses snaking out of the engine before diving below the running boards. In the full sunlight, Janus could see that what at first looked like a big black car was actually a deep, dark blue. August and imperious, sleek and sinister, this limousine, he was assured, had been the pride and joy of the most hateful man the century had yet produced. And now it was his, all his.

The crane whirred and lifted the Mercedes over the *Stockholm*'s gunwale. The dockers pulled at the ropes to keep the limousine's right front fender from grazing the pier shed, whose reflection danced ominously close in the car's glossy paint. When the crane finally landed the tires on American asphalt, Janus pulled open the limousine's leaden door and climbed in. He obliged the photographers by sitting on the back of the driver's seat and waving. He seemed either giddy or overwhelmed. It was probably both.

"What did you pay for the car, Mr. Janus?" asked a reporter.

He wouldn't say.

"What do you plan to do with it?"

"I don't know what I am going to do with it," Janus said.[4]

He looked down at the car's dashboard, an ivory-white field of forty chrome dials and switches. The steering wheel was as big as a life preserver. The shifting rod, a stalk of glistening black steel, jutted out of the transmission below the floor, its eight-ball-size knob etched with the boxy footprint of the car's six speeds—five forward, one reverse. It must have occurred to Janus then that he had no idea how to operate the goliath beneath him.

Janus slipped down and attempted to start the car, but the engine would not turn over. He had no way of knowing it, but it took seven steps to start the engine of a Grosser Mercedes 770K, and this one also had a hidden master switch behind the instrument panel to foil intruders.[5] The impasse left no alternative: Stevedores ganged up and began to push the Mercedes toward the headhouse. His media moment over, Janus made a quick exit in hopes of finding license plates, gasoline—plenty of that, since the Grosser had a fifty-two-gallon tank—and, of course, someone who could teach him how to drive his new car.

Fortunately for him, help wasn't far away. Zumbach Motor Company on West Fifty-third Street was the official Mercedes-Benz agent for the United States. Its mechanics would, he hoped, know what to do with a custom-built armored touring sedan. All Janus had to do was get the Mercedes down to Zumbach's garage. Someone conscripted an old Buick, which managed to tow the recalcitrant limousine a few blocks downtown.[6]

The next morning's newspapers had a field day with the story, especially the details about the automobile's construction. The bulletproof glass was "thick as a cheese sandwich," the car so big that Janus had to "make sure Hitler [wasn't] in it."[7] The *Los Angeles Times* called the hulking limousine "a getaway car that would be far beyond the wildest dreams of a prohibition era gangster—and the former property of the arch gangster of all time."[8]

Even in a city like New York, stories this unusual didn't happen every day. It was enough to stir the editors at *The New Yorker* from their high-culture perch on West Forty-fourth Street. Philip Hamburger, from the magazine's Talk of the Town department, tracked Janus down to ask if he might have time to give a few of his colleagues a spin in this big car of Hitler's—say, in Central Park? Of course, Janus said.

The writers met him at Zumbach Motors, whose tall brick garage loomed between Sixth and Seventh Avenues. There they found the ebullient Chicagoan beside his Hitler car, now sufficiently gassed up and otherwise mechanically readied. "I haven't had so much excitement since I was voted the Blue Ribbon Baby of Charleston, West Virginia," Janus told his visitors. Janus was also savoring his perverse triumph over the much-hated waiting list for new cars from Detroit. "I've been trying to get an American car for eighteen months," he said. "Took me only thirty days to get Hitler's."[9]

By now Janus had had time to do some exploring inside the car, and he showed the visiting writers some of what he'd discovered: In the passenger-side door was a secret compartment (in all, the car had thirteen of them) for a Luger pistol. A sheet of armor plating, covered in leather, could be raised behind the backseat with four hundred turns of a crank. Three additional seats folded down just behind the driver, bringing the total accommodation to eight passengers ("or four Görings," *The New Yorker* quipped).

Zumbach Motors was supposed to have given Janus driving lessons, but he wasn't confident enough to take the wheel yet. Presently, the garage's mechanic slipped into the driver's seat and started the engine. The eight cylinders purred low and softly. The men piled in, and the limousine pulled out onto Fifty-third Street, hooked onto the avenue, then headed north to Central Park.

"My wife is a little suspicious," Janus told his passengers. Word of the Hitler car had reached the buttoned-up suburb north of Chicago where the Januses lived. "She thinks I'm getting to be known as the screwball of Winnetka," he said.[10]

One thing Janus didn't mention to his guests was that many members of the public didn't share his gee-whiz attitude toward his new car. He'd first noticed this fact the previous day. As the stevedores swung the Mercedes from the dankness of the ship's hold, some began jeering at it. One of the booing wharfies was a man named Paul Purpi, who'd survived his four years in the Wehrmacht, emigrated to America, and didn't much appreciate a reminder of *der Führer* in his new home. Reporters took note, and some had made it the lead of their stories. The following day's *Chicago Tribune* ran the headline HITLER'S CAR BOOED AND HISSED AS IT REACHES NEW YORK.[11] Now again, as Janus and his guests rolled around the leafy, curving lanes of Central Park, "everybody seemed to wave at us," he said, "although some people booed as well."[12]

In short order, the car's appearance would also reawaken very recent memories of American men who'd been in the European theater and, with those memories, all the familiar venom for Hitler. "Your sweatful reporter took more than a passing interest in the arrival here of Hitler's car," scoffed International News Service columnist Bob Considine, who'd reported out of Germany during the war and remembered GIs capturing an armored Mercedes-Benz in its final weeks. "I took a ride in it once upon a time," Considine wrote. "Hitler wasn't with me. He was detained somewhere suffering from a slight case of suicide."[13]

Janus took the derision in stride. Still, it was a taste of what he'd gotten himself into by purchasing an automobile associated with a figure so despised. A strange aura seemed to hang about the big car. As the shiny steel beast prowled the lanes of the park, *The New Yorker* writers couldn't help but remember Leni Riefenstahl's infamous footage of Hitler standing straight as a matchstick behind the windshield, giving the Roman salute to delirious crowds spilling over the curbstones of Nuremberg. But now Hitler was dead, Germany's cities lay in ruins, and history's deadliest war was already three years in the past. During the surreal drive in the park, there were "no crowds, no salutes, no *heil*s," said the magazine. "It was a funny feeling."[14]

Janus's earlier insistence that he had no idea what to do with the car wasn't really true. Clearly, he was just baiting the hook for more publicity opportunities. Within hours, he had them. Offers came in from one Hollywood star, a movie studio, a Chicago gangster, and two circuses to buy the car outright. Janus turned them all down. Then came an invitation to put the car on short-term exhibit at Rockefeller Center. Janus accepted.

The Museum of Science and Industry was part of what tourist brochures advertised as a "full day's entertainment" in Rockefeller Center.[15] Nested in the lower floors of the RCA Building, the tallest of the complex's fifteen limestone towers, the museum was a quirky place that touted "discoveries, inventions, and developments of the scientific world."[16] Its marvels included push-button aroma machines, lightning generators, and, during the war years, an enormous—and presumably defused—bomb that boys could straddle and ride like a pony.[17] Despite the glamour of neighboring Radio City Music Hall and an exhibition space designed by Edward Durell Stone, the museum's "scientific" attractions often swerved suspiciously close to the stuff of traveling sideshows, making Rockefeller Center's conservative management wary. A bubble-gum-chewing contest proposed for 1948, for example, got the kibosh for being "very offensive."[18] But Hitler's high-tech Mercedes—"the most famous used car in the world," as it would be billed—was deemed a good thematic fit.[19]

It was not, however, a good physical fit. Because the exhibit space lacked a freight elevator, the only way to get the Mercedes up to the museum's second-floor concourse was to remove the plate-glass window at 60 West Fiftieth Street and hoist the five-ton limousine in. The operation took place on or around June 8, when an enormous crane anchored itself just across from the Music Hall's vestibule doors, closing off the entire street. At the foot of the RCA Building, beneath the heavy neon marquee proclaiming the Rainbow Room restaurant and the NBC studios, ordinary New Yorkers lacking the money to dine in the former and the status to enter the latter watched as the boom threaded the limousine through the opening. Museum president Robert P. Shaw was watching, too, uneasily. "By hoisting the car into the building," read his sheepish memorandum to Mr. Rockefeller, "considerable public attention and unnecessary agitation on the part of Rockefeller Center was created."[20]

Still, given the fiscal straits that the museum was in (Rockefeller Center had been jacking its rent yearly since 1945), Shaw was probably all too happy to book a headline-generating attraction like the Hitler Mercedes.[21] Janus most certainly was. The exhibit gave him his first chance to try out his business plan of deploying the car for the benefit of charity—in this case, some four hundred war orphans enrolled at Athens College, an American school in Greece. During the war, the Nazis had appropriated the college's campus and burned its books for fuel, leaving it a blackened shell when they retreated. Janus made the most of his opportunity, handing over this bit of prepared copy to the Rockefeller Center Press Office: "Hitler's armored automobile is more than a vehicle owned and used by the most wicked and infamous tyrant of all time. The fact that the car has now come to the greatest free country in the world makes it a symbol that free men always win out, and that bad characters, whether dictators or common hoodlums, cannot long shield themselves behind armor plate, bulletproof glass or iron curtains."[22]

That "iron curtain" bit was a reference to Winston Churchill's recent characterization of the Soviet Union's partitioning of Europe—a muddled reference at best, given that Hitler had loathed Communism and the Soviet land grab had started after the war's end. But why split hairs? Janus's purple prose had shrewdly grouped America's new Cold War foe together with its former wartime one and achieved something singular: In just a few lines he'd managed to elevate his car from a dented war relic to a teachable lesson in democracy, American moral certitude, and the evils of the Fascist state. Simplistic and reductionist, sidestepping the question of how dubious it was to gawk at a mass murder's automobile in the first place, Janus's marketing touch fearlessly anointed a visit to the car as a wholesome pledge of patriotism.

And it worked. Word spread quickly, and New Yorkers flocked to the museum. When Spyros Skouras had argued that nobody would pay to see Hitler's car because Hitler was "the worst person who ever lived," he overlooked a small but critical truth of human nature: Hitler's being the worst man who'd ever lived would be the main reason people *would* pay to see his car.

After handing over their thirty-cents admission, visitors filed up the broad white ramp and found the huge car below the museum's rotunda, cordoned off by stanchions and rope. One of those visitors was Mrs. Michael Yanik, who shook her head in disgust as she peered at the long, gleaming automobile—one, the accompanying placard explained, that had belonged to Adolf Hitler. "Huh," she said. "He might have had inch-and-a-half-thick windows and armor plate, but it didn't stop us none from getting him."[23]

Her husband nodded his assent. "I'd rather ride in my Ford anyhow," he said.

But other visitors were impressed by the machine. A man named Albert Reiger told a reporter from the United Press that he didn't care "if the devil himself" had ridden in the Mercedes. "It's a beautiful job," he said. "I wish I owned it." Nearby, a man in his twenties, named D. E. Ward, whistled long and low as though he were admiring the curves of a bathing beauty and not a Mercedes. "Know what my ambition is?" he volunteered. "To stand up in the front seat of the car, just on the spot Hitler stood. Wonder what I'd feel like."

Standing nearby was Allen Bailey, at the exhibit to represent Athens College, which would receive the proceeds from the exhibit to pay the tuition of students whose parents had been murdered by the death squads of *Reichsführer* Heinrich Himmler's *Schutzstaffel*, or SS. Bailey, overhearing Ward, sadly shook his head.

While the public's reception was mixed, the car had no trouble attracting a paying audience, and its thirty-day residency on Fiftieth Street was a huge success. Before the crane returned to lift the big Mercedes back out the window on the second week of August, one hundred thousand people would come to see it. Most were ordinary citizens. Some, like the comedy actor Roland Young, were famous. One was not even human.

A surviving publicity photo shows four children piled into the limousine's backseat below a cluster of balloons. Behind the steering wheel is TV host Bob Smith and, standing in the right front passenger seat—Hitler's usual spot—was none other than Howdy Doody.[24]

Though it had only been in the country for a few weeks, a powerful mythos was developing around the car, a mixture of fact, embellishment, and supposition. That the limousine weighed five tons, boasted an engine capable of 230 horsepower, and had been obtained in a business deal gone awry—that much was provable.[25] But Janus had also been playing it a bit loose with his facts, probably in an effort to patch over what he didn't know or to make a good story better.

Newspapers reported, for example, that Janus's car could hit a top speed of 130 mph. If a ten-thousand-pound armored limousine could go that fast, it should have been world news: The fastest production car on the planet, Jaguar's two-seater XK120, strained to hit 132.[26] Published stories also proclaimed that Janus's Mercedes hadn't just been owned by Hitler but had been personally designed by him, too, purportedly to "whiz the dictator over Germany."[27] That Hitler was hardly an automotive designer, and generally used trains or airplanes to cover long distances, did not intrude upon these savory details. Nor did the fact (one Janus would soon discover) that the car risked blowing out its tires if the speedometer needle crept much past 50 mph.[28]

In time Janus would also maintain that the car was Hitler's "pet limousine,"[29] and that he had used it "to go with Eva Braun, his mistress, from Berlin to Berchtesgaden," a reference to the alpine retreat in Bavaria where Hitler had built a house.[30] How an ordinary American businessman was privy to such detailed information about Hitler's romantic life was anyone's guess.

But most confusing was the car's origin story. Janus insisted that the big Mercedes "was used in parades and other ceremonial functions for Hitler."[31] But he also explained to the papers that Hitler had given the car to Carl Gustaf Mannerheim, the brilliant military leader and father of modern Finland, as a seventy-fifth-birthday present.[32] Mannerheim, Janus continued, had sent the car to Sweden when the Soviets attacked his country, which was how he'd eventually obtained it.

At best, these historical details felt a little shaky. A military leader whose country was attacked might well send his wife and children abroad to protect them—but his convertible, too? And if Hitler had indeed been shopping for a birthday present, why didn't he give Mannerheim a *new* car? Yet Janus apparently detected no soft spots in his account. Nor, apparently, did any of the reporters think to ask. So the story stood, for the time being.

While his car did its part for good causes, Janus returned to Chicago to consider the problem of where and how he'd display his four-wheeled prize locally. Then, it seems, his angel stirred once more. The telephone rang. On the line was Governor Dwight H. Green, inviting Janus to bring his car to the Illinois State Fair. Green told Janus he'd meet him there personally. Was he interested?

There were probably ulterior motives for the call. Since 1941, the governor had pulled the levers of the infamous "Green Machine," a greasy political apparatus rife with payoffs, patronage, and ties to downstate racketeers.[33] The *St. Louis Post-Dispatch* had been exposing Green for years, and now Democratic reformer Adlai Stevenson was after his job in the coming election. Sponsoring the car would mean good press for a change, and Governor Green needed plenty of that.

Janus liked the idea of bringing his car to the fair, though the invitation didn't help him solve the logistical troubles of driving his Mercedes from New York to the heartland. It wasn't just that operating the car was expensive, it was potentially perilous: How many garages stocked parts for a custom-built German limousine? His experiences in New York had also made clear that security would be a good idea, but how was he to arrange for a law-enforcement detail to cover six states?

These questions shadowed the prospective trip, until the fair's public-relations chief stepped in with a solution: "Why don't we have the car driven from New York to Springfield and have [New York City] Mayor O'Dwyer give some kind of Freedom Torch as a symbolic gift from the mayor of New York to the governor of Illinois?"[34]

It was a cheeseball idea. And both politicians went for it.

With Illinois's highest-ranking official now throwing his weight behind the drive, Janus's Mercedes would enjoy a police motorcycle escort the whole way. But Governor Green was hardly finished. He ordered up a special set of vanity license plates for the trip that read XX-HITLER, which many interpreted to mean double-crossing Hitler. Not one to miss a publicity opportunity, Janus posed with the dark-blue-and-off-white plates for several newspapers, one of which applied the headline THIS MUST BE DER TAG.[35]

Janus decided to retain the Amusement Corporation of America to handle the car's subsequent tours. Clif Wilson, who cut his teeth as an exhibitor at the 1939 World's Fair, came aboard as the manager of the Mercedes. In late July, *Billboard* reported that Hitler's limousine was "expected to prove a powerful Midway attraction," not least because it had enjoyed an "avalanche of publicity in newspapers, over the radio, and in class magazines."[36] But the drive back to Chicago was clearly one that Janus wanted to undertake on his own.

The car's engagement at the Museum of Science and Industry ended on Monday, August 9. Come Tuesday, Janus, now back in New York, was on a tight schedule. He wanted to be on the road by afternoon, but getting the car out of the RCA Building proved every bit as fraught as coaxing it in had been. While the three-thousand-dollar-a-day moving crew tried to wrestle the Mercedes to the window, the five-ton car broke loose and squashed a nearby Baltimore & Ohio train. Fortunately, it was just a cardboard display, but the implication was still amusing: If there was any automobile in America big and mean enough to face down a train, this one was it.[37]

Before Janus could set off, his car was due down at Times Square for a joint recruiting drive hosted by the U.S. Army and Air Force, which President Truman had made into separate military branches just the year before. While attendees milled around, film star and former vaudevillian Edward Everett Horton showed up in a derby, hopped into the front seat, and mimed a panicked driver at the wheel.[38] The photo op over, Janus's Hitler car had an appointment downtown at city hall for an official send-off from Deputy Mayor John J. Bennett.

The sixty-block trip down Broadway turned into an event unto itself. Janus had invited his old friend, the newspaper columnist Jack Mabley, to come to New York in time to join him in the Mercedes for the big trip home to Chicago. "I was late getting to the car at Times Square," Mabley recalled, and the backseats were already filled.[39] One of the passengers was John Schneider, an eighteen-year-old Manhattan boy who'd just signed up for a "three-year hitch" and was being rewarded with the ride of his life—first down Broadway, and then all the way to Chicago. Schneider's enrollment was a twofer: The teen told reporters that Peggy Marshall, his "best girl," planned to enlist in the Women's Army Corps.[40] The United Press hailed that Hitler's car had been made into a "recruiting steed."[41] For his part, Mabley just needed a ride. He jumped into the only spot still open—the front right passenger seat.

The group set off down Broadway with an escort of Jeeps. Mabley stared through the bulletproof windshield in amazement. Thousands of people had turned out to see the car. Many of them looked at Mabley—who was, he now realized, occupying Hitler's former spot—and shot him strange looks. The parade was "the nuttiest ride of my life," Mabley later said. "It was embarrassing."[42]

And it was only the beginning. Down at city hall, a crowd of several hundred people gathered as Janus showed off his car to the deputy mayor—the secret pistol compartments, the layers of bullet-proof glass, all the gizmos. Then it was time to go. By now Janus had driven the beast a few times by himself and concluded that wrestling with a twenty-foot-long car without power steering was "quite a chore," as the *Chicago Tribune* put it.[43] So he'd hired Joe Zenber, a mechanic who knew his way around Mercedes-Benzes, to do the driving. And since an eight-passenger limousine was going to be making the 827-mile run to Chicago empty or full, Janus saw no reason not to make a party out of it. Waldo Logan, another Chicago friend, joined the car in New York, as had Charles Raphael, a Wall Street attorney. The fresh-faced Schneider, his wiry frame folded into the backseat, was along in the official capacity as bearer of the Freedom Torch.[44]

As Tuesday afternoon's sun lengthened the skyscraper shadows, Hitler's Illinois-bound limousine purred out of Manhattan with a police escort.

The era of great American road trips—Kerouac's, Kesey's, Steinbeck's—was still several years in the future, but between August 10 and 13, 1948, Christopher Janus and his cohorts would blaze a pioneering (if now-forgotten) trail. And if the six men riding in the Mercedes weren't exactly larger-than-life figures, the Mercedes certainly was. As Mabley would reflect, "Since this car arrived in America it has provoked a mild sensation."[45]

The security escort had been all worked out, and the presence of Zenber was at least moderate insurance against the car's breaking down. "It won't break down," Zenber insisted. "Anyway," he added, "I've got a book called *Betriebsanleitung für Mercedes-Benz Personenwagen*"—"Operating Instructions for Mercedes-Benz Passenger Cars."[46] The only trouble, Zenber admitted, was that he couldn't read German.

At least Janus and Zenber had plotted the route. Motoring out of New York, they'd swing down through Elizabeth and Newark,

New Jersey, hook west to Harrisburg, and then take the Pennsylvania Turnpike all the way to Pittsburgh. From there they'd follow the old National Road west through Ohio and Indiana, then on into Illinois. In this, the era before interstate highways, two-lane routes that meandered through the countryside were the only options for the long-distance motorist.

Such roads weren't safe for the Mercedes to speed on, but the fact didn't stop the men from speeding.[47] Janus was eager to put the machine through its paces and, as the westward adventurers found themselves on suburban roads, here at last was the opportunity. The experience of gunning an armored Mercedes 770K—longer and heavier than any automobile made in America—was heady stuff. The renowned automotive writer Ken W. Purdy was not along for the Chicago trip but would get his chance at the wheel a few months later, and he recounted what it was like to drive the beast: "With hardly a sound from the starter, the big (468-inch) straight-eight overhead-valve engine fires and warms up quickly at 1,200 rpm," Purdy wrote. "You shove the long gear lever forward and left for first, the clutch comes in like velvet, and you're off." Purdy was mesmerized. The shifter was long as a golf club, yet "smooth, oily, and dead silent." Floating on its independent suspension, the Grosser's mass rendered velocity imperceptible. "When it's moving, rolling along in fifth, it hands out a ride quite beyond comparison with anything else on wheels," Purdy wrote. "The sensation is simply that of a moving house."[48]

As Janus and his crew flew down the highway, the speedometer reached seventy-five. Zenber decided to give the supercharger a try. He mashed the accelerator to the floor.

In straight-eight Benzes of this vintage, the sound of the "blower" kicking in was so loud it was known to force other motorists off the road with its "ear-assaulting, scalp-lifting Mercedes scream," the writer and humorist Ralph Stein recalled, "not unlike that of a lighthouse diaphone at close quarters."[49] Now a creature possessed,

Janus's limousine lunged down the asphalt, its speedometer needle tickling ninety-five as New York State whizzed by, slightly distorted in the bulletproof glass.[50]

Letting the engine flex its muscles was thrilling. And truly stupid. No sooner had Janus pushed his car to its limit than the tires began blowing out.[51] Janus had two spares nudged into the crooks of the fenders, but the car ate them like lozenges. The group had hoped to make Bedford, Pennsylvania, by dark, but there was simply no way. As Tuesday night fell, the famous Hitler limousine limped into a Harrisburg service station, where Janus had all four tires replaced again.[52] His gang had made it all of 150 miles.

As things would turn out, stopping at gas stations would become necessary simply for the fluids. The big Mercedes burned a quart of oil every sixty-six miles and gulped a gallon of petrol every four to seven. Station attendants were happy enough to top the car off, but allowing the monster into the garage was another matter. "When we needed some minor service in a town in Pennsylvania," Mabley later recalled, "they wouldn't let us drive into the service department because the car was so heavy they feared it would go through the floor."[53]

Hunkered down inside the "monster," as he called it, Mabley began to fire off dispatches for his newspaper.[54] His datelines would allow *Chicago Daily News* readers to experience this peculiar adventure from the safety of their armchairs in Pulaski Park and Lake View. When he couldn't find a dateline city, he simply filed from "Somewhere in Hitler's Car."[55]

Leaving Harrisburg Wednesday morning, the Mercedes grumbled onto the Pennsylvania Turnpike. Completed eight years earlier, the highway threaded its way through the Allegheny Mountains via seven deep tunnels. Fortunately, the car was superbly equipped for driving in the dark. It had headlights, spotlights, fog lights, parking lights, and flashing red lights, too. Motorists on the road could only stare slack-jawed at the Mercedes, a make not yet common in the United States, lit up like a parade float and about as big as one.

"Sooner or later, everything turns up on the Turnpike," marveled the *Bedford Gazette*, "—even Hitler's private automobile."[56]

Word of the car's approach moved faster than the car itself, and throngs of bystanders lined the highway and snapped photos as the group passed. "Whenever we stop for lunch we eat in solitude," Mabley wrote, "because the restaurants empty when the auto drives up."[57]

Sometime on Wednesday, Zenber moved over to let Mabley have a turn at the wheel. "Driving Hitler's armored auto is like driving a cross between a jet plane, your family bus, and Hook and Ladder 37," the reporter wrote. The car's twenty-foot length took getting used to, but the supercharger was great for hills, and Pennsylvania had lots of those. Soon Mabley sunk into the soft leather of the driver's seat and relaxed. "Swings around corners like your old Ford," he said.[58]

Chancy as the road trip must have felt to these well-heeled townies, they were never far from aid. Thanks to Governor Green, the Mercedes stayed in watchful eyes of the cops, who motored alongside and guarded it during stopovers. Since Illinois police had no jurisdiction in New York, New Jersey, Pennsylvania, Ohio, or Indiana, the state's Department of Public Safety sent letters out to the cities along the route requesting "escort and proper protection" for Janus and his Hitlermobile. "Because of the peculiar nature of the vehicle and the reactions it might arouse," the letter stated, "it is necessary that law enforcement officials co-operate to escort it safely."[59] One state's troopers would trail the car as far as the state line, then hand it over to the next group of police awaiting its arrival.

The Illinois State Fair's publicity people were eagerly awaiting Janus's appearance, but the man was in no hurry. Janus would stop when he could to let the curious get a closer look at the car while he talked to local reporters. "We achieved fantastic publicity," he later remembered. "The Hitler car was on the way to becoming known all over the country."[60] While Janus had a decidedly Barnumesque side, it was his common touch that made for good copy. Far from being protective of his Mercedes, Janus allowed the young Schneider to take the wheel. The teenager helmed the colossal car through Cambridge City, Indiana, on the morning of August 12.

Mabley calculated that it had taken the group twenty-one hours of driving to get from Harrisburg to Indianapolis, meaning Hitler's limousine was barely making 16 mph as an average cruising speed. But that was hardly the only annoyance. It took a cloudburst over Ohio for the men to discover that the car's windshield wipers did not work. Hastily buttoning down the car's mohair top, the men found the interior suddenly suffocating. "It is like riding in a hearse with the doors closed," Mabley groused.

Soon they found the real source of the trouble: Hitler's seat was—appropriately, enough—hotter than hell. "The best theory is that there is a heater going," Mabley said, "but no one can find the button to shut it off." The men began to discuss the possibility that Hitler's ghost was still in the car.[61]

Sometime Thursday afternoon, Janus pulled into the fairgrounds in Springfield, Illinois. His group had been on the road for two days. As promised, Governor Green was waiting, sporting a fedora and a double-breasted suit, his big-bellied associates joining the crowd of onlookers. Smiling for the press photographers, Janus took the eighteen-inch liberty torch from Schneider and presented it to Green.

The limousine stayed at the fair for its ten-day run. On closing day, a tiny item appeared on page 36 of the *Illinois State Journal*: "The radiator cap was stolen from Adolph* Hitler's automobile now on exhibition at the Illinois state fair. Authorities blamed souvenir hunters for the theft. A $20 reward has been offered for its return."[62]

By the end of September, Janus had owned the big Mercedes for just three months, but the car had already changed his life. The

---

*Note the American spelling "Adolph" (as opposed to the German spelling "Adolf").

crowds and media attention had thrilled him, as had—perhaps a little less—the crackpots and misfits the machine seemed to draw magnetically. A U.S. Marine veteran had called from California, offering Janus the chance to buy Hitler's Luger pistol for five hundred dollars (he declined).[63] The Lincoln Park Zoo had requested one of the enormous Mercedes tires for its gorilla, named Bushman, to play with. A psychiatrist had called, not to examine Janus but to psychoanalyze the Mercedes. Between forty and fifty calls and letters a day had arrived at Janus's office, all of them about the car. He'd received two marriage proposals and several dozen letters warning him that "Hitler's ghost still may be hovering about the automobile."[64] Perfect strangers had sent him presents, often perplexing ones. "The one that mystifies me most," Janus said, "is the gift of a dozen girdles."[65]

But the car had also opened a kind of experiential side door, permitting Janus a glimpse of the postwar human condition that he hadn't bargained for. Janus would long remember the air force pilot from Syracuse, New York, who'd flown down to New York City the same day he heard about the Hitler Mercedes on the radio. Approaching Janus while the car was parked in Times Square, the airman had explained that he'd dropped some of the bombs that had razed Berlin to the ground. The pilot had never seen Hitler but could not suppress the need to see his car.

There was Don Limburg, a radio announcer in Pasadena, who suggested on the air that Janus send the car to the newly created state of Israel, where it could be converted into an ambulance. Limburg had only been joking, but within fifteen minutes the station had one hundred calls with offers of money to ship the car over.[66]

And then there was the woman who appeared like a wraith at Janus's office door. As she approached, she rolled up her sleeve to show him the numeric tattoo that had been etched on her arm at the concentration camp where her parents and brother had died. "Please let me see the car," she said, her voice heavy with a Hungarian accent. "You won't understand. But I just want to stand and look at it."[67]

"When I asked her why," Janus recalled, "she said it was a feeling she couldn't explain."[68]

It had taken a while for this particular feature of the automobile to manifest itself. All the while, Janus and the reporters who chased him had assumed that the simple presence of Hitler's Mercedes on American soil was the story. As the weeks wore on, however, it grew increasingly clear that something else, something ineffable and quite beyond the physical fact of the vehicle—its enormous engine and many hidden features—was drawing people near.

Or keeping them away. Syndicated columnist H. I. Phillips penned an open letter to Janus, warning him, "I am afraid you will not find riding in *der Fuehrer*'s old car any too comfortable. . . . There is bound," he said, "to be a certain aroma in it. . . . No matter how often you go over the motor you will not be able to get all the swastikas out of the valves," Phillips continued, adding: "It is bound to be a very noisy car. How could it be otherwise? Even with Hitler dead three or four years we can still hear him."[69]

Phillips was one of the few voices in the media to suggest that there was a moral and symbolic complexity to the automobile. It was one that reached beyond the conqueror's privilege of owning a piece of a defeated foe and touched on a thornier idea: that anything so inextricably linked to Adolf Hitler, even a car in which he may have ridden, was a kind of poison and perhaps something that *nobody* should own.

It's worth pointing out that Phillips's evocation of Nazi barbarism did not include a specific reference to the Holocaust. Nor, indeed, did any account of the car during this period. The reason is not because Americans were unaware of Nazi atrocities as such. Certainly, the 137,450 Jewish refugees who'd emigrated to the United States were aware of them, and millions of radio listeners had heard Edward R. Murrow report from Buchenwald in April of

1945. But in these immediate postwar years, public discourse about the war's human toll tended to focus on the killing or wounding of over one million U.S. servicemen above all else.[70] In addition, the American popular conception of the Holocaust—the point at which it acquired its capital "H" and was broadly understood foremost as a crime against Europe's Jewish population—was still several years in the future.[71] Indeed, Phillips's reference to Janus's Mercedes limousine being used by "Nazi warlords" extended only to their "blueprints for blitzes," not their genocide.[72] Nevertheless, his broader point was clear enough: The personality of Hitler represented a human toll of appalling scale, and Janus, as the possessor of a tangible piece of the Nazi legacy, would do well to handle it with caution if he was to handle it at all.

In that unique custodianship, Janus sometimes succeeded and sometimes he did not.

Some of his exploits, especially viewed with the benefit of hindsight, seem naïve, if not vulgar, as though Janus failed to fully grasp the dark significance of the relic he possessed. When the Mercedes was not out on tour, for example, Janus used it as his family car. He parked it in the Winnetka house's two-car garage (where it took up both spaces), driving it to the office and the grocery store as though it were Grandpa's Studebaker and not the former conveyance of the man who'd started a war that killed fifty million people. Jutting out from the front of the limousine's grille was a large chrome siren, louder than the wolves of hell. Janus found the horn was handy when his car got stuck in traffic. The fears that Janus's wife, Beatrice, had expressed about him becoming known as the "screwball of Winnetka" were, if anything, prescient. By one account the "abuse" the family took over the car drove her "crazy."[73]

Given the dubious nature of the whole enterprise, it's tempting to presume that Janus may have harbored some secret admiration for Hitler—but nothing in the record suggests as much. Janus openly disparaged "sick individuals who idolize Hitler," and was personally and painfully acquainted with the toll of racial hatred.[74] As a child of Greek descent in the Deep South, Janus had grown up with the Ku Klux Klan—"During the fifteen years that the Janus family lived in Montgomery," he recalled, "several crosses were burnt in our front yard"—and he never forgot the fear that bigotry bred in him.[75] When he'd studied with Santayana in Rome as an Oxford graduate student, Janus was heavily influenced by the philosopher's promulgation of kindness and tolerance. Janus had also helped Franz Wangemann, a Jew who'd escaped Germany as Hitler rose to power, establish himself in the American hotel business. At a time when socializing with heavily accented immigrants (Jews or otherwise) was hardly fashionable in a *Social Register* neighborhood like Winnetka, Janus became Wangemann's close friend. Later, when Janus married, Wangemann—who'd eventually rise to manage New York's landmark Waldorf Astoria Hotel—paid the tab for the Januses' weeklong stay at the Greenbrier Resort in White Sulphur Springs, West Virginia.[76]

While the depth of Janus's involvement with the car was unusual, his devotion to it was not adulatory so much as pragmatic. Having seen the difference he could make in fund-raising for Greece during the war, it seems clear that Janus saw the car largely as a publicity boon and, secondarily, as an excuse for some adventure. "Despite much initial criticism," he would write many years later, "I took a chance, made the trade, and brought the limousine to America."[77] Thanks to his many connections and having married well, it's unlikely that Janus worried much about the high cost of keeping the car on the road.[78] He was free to experiment and took pleasure in doing so. "My education and my background have taught me that there are many things in life more important than money," he said. "I have never shied away from the unusual or the unfamiliar. Risk taking, I guess, is second nature with me."[79] He'd put the sentiment more succinctly as he reached old age: "I love to gamble."[80]

Yet to chalk up Christopher Janus as just a gambler—a "businessman-philosopher who dabbles in adventure," as the *Chicago Tribune* said—would be to underestimate him.[81] Unpalatable as some of his antics may have been, Janus's determination to use the limousine as an engine for charity was genuine and successful. To the war orphans of Greece went the proceeds of the Rockefeller Center exhibit—twenty-five thousand dollars, a considerable sum for the time—and by the fall of 1949, Janus reported that the Mercedes had raised over one hundred thousand dollars.

In time Janus would set up a trust he called the Fight the Dictators Fund, through which he'd distribute the piles of cash that the limousine would generate.[82] As 1950 approached, Janus's Hitler car had traveled twenty thousand miles and stopped in forty cities, and in the following two years it would crisscross the country three times. The hulking automobile stopped at county fairs, rolled in parades, and parked as the guest of local auto dealerships. The admission fees—always voluntary—benefited a staggering array of causes. Janus funneled money to Detroit's Mercy Hall Cancer Hospital, the Hines Hospital in Chicago, Camp Reinberg's program for underprivileged children in Cook County, Illinois, and the Welfare Fund of the Variety Club of Washington, D.C. He contributed to the Illinois Police Fund, the American Legion, and the Military Order of the Purple Heart. Proceeds from the car helped poor cancer patients in Detroit and raised a barn on an orphan boy's farm in Georgia. A young lady in Athens whose parents had been murdered by the Nazis was due to get married; Hitler's Mercedes paid for her wedding dress.[83]

Late in his life, when Janus looked back on his exploits with the limousine, he estimated it had raised one million dollars for 150 charities.[84] The whole point, he had long before explained, "was to have the car do some good."[85]

3

THE GREAT MERCEDES

The very idea of Hitler's car doing *any* kind of good doubtless struck many spectators as a strange turn of things—as indeed it was. When Americans of the postwar period conjured an image of the Nazis, they saw them wearing red armbands, clicking their heels, and, as often as not, stepping into Mercedes-Benzes. The day after ten of Hitler's senior henchmen swung from the gallows in the Nuremberg Tribunal's jail on October 16, 1946, columnist Victor H. Bernstein scorned the war criminals as the men who'd packed the gas chambers of Auschwitz even as they were "having a very good time [as] they drove in very powerful Mercedes cars."[1]

That this was the image many Americans had of the Nazis was only fitting: By now they'd seen the same agitprop that Hitler had foisted on Germany. As masters of their own brainwashing, the National Socialists had methodically built an arsenal of emblems to deploy in photographs, posters, film, and daily life. And though the eagle, the swastika, and the Iron Cross were dominant motifs, Mercedes-Benz kept them company in the ideological tool chest. Mercedes-built trucks, cars, and aircraft engines were central to the conduct of the war itself, but the firm had an equal or even greater value as a symbol—not just of the technological might of the "New Germany," but of the party itself. Thanks in part to Mercedes advertising (which routinely intertwined the Third Reich's imagery with its own), "the three-pointed Mercedes emblem and the Nazi swastika," the critic Herbert Mitgang has written, "were paired in the eyes of the German *volk*."[2]

Mercedes and the German state were paired in the eyes of visitors, too. When the fresh-faced boys of the 1936 United States Olympic crew team returned home to Washington State from Berlin, they remembered the bratwurst, the fräuleins, and the long black Mercedes limousines packed with SS men.[3] In 1938, Colonel Noel Mason-MacFarlane, the British military attaché in Berlin, stopped for gas at a station outside of Linz, Austria, and later described the unexpected drama of being passed by two Mercedes-Benzes "filled with SS bristling with tommy guns and other lethal weapons . . . closely followed by half a dozen supercars containing Hitler and his immediate entourage and bodyguard."[4]

Even the Soviets had observed the central role Mercedes played in the Hitler government, regarding the car as proof of the regime's corruption and Western-style decadence. The secret report on Hitler prepared for Stalin after the war makes pointed reference to Hitler's "enormous and comfortable vehicle," and notes that Hitler's Mercedes limousine was the chariot of conquest he rode into Prague after the Wehrmacht crushed Czechoslovakia.[5]

But the most indelible images of the Mercedes-Benz, the ones that cemented its identity as a vehicle of state, would be found in the Nazi Party's ubiquitous parades and rallies. Motorcades moved in the center lane of the propagandist imagination, and while there was spectacle aplenty at party events—brass bands, men marching by torchlight, banks of blue spotlights trained at the clouds—the biggest prop in this theater of Fascism was a Mercedes: It alone was entrusted to carry *der Führer* himself. Writing in his diary after attending the 1934 Nazi Party Congress in Nuremberg, journalist William Shirer recalled how Hitler stood "like a Roman emperor" in his limousine, rolling "past solid phalanxes of wildly cheering Nazis who packed the narrow streets."[6]

The hypnotic sway that Hitler held over crowds, his ability to keep spectators spellbound and then whip them into a state of devotional ecstasy, was one he could easily practice while standing at a podium. But the addition of an expensive, powerful limousine intensified the sorcery. This effect was centrally planned. A 1939 report prepared by the Propaganda Ministry dissects Hitler's fiftieth-birthday festivities in Berlin minute by minute, including the part where "with screaming engines the great automobiles leave the Wilhelmstrasse: Hitler and his entourage depart for the parade."[7] Propaganda chief Joseph Goebbels considered one of his biggest achievements to be "the style and technique of the Party's public ceremonies"—of which the Mercedes motorcades were the most stylish touch of all.[8]

Aware of the uses to which its special limousines would be put, Daimler-Benz had equipped them with chrome stanchions on either side of the grille. Hitler's car flew the "*Führer* Standard," a garish flag of eagles and swastikas he'd designed himself. Mercedes also built in a special option that only a dictator could appreciate. The right front passenger seat flipped upward on a hinge to reveal a rectangular platform bolted to the floor. Thanks to this feature, the head of state standing atop it would appear six inches taller—in Hitler's case, turning his ordinary five-foot-eight-inch height into a statuesque six-foot-two. Ever mindful of the details, designers at Stuttgart had also fitted the inside edge of the windshield bracket with a heavy chromed handle, so that the standing ruler might steady himself.

Thus deified, rising like a vision from a miasma of exhaust smoke and tossed bouquets, *der Führer* seemed to levitate through the conflux of his faithful. Witnessing this pseudo-religious pageant at the

1936 Olympics, Thomas Wolfe rendered it in the pages of *You Can't Go Home Again*:

> *At last he came—and something like a wind across a field of grass was shaken through that crowd, and from afar the tide rolled up with him, and in it was the voice, the hope, the prayer of the land. The Leader came by slowly in a shining car, a little dark man with a comic-opera moustache, erect and standing, moveless and un-smiling, with his hand upraised, palm outward, not in Nazi-wise salute, but straight up, in a gesture of blessing such as the Buddha or Messiahs use.*[9]

If the full Hitler experience, as it were, unfolded from a seat in the stands, it was even more intense from a seat in the car itself. Some of the most dramatic footage from *Triumph of the Will*, shot during the 1934 Reich Party Congress, comes from the camera in the limousine's backseat, its lens peering over Hitler's shoulder as the mammoth automobile rumbles down the cobblestones, parting a sea of feverous acolytes.

Hitler's architect Albert Speer was often aboard for such rides, and the memory was still fresh as he scratched out his memoirs in Spandau Prison after the war. "The front seat was folded back, and [Hitler] stood beside the driver, left hand resting on the windshield, so that even those standing at a distance could see him," Speer wrote. "The car moved at a snail's pace through the throng. I sat as usual on the jump seat close behind Hitler and shall never forget that surge of rejoicing, the ecstasy reflected in so many faces."[10]

Richard Helms, a cub reporter for the United Press, was the rare American to be afforded a seat like Speer's. He, too, would never forget the surreal quality of the enormous car floating through the tide of upturned faces and reaching hands. There was, Helms wrote, "something mesmerizing about this ride. Only a seasoned movie star might have resisted the weird, vicarious sense that somehow some of the blind adulation of the crowds, who could have had no idea who was riding in the limousine directly behind Hitler, was meant for oneself." No matter one's feelings about the Nazis—and Helms avowedly detested them—he was loath to admit that a trip in Hitler's car "was heady stuff."[11]

"We come like wolves," Goebbels had written, "descending upon a herd of sheep."[12] The Nazis had come, all right, riding in Mercedes-Benz limousines.

Adolf Hitler loved automobiles (unlike trains, he proclaimed, cars were instruments of the individual will), but his devotion belonged to the Mercedes marque.[13] The affair had started early. Hitler owned his first Mercedes at age thirty-four, the red Benz he drove to Munich's *Bürgerbräukeller* on the night of November 8, 1923, to stage the failed coup later known as the Beer Hall Putsch.[14] Despite the charge of high treason, a malleable judge sentenced the Austrian to just five years—only eight months and nineteen days of which he'd end up serving. In Landsberg Prison (hardly a prison in the traditional sense) Hitler dictated his reactionary gospel to bushy-browed secretary Rudolf Hess while admiring the countryside out the window and dipping into a hamper of treats sent by a smitten Winifred Wagner, daughter-in-law of Richard Wagner.

Hitler's notable jailhouse compositions included the first volume of *Mein Kampf,* and also a letter to Jakob Werlin, the Mercedes-Benz representative in Munich. In his September 13, 1924, petition, Hitler expressed his desire to purchase a new Mercedes (a model 11/40, preferably in gray and with wire wheels) on credit, the hoped-for earnings from his book serving as a promissory. "The hardest thing for me at the moment lies in the fact that the biggest payment for my work is not expected until the middle of December," Hitler wrote. "So I am compelled to ask for a loan or an advance."[15]

Hitler got his car, though it appears that the paltry budget of the then-nascent National Socialist Party paid for it. Four days before Christmas of 1924, a shiny new Mercedes pulled up to Landsberg's front gates to collect Hitler. Numerous accounts say the driver was Werlin, though his family has denied it.[16] Whoever was at the wheel, Werlin and Hitler were known to be personal friends, and in the coming years Werlin would become a regular at the Berghof, Hitler's alpine house in Berchtesgaden, and discreetly arrange for senior Nazi officials to receive Mercedes-Benz cars at steep discounts.

On the afternoon of March 13, 1930, Hitler had just concluded an inspection of the Luitpoldhain, the open-air preserve southeast of Nuremberg, which he planned to turn into a rallying ground for the party, when a Magirus truck collided with his car. "The truck's frame and springs must have taken hold of our Mercedes and shoved it diagonally across the open triangle, a distance of about twenty meters, as far as the street corner, only to come to a stop at last at the instant when our left wheels were already touching the curb," recalled Otto Wagener, who was in the backseat.[17] Had the truck not exhausted its momentum, it would surely have eviscerated the future chancellor of Germany—as, indeed, many have subsequently wished that it had. For his life, Hitler thanked not luck but Mercedes-Benz. "The other car was totally wrecked," Hitler recollected to his associates; "on mine only the bumpers and running board were damaged. It was then I decided to use only a Mercedes for the rest of my life."[18]

Fortunately for him, Mercedes was just then getting ready to introduce the finest prewar automobile it had ever built.

As the 1920s drew to a close, Bugatti, Duesenberg, and the rest of the world's leading automakers had struck on the winning formula of dropping enormously powerful engines into long luxury cars. Rolls-Royce unveiled its sumptuous Phantom II in 1929, right on the heels of Maybach's new DS7 V12 Zeppelin limousine. Executives at Mercedes had watched the launching of these lavish land yachts with apprehension, knowing they had no car to compete. Finally, by 1930, they had caught up. Behind the factory gate, officials designated the new automobile as the Type 770 (signifying the presence of a 7.7-liter engine) model W07. To the outside world, however, it would be introduced as the Grosser.

Hand-built by special order, the Grosser Mercedes (in translation, "Great Mercedes" or "Super Mercedes") addressed itself to heads of state and the cream of the merchant classes—people, said the company's advertising, "who desired a car which was quite outside the ordinary run of things."[19] And this car was. At 18.5 feet, 3.9 tons, and 152 horsepower, the Grosser W07 series turned heads when it debuted at the 1930 Paris Motor Show.[20]

The Grosser was designed to impress onlookers, not charm them. Indeed, a whiff of menace seemed to hang about its muscular valances and jutting, V-shaped grille. One critic dismissed the car's "aggressive styling and Teutonic arrogance."[21] The Grosser came in a choice of six body types and features that included velvet upholstery, a liquor cabinet, and an intercom system to call the chauffeur up front. Japan's Emperor Hirohito became one of the Grosser's earliest customers. He ordered seven of them.

Hitler began using Grosser limousines in 1933, when his ascendency to the chancellorship removed any and all limits to his automotive indulgences. Hitler proclaimed he could "not tolerate a car manufactured by another company" as his own limousine, nor any of the others that began to form the column of security vehicles that accompanied him.[22]

Though Hitler's fealty to the Grosser arose mainly from its styling and performance, there was doubtless a nationalistic side to it as well. Hitler drove Mercedes, owned stock in Mercedes, and even claimed to have influenced the designs at Mercedes.[23] For a man obsessed with parentage and race, it would have been no small satisfaction that his Daimler-Benz's lineage reached back to the founding of the motorcar itself; it was as German as King Ludwig.

In 1883, working secretly in his garden shed in Stuttgart, Gottlieb Daimler had perfected the world's first high-speed, four-stroke engine. Three years later, mechanical engineer Karl Benz turned loose his one-cylinder, one horsepower *Motorwagen* (generally agreed to be the world's first automobile) on the leafy lanes around Mannheim. These two automakers—incorporated as Daimler Motoren-Gesellschaft and Benz & Cie.—competed for customers until 1926, when the post–WWI German economic crisis forced a merger, creating Daimler-Benz AG. The union of the companies also enshrined the three-pointed star radiator cap (a symbol of Daimler's ambition to unite land, sea, and air under motorized power) and the name Mercedes itself—an homage to the daughter of Emil Jellinek, one of Daimler's earliest and wealthiest patrons.[24] It must have escaped *der Führer*'s attention that Jellinek happened to be Jewish.[25]

In 1936, six years after unveiling the Grosser W07 series, Daimler-Benz proclaimed the car outdated and sent its engineers back to the drafting table with orders to magnify everything. They began by stretching the wheelbase to nearly thirteen feet and boosting the supercharger's output by 15 percent. Into the new prototype went independent suspension, a five-speed gearbox and, critically, power-assist brakes. With the Mercedes flagship sedan now tipping the scales at 7,804 pounds, few mortals could have stopped the thing otherwise.[26] Among the technological improvements reportedly considered for the new Grosser was an onboard toilet. "Why it was passed up, history recordeth not," an American journalist quipped in the years after the war. "The space is there."[27]

Meanwhile, stylists attended to the body, widening and rounding the lines until the fenders bulged and rolled back to the A posts like ocean waves before flattening out into running boards as wide as the sidewalk. Or seemingly so. For no trick of the draftsman's pencil, no stylish rake of the windshield or bracketing of chrome trim could conceal the naked fact that the car was simply enormous—"bigger, faster, and more elephantine than ever," as the automotive historian Graham Robson later characterized it.[28]

Mercedes designated this second, and final, 770 Grosser model as the W150, pricing it in the stratospheric realm of forty-four thousand reichsmarks—enough money at the time to purchase five Packards, seven Cadillacs, or sixteen Fords.[29] Few customers anywhere were possessed of the financial resources and raw self-importance necessary to even inquire about the new W150. Mercedes, however, had an inkling of whom one such customer was.

In the district of Charlottenberg, a radio tower called the *Berliner Funkturm* pierced the sky with a finger of latticed steel. A warren of gardens and pavilions huddled around the tower's anchorage, and some of Europe's most important business and trade events booked the space year-round. Each February, the much-anticipated International Automobile and Motorcycle Exhibition took over the complex, filling the halls with bunting and trace whiffs of axle grease. It was here, in 1936, that the world learned of Ferdinand Porsche's plans to build a socialist buggy called the Volkswagen. And it would be here, in 1938, that Mercedes would take the wraps off its W150 Grosser limousine.

Mercedes enjoyed prime floor space within the *Funkturm* complex. Below the skylights and the swastika banners strung from the roof trusses, the massive automobile stretched out on the carpet, its muscular body drawing eyes away from the more modest Horchs, BMWs, and Maybachs parked nearby. To show off the car's advanced engineering, Mercedes had one W150 stripped down to its frame, exposing the chassis, drivetrain, and engine—and also the device that gave the Grossers their fearsome reputation on the road.

Bolted to the lower right side of the engine block was a finned metal casing fed by an air channel branching off the intake. This was the *Kompressor* (what the Americans called a supercharger)—an angry pair of aerodynamic screws, driven off the crankshaft, that forced air down through the twin-choke carburetor.[30] Drunk on a volatile cocktail of gasoline and pressurized air, the engine's output would surge from 155 horsepower without the supercharger to a monstrous 230 (one source even ventures 284) with it.[31] At the top of the engine, a pair of fat chrome hoses slithered down and away, expelling the exhaust with a blend of high industrial style and clinical German efficiency.

The *Kompressor* wasn't just a formidable piece of hardware; it was part of what would give the Grosser a name that many admirers preferred. Since "Type 770 model W150 Grosser" didn't exactly roll off the tongue, a popular shorthand developed that combined the 770 series number with "K" (to stand for *Kompressor*) to form 770K. When the Grosser found new audiences in America after the war, this would be the name most often applied to it.

And indeed, the new Mercedes limousine might have easily stolen the headlines on this day, too, were it not for the appearance of an even louder piece of machinery in the hall. "Herr Hitler . . . amid scenes of marching troops and impressive pageantry, opened the exhibition in person," reported the British magazine *Motor Sport*.[32]

With his entourage in tow, Hitler found his way to the Mercedes patch of carpeting. German race-car driver Max Seiler, employed by the company as its technical director, pointed out the new car's features as Hitler gripped the dashboard and admired the latest Mercedes machine, its straight-eight engine chromed and lacquered to a jackboot shine.

Hitler was already a connoisseur of the Mercedes supercharger. He had fond memories of how his driver, Julius Schreck, had used the booster under the hood to bully other cars off the road. "Our supercharger is good for over a hundred," Hitler once blustered. "What fun we had teasing the big American cars. We kept right behind them until they tried to lose us. Those Americans are junk compared to a Mercedes."[33]

One of Hitler's regular companions in the early days was Ernst Hanfstaengl—"Putzi" to his friends—a Harvard-educated raconteur who served as Hitler's press secretary and invariably rode in the backseat. But Putzi's memoirs, penned after he fell out of Hitler's favor and fled to America, make no mention of superchargers or Schreck's fast driving. Instead, his lingering memory of the big Mercedes was *der Führer*'s filling the car with his farts.[34]

Back at the motor show, the British racing magazine didn't think much of the newest Mercedes limousine, since its top speed was merely 103 mph. The Grosser was, sniffed the editors, "a luxury carriage for . . . the use of State potentates."[35] It was a slight to be sure, but a prescient one. Within days of the motor show's closing, after some last-minute tweaks at the factory, a driver delivered the brand-new Grosser 770K W150 limousine to Hitler's office at the chancellery—a birthday gift.[36]

Mercedes' new top-of-the-line model came in six different body styles, from four-seater cabriolets to hardtop Pullmans, but Hitler preferred the *Offener Tourenwagen*, the open touring car big enough for eight passengers. In the years ahead, this vehicle would become associated with him almost exclusively. Hitler liked to give the touring cars as gifts to the few foreign heads of state he favored, and, of course, he liked to use the limousines himself even more. The minimum vehicular complement required to transport Hitler was one 770K *Tourenwagen* and two escort vehicles, but at times his motorcades would stretch to twelve Mercedes-Benzes stuffed with bodyguards and cronies, photographers and valets.

In addition to Hitler himself, senior-level officials were entitled to the use of a staff car and chauffeur. The result was that the Berlin Chancellery, Hitler's Berchtesgaden house, and any of his numerous far-flung field headquarters crawled with party bosses and their drivers. Because Hitler placed loyalty and ideological purity far above the demonstration of competence or intellect, most of these ministers were little more than semiliterate goons in tailored uniforms—"nobodies in their shirtsleeves playing at being [Austrian Prince] Metternich," Hanfstaengl scoffed.[37] Architect Albert Speer shared this view and referred to both the drivers and the bureaucrats they hauled around as the "*Chauffeureska.*"[38]

Responsibility for this rolling Reich fell to Erich Kempka, who bore the cumbersome title of *Chef des Kraftfahrwesens beim Führer und Reichskanzler* ("chief of the Fuehrer's and Reich chancellor's fleet of cars"). Kempka had become Hitler's principal driver in 1936, after longtime chauffeur Julius Schreck died suddenly of meningitis. As a youth Kempka had worked for an automobile distributor before the Gauleiter of Essen hired him as his driver, then put in a good word for him further up the chain of command. By 1932, when Kempka began driving Hitler, he was all of twenty-two years old. Though he routinely handled the finest Mercedes automobiles, Kempka never forgot the tingle of excitement he'd felt when he first climbed behind the wheel of a supercharged eight—so huge he had to sit atop rolled-up blankets to see over the hood. "The mere sight of this vehicle excited my admiration," Kempka remembered. "I had never seen anything like it before."[39]

Kempka had driven candidate Adolf Hitler back and forth across Germany right up until the 1933 elections that would sweep the Nazis into power. During those long road trips, the future chancellor showed himself to be more comfortable in an automobile than in most social settings. Hitler would sit up in front, a road map spread across his knees, and talk to Kempka for hours. Hitler prepared box lunches for his driver and saw to it that Kempka had proper quarters in which to spend the night. "My drivers," Hitler said, "are my best friends."[40] Which was to say: Drivers were as close as Hitler came to having friends.

For his part, Erich Kempka liked Adolf Hitler a great deal, though for a man of Kempka's character, that was not difficult. As coarse and ignorant as he was strapping and handsome, Kempka was the sort of Aryan exemplar that the National Socialists worshipped with calipers and anatomy charts. Of Kempka's three loves in life—automobiles, prostitutes, and liquor—the first two were fine with Hitler, who liked bruisers behind the wheel, preferably with their seminal vesicles emptied. "A good sex life," preached Hitler, "relaxes chauffeurs."[41]

It was Kempka who'd tried to convince Hitler to have Daimler-Benz make a bulletproof version of the Grosser 770K for his use. Hitler had initially resisted the idea, proclaiming he had nothing to fear from the German *Volk*. At considerable risk to his career, Kempka took the initiative and commissioned Daimler-Benz to build an armored Grosser anyway, paying for the car himself with money raised in affluent Nazi circles. Once the car was finished, Kempka stashed it in his garage, waiting for the right moment to bring it out.

That moment came in November of 1939, after an aggrieved carpenter named Georg Elser had hollowed out a column in Munich's *Bürgerbräukeller*—where Hitler was due to speak on the sixteenth anniversary of the failed Beer Hall Putsch—then packed it with dynamite and a timing mechanism. Had the speech not been one of the rare ones that *der Führer* decided to keep short, leaving the hall twelve minutes before the explosion, Hitler almost certainly would have been killed. When a shaken Hitler returned to the chancellery in Berlin, Kempka motored up into the portico with his armored Grosser and showed off some of its security features: the electromagnetic door locks that could be opened only from the inside, the twenty-chamber bulletproof tires, the 1½-inch-thick *Sicherheitsglas* ("safety glass") windows, and the heavy steel armoring—in the doors, the undercarriage, and even the spare tire covers. Hitler was thrilled. "In the future, I will use only this car," he announced, "for I can never know when some idiot might throw another bomb."[42]

From 1939 onward, all of the Mercedes limousines Hitler would use would be Kempka's new, armored type. Aware that the added ¾-inch armor plating and 1½-inch bulletproof glass got close to making the car too heavy to drive, Daimler tried to offset the loads by forging the Grosser's body panels from aluminum.[43] Even so, the protective steel had added 2,690 pounds to the car, nudging its final weight to nearly five tons.

Lavish, corpulent, and tanklike, these armored Grosser 770Ks both served and symbolized Hitler's regime at the peak of its power and excess. They could sail past a sniper and glide over a grenade, even as they pampered high Reich officials on seats of goose-down-stuffed glove leather.

Though he'd become the most powerful man in Europe, Hitler never lost his almost boyish delight with his Mercedes-Benzes. Indeed, some believed he was more attracted to his limousines than to women, with whom the chancellor remained shy and awkward. The Bavarian psychiatrist Jutta Rüdiger, who'd headed up the Nazi League of German Girls in the war years, would recall a chance meeting with Hitler during a reception in 1938. Hitler looked the budding fräulein up and down, then said: "I've always told the Mercedes people that a good motor isn't enough. You need a good body, too. But a good body alone isn't worth anything either."

In later years, Rüdiger would try to decipher the meaning of Hitler's words. "Mercedes cars were his great love," she concluded. "I suppose he thought he was honoring us with the comparison."[44]

Though the irony was most likely lost on Hitler, his Mercedes fleet's singular ability to embody the authoritarian might of his Reich would be equaled only by its capacity to symbolize—indeed, to participate in—its fall.

As early as 1941, Hitler had already made two decisions that would ensure Germany's defeat: opening a second front against the

Soviet Union in June, and declaring war on the United States in December. The last of the Nuremberg rallies had already ended in 1938, and Germans would see less and less of their *Führer* after 1940. The high ornamental purposes for which the Grossers had been built essentially ended with the onset of the war, reducing the 770K to mere transportation. Soon, the government Mercedes fleet would be reduced to far worse than that.

When Allied bombers began the systematic leveling of German cities in 1944, Hitler ordered the windows of his private train to be painted black to spare him the increasingly common view of streets reduced to rubble. By pulling the curtains tightly closed, Hitler avoided these same views while traveling in his limousine.[45] As Hitler turned his back on his own people, his henchmen began killing them. Thousands of ordinary Germans who'd once turned out to cheer the SS now shuddered in terror as the SS paid visits to them in the form of "flying court martial" squads. These tore around the fractioning Reich, summarily executing anyone for perceived disloyalty. With drawn guns and knotted ropes, the executioners invariably arrived in Mercedes staff cars.[46]

With their elongated bodies and black mohair roofs, the Grosser 770Ks had always borne a certain resemblance to hearses. And as death's hand reached for the necks of the top Nazis, the giant limousines became those chariots of death. When Joseph Goebbels evacuated his family from his Ebertstrasse villa on April 22, 1945, he used a pair of 770Ks to take them to Hitler's bunker below the chancellery, where he would shortly murder his six children.[47] Three days later, SS *Gruppenführer* Hermann Fegelein, the dashing horseman who was Himmler's liaison to Hitler—borrowed two of Kempka's surviving Grosser limousines in an attempt to flee Berlin with cash-stuffed bags and a drunken woman who was not his wife. Fegelein was captured and shot.[48] A 770K limousine would also furnish a final ride to Marshal Pétain, architect of Vichy France's capitulation to the Nazis, who rode in the back of the giant limousine as he crossed the German border in April of 1945 to face a death sentence in France.[49]

Hitler's final earthly trip would be taken in a Mercedes 770K limousine as well. On March 15 or 16, 1945, Hitler insisted on making a mad, fifty-mile dash to the Oder front to visit his troops. "On the drive back," Kempka recalled, "he sat next to me sunk in thought, the gravity of the situation casting its shadow over his features."[50] After the chauffeur deposited him back at the Reich Chancellery, Hitler shuffled to the bunker beneath the garden, where he would put a bullet in his brain forty-six days later. Yet even after the event, Hitler's chauffeur and his Mercedes would attend to him, in a fashion.

"Petrol—Erich—*Petrol*!"

Hitler's adjutant Otto Günsche was yelling into the telephone receiver Kempka pressed to his ear, trying to make out the words over the roar of Soviet artillery eviscerating Berlin. Holed up in his subterranean garage, Kempka couldn't believe the order Günsche was barking at him: fifty gallons of gasoline to be hurried over to the chancellery bunker immediately.[51]

Kempka knew the mission was unthinkable: His only remaining gasoline reserves lay hidden in tanks buried below the Tiergarten, the large formal park that stretched across the center of the city. It lay just to the west across Hermann-Göring-Strasse, but with Berlin ablaze and the skies thick with shells, there was no surviving up there—certainly not by toting ten jerry cans of gasoline around.[52] Instead, Kempka surveyed the ruins of his garage. All but two of his Grosser limousines were now "wrecked vehicles," he later wrote, "crushed and covered with masonry from the caved-in concrete roof."[53] Only one option remained open: Kempka ordered his men to siphon off what gas remained in the tanks of the cars.[54]

When Kempka stumbled into the chancellery bunker, he learned that Hitler was dead. Eva Braun, who'd married Hitler the day before, had chosen to end her life with him, and now Kempka carried her body up the twenty concrete steps to the bunker's emergency exit. Hitler's physician, Dr. Stumpfegger, and his valet, Heinz Linge, shared the burden of his body just behind.

When the group reached the garden, the flying shrapnel, phosphorus, and smoke were so heavy they could do little more than hurl the bodies into a bomb crater near the doorway. His corpse contorted in death, Hitler lay in the dirt with his right foot bent inward. "I had often seen his foot in this position when he had nodded off beside me on long car drives," Kempka later recalled. The chauffeur soaked Hitler's body with petrol he'd siphoned from Hitler's limousines, and tossed a lit match.[55]

4

"THE GÖRING SPECIAL"

As Christopher Janus readied his rolling Hitler relic for its national tour at the start of 1950, he may or may not have been aware that his was not the only Mercedes 770K from the Third Reich that had found its way to the United States. Nor was it the first.

As Janus's *Offener Tourenwagen* brooded in the garage of his Winnetka home, there was—631 miles away in Aberdeen, Maryland—another car almost completely identical to it. It, too, was sitting in a garage, where the United States government had mothballed it in 1946. In time, the destinies of the two cars would switch places, but not yet. For now, as the dust thickened on its hood and the tires' pressure drained, this other big Mercedes was the one nobody remembered. In time, however, it would yield a story that nobody would forget.

In the spring of 1945, Joseph Jerome Azara was an ordnance technician, third grade, and three years with the Twentieth Armored Division of the Seventh Army. He was old for the army—thirty-three, and already married. Azara's wife's name was Jackie, but he always called her Blondie. They'd run off to get married in Nebraska before the war, and when it came she didn't want him to go. But what wife did? Azara sweated through basic training at Fort McCoy in Wisconsin, then he shipped out. Now Azara was forty-five hundred miles away in Germany, using his M1 to slay what remained of the Wehrmacht.

The Twentieth Armored Division was a latecomer to the war, landing at Le Havre on February 18, 1945, to join in the final push on Munich. Motoring in a high arc through liberated France and Belgium, the division wet its feet in the Rhine on April 10 before crossing into Hitler's Reich. Or rather, what was left of it: Though the Twentieth was a highly trained combat division, most of the enemy forces it encountered had their hands in the air. Townsfolk doused the Americans in wine, flowers, and cookies.

Nevertheless, as the Twentieth plunged deeper into the dark heart of Germany, the men would discover that there was plenty of war left for them. The division ran into vicious firefights at the München-Reimann barracks on April 29, and the following day it reached Dachau. After the war, the Twentieth Armored's unit history would devote eight angry, agonizing pages to trying to make some earthly sense of what the Americans found at the former munitions factory ten miles from Munich—the forty boxcars filled with corpses outside the camp gates, and inside of them, the "dead, bone-thin bodies stacked like cordwood."[1] By the time the division turned for Salzburg, the shaken men girded themselves for the unknown.[2]

Where they were going, they had reason to expect the worst. Since late 1944, Supreme Allied Commander Dwight D. Eisenhower had chain-smoked over reports from the Office of Strategic Services (or OSS, the forerunner of today's Central Intelligence Agency). These dispatches predicted a German National Redoubt—a last stand of fanatical Nazis prepared to fight to the death in the high alpine terrain of southern Bavaria. Each day the intelligence had grown more chilling: of two hundred thousand seasoned troops and stocks of poison gas, of fortresses connected by subterranean railways, and of specially trained killing squads called Werewolves. "All indications suggest that the enemy's political and military directorate is already in the process of displacing to the Redoubt in lower Bavaria," read a memorandum from the Twelfth Army Group on March 12, 1945.[3] So convinced was the Allied high command of a final, bloody holdout in the mountains that, near the end of March, Eisenhower chose to abandon his drive for Berlin and wheel his forces southward.

By the start of May, Azara's unit found itself in Laufen, a medieval *Altstadt* of whitewashed houses with red slate roofs perched on a bend of the Salzach, a river of snowmelt that gurgled down from the Kitzbühel Alps through Salzburg, eleven miles to the south. The fearsome Redoubt had yet to materialize (nor would it; Germany was mere days from surrendering), but Azara later recalled how the road he scouted behind the wheel of his Jeep was "full of snipers."[4] The sergeant rolled on cautiously, his gaze sweeping the forward terrain.

Then he spotted something.

Off in the distance, some seven hundred yards, was a large automobile lashed with cable to the back of a flatbed railroad car. At this stage of the war, abandoned vehicles littered the German countryside and were hardly a new sight to the men of the Twentieth. But this car was clearly different. It was immense, with civilian curves, and the glint of its chrome made clear this was no *Kübelwagen*. Even from far away, Azara knew he was looking at a fancy car—"some big shot's job," he later said.[5]

Despite the danger, Azara decided to take a closer look. Stashing his Jeep out of sight, the sergeant grabbed his carbine, dropped to his belly, and snaked through the undergrowth. At 250 yards off, he counted four Wehrmacht soldiers by the railroad track. Azara opened fire, wounding one of the Germans, who crumpled and fell. Shifting position, the sergeant shot another through the knee, dropping him as well. The two remaining soldiers scrambled up inside the big car and fought it out with Azara for the next two hours before giving up.

After marching the prisoners back to his outfit, Azara borrowed a truck and returned to the rail siding with a buddy, where he finally got a chance to look over his hard-won prize. The machine, it turned out, was a Mercedes-Benz—a big one, plush and well cared for. Its soft leather seats were fit for a monarch, the carpeted floor of the backseat expansive enough to walk around in. Though the car had appeared to be black from a distance, Azara could see now that it was actually a deep, dark shade of blue, glistening like cobalt amid the grass and wildflowers of the alpine foothills. The limousine, Azara later recalled, looked "like it had just come from the factory."[6]

Well, almost. There were seven bullet holes in the Mercedes— four in the dashboard and three near the trunk, where Azara discovered thick steel plating below the body panel. The windshield and front passenger-side window also bore extensive cracks from rounds that had struck the car, at least one of which was Azara's.[7] But the glass, well over an inch thick, had held. Obviously the car was armored and had been built for someone important.

Sergeant Joe Azara of Wentworth Avenue in Cleveland did not know what a Grosser Mercedes-Benz 770K model W150 *Offener Tourenwagen* was, but he had just found himself one.

Still bolted to the car's fat chrome bumper was a license plate. Its designation—IAᵛ148697—meant nothing to a technical sergeant from Ohio. Nor would it mean anything to any of the other soldiers or the officers of the Twentieth Armored Division.

A gleaming straight-eight engine hunkered beneath the hood and, incredibly enough, it turned over—an odd thing, since Azara's prisoners had claimed that the car had run out of gas.[8] After freeing the anchor cables and ramping the limousine down to the ground, Azara climbed into the driver's seat and motored back to his outfit. (His entry into a U.S. Army camp behind the wheel of a convertible limousine can only be imagined.)

There's no such thing as a bad time to find a free Mercedes, but Azara's timing was especially propitious. Having reached Salzburg on May 4 and encountering little of the fighting that had been predicted, the Twentieth Armored had seen the last of its combat for the war. Major General Orlando Ward had installed his troops on the shore of the Chiemsee, an ice-blue lake lying like a mirror below the jagged horizon of alpine peaks. The American boys rubbed their eyes at their splendorous outpost. "It was one of those abrupt changes of fortune that sometimes occur to combat units," wrote Ward's biographer Russell Gugeler, "from combat rations to champagne, from cold and mud to a warm bath, or from combat to the Chiemsee resort area when both peace and springtime had spread across the Bavarian fields and mountains."[9]

In this mystical woodland during weeks to follow, Azara could be found beneath the hood of his Mercedes. By now, three buddies were helping him: Edwin J. Lasko, a sergeant from Centerville, Michigan; Lieutenant John J. Cole of Bristol, Pennsylvania; and Corporal James A. Pendas of Plaquemine, Louisiana—a particular asset to the team, since Pendas had worked as a mechanic in civilian life. Eventually, the four men got the car's motor pulling like a dray horse, a point of obvious pride for Azara. In time, he'd later say, "everybody knew about my souvenir."[10]

A twenty-foot-long Mercedes was awfully big for a souvenir, but Azara applied the term without sarcasm. The taking of battlefield trophies was a tradition as old as combat itself. As General Omar Bradley famously remarked, "in war there is no prize for the runner-up"—but for the victor, the prizes lay about in virtually unlimited quantities.[11]

For American GIs, the most coveted souvenirs were Wehrmacht tackle—Lugers, daggers, helmets, and especially swastika flags. The men frequently nabbed these items for loved ones back in the States. In his book *Soldier from the War Returning,* Thomas Childers recounts the story of B17 navigator Michael Gold, homeward bound with a "cache of Nazi souvenirs for his younger sibling Lenny," including a German helmet, a swastika armband, and a Walther pistol—treasures that would make his kid brother "the prince of the eighth grade."[12] One U.S. officer somehow came into possession of Hitler's gold-plated pistol, a fact discovered only when he tried to mail it back to his parents in Brooklyn, New York.[13]

But the desire for souvenirs was driven by far more than the want of a keepsake, for proof that one had seen action. As the philosopher and military historian Jesse Glenn Gray has written, souvenirs assumed a near-talismanic significance because they "appeared to give the soldier some assurance of his future beyond the destructive environment of the present. They represented a promise that he might survive."[14] Army brass understood this psychology well enough to give its official sanction to souvenir collecting. Form No. 33—colloquially known as a capture document—permitted GIs to take official possession of enemy matériel. It went far enough to include machine guns.[15]

While technically speaking there was a difference between "legitimate" souvenirs plucked from the battlefield and items looted at will (frequently from civilians), the distinction blurred in practice. Sticky-fingered MPs won the moniker the "Lootwaffe." A dispatch from the Twenty-Ninth Division trekking across Westphalia read, "Advancing as fast as the looting will permit." Even Azara's division would come to be known as the "Lootin' Shootin' 20th Armored."[16] "Looting is irresistible to anyone who has not a real indifference to possessions or a rare sense of duty," wrote Colin MacInnes in his wartime novel *To the Victors the Spoils*. "Even for those who are not thieves by nature, the attraction of what seems at first a delightful game, is overwhelming."[17]

To the soldier, of course, the term was not "looting," it was "requisitioning" or "liberating"—and the grandest object a fighting man could liberate was an automobile.[18] By one account, most British officers storming through the Reich near war's end had acquired a car, and some of them two or three cars. One advancing division swelled to double its original length owing to all of the Axis vehicles added to the column.[19] As the dominant force in Europe, the Americans naturally indulged in automotive acquisitions, too. U.S. generals could be seen racing up and down the autobahn in cars that had belonged to senior German officials. One twenty-two-year-old staff sergeant with the Army Counter-Intelligence Corps relished motoring around Bensheim in a requisitioned white 1938 Mercedes-Benz. His name was Henry Kissinger.[20]

It was no surprise, then, that Sergeant Azara regarded his Mercedes 770K Grosser limousine as a war trophy, albeit a very large one. "Most GIs overseas confined their souvenir collections to something that could be packed in a barracks bag," a local newspaper back home later wrote. "But not so with Tech. Third Grade Joseph Azara."[21]

Azara's joyrides on the roads around the Chiemsee came to an abrupt end when a hellish noise shot from under the hood: The big Mercedes had broken a connecting rod. Now the sergeant was in a fix. Where in the Alps was he supposed to find spare parts to rebuild a 7.7 liter supercharged Mercedes engine? Incredibly enough, the answer lay just twenty miles to the south in a town called Berchtesgaden.

Tucked into a pocket of spruce and larch amid the limestone

mountain peaks, Berchtesgaden was so tiny it was tough to pinpoint on a map. Nevertheless, it was famous throughout Europe and known to Pentagon officials in Washington, D.C.: Berchtesgaden was Adolf Hitler's country retreat.

Hovering twelve hundred feet in the piney air above the village was the mountain region of Obersalzberg, a place of near mystical beauty that enchanted many a visitor. In 1923, one of them had been "Herr Wolf," a cover name Adolf Hitler used in the Nazi movement's early days while hiding from the police. There, Hitler rented, and later purchased, a small house. By 1936, near the peak of his political and financial power, Hitler remodeled his domicile into the Berghof ("Mountain Court"), a monumental chalet whose roofline jutted into the alpine mists like the prow of a warship. In the front of the house, Hitler installed an oversize picture window that enabled him to gaze across the valley to the rocky face of the Untersberg, a mountain where ghosts of the Holy Roman Empire—the red-bearded Frederick I and the armies of Charlemagne—were said to move among the snow-dusted firs. "By night," Hitler said, "I often remain for hours with my eyes open, contemplating from my bed the mountains lit up by the moon."[22]

While Hitler schemed by moonlight, party secretary Martin Bormann set about turning the Obersalzberg into a rustic version of Berlin. As the Nazi high command hastily raised their own chalets to be close to Hitler, Bormann built guardhouses, administration buildings, SS barracks, dining halls, shooting ranges, and, to hold the fleet of Mercedes limousines that had carried Hitler's entourage up into this alpine aerie, a voluminous garage. In this way, the isolated village of Berchtesgaden became the spiritual heart of the Third Reich—or what Private David Kenyon Webster would call "the Nazi's Valhalla."[23]

Webster, a rifleman with the 506th Regiment of the U.S. Army's 101st Airborne Division, would be among the first Americans to see the place. The 101st rolled into the town on the afternoon of

May 4, 1945, to find white bedsheets fluttering from windows of Castle Square: Berchtesgaden had surrendered without a fight. Climbing up into the Obersalzberg above town, its forests splintered by the concussion waves of Royal Air Force bombs, the Americans sifted through the remnants of the Nazi kingdom. Hermann Göring's private train, its parlor cars appointed with double bedrooms and tiled baths, stood abandoned in a clearing. Still smoldering from the fire set by fleeing SS, Hitler's Berghof disgorged the evidence of the Fascist high life: phonograph records, fine linen, and silverware monogrammed A. H. Domestic wealth aside, there was genuine treasure in Berchtesgaden, too: a fortune in cash in twenty-three currencies squirreled away in a barn, and "Aladdin's Cave"—a sealed tunnel packed with five hundred million dollars' worth of oils by the likes of Rembrandt, van Gogh, and Rubens, along with tapestries, statuary, and gold chalices. Picking his way along the mountain district's ruins, where icy waterfalls spilled over books blown from the libraries of Nazi autocrats, a U.S. colonel remarked, "It looks to me like they were expecting to defend this place with wine bottles."[24]

Of most immediate use to the soldiers, however, was Berchtesgaden's motor pool, as huge and varied as the liquors in Göring's cellar. "The Regiment," Webster wrote, "always so short of vehicles that it had to use farm carts . . . suddenly found itself completely motorized, with every man who could drive the proud owner of his own near-new vehicle."[25] The U.S. Army's hierarchy determined how the wheels found on the mountain got divvied up: trucks, Volkswagens, and ambulances went to the enlisted boys, while the brass quickly laid claim to the elegant Mercedes-Benzes.

At least three of these were 770K Grosser limousines. Colonel Robert F. Sink, commander of the 506th Parachute Infantry, appropriated the first. "This magnificent black cabriolet was a hoodlum's dream," Webster recalled. "It had bulletproof glass and a bulletproof body, one of the smoothest, most powerful engines on earth, and a glittering, silver front as imposing as any Rolls-Royce's."

Installing a young private behind the wheel as his chauffeur, Sink "drove through the Alps in oriental splendor," Webster continued, "smoking cigars back in the rear seat, king of the world."[26] Only too happy to ditch his Jeep, General Maxwell Taylor claimed another 770K.[27] The third limousine went to Captain Ronald Spiers, but not for long. After a jealous battalion commander ordered him to turn over the car (shooting out a few windows with an M1 to make his point), a furious Spiers retaliated by starting the 770K's engine and sending the empty limousine off a cliff.[28]

The 101st found so many abandoned vehicles in Berchtesgaden that eventually the division set up an auto dump in a clearing at the base of a mountain. The yard had "the Sunday air of a giant used-car lot where everything was free and nothing was guaranteed," Webster wrote. "Amateur mechanics had a field day."[29]

Apparently, one of those amateur mechanics was Sergeant Joe Azara from the Twentieth Armored, who appeared one day to look for a new connecting rod for *his* 770K limousine.

Ever concerned with keeping up his men's morale, General Ward had arranged for sightseeing tours in the area, which is most likely how Azara had found his way from the Chiemsee down to Berchtesgaden. Azara probably knew that his moving among the 101st's captured vehicles looking for a specific part (one for a straight-eight supercharged Mercedes engine, no less) was bound to arouse suspicion. But the sergeant from Cleveland had the gift of gab, and he knew how to use it: Not only did Azara find his new connecting rod, he managed to get his hands on a complete supercharged motor. "I had to do a little fast talking," he said, "to get that engine away from the 101st Airborne boys."[30]

Azara's luck got even better. While in Berchtesgaden, the sergeant found his way to the "Hitler garage" (probably the long automotive complex Bormann had built opposite the SS barracks), where he encountered a mechanic.[31] Azara told the man about the big Mercedes he'd captured, and the mechanic (having been captured himself) was in the mood to be helpful. He told Azara that his Mercedes had probably broken a rod because American motor oil was too light for the 770K's engine. He'd need a heavier grade if he didn't want to break another rod.

This was a critical piece of intelligence for Azara, as was the next thing the mechanic told him: The Mercedes-Benz he'd found on the back of that railroad car up in Laufen? It had, he said, been Hermann Göring's automobile.[32]

Azara headed north to Trostberg, about eight miles away from his division's headquarters on the Chiemsee, where he and his buddies switched out the engines.[33] Before they finished, Azara decided to remove the metal identification tag from the firewall of the donor Mercedes. Perhaps the sergeant wanted the identification numbers for future reference. Or maybe he was just looking for another souvenir. By now Azara had quite a few of them. During his visit to Berchtesgaden, he'd found his way to the ruins of the Berghof, where he'd helped himself to one of Hitler's lace table runners and a fistful of *der Führer*'s chandelier crystals, too.[34]

Thanks to the heavier-grade oil, Azara soon had the Mercedes running like new. The sergeant was obviously proud of his car and of its unlikely resurrection. A photo from this time shows him behind the wheel. Azara wears his combat helmet. The 770K wears a thick coat of mud. Evidently, the sergeant from Cleveland had done some off-roading.

By all accounts, Joe Azara was a highly likable soldier—a good guy to have a drink with, who played the drums and also loved animals. On this last score, Azara had a way with all creatures great and small that would have made Saint Francis envious. At some point during the Twentieth Armored's encampment in the Chiemsee, the sergeant acquired a pet duck, probably one of the countless mallards that called the alpine lake home. Azara named the duck

Goo Goo and gave her a place of honor in the Göring Mercedes. "The duck would come when he called, and he would drive around with Goo Goo—she'd sit in the front seat," Azara's daughter Debra Weidrick recalls.[35]

Goo Goo would not keep her choice spot for long. In time, Cornelius M. Daly, commanding officer of the Twentieth Armored's Combat Command A, heard about Azara's souvenir Mercedes. So it came to pass, apparently, that a brigadier general approached an ordinary sergeant and asked if he could borrow the car. Wisely, Azara acquiesced. The 138th Ordnance Battalion showed up and covered the car's glossy blue paint with a flat coat of olive drab, adding an oversize white star on each of the rear doors and on the mohair convertible roof.[36] As a finishing touch, the ordnance boys lettered 7A-CAP on the front fenders with white paint, to indicate that the Seventh Army had captured the car.[37]

On May 24, *The Dispatch*, the Twentieth Armored's newspaper, carried a front-page story about the car's new assignment: "The swank, powerful convertible sedan that carried Goering* through his vicious, vain days of all-out aerial war in 1940 until he abandoned it because of no gas and was himself captured, soon will be ridden by his exact opposite, Brig. Gen. Cornelius N. Daly, modest, wiry, commanding general of Combat Command 'A,' 20th Armored Division."[38]

To the men of the division, the car immediately became known as the "Göring Special."[39]

If Azara had any regrets about loaning his dream car to the general, he couldn't have held on to them for long. In a surviving photo snapped just outside the Hotel Gablerbräu in Salzburg, the Göring Special appears to have become rather the party car—stuffed with smiling GIs in the back, Azara's buddy Edwin Lasko at the wheel, and, to his right, Brigadier General Daly along for the ride.

---

*Note the American spelling "Goering" (as opposed to the German spelling "Göring).

(There is no sign of Goo Goo.) "The general got quite a bang out of riding around in Goering's car," Azara remembered. "He used to like to ride in front and push the button that worked the dual horns."[40]

Edwin Lasko loved driving the big limousine, but he chafed at General Daly's refusal to let him put the car through its paces. "Keep it down, sergeant, keep it down," Daly would say each time the needle neared 35 mph.[41] Such granny driving struck young Lasko as ridiculous. "Gee whiz," he groused. "We had a supercharger and everything . . . and those great big beautiful straight roads."[42]

Lasko tried to trick Daly into letting him speed by claiming the supercharger would rust if they didn't use it, but the general wasn't buying it.

Had the Göring Special really once belonged to Hermann Göring? Given the sheer number of automobiles that the 101st Airborne had found in Berchtesgaden, nobody was in a position to know for sure—or, frankly, to care. To what end? The fighting was over and the boys were living high in the land of the Nazi kingpins. Liquor flowed, souvenirs were free, and the henchmen they'd driven out were essentially interchangeable. For example, when Azara later told the story of visiting the Berchtesgaden garage, he claimed to have spoken with Göring's mechanic in one version and Hitler's mechanic in another.[43] David Kenyon Webster even poked fun at the take-your-pick nature of attributing certain treasures to certain tyrants. Colonel Sink had gotten Göring's Mercedes, he said—"or was it Hitler's or Himmler's?"[44]

Azara had seen no reason to doubt what he'd been told by the captured Wehrmacht soldiers and the garage attendant—that Göring's car had been put on the Munich-bound train because there was no more gasoline to be had in Berchtesgaden.[45] Yet evidence abounded that that explanation was suspect. Driving their captured cars around town, GIs were pulling into ordinary filling stations to top off their tanks, so where was the petrol shortage?[46] And if the Göring Special had indeed been the Reichsmarschall's personal vehicle, how could one explain that, just days after Azara captured his big Mercedes in Laufen, Göring himself turned up in his *own* chauffeur-driven Mercedes limousine outside of Salzburg, surrendering to General Robert Stack of the U.S. Thirty-Sixth Infantry Division?[47]

No, there was just no telling if the Göring Special had really been Göring's. But for now it was what everyone needed it to be: a great story.

With the war in Europe now over, it was clear the men of the Twentieth Armored would soon be heading back to the States. Azara would be among them, of course, but leaving Europe raised the troubling thought of leaving his prized souvenir behind. Azara had lent the Göring Special to General Daly in good faith, and now he approached his commanding officer for a favor in return. "When we started home," Azara later recalled, "I asked the general to book passage for the automobile on the ship with us and get it home for me. He said he would try, and did."[48]

In fact, it would take an additional star to make it happen. Major General Orlando Ward, commander of the Twentieth Armored Division, did not condone the army's practice of freely appropriating German motor vehicles, but he made an exception for Sergeant Azara's five-ton souvenir.[49] On a late-July day in 1945, the Liberty ship *George Shiras* steamed out of Le Havre, bound for American shores. Somewhere in one of the ship's five holds was the Göring Special.

Sergeant Azara returned to America aboard the USS *Hermitage*, originally the Italian luxury liner *Conte Biancamano* before the navy converted it to a troop ship. Azara had wanted to take his duck back home, too, but the U.S. Army wasn't going for that. To this day, the Azara family tells the story of how, as the *Hermitage* left Le Havre on July 25, 1945, so did Goo Goo—swimming after the ship in an attempt to come along. But webbed feet were no match for the *Hermitage*'s twenty-four-thousand-horsepower-geared turbines. "Finally they got so far out that Goo Goo turned back," Azara's daughter Debra Weidrick relates. "He wanted to take that duck back, but they wouldn't let him."[50]

The *Shiras* called at Boston's Castle Island on the afternoon of August 8, sidling up to berth seventeen, where a boom swung the Mercedes over the gunwale and winched it down to a lighter beside the quay.[51] Two months after it had been discovered on a railroad car in Bavaria, the Mercedes-Benz limousine of Reichsmarschall Hermann Göring (or whichever Nazi had used it) was in Beantown.

And it was a mess. The Twentieth Armored had evidently had plenty of fun with the limo, which now bore rust pits on its chrome and a nasty dent on the right fender just behind the headlight. The spare-tire covers had disappeared, as had the sun visors and the front license plate. To keep the sea air from rusting the rest of the car on the passage over, the shipmen had slathered the body in a thick coat of brown grease. Out at sea, some of the men finger-painted in the grimy film. One of them—"Okie"—left his name on the left-side quarter panel. A reporter for *Newsweek* called the Göring Special a "battered trophy of war."[52]

And there were plenty of reporters on hand. No relic of *this* magnitude had yet made it back from Germany, and photos of the big car would be all over the next morning's newspapers. The *Brooklyn Eagle* hailed the arrival of "Goering's Chariot."[53] The headline of *The Boston Daily Globe* scoffed that the car's slab-glass windows and armor plating had been made "to Protect Fat Marshal's Hide." For all their disdain, the men were also fascinated by the Grosser 770K, in particular its independent, four-wheel suspension. "It is slung exceedingly low," said *The Globe*, "and rocks on its springs like a baby carriage."[54]

The official paperwork noted that the odometer—which was broken—was frozen at 13,900 kilometers.[55] This was a minor detail at the time. There was a day waiting when it would not be.

That the car was already getting this much attention should have been a sign for Azara that his plans to take his souvenir home to Cleveland might not go as he'd planned. And, in fact, no sooner had the *Shiras* tied up than the sergeant would get some bad news about his Göring Special. "Military Intelligence tapped me on the shoulder," Azara would later recall, "and said it was too big a souvenir for me to keep."[56]

In fairness, it was. Permitting GIs to take home a dagger or a pair of binoculars was one thing, but war trophies of automotive size were something else—specifically, they were U.S. government property, according to Michael McAfee, curator of history at the West Point Museum. "When it was something of obvious significance," he explains, "it was treated differently than a Nazi flag pulled down from a pole."[57] The fact that a two-star general had ordered space for a Nazi limousine aboard a Liberty ship made clear that higher-ups in the government had plans for the car.

For now, the public learned only that the limousine would be sent 330 miles down the coast to the Aberdeen Proving Ground, the army's ordnance facility in Maryland, where it would be "tested with other captured enemy equipment"—whatever that was supposed to mean.[58] The moment couldn't have been an easy one for Joe Azara, but it did not mean good-bye, either.

The United States Army had zero use for a beat-up Mercedes-Benz. But it had ferried the car home for one reason: The United States Treasury Department *did* have a use for it. In a rare example of intragovernment cooperation and insight, Treasury's War Finance Office had requested the Göring Special for a new and entirely domestic mission: fund-raising.

Fighting the Second World War had cost the United States government three hundred billion dollars, much of it financed through the sale of war bonds. The securities sold well on their own, but to stimulate additional interest, the government held periodic Victory Loan Drives, setting sales quotas for each state that encouraged cities and towns to compete with one another. Seven such drives had been held since 1942. The eighth, and last, would begin on October 29, 1945. But with the war already won, it would not be easy. "Absent will be the sense of urgency and need that has characterized the earlier campaigns," a Federal Reserve publication pointed out.[59]

Uncle Sam had dangled various carrots during earlier drives, selling bonds for a shot at winning prizes like Jack Benny's violin or Betty Grable's stockings.[60] This final time, the incentive was as big as it got—a chance to take a spin around the block in Hermann Göring's limousine.[61]

The plan was simple and, for a public flushed with the success of victory, perhaps even inspired. For a marathon, four-week tour, the Göring Special would ply the eastern seaboard, stopping in cities and towns and rewarding those who bought a new bond with a souvenir photo. The Mercedes would stop at town squares and main streets, five-and-dimes and factories—anything to get the car before the public. The junket wouldn't just give ordinary Americans a chance to see and touch a genuine Nazi artifact, but a chance to meet the men who'd captured the thing. The U.S. Army's loan to the Treasury Department was a package deal: the Grosser Mercedes, plus Azara, Cole, Pendas, and Lasko. In fact, Lasko would be doing the driving, just as he had in Germany.

Chaperoning a souvenir recently confiscated from him was asking a lot from Sergeant Joe Azara. Still, the brass had given him a concession. Azara had asked his superiors to be notified if and when the army was finished with the car—and apparently received assurances that he would be.[62]

In the meantime, the tour was the sweetest deployment Azara and his fellow soldiers could have hoped for. The original plan for the men of the Twentieth Armored was to report to Camp Cooke in California, where they would prepare to join the Allied invasion of Japan slated for October.[63] But on August 6, when the *George Shiras* was still two days out of port, the Americans had dropped the atomic bomb on Hiroshima. Nine days later, World War II was over. For Sergeant Azara and the buddies who'd helped him get the Göring Special running, this turn of events meant that instead of storming the cliffs of Honshu, they'd be riding a convertible through Maryland. The trade-off wasn't a bad one.

The Victory Loan Drive began on November 2, three blocks away from the White House. The Göring Special received a stream of curious locals, many of whom had read about the car's arrival in the pages of *The Washington Post*. "Manning the 8,300-pound, 160-horsepower vehicle, which carries 70 gallons of gas in two tanks, will be Sgt. Joe Azara of Cleveland," announced the paper, "who captured it on a railroad siding while under fire of enemy snipers."[64] Azara wore his dress uniform, smiled, answered questions, and posed for photos. It was exciting stuff.

Whether or not Azara and his buddies knew it, the Göring Special was actually just a part of what can only be described as a traveling Nazi auto show.

In the course of its European campaign, the U.S. Army had picked up plenty of the Reich's opulent staff cars. As mentioned above, the 101st Airborne had captured at least three Mercedes-Benzes on its romp through Berchtesgaden, including the 770Ks appropriated by General Taylor and Colonel Sink. Sink had also helped himself to a sky-blue 540K roadster.[65] Twenty-four miles to the south, the 90th Infantry Division confiscated the limousine in which Göring had surrendered at Zell am See.[66] In Paris, Brigadier

General William T. Sexton of the 3rd Infantry Division was also in possession of a bulletproof Mercedes limousine. It was "just a few feet shorter than the *Queen Mary*," cracked Bob Hope, who borrowed the car one night to carouse in Montmartre. "We were touring in Herman Goering's private taxi," Hope recalled. "I should have guessed when I saw how wide the seats were."[67] Rounding out the roster was the Twentieth Armored's Göring Special, care of Technical Sergeant Joe Azara.

Nobody knows how many of these vehicles the army still held at the war's end, but it wound up sending three of them over to the United States for the Victory Loan Drive. The Göring Special, which had landed in Boston on August 8, was the first. By October 20, two additional vehicles arrived—this time in New York, sent over by the 101st Airborne Division: a Grosser limousine and the light-blue Mercedes roadster.[68] All three cars converged at Maryland's Aberdeen Proving Ground, where mechanics cleaned off the nautical grease and got the machines ready for the upcoming drive.[69]

The story makes sense up to this point, and then it swerves headlong into a ditch. A publicity photo released by the U.S. Army Signal Corps on October 30 pictured two glistening Reich autos—a 770K Grosser limousine and a 540K roadster—loaded up with smiling GIs and all ready for the bond tour. But the caption reversed the identities of the two cars, and, more confusing still, the Göring Special and Azara's crew had been left out entirely.[70]

More confounding was the fact that, from day one, neither the army nor the Treasury Department troubled itself to keep any of the cars' identities straight and, in fact, seemed comfortable with using them interchangeably. While the Signal Corps's photograph identified the roadster as Hitler's and the limousine as Göring's, an article in *The New York Times* ten days earlier identified the roadster as Göring's and the limousine as Hitler's, even though the Victory Loan Drive, in fact, had *two* limousines and one roadster—three cars in total—and scant evidence of whom any of them had belonged to in the first place. And because local newspapers only compounded the confusion by using imprecise descriptions and inconsistent attributions, to this day it's impossible to say with certainty which car stopped where on the ensuing Victory Loan Drive.[71]

This much is (mostly) clear: The Treasury Department put each of the cars on its own circuit, starting with the powder-blue roadster, which took off through the center of the country: Pennsylvania, Ohio, Indiana, Illinois, and Iowa.[72] The 101st Airborne's Grosser limousine appears to have ventured farther west, making stops throughout Missouri, Kansas, Colorado, and Nebraska.[73] That left Azara's crew to cover the all-important East Coast stops in the Göring Special, which now wore a fresh coat of dark-gray paint.

A government that had just won history's biggest and most strategically complicated war ought to have been able to take a head count of a few Mercedes-Benzes. Clearly, the army and Treasury Department were more interested in the publicity it took to sell war bonds than in worrying about the provenance of its captured Benzes. In Uncle Sam's defense, there was never any evidence to go on in the first place. "No history of any of these vehicles was furnished this office," Aberdeen's curator Karl F. Kempf would admit years later.[74] What's more, the American public didn't seem to care whose Mercedes was whose, anyway. They were Nazi cars, certainly, and that was enough.

"When these [automobiles] were first brought to our attention we discounted them as war propaganda," read an editorial in the *Statesville* [North Carolina] *Record & Landmark*. But the Nuremburg Trials' charges of Nazi human-rights atrocities, which Americans were just then reading about, were so horrible, so difficult to fathom, that the distinctions between a figure like Hitler and one like Göring faded to insignificance: They were all butchers. If the charges were proven, said the paper, "we won't need the long, sleek cars of the Nazi gangsters to sell Victory Bonds. The people of America, grateful for having escaped the miserable fate that overtook millions of Europeans in occupied countries, will oversubscribe the issue in record time."[75]

As it turned out, the American public *did* oversubscribe the issue in record time—blowing past the nine-billion-dollar quota by buying twenty-one billion dollars in bonds in just forty days. The touring Nazi cars played a big part in generating that turnout.[76] After the weekend kickoff in Washington, Sergeant Lasko took the wheel and started the Göring Special on its swing up the coast.

From the first stops in New Jersey, it was clear that the Treasury Department had accurately taken the temperature of a populace fevered by war and hungry to see a piece of the defeated Reich. The tone of this story from *The Jersey Journal* would become typical: "Hermann 'Call-Me-Meyer' Goering's bullet-proof auto, in which the No. 2 Nazi used to travel about the deluded Reichland until his fuehrer, and the other Germania screwballs fell foul of American might and the auto was captured by American GIs, is to be on display at Journal Square tomorrow."[77]

With Azara, Cole, Lasko, and Pendas on hand to tell stories and pose for photos, thousands of people—"wondering and admiring crowds," said *The Jersey Observer*—lined up to see the Göring Special.[78] In Trenton, a man named Samuel Tankle purchased a two-thousand-dollar bond just for a chance to have his photo snapped with Joe Azara beside the monstrous car.[79] Lasko motored over the Hudson River to New York City, where on November 8 the limousine joined seventy Jeeps and the Fort Slocum Band in a torchlight procession down Broadway to Times Square. After a stop in Brooklyn, Lasko wheeled the Mercedes toward Upstate New York.

In Elmira, the Treasury Department rewarded citizens who bought five hundred dollars or more in war bonds with an actual drive in the car, which now wore a huge tent on the roof that announced "The Fat Pig Herman Goering [*sic*] Automobile." As would be the case with Christopher Janus's Mercedes, many observers noted how the once-nefarious duties the big car had performed had now been inverted. "Once upon a time, Hermann Goering, second only to Hitler in the Nazi sty, used to ride around in this king-size automobile," growled *The Elmira Advertiser*. "Now the car is being used in a good cause."[80]

By November 20, the limousine had double backed through D.C. and stopped in Frederick, Maryland. Azara and his three buddies rode the car in parade-float style down North Market Street, towed by the town's fire engine. Speaking into a PA system to a crowd near city hall, Azara told the story of how he'd captured "the biggest souvenir of WWII" while local police guarded the car as it sat behind a rope cordon.[81] With each day's new appearances, Sergeant Joseph Azara—"G.I. Joe," the papers were now calling him—was becoming every bit as famous as the Mercedes he'd captured.[82]

"For a certain amount of money, you could sit in the car with my dad and he'd tell you the story of what happened. And for more money, he'd drive you around the block," Azara's daughter Debra Weidrick recalls. "He got the key to Baltimore. And he and my mom would go to dinner with mayors and senators."[83]

Azara's heightened social status didn't change his easygoing manner, but it does seem to have hardened his resolve to take the big car home when all of this fund-raising business was done with. "Sure I'm glad to have it used to sell bonds and I don't mind telling my story to spectators," the sergeant said. "But I'm still on the record that I captured that job, it's mine and when it sells a big quota of bonds, I'll still be there fighting to get a clear certificate of title."[84]

In Cumberland, Maryland, some twenty-five hundred people stood in line despite a heavy downpour to see Azara and his car out in front of McCrory's five-and-dime. In Charleston, West Virginia, interest was so high that the Tag Galyean Chevrolet dealership sold tickets for a "Special Exhibit: Herman [*sic*] Goering's Private Sedan with Sgt. Joe Azara—Who Captured It."[85]

As the Göring Special motored deeper into the South, the reception grew steadily more patriotic and impassioned. The *Aiken* [South Carolina] *Standard* nudged its readers to welcome the Twentieth Armored boys and their big Nazi car by pointing out that they had made sacrifices enough: "Sergeant Azara had his troubles getting that car here," said the paper. "All you have to do is buy a bond and Dr. Quattlebaum will take your picture in it. That will be a picture for posterity. Imagine you in Herman [*sic*] Goering's car!"[86]

Photos that survive from this tour only hint at the gravitas with which spectators viewed the hulking artifact from the Third Reich. Some citizens posed alone with Azara, and some in groups. Invariably, they are stone-faced and wearing their Sunday best. Occasionally, Azara's lips are set in a satisfied smirk, as possibly he recalled his derring-do in acquiring this piece of machinery. In Lumberton, North Carolina, a writer for *The Robesonian* picked up on a curious duality: the limousine's ability to maintain a foreboding presence despite the enthusiastic crowds and the celebratory barn dance at the American Legion that welcomed the car's arrival.[87] "Vast, but sleek; luxurious, but ominous appearing," the paper said, "the car gives full expression to the cunning and ingenuity of the enemy defeated in the fields of Europe. In the thick glass and steel sides it expresses the 'gangster' brutality that has been stamped out."[88]

Christmas of 1945 came and went, and after so many weeks in the public spotlight, the Göring Special disappeared from the headlines as quickly as it had made them. The car vanished into one of the cavernous warehouses of the Aberdeen Proving Ground to join hundreds of pieces of foreign military equipment captured during the Second World War.[89] The army took Joe Azara's souvenir back out of the garage in the spring of 1946, this time to drive it sixty-three miles down to the Barry-Pate Motor Company in D.C. to help with a recruiting drive. The limousine sat on the checkerboard showroom floor behind the neon Chevrolet signs in the windows looking out on Connecticut Avenue, its hulking mass never failing to turn a few heads in any crowd.

By now, however, some had begun to question publicly whether the car had ever belonged to Göring at all. During the Victory Loan Drive, Azara had told a local newspaper reporter that the mechanic he'd met at the Berchtesgaden garage had shown him "the special order checking my souvenir as having been built for and assigned to the Reichmarshall [sic]."[90] But the nature and whereabouts of those papers—assuming they had actually shown a link to Göring in the first place—were unknown.

Unable to furnish proof, the army began to inch back from the claim. The newspaper ad announcing the limousine's stay at the Barry-Pate dealership spoke of "the car *allegedly* owned by Herman [sic] Goering" (emphasis added).[91] On the showroom floor, a large placard now stood by the running board. THIS CAR WAS FORMERLY PUBLICIZED AS BELONGING TO HERMANN GOERING; MADE A BOND TOUR THROUGHOUT THE UNITED STATES UNDER THAT PUBLICIZATION [sic], the sign read. HOWEVER SINCE THAT TIME THERE IS SOME DOUBT AS TO THE AUTHENTICITY OF THAT STATEMENT. THERE IS A COMMISSION IN GERMANY AT THE PRESENT TIME INVESTIGATING THE FACTS. If there was indeed such a commission, it left no record of its existence.[92]

The car would be in the headlines one more time. In the summer of 1946, Pottstown, Pennsylvania, held a Victory Homecoming parade. The Göring Special carried the vets who'd endured amputations. At the wheel was a corporal named John Hicks, who apparently decided to take the car on a drive after the parade was over. Then Hicks and the Mercedes disappeared. That was June 8. On June 10, Hicks left the huge car in a parking space at the Elks Home at 61 High Street in Pottstown. State police later determined that the Mercedes had been in a three-car accident in New Berlinville. While Hicks faced AWOL charges, the huge car—now with a few new dents and damage to its siren and fog lamps, was returned to the garage at Aberdeen.[93] It would not see daylight again for ten years.[94]

If the end was rather unspectacular, at least the Nazi Mercedes had done its part for the Allies. It had helped to pay for a war that had spared the planet of slavery under National Socialism. It had helped to replenish the ranks of the military once that war was over. And it had given tens of thousands of Americans on the home front a rare glimpse of a regime that all their years of scrimping, saving, and doing without had helped to defeat. The public's enormous and emotional response to the car—a mixture of smugness, wonder, and disgust—was a foretaste of a regime that Christopher Janus would witness three years later. But Janus's experience would be more intense, more authentic. After all, *his* Mercedes 770K had belonged to Hitler himself.

Or had it?

5

THE FINNISH CONNECTION

Christopher Janus had never doubted for one moment that the car he'd bought was just as the man from Stockholm had advertised. "He said he had a Mercedes limousine that had been the private touring car of Adolf Hitler" is how Janus remembered it.[1] Naturally, some were curious about that claim. During their spin in the big Mercedes in Central Park, the writers from *The New Yorker* had queried Janus about the car's provenance. But he swatted the question aside. "Janus is perfectly sure that it's Hitler's car," the magazine reported.[2]

It's reasonable to assume that Janus knew about the Nazi autos of the 1945 Victory Loan Drive, including the Göring Special, which had generated so much publicity in the years before he imported Mannerheim's 770K. And if he had known about the loan drive, Janus would also have known that salvaged Mercedes limousines with an alleged Hitler pedigree were not new in the United States. Yet in the many interviews he gave, and in the memoirs he wrote, Janus never mentioned any vehicle but his own. Evidently, he believed that his 770K was different. It hadn't been hauled back to America by a bunch of GIs who didn't know Heydrich from

Himmler; his Grosser came with bona fides, a pedigree: It was *der Führer*'s personal vehicle.

Janus was not a naïve man. He would long recall how he'd been conned—once—while importing a pair of Abyssinian cats for a client in Chicago. As the expensive felines moved through a transfer point in Cairo, a bandit nabbed them and substituted a pair of common alley cats in their place. Fortunately, Janus had gotten the creatures at a good price from Emperor Haile Selassie, and his losses were modest. Experiences like this, Janus believed, made him wise to the shenanigans of the import-export business. Yet when it came to the Hitler Mercedes, he felt no tug of doubt. "When I bought Hitler's car," Janus said, "I got the real thing."[3]

At the start of 1950, Janus's car had begun another ten-thousand-mile "patriotic drive" of the United States.[4] He'd invested in a trailer, since the car itself was showing some road wear—including a chip in the windshield left by an Indiana state trooper who'd decided to put the bulletproof glass to the test with his .45 service revolver. By the end of January, the rig's driver was rolling out of El Paso, Texas, hauling the overworked limousine west to Tucson, Arizona. In a few more days, Californians from San Bernardino and Bakersfield would flock to see "Adolph's Big Car."[5]

Janus's 770K had now been in the headlines for two years. And in the course of that time, it had accumulated enough lore to fill its capacious trunk. Not only had the car belonged to Hitler, the newspapers said, it had been Hitler's "personal car," and one "in which he toured conquered areas of western Europe in 1940."[6] The limousine hadn't just "whisked Adolph Hitler over the Third Reich's autobahns,"[7] it had "belonged to Adolf Hitler at the height of his power and at his death when his empire was crumbling."[8] It was Hitler's showcase automobile, "the car in which the former German dictator was often seen during important events of his career."[9] And to top it all off, the car was even "designed by Hitler" himself.[10]

Where had all these tasty morsels of newspaper copy come from?

The reporters, feeling the heat of their deadlines, had evidently printed the details that Janus fed them. And Janus, in turn, had gotten his information from the man in Stockholm. An example: "The Swedes told Janus that Hitler normally did not enjoy driving," reported the *Chicago Daily News*. "However he did like to drive this car because its power gave him exhilaration."[11]

Janus also claimed to have conducted his own "investigation" into the Grosser's past—one that, by whatever means, yielded still more colorful details. There was this chestnut: "Janus said his investigation showed that Hitler's mistress, Eva Braun, who loved fast driving, persuaded him to get the car. Timid Goebbels hated driving in it, Janus said. . . . Hitler got a thrill on the few occasions when he took the wheel."[12] And this one: "Adolf used the auto primarily for state occasions. It was said that once he ran it 100 miles per hour while a frightened Goebbels traveled with him."[13]

The longer the car was in Janus's possession, the more melodramatic its past became. In 1951, a local newspaper in Washington State would report how "this eight-passenger convertible was supposed to have [been] an important part in Hitler's plan of escape. He reputedly had ordered it to be in readiness with a full supply of gasoline, a supply of firearms, foods and items that Eva . . . wanted to have included."[14]

A knock-kneed propaganda minister? A lead-footed *Führer* and his materialistic mistress? The anecdotes about the car were comical, startling, and altogether incredible.

And not a single one of them was true.

Setting aside the obvious problems with these attestations—that a 1941 Mercedes could not have toured anyplace in 1940; that Joseph Goebbels was hardly a timid man; that Hitler chose not to escape Berlin (and, even if he had, it's hard to imagine his mistress reduced to packing guns and sandwiches for the trip)[15]—one has to wonder why Janus himself did not regard these particulars with more skepticism. After all, he'd done a stint as a reporter for *The*

New York Times before the war, and the man from Stockholm, obviously desperate to unload the car, had every reason to embellish its past.

And what of paperwork, of a documentary link between the car and Hitler? The young Chicago importer had none. But in lieu of documents, Janus produced a photograph that, he said, clearly showed Hitler riding in the Mercedes. Had Janus examined that photo more closely, however, he might have noticed a problem. The long, smooth hood of the pictured 770K differed significantly from the hood of Janus's machine, which featured twenty ventilation slits on both sides of its center hinge: The car in the Hitler photo wasn't the same car that belonged to Janus.[16]

It's impossible to say, now, whether the man in Stockholm had hoodwinked Janus, whether the Chicago businessman permitted himself to be hoodwinked, or whether he had gilded parts of the story on his own. Very possibly, it was some combination of all three. But Janus's account of the car's past did contain one detail that turned out to be cold, hard fact: The machine had come to him from Sweden, where Field Marshal Mannerheim of Finland had sent it.

In that single detail lay the car's murky past.

In June of 1939, the German company Soennecken—maker of notebooks, fountain pens, and other fine writing supplies—placed an order for a model W150 Grosser 770K limousine with the Daimler-Benz factory in Stuttgart. Perhaps the car was to be used for a senior executive or for corporate purposes as needed. Whatever the case, Soennecken's timing was bad. Three months after the firm ordered its car, Hitler invaded Poland and touched off the Second World War. Mercedes, beset with military orders from the German government, halted work on Soennecken's limousine. At the Mercedes Sindelfingen plant, a sprawling complex about nine miles southwest of Stuttgart, where the Grosser limousines were built by hand, workers in the special-orders department set the incomplete chassis aside.[17]

Two years later, on June 27, 1941, the factory received an order for a new W150 Grosser limousine, open-topped and armored.[18] This order, like so many of the others, had come in from Hitler's adjutancy in Berlin. But this particular 770K was not to be Hitler's. Scribed in thick fountain-pen strokes on the purchase order is a note that commission no. 398150 was a *Geschenkwagen* ("gift car"), and the recipient of this not inconsiderable gift was to be one Field Marshal Mannerheim in Helsinki.[19]

Frequently referred to as the George Washington of Finland, Carl Gustaf Mannerheim was a revered statesman and brilliant military leader who'd become a national hero in 1918 by leading the White Army's rout of the Bolsheviks and securing Finnish independence. Ever wary of the new nation's belligerent neighbor to the southeast, Mannerheim laid a chain of fortifications—later known as the Mannerheim Line—across the Karelian Isthmus, twenty miles from Leningrad, in case the Soviets decided to come back. On November 30, 1939, the Soviets did, sending a million men storming up the marshy neck of land. Though ill-equipped and hopelessly outnumbered, the thirty thousand Finnish soldiers under Mannerheim were tenacious and fiendishly resourceful. Focusing their fury on the Soviet foreign minister Vyacheslav Molotov—who'd claimed on the radio that Soviet bombs dropped on Helsinki were really just food parcels—the Finns fought back with everything at hand, including gas- and kerosene-filled bottle bombs they nicknamed "Molotov cocktails."[20] After four months of combat, the Finns wrestled the Russians to the negotiating table, and the Winter War, as it became known, was over. "Only Finland—superb, nay sublime—in the jaws of peril—Finland shows what free men can do," said Winston Churchill, deeply impressed.[21]

Churchill was not the only one. In August of 1940, Mannerheim received a confidential communiqué from Reichsmarschall Hermann Göring, suggesting that Finland and Germany might begin quietly cooperating against the Soviet Union, which both regarded as a foe.[22] The letter would open the door to Finland's WWII partnership with Germany as a "co-belligerent."

It was an uneasy coalition. Mannerheim disliked the Nazis and refused, along with his government, to cave to German pressure to persecute Finland's Jewish subjects.[23] But faced with a Soviet menace in the east, and its Baltic supply route already controlled by Nazi-occupied Norway and Denmark in the west, Mannerheim picked his poison. He remembered the chilling words Stalin had spoken to him the year before: "I well understand that you wish to remain neutral, but I can assure you that is not at all possible."[24]

Finland wound up serving as one of the staging areas for Hitler's attack on the Soviet Union on June 22, 1941. Five days later, a grateful Hitler decided to buy Mannerheim a Mercedes-Benz.[25]

At the Sindelfingen plant, frugal Mercedes executives decided to fill Hitler's order by taking the unfinished Soennecken chassis—moldering in the corner since 1939—and completing it. Four months and seventeen days later, the car was ready. Hitler lavished time and energy on the giving of presents, and it is a testament to his utter dictatorial power that he could hand out Mercedes limousines as though they were boxes of chocolates. Such cars, chauffeur Erich Kempka recalled, "were always under construction under my supervision, as gifts from Hitler to foreign Heads of State."[26] Kempka had delivered Grosser limousines to Prince Regent Kyril of Bulgaria and to Spain's General Franco. And on November 15, 1941, he drove to Berlin with a new limousine for Gustaf Mannerheim of Finland.

Hitler was not home. He was at the *Wolfschanze*—the "Wolf's Lair"—a sprawling complex of low timber buildings huddled among the hemlocks in the forests of Rastenburg (today Kętrzyn in northeast Poland). Long fond of using "Wolf" as a cover name, Hitler had moved to his swampy hideout in June to conduct his war campaign in the east.[27] Some two weeks after taking Mannerheim's gift car to Berlin, Kempka arrived at the *Wolfschanze* with it: Hitler would need to inspect the limousine before Germany could give it as an official present.

Dressed in his black SS uniform, Kempka snaked the huge car around the compound's narrow, curving roads and brought it to a halt near Hitler's bunker. *Der Führer* emerged with a small entourage. Kempka had made sure the limousine was fully dressed for the meeting, with blackout covers pulled down over the headlights, and the grille sporting a leather bonnet. Polished to a mirror shine, the Grosser's black and blue paint reflected the evergreen canopy high above. The car was a sinister masterpiece.

His hands thrust deep in his coat pockets, Hitler looked over the twenty feet of Mercedes machinery. The chauffeur turned the chrome handle and hoisted the hood's right wing so his boss could inspect the engine. Then the verdict: approved. Hitler returned to his bloody business, and Kempka busied himself with getting the limousine to Finland.

From the wharves of Stettin (on present-day maps, Szczecin, in Poland), the Germans ferried the limousine north over the icy Baltic to the port city of Vaasa. Accompanied by representatives from the Wehrmacht and Daimler-Benz, Kempka drove the Grosser 230 miles southeast across Finland to a two-story stucco building on a narrow street in Mikkeli, where Mannerheim had established the headquarters of the Finnish Army. They arrived on December 16, a gray Tuesday, the snow thick on the ground. Resplendent in his fur-trimmed field coat, Mannerheim emerged from a slender wooden door and crunched through the snowpack to receive his eight-cylinder gift.

The Finnish commander looked far younger than his seventy-four years, his hooded eyes and trimmed mustache still recalling the dashing lieutenant general he'd been in Tsar Nicholas II's army.

The world had become complicated for him since then. Tall and officious in their death's-head visor caps, the Germans circled like wasps while a state photographer snapped frames for posterity. As Kempka expounded on the 770K's attributes, Mannerheim's face wore a look of unabated fatigue. Then the Germans departed.[28]

Kempka had taught Mannerheim's chauffeur, Kauko Ranta, how to drive and care for the enormous car, and the Finns wasted no time removing the SS license plates that had been bolted on in Germany.[29] Replacing them were ones that read sa1, the letters short for *Suomen Armeija*, or "Army of Finland." It was the badge that Mannerheim put on all of his automobiles.[30] The field marshal's love of fine cars was well known, and it pleased him to park the Grosser alongside his other trophies: a Packard V12 touring limousine and a Mercedes-Benz 320. Both were impressive machines, but the 770K was unlike anything Mannerheim had ever owned.

The car was a cabinet of wonders. There were hidden compartments for pistols. Engine tools rested in velvet-lined leather trays that slipped into a hidden compartment behind the firewall. There was a chauffeur's valise complete with a shaving razor and clothing brush. The Grosser even came with a medical kit equipped with remedies ranging from headache powder to treatments for poison-gas inhalation.[31] One has to wonder if the hideous paradox of that touch was lost on the field marshal or not.

Because Mannerheim's limousine was built to the same specifications as the 770Ks that Hitler used, it also came with the standard *Führer* option. The right front passenger seat tilted up to reveal a platform for standing. But the unobtrusive Mannerheim did not want to make a peacock out of himself. Riding in the back—seated—was fine with him.[32]

Though Mannerheim did not like Hitler, he liked *der Führer*'s gift very much. The limousine was immense and comfortable, its ferocious heating system keeping the interior warm as a greenhouse, even as temperatures outside plunged to twenty below. Far from treating the Grosser as an ornament for state occasions, Mannerheim made it the steed of his daily commute to the office.

That choice saddled Ranta with many burdens. While the chauffeur relished the big Mercedes supercharger (goading the beast up to 106 mph on one occasion), the care and feeding of this exotic pet was considerably less fun. Routine service appointments required a Mercedes-Benz technician—one Mr. Katzenwadell—to cross the Baltic Sea from Germany. The car's ridiculously bad gas mileage and taste for high octane forced the Finns to stockpile German petrol in special dumps all over the country. The monster limousine was too wide for Finnish roads, it destroyed snow chains, and washing it took Ranta no fewer than four hours.[33]

On June 4, 1942, Mannerheim was hoping to spend the day in relative peace. The fact that it happened to be his seventy-fifth birthday made little difference to him: Holding a celebration while Finland was at war was, he believed, in poor taste. Mannerheim's engineer had parked his private train in a stand of birches on the southern shore of Lake Saimaa, near the Immola Airfield. It was a quiet place, though Mannerheim's birthday was not destined to be quiet: Out of the blue came word that a guest would be arriving—uninvited, within the hour. It was Hitler.

The fact of the visit itself was remarkable. Apart from a handful of trips to Italy and to a conquered France, Hitler never left Germany. But he was coming now to Finland. And Mannerheim, not a little piqued by Hitler's presumptuousness, had no choice but to receive him.

Regardless of what the news dispatches later said about this trip, *der Führer*'s visit had little to do with birthday greetings and everything to do with keeping Finland in a war that was not going well for Germany. Eleven months and thirteen days after invading the

Soviet Union, Hitler's troops were clearly in trouble. Despite the initial success of the blitzkrieg, the Red Army had regrouped and hurled itself back on the Wehrmacht. The Russian winter blew in, pinning down Hitler's underequipped divisions with the miseries of hunger and frostbite. By November of 1941, the Germans had suffered 730,000 casualties.

If the German boys conscripted to freeze to death on the Russian plain wanted no part of Hitler's war, neither, increasingly, did Finland. The country had already ceded all of Eastern Kavelia to shape an armistice with the Soviets, and with each passing day Mannerheim had fewer reasons for adhering to his country's "co-belligerent" pact with Germany. Feeling the Finns slipping away, Hitler performed an act unfamiliar to him: He would attempt to be charming.

At Immola, Hitler's Focke-Wulf 200 leveled off on its approach and touched down on the grassy field.[34] A hatchway with a curtained window sprung open, and Hitler clomped down the ladder and into the handshake of Finnish president Risto Ryti. Then a long car drew up that looked familiar to Hitler: It was the *Geschenkwagen*—Mannerheim's Grosser 770K—that Hitler had inspected at his eastern headquarters not six months earlier.

Here again, Adolf Hitler and the limousine that would eventually belong to Christopher Janus crossed paths. Hitler climbed into the backseat along with Ryti, and the giant car lumbered off the airfield.[35] When they reached the railroad tracks, the car stopped; the ground was too marshy to support the 770K's enormous weight. Hitler and Ryti had to walk the rest of the way to the field marshal's train.

Mannerheim approached Hitler on the narrow pathway beside the tracks. Hitler gripped the field marshal's hand and shook it as though he were hammering a nail into place. Mannerheim bowed slightly and said little. Not once during the visit would Mannerheim return the *Sieg Heil*s directed at him.[36]

In the train's dining car, Hitler sat across from Mannerheim at a linen-draped table with the thick woods of Imatra filling the window. The marshal listened, sipping wine, as Hitler railed against the treacherous Soviets, the unreliable Italians, and his own army's inability to fight in cold weather. "You cannot wage war in winter," Hitler complained to the Finnish commander who'd successfully waged war in winter.[37] Hitler's attempt at charm was as bad as his haircut.

Hitler awarded Mannerheim the Grand Cross of the Order of the German Eagle, a gold decoration that did not impress the field marshal. In Nazi Germany, medals were a cheap way to buy loyalty; Hitler kept a whole box of Knight's Crosses on hand for convenient dispensing.[38] A German newsreel of this meeting would soon bleat about "the spirit of the warm friendship between Germany and Finland," and a "historic brotherhood-in-arms."[39] But the statements were as empty as all the others that skulked out of Goebbels's propaganda ministry. The Finnish-German pact, a marriage at gunpoint, would disintegrate before 1944 was up.

When the meeting ended, the Finns returned Hitler to his waiting plane in the field marshal's Grosser Mercedes.[40] The ride in the 770K would be the third time Hitler had seen the car and the second time he would ride in it.

It was also the last contact Hitler would ever have with Mannerheim's limousine.

With the end of WWII nearly in sight, the Finns only clung tighter to the man who had delivered them through the maelstrom. In 1944, Finland elevated Mannerheim to the presidency. But when the old soldier arrived for the inauguration ceremony, he stepped out of his Packard 12. The 770K, so familiar to Mannerheim's admirers over the preceding two years, had disappeared.

Nobody knew better than Mannerheim himself the treacherous games of diplomacy that had been necessary to play with Germany in the name of preserving Finland, and nothing reeked of that odious pact more than the Mercedes-Benz from Hitler. Whatever his personal attachments to the car, Mannerheim knew he could never be seen again with it, since it had never been *just* a car to start with. The Grosser "had always been associated with its donator," is how the Finnish government has since explained things. "It would have been impossible to use it for political reasons."[41] Hitler notwithstanding, nor would it have been appropriate for the president of a country broken by war to be seen motoring around in a plush limousine.[42]

For all of 1945, the troublesome automobile remained out of sight. Increasingly, so did Mannerheim. Now age seventy-eight and plagued by lung and intestinal ailments, Mannerheim submitted his resignation in March of 1946. The time had come to write his memoirs. Mannerheim retired to Switzerland, and he sold the big Mercedes.

The car surfaced in Stockholm a year later, sitting behind plate glass on the Birger Jarlsgatan, the opulent boulevard of shops in the central city. Gustaf Byrenius AB, the dealership that purchased Mannerheim's armored limousine, understood that the cars hardest to sell are also the ones that eventually sell themselves. And so it happened: The crowds clustering at the showroom windows day in and day out came to include a man named Gösta Sverdrup. A collector of luxury automobiles, Sverdrup fell for the Grosser even before he wheeled the monster out onto the cobblestones for a test drive. Its price must have been dear: Sverdrup, who owned a brewery, traded in his Mercedes 540K to swing the purchase. But after transplanting his roadster's large chrome siren onto the Grosser's front bumper, Sverdrup completed the paperwork and Mannerheim's archaic Mercedes, onetime gift from Adolf Hitler, was his.

One must suppose that Sverdrup was happy with his new limousine, for a while at least. But the collector quickly learned—as all the car's subsequent owners inevitably would—that the 770K was a demanding mistress. Its abominable gas mileage was a hardship, even for an affluent man, in a country suffering a severe petrol shortage. Crowds dogged the limousine everywhere, gathering so thick and deep around the running boards that Sverdrup often had to elbow his way to the driver's seat. His family pressed him to sell. By the summer of 1947, Sverdrup had had enough. The Mannerheim Mercedes found its next owner in Arne Gustafsson AB, an automotive dealer in Sweden's southeastern city of Eskilstuna.

Gustafsson gave the Grosser Mercedes a prominent place in his showroom, but Eskilstuna was not a big city: Months elapsed and no buyers appeared. Finally, nearly a year after acquiring the car, Gustafsson found a way to unload it. An automotive-parts firm in Stockholm called Bildels AB had run into trouble financing its ball-bearing import from Christopher Janus, and the solution revealed itself immediately: Bildels purchased the limousine from Gustafsson, then offered it in trade to the Chicago exporter.[43]

It remains unclear exactly how the story that the Mercedes was Hitler's personal car got started—but it surely got started here.[44] Perhaps the man from Stockholm recounted the car's ownership details accurately and Janus misunderstood because of the language barrier. More likely, though, drawing from the rich and varied traditions of used-car salesmanship, the seller embellished the car's credentials a little. Or a lot. In the course of a brief telephone call, Field Marshal Mannerheim's old limousine took on the identity and full notoriety of the despot who'd inspected it once and ridden in it twice: "It's not *just* a car," the man from Stockholm told Janus over the costly international call. "It is Hitler's."[45]

Bildels dispatched the car to the city of Gothenburg on Sweden's west coast, where the liner *Stockholm* called on its transatlantic runs. On June 18, 1948, the *Stockholm*'s distinctive white hull rode in the chilly water of the Göta älv estuary, its long flank shouldered into the Gothenburg staith. A freight crane threw a latticework of shadows across a small crowd below. They watched as the stevedores fastened rope slings to each of the car's enormous wheels and then hooked them to the hoisting tackle. A crane coughed and lifted the five-ton limousine off the ground, swinging it out over the watery breach. Tipping its trunk to Europe, the car disappeared into the hold. Its American journey had begun.

By January of 1950, as the tractor-trailer hauling Janus's Hitler car swung west for California, an unlikely character reentered the picture. He was the man who'd pleaded with Janus not to go near the machine in the first place. Now that man wanted very badly to get his own hands on it.

Spyros Skouras wanted to cast the car in a Hollywood movie.

Two years had passed since the 20th Century–Fox president had admonished Janus to stay away from the Grosser said to be Hitler's. But Skouras had since experienced a change of heart when an unexpected project had landed on his marble-topped desk.

It had come from Darryl F. Zanuck, Fox's cigar-chomping, skirt-chasing production chief. In February of 1950, Zanuck was finalizing his acquisition of the film rights to *Rommel,* a bestselling biography of Erwin Rommel, the Wehrmacht's brilliant tactician and foremost apostle of the blitzkrieg. Having spent years turning out censor-approved rah-rah films for the Office of War Information, Hollywood would normally never have touched a sympathetic portrayal of a German military chief, but this book was different.

Its author was Desmond Young, a British lieutenant colonel who'd been taken prisoner by Rommel's forces in North Africa. Once in the Wehrmacht's clutches, Young expected to be executed. Instead, he and his fellow prisoners were fed, given medical attention, and treated with respect—all at Rommel's insistence. Young had known that Erwin Rommel was the legendary "Desert Fox," the wily commander who'd run the British out of Libya. What had surprised him was that Rommel had behaved like a gentleman.

After the war ended, Young began to research the enigmatic

field marshal. He learned how Rommel had defied Hitler's order to hold Germany's North African position at El Alamein—with British forces bearing down, it was a veritable suicide mission—opting to evacuate and save his men instead. Rommel had also risked his career by advising Germany to negotiate terms of surrender rather than attempt the pointless defense of the French coast. But Young's most surprising discovery was how the field marshal's disillusionment with Hitler ("The *Führer* must be a complete lunatic," Rommel had told his men) led to his role in Operation Valkyrie, the failed plot to assassinate Hitler in 1944—an implication that ultimately cost the commander his life.[46]

That Rommel was a literal German Brutus must have made his story irresistible to a practitioner of melodrama like Darryl Zanuck. Still, *The Desert Fox,* as the film was to be called, would be "the first Hollywood effort giving the enemy's side of World War II," said *The Hollywood Reporter.*[47] With the war so recent a memory, the proposition was a shaky one. Zanuck announced he had the "full authorization and cooperation" of the State Department to make his movie.[48] He also stressed that the film he was making was his-torically accurate.[49] Zanuck spliced in actual battle footage, used a voice-over of Winston Churchill, and even signed on Rommel's widow as a technical advisor. Director Henry Hathaway didn't just follow the account in Desmond Young's book, he cast Young to play himself.[50]

Still, historic accuracy was a tough sell for a film where Field Marshal and Frau Rommel were played by James Mason and Jessica Tandy; a film that featured hardened Wehrmacht officers slinging American English; a film whose North African scenes were actu-ally shot in Borrego Springs, California. To spur ticket sales, what *The Desert Fox* really needed was a true artifact, something that be-longed to Hitler himself—a vehicle, perhaps? The final scene called for Rommel, his conspiratorial role uncovered, to be driven to his death in an official Nazi staff car.

And one man in America just so happened to have one.

Janus was happy to loan the Fox film crew his big Mercedes, and he temporarily took the limousine off its western tour for the shooting. For Janus, the opportunity must have seemed like an awfully nice touché after the grief he'd gotten from Skouras over the car. Certainly, Janus got that point across with the invoice. "I charged $2,500 a week for three weeks," he later boasted.[51] The effect that the seventy-five-hundred-dollar bill must have had on the scrimpy Skouras can only be imagined.

In the movie, as in actual events, three generals confront Rommel with charges of treason and give him a "choice" of committing suicide or seeing his family destroyed. (It was the sort of transaction that only a regime like Hitler's could have produced.) The real-life Rommel had chosen the former, bitten into an ampoule of hydrogen cyanide in the staff car's backseat, and slumped over dead. But the Motion Picture Association of America censors would never have let Fox get away with a scene like that. So Hathaway just left the graphic part off: The film closes with a doomed Rommel bidding farewell to his wife and son, stepping into the Mercedes, and disappearing down the driveway. THE END.

Predictably, the studio's publicity department made the most of the car's inclusion. "Adolph Hitler's fabulous 10,000 pound bulletproof car was obtained by Twentieth Century–Fox for use in the filming," enthused the movie's press booklet—brimming with prewritten "articles" that the Fox publicity office encouraged newspapers to drop right into their morning editions.[52]

In the end, however, the presence of an interesting historic prop was hardly enough to absolve the movie of its highly selective memory.[53] As film critic Gynter C. Quill wrote in 1951, "there will be many to take offense at what they might with some justification term a glorification of a recent enemy"—one, Quill added, "who ceased to support the military politics of Adolf Hitler only when he was convinced that the continuation of those politics meant the destruction of Germany."[54]

Other critics of the film (war veterans and Jewish organizations, especially) decried a "whitewash of the Nazis" and the portrayal of Rommel as a "pinup general."[55] The Warner theater chain refused to screen *The Desert Fox* at all. The movie prompted protests in New York and even four days of riots in Vienna. Then as now, however, controversy is great for ticket sales, and *Variety* reported "biz socko" for the movie in many cities.[56]

Business was certainly socko for Christopher Janus, who'd booked his Hitler car for appearances in Colorado, Oregon, Washington State, Arizona, and Texas. Not long after Janus sent his bill to 20th Century–Fox, his telephone rang. The voice on the line was familiar.

"You lucky bastard," Spyros Skouras barked. "Only you could have pulled it off."

Ever the hard-nosed businessman, Skouras seemed more proud of Janus than angry with him. Janus had, after all, ignored his mentor's advice and taken a big risk that paid off. The car had raised a fortune on exhibit and made Christopher Janus famous in the process. He could hardly have done better if he'd been in the movies.

Skouras congratulated him on everything. "Next time I come to Chicago," he said, "I want to ride in that awful machine!"[57]

6

MEN WITH CARS

Skouras would never get the chance. By the summer of 1952, Janus had decided that nearly four years of owning a five-ton bulletproof limousine linked to a genocidal despot was enough. Later, when he looked back on this period, Janus would reflect that he'd gotten a good ride for thirty-five thousand dollars in ball bearings. He'd become a charity benefactor, a regular in the newspapers, even a celebrity of sorts. What Janus didn't know was that the car's notoriety had already cast a shadow long enough to shade the rest of his life. Over four decades later, Janus would write, "To this day, I am labeled 'the guy that bought Hitler's car,' and I'm a bit tired of it."[1]

He was, obviously, even tired of it in 1952. Still, the excitement of owning a famous car wasn't a feeling that Janus was quite ready to let go of. It is the reason he was in New York on a Friday night in 1952 to meet with a fellow named Waterman. Christopher Janus, true to form, wanted to do a deal.

George H. Waterman Jr. was a collector's collector, a man, it was said, with gasoline running in his veins.[2] This was no common thing in Waterman's time. Born to an affluent New England family, Waterman began collecting old automobiles in 1925 when he purchased his first Maxwell. He was thirteen. Few Americans of the era saw the point of preserving old cars, which most regarded as junk. "He was way ahead of his time," says veteran automotive journalist and publisher Michael Lamm. "There weren't many people who did that sort of thing. I admired him for it."[3]

Waterman's family members were apparently not among his admirers, as a contrite letter he penned to his older sisters in November of 1926 illustrates: "I will agree not to keep the Metz in the garage, will dispose of it by June 10th, and I will do my best not to get in a temper if things don't go write [sic]," the fourteen-year-old Waterman wrote. "I will not crank it without the permission of my parents. I will dispose of the old Ford engine, and unnecessary parts at once."[4]

The early twentieth century produced very few teenagers like George Waterman—but it did produce another worth noting here. His name was Kirkland Gibson—K. H. Gibson in formal address. Gibson was Waterman's childhood friend, born the same year and raised, like Waterman, on Hammond Street in Boston's suburb of Chestnut Hill. Gibson too regarded outdated cars as creatures worth protecting. "He called them invalids," says Gibson's son K. H. Gibson III (Kirk to his friends), who is today a petroleum entrepreneur living in Pennsylvania. The senior Gibson's love of automobiles had started in adolescence, as Waterman's had, though under less auspicious circumstances than his friend's.

"He developed polio, *and* he had an accident that mangled his leg," Kirk Gibson says of his father. "The accident shortened one leg by two inches and the polio shortened the other. Ultimately, he got out [of it] symmetrically. But he spent a lot of time on his back. And during that time, he read everything he could about cars."[5]

As they grew, Waterman and Gibson began rescuing old cars together.[6] They had penny postcards printed up that read "Information regarding location of antique cars wanted. Please write: Waterman & Gibson, Chestnut Hill, Mass."[7] The boys gave the cards to rural mail carriers with instructions to leave one in the mailbox of any property with a barn. Often, after the youths had extricated their prizes from the cobwebs, the owners let them have the old junkers for nothing.[8] By these and other methods, George Waterman and Kirkland Gibson assembled a staggering collection. One source numbered it at 158 cars, another at 200. It could well have been larger.[9] "We had one garage that held 15 cars and one that held three and another that had several sections that had 14–15 cars," recalls Waterman's son, George H. Waterman III, who is today a real estate investor in New York. "We had an old warehouse in West Warwick with *hundreds* of cars."[10]

Inevitably, in the course of their manic collecting, Waterman and Gibson acquired some very important automobiles. Their finds included an 1866 Dudgeon steam wagon, among the earliest self-propelled vehicles in the United States.[11] Gibson got his hands on the famed Renault racers of William K. Vanderbilt Jr., who'd created the Vanderbilt Cup, America's first international driving competition. Waterman once talked the Astor family's chauffeur into selling him a 1908 Mercedes for eighty dollars.

Waterman and Gibson remained collectors and friends into adulthood, though the former (whose pockets were deeper) became the more acquisitive. Some time after the death of Franklin D. Roosevelt in 1945, the well-connected Waterman found himself in contact with former First Lady Eleanor Roosevelt. The exchange is one that George Waterman III can still recount: "He said, 'What are you going to do with FDR's armored Packard?' And she said, 'You can have it if you let the public see it.'"[12]

Here is where Christopher Janus of Chicago entered the lives of the famed car collectors from New England.

Though he was over and done with the Hitler business, Janus was bent on continuing his "hobby" of putting a famous car on the road to raise money for charity.[13] That is why Janus was interested in FDR's old 1939 Packard V12 in the garage of George Waterman. And Waterman, for his part, had more than a casual eye on the 770K Mercedes in the possession of Christopher Janus.

Waterman's interest in the 770K was more mechanical than political. According to his son, Waterman was not sentimental about motorcars. He regarded automobiles as works of engineering, the natural avocations of worldly men, and he was especially fond of Mercedes-Benzes. "He had many Mercedes. He liked Mercedes— or, as we called it, 'the Mehr-*sehd*-eez,'" Waterman says, evoking his father's New England elocution.[14] With all the publicity that Janus's Mercedes generated, it's no surprise that George Waterman heard of it, nor is it surprising that he wanted it. "Once my father got his mind set on something," Waterman III says, "he was enthusiastic about getting it."[15]

On the evening of March 21, 1952, Waterman and Janus swapped cars.

Janus would put the ex-presidential Packard on a two-year public tour starting that summer. Somehow, he also located a direct descendant of FDR's Scottish terrier, Fala, and put the pooch on the road with the Packard.[16] Waterman and Gibson became the latest custodians of Field Marshal Mannerheim's old Mercedes.[17]

Yet while Janus left the picture at this point, the dubious marketing touch he'd added to the Grosser would travel with it from that day forward. For the next four decades (and well into the fifth), the 770K would be known, invariably and erroneously, as Adolf Hitler's personal automobile.

The spooky German limousine that Waterman brought to his garage in 1952 was now over a decade old. It was in original condition, too, less a few parts. As mementos, Janus had decided to keep the license plates and the headlights' blackout covers—hoods of black wool with narrow slits cut in them. In time he sold them both (the plates for twenty-five hundred dollars and the covers for a thousand dollars) and gave the money to charity. Janus said he was "glad to be rid" of these items, though it's a good bet Waterman would have liked to have had them.[18]

Toward the end of 1953, the realization dawned on Waterman and Gibson that often dawns on many a collector: Once the thrill of acquisition fades, the prized purchase devolves into the object you stub your toe on. Floor space was already at a premium for the men, and here was a car taking up 140 square feet of it. As Kirk Gibson puts it, "During that time, they were saying, 'What are we going to *do* with this damned thing?'"[19]

What indeed. Though Janus had made a second career out of touring the big Mercedes around the country, George Waterman couldn't be bothered with such exploits. Gibson, however, saw things differently. It didn't take an economics degree to see the financial potential of a limousine associated with Adolf Hitler. With the war now eight years in the past, Americans may have tired of hearing about Hitler, but Gibson wagered they had not tired of gawking at his car.[20] "Gibson was a bit of an eccentric," George Waterman III says when asked about his father's role in the subsequent road show. "He had off-the-wall ideas. My father wouldn't have done it without him."[21] Nevertheless, Waterman acquiesced to Gibson's plan, and Gibson made no small plans.

Gibson contacted the Trailmobile Corporation of Cincinnati, Ohio, and commissioned a custom semitrailer—a sleek streamliner painted up as bright as a Wrigley's billboard. The left flank screamed in block capital letters: HITLER'S *PERSONAL* ARMORED CAR, just below a tricolor banner announcing a NATION-WIDE TOUR. Gibson detailed the lower strip with eye-popping facts about the car: WEIGHT 10,000 LBS. ★ ½-IN. STEEL ARMOR ★ 1¼-IN. BUL-LETPROOF GLASS ★ 135 MPH ★ 235 HP. Gargantuan swastikas—their arms broken off for added effect—flanked either side of the headline-style lettering. Trailmobile equipped the rig with metal stairs to allow visitors to climb in on the right side, where the decking extended outward, camper-style, to create a shaded arcade. Here, Gibson had the fabric awning lettered with OFFICIAL STATE CAR OF "DER FUEHRER", in the unlikely event that queuing visitors needed reminding.

Since the Grosser's faded exterior no longer suggested a car of state, Waterman and Gibson had the limousine repainted, retaining the two-tone scheme of jet-black fenders and a cobalt-blue body. The interior they left untouched—"for the sake of history," said a later account.[22] Gibson equipped the pistol compartments in the doors with replica Lugers. And when the Grosser and its new trailer were all ready, he made a few management decisions.

To set up the itinerary, Gibson needed an experienced road manager. He found his man in Jack W. Burke, who'd cut his teeth booking the Ripley's Believe It or Not! tours. Ripley's traveling "Odditorium" had filled a pair of trailers and included curiosities such as a two-headed goat, an African hate god, and the shrunken head of a Chinese missionary.[23] If Burke was comfortable with happy little horrors like that, he wouldn't have had much trouble hawking Hitler's wheels. Burke would soon take out classified ads in the back pages of *Billboard* in search of "young men—single, honest, [and] neat" to help out. Cognizant of what sort of young men such ads tend to attract, Burke specified, "No drunks considered."[24]

Once again, Hitler's car was a hit with the public—at least if bookings are any measure. By Christmas of 1954, the car had logged fifty-three straight weeks on the road, following the neon-lit migration path of carnival midways: summers up north, winters in the south. Burke landed county fairs when he could, but sometimes the huge trailer simply grabbed the street in front of a five-and-ten and drummed in the locals.[25] A handful of photos from the time show the trailer set up in town squares, where lines of T-shirted boys and men in black shoes waited their turn. To the left of the entry stairs hung a wooden sign in the shape of an arrow: WALK RIGHT IN, it read.

Often, it would be Kirkland Gibson himself hanging up that sign. Gibson's son treasures a yellowed snapshot dated September 1958, showing his father on a fairground somewhere. A slender man in short sleeves, Gibson stands on the grass in the trailer's shadow, arranging the arrow sign as a cigarette dangles casually from his lips. His chinos and canvas tennis shoes betray a Yankee pedigree, but Gibson wasn't afraid to mingle in the world of claw machines and cotton candy. In fact, it's where he'd found the rig's driver, a man named Ray Ehlert. Ehlert was great behind the wheel and, just as important, great with a megaphone. He barked with the best of them, though usually the big Mercedes drew a crowd all by itself. "Oh, it was popular," Kirk Gibson says. "There would be a line formed." He pauses. "It's *not* like this was the bearded lady."[26]

The moment visitors climbed up into the trailer, the Mercedes confronted them with its menacing chrome face, the hood opened to permit inspection of the engine. The sheer length and size of the 770K was a staggering sight, its effect heightened by a wall of fencing enclosing the car as though it were a beast that had been caught. An opening allowed spectators to slip a hand through and squeeze the window glass's two-inch girth. Every few minutes, the car's siren terrified visitors with its bloodcurdling scream. The siren also did a good job of drawing still more people into the trailer.[27]

Kirk Gibson relates that if anyone objected to a Nazi artifact so casually put on public display, he never learned of it. There was a tempering mechanism in place, too: Proceeds from the admission went to benefit worthy causes. A VFW or local chapter of a service organization invariably sponsored the car's appearance, displaying its banner by the entry stairs. In turn, the group received half of the contents of the fishbowl. Admission to the trailer was always by donation. "A club sponsoring the thing made it respectable to go in," Gibson explains. "Who would argue with that?"[28]

Surely nobody Kirk Gibson saw—and he was in a position to know. A teenage Kirk Gibson accompanied the car on one of its summer tours in the mid-1950s. He still fondly recalls the week he spent living in the mystical realm of flickering bulbs and zeppoli carts. And even though young Gibson missed the chance to slumber in the limousine's backseat, the sleeping bag he unrolled beneath the trailer provided adventure enough. "I had a nice time mingling with the carnival people," he says coyly, "and we'll leave it at that."[29]

At the time, none of the spectators packing the trailer would have known that the limousine's terrifying siren, so evocative of the Nazi police state, had, in fact, been installed after the war by a Swedish brewery owner and had never once sounded on German soil. Visitors gazing at the reproduction *Führer* Standards hooked onto the limousine's stanchions would not have known that this 770K had, in fact, never flown them. Nobody would have questioned the lettering on the trailer's rear door proclaiming that the car within was used in a "Berlin Victory Parade of 1942"—though that was an impossibility, given that the car had been whisked to Finland in December of 1941.

This none-the-wiser crowd all but surely included Kirkland Gibson himself. If he was hyping the car's reputation, it was a reputation he had inherited. Hadn't the newspapers printed that this was Hitler's personal car? They had. Did paperwork exist that would have proven otherwise? Yes—but it was nothing that Gibson could have laid his hands on at the time. The big scary limousine might have toured the midways of America under Gibson's auspices, but the author of its mythology had been its first owner.

Christopher Janus was also the apparent author of a souvenir booklet—rendered, like the Nazi *Blutfahne*, in white, black, and red—which visitors could take home for $1.50. Lavishly illustrated and ornately styled, the booklet brimmed with facts, and a good many not-quite facts.

The pamphlet's basic version of events—the car was ordered by Hitler and given to Mannerheim—was true, as were the accounts of the car's residency at Rockefeller Center, its touring America, and its raising money for good causes. But many of its details (including Hitler's traveling to the Mercedes plant to "personally test the armor by firing a pistol at it" and using the Mercedes as his "getaway" car) ranged from dubious to ridiculous.[30]

The souvenir booklet also treated its purchaser to several photographs of the big Mercedes—though the Grosser 770K limousines in the pictures were, alas, often of a car that wasn't the one sitting in the trailer.[31]

While Kirk Gibson believes his father may have had a hand in producing the souvenir booklet, it's more likely that the elder Gibson was simply redistributing the publication originally produced by Christopher Janus for his tours in the late 1940s, maybe with a few edits.[32] Not only were the articles in the booklet Gibson sold virtually identical to those that Janus published in his (including a thirteen-page disquisition into whether Hitler was still alive), the preachy and purple prose felt uncannily Janusesque, too.[33]

But whatever the booklet's shortcomings as a monograph, it did manage one poignant observation: "Hundreds of thousands of people have walked around this car, looking and thinking, each with a different thought."[34]

It was true. Absent a few hiatuses in the garage, the car had been crisscrossing the United States for six years. People had come in droves to see it. They were still coming.

Why? Why were so many people drawn to the car?

Obviously, thousands of Americans were not queuing up simply to stare at an old Mercedes-Benz, even an armored-plated curiosity like this one. Early on, many who'd come to Janus's exhibits realized that something more complex was going on. A United Press dispatch from the car's 1948 stay at Rockefeller Center expressed it this way: "The people Adolf Hitler swore to subjugate crowded curiously around one of the last remaining symbols of the fuehrer today, and the significant fact seemed to be: They were here and he wasn't."[35]

There was a great deal to that statement. By its very presence on American soil, the car was proof of the Allied triumph. And with 405,399 of their number killed and 670,846 wounded in the war, Americans had earned the right to savor that triumph.[36] For many, then, a visit to Janus's (and later, Gibson's) exhibit was an opportunity for Americans in high dudgeon to get the closest they would ever come to the man responsible.

On top of this, the fact that admission proceeds would benefit charities imparted the comforting knowledge that a great wrong was beginning to be righted, however incrementally. Hammy as he could be, Janus understood and respected the importance of that dynamic and gave it a clear voice: "I felt the more good [the car] did, the worse Hitler would have liked it," Janus had said. "In fact, most of the things I did I am sure Hitler would not have liked."[37] The public would naturally have liked participating in anything that Hitler would not have liked.

But to say Americans turned up in the tens of thousands just to gawk and gloat would be to miss yet another probable reason the car drew so many spectators: It was a genuine, physical artifact from a conflict about which civilians had only a fuzzy understanding.[38]

For Americans on the home front, WWII was a censored war, its view clouded both by those who conducted it and those who fought it. A true sense of the war's horrors could not be obtained, for example, in letters from the front. "One reason soldiers' and sailors' letters home are so little to be relied on by the historian of emotion and attitude is that they are composed largely to sustain the morale of the folks at home," Paul Fussell observed in his influential book *Wartime*. "No one wrote: 'Dear Mother, I am scared to death.'"[39]

Nor could Americans necessarily expect a sense of the war's ugly depths from newspapers, radio, or newsreels, all of which were officially sanitized. In 1942, a writer for *Variety* decried the "buoyant roseate picture of the war" presented by the newsreels, with their "anemic and Pollyanna slant."[40] Reporters and editors railed against the restrictions, decrying the "dry cleaning" of the news, even as NBC admonished its own reporters not to file anything "unduly harrowing" from the battlefield.[41]

Even when, late in 1943, media coverage was permitted a measure of realism, Americans' grasp of the enormity of the war was still bounded by the limitations of the media itself. "The camera tells the truth but it doesn't give any idea of how it smells," is how Marine combat photographer Sergeant Norma Hack phrased it.[42] "Only the soldier really lives the war. The journalist does not," said CBS correspondent Eric Sevareid. "This war must be seen to be believed, but it must be lived to be understood."[43]

Obviously, the folks back home could neither see nor live World War II where they were. But the opportunity to see—or perhaps even touch, feel, and smell—the limousine ascribed to Adolf Hitler himself? *That* was an opportunity.

Whether or not all those who flocked to see the big Mercedes felt this way (and, doubtless, many people felt many ways), the fact remains that the limousine was unique because of the emotional access it provided visitors to the biggest event of the twentieth century: It was a visceral link to the war's very origin and a chance to face, if only by proxy, the architect of its horrors. "Relics of the past," the late historian and curator Brooke Hindle has written, ". . . provide direct, three-dimensional evidence of individuals who otherwise exist only as abstractions." Everyone has a need to "touch the past" in order to develop some understanding of it. "By providing a three-dimensional reality," Hindle argues, "these objects play an important social role."[44]

The limousine drew not only the home-front citizenry who hadn't gone to war, but plenty of soldiers who had—veterans who, by the early 1950s, had become new fathers. They brought their families to see the car, perhaps as a way of explaining a war they could not bring themselves to speak about. In Texas, the *Abilene Reporter-News* ran a story about children who'd stared wide-eyed at the long dark limousine, then looked up to ask, "Who was this guy Hitler?"[45] So powerful was the desire to confront, in effect, the man historians have called "the Demon King of history," the "quintessential hate-figure of the twentieth century," that even a Mercedes limousine associated with Hitler's henchman Hermann Göring would be enough—as Joe Azara and his buddies had discovered—to bring out crowds willing to wait for hours merely for a few moments with, and a photograph in front of, an old Mercedes-Benz.[46]

The American population for whom the Grosser limousine would have carried the gravest meaning is also the one whose response to it is hardest to judge, at least in this period. To be sure, Jewish communities in the United States were aware of the Hitler car's presence. *The Jewish Daily Forward*, the hugely influential Yiddish daily with a national circulation around two hundred thousand, was among the newspapers that covered the Mannerheim car's arrival at Pier 97 in 1948. Referring to the big Mercedes as "Hitler's 'getaway car,'" the *Forward* had pointedly run a photo of Wehrmacht soldier-turned-longshoreman Paul Purpi thumbing his nose at the 770K as it dangled in the deck crane's tackle.[47] Yet in all of the newspaper ink that the Mannerheim car generated during its first decade on U.S. soil, a Jewish perspective on the car is largely lacking—most probably because, in the face of events like the fate of displaced persons and the founding of the state of Israel, the Jewish press had far more important things to write about than Hitler's used car.[48]

Which is not to say that Jewish Americans—including those

who'd escaped the Nazis themselves—ignored the notorious limousine. Many didn't. The young Hungarian woman who'd shown Janus her numeric tattoo and asked to look at the car was not an isolated case. Enough survivors came forward that Janus elected to acknowledge them in his souvenir booklet: "Visitors to this exhibit have rolled up their sleeves," he wrote, "and showed us tattooed arms bearing concentration camp numbers, saying, as slave laborers they helped build this very machine."[49]

It was a vital and gripping narrative, the idea that men and women forced to build the hated limousine would return years later, as free citizens, to gaze upon its hulk. But while Nazi victims certainly numbered among those who went to see the car, none of them would have been involved in building it—at least directly.

It is a fact that Daimler-Benz made widespread use of slave workers (including European Jews) in its factories, but the evidence suggests that the automaker did not use compulsory labor to build the 770K limousines.[50] Not that a matter of degree constitutes justification: The fact that the corporate parent of the Grosser fleet only used *some* slave labor—in one factory but not another, on this assembly line but not that one—did nothing whatsoever to diminish or excuse the company's complicity in war crimes and, by extension, did not make the 770K limousine anything less than a manifestation of the Nazi regime in both symbol and fact.[51]

And this raises a final point about the curious drawing power of the Mannerheim Mercedes. In a sense, the car's transformation into a public attraction transcended the question of whether or not the automobile—ordered in Hitler's name, yet in only brief contact with him—was "his" car or not: Spectators *believed* that it was. As such, the chilling effect that the car had was quite real, even if the car's provenance did not entirely support it.

What's more, seeing the car set up as a county-fair curiosity or pulled by a circus trailer did smack of a certain poetic justice. "As a symbol of a toppled dictator, the limousine was a side show freak,"

reflected one writer in 1961. "It was exhibited the way Hitler franti-
cally feared he himself would be exhibited if captured alive by the
Allies."[52] The Nazis had always mingled myth with symbolism to
turn the false to the fantastic, to reward belief with deceit. Maybe a
weedy lot on the midway between the Fiji mermaid and the rigged
game of ring toss was the one place where this Hitler relic—*any*
Hitler relic—actually belonged.

In 1956, the Rhode Island Department of Public Works was busy
laying the first sections of Interstate 95 up as far as East Greenwich
and Warwick. Work crews had finished blacktopping the northern-
most stretch, but the lanes hadn't yet opened to public traffic. One
day, as Kirk Gibson tells the story, local officials decided to grant
his father an opportunity to give this tract of I-95 a test drive. The
cops would furnish an official escort. Gibson chose the Hitler car
for the occasion.

The men removed the five-ton beast from Waterman's garage in
East Greenwich, where it hibernated during the off-season. When
it was his turn to drive, young Kirk—now fifteen and still a year
away from obtaining his driver's license—slipped behind the wheel.

Fortunately, the boy was tall for his age, so he could see over the
long hood to the road ahead. He'd need to summon every bit of his
wiry muscle, too, because the 770K lacked power-assist steering.
Gibson knuckled the stick into gear and eased off the clutch. "It felt
like a *very* heavy car," he remembers. "There was nothing subtle about
that car."

Gibson let the limousine taste a few hundred feet of I-95's fresh
asphalt, keeping the beast under tight reign, at least for a little
while. "This thing was truck-y at lower speeds," he says. "But once
you kicked in the supercharger it took off like a missile. That's an
overstatement—but it's the memory of a fifteen-year-old boy."[53]

A few gearheads and a few cops—the only witnesses to the time when a car that had carried Adolf Hitler—rolled through the undulating green hills of Rhode Island.

To this day, Kirk Gibson—a seasoned car collector in his own right—shrugs off the notion that there was anything particularly outstanding about the Mannerheim Mercedes apart from its titanic size. "I had my first car, a 1929 Chevrolet, when I was a kid. I drove it through the woods, and I had driven Waterman's old wrecks," he says. By 1956, Kirk Gibson had tooled around in countless antique cars. The Mannerheim Mercedes, he says, "was just another one."[54]

To others, however, the limousine would never be just another car. It was still the Mercedes with an obscene past, the one with the out-of-control (and hellishly hot) heater beneath the front seat, the car that had prompted a daily deluge of calls and letters to Janus's office, whispering of curses and warning that Hitler's ghost had never left.[55]

On July 25, 1956, eight years after delivering the Mannerheim Mercedes to Janus, the MS *Stockholm* steamed away from Pier 97 on a routine run home to Sweden. Grinding through a heavy fog at 11:22 that night, the *Stockholm* rammed headlong into the *Andrea Doria*, killing forty-six passengers and crew and sending the Italian liner to the bottom of the Atlantic.[56]

Sometime around 1958, Gibson's trusty driver and barker Ray Ehlert fell ill. Gibson decided not to replace him. He took the 770K off the road. Meanwhile, Waterman had found the big Mercedes a new place to stay.

It was the old Weld Estate, sixty-four lush acres in the town of Brookline, Massachusetts, a few miles southwest of Boston. Isabel Weld Perkins had become the richest woman in America in 1881 when, at the age of five, she inherited a shipping fortune worth seventeen million dollars. In 1897, a twenty-one-year-old Perkins married Larz Anderson, a strapping diplomat she'd met at the United States embassy in Rome. The Andersons were global travelers, and enthusiastic automobile buyers. Nearly every year while abroad, they purchased a new one, retiring its precedessor to the carriage house on the property. By the time of Perkins's death in 1948, there were upwards of 32 cars in the garage, and the town of Brookline found itself holding title to all of them—in fact, the entire estate—as the Andersons had had no children.

Brookline would turn the property into a park but had no idea what to do with the automobiles. The solution would come from the Veteran Motor Car Club, a group that Waterman had founded in Boston some years earlier. In 1949, the club took the cars off the town's hands, and in exchange Waterman's group got the keys to the carriage house. The Antique Auto Museum at Larz Anderson Park opened its doors later that same year.[57]

The opulent building, modeled after France's Château de Chaumont-sur-Loire, made a stately museum, but its attraction for Waterman and Gibson was more practical. "It was a good place to keep cars," Kirk Gibson says.[58] Not long after the Mannerheim Mercedes left the tour circuit, it quietly slipped beneath the rafters of the Weld's old carriage house.

Regrettably, the limousine's residency in a museum would do nothing to correct the mistaken belief that the car had been Hitler's. If anything, the tale would take deeper root. *The Boston Globe*'s reporter Anne Wyman showed up at the museum in November of 1963 to write a human-interest piece on the collection. When the story appeared, it included a photo of a ten-year-old local girl named Mary Lynch standing atop the platform in the Grosser's front passenger seat, using two fingers of her left hand to fashion a Hitler mustache and giving a robust *Sieg Heil* with her right.[59] The photo—which somehow manages to be amusing and abhorrent at the same time—also showed the car flying Hitler's personal standard from its stanchions. There was no mention made of Finland's Carl Gustaf Mannerheim, nor that the Mercedes had really belonged to him.

Five years later, the auto museum anointed the 770K its Car of the Month. The press release stated unequivocally that the limousine "was Adolph Hitler's personal vehicle, from which he reviewed his goose-stepping troops and in which he traveled all over Nazi Germany during World War II." Then the release took the car's story on yet another scenic bend around the trees, erasing the years of Christopher Janus's ownership by stating that the big Mercedes had been "brought to America directly after the war by George H. Waterman, Jr."[60]

In one fell swoop, the museum enshrined the car's Hitler myth while removing the man largely responsible for its mythmaking.[61]

One day in 1965, the enormous Grosser limousine had a visitor.[62] His name was Jan Melin. Born in Sweden, where he sometimes gigged as a jazz pianist, the twenty-eight-year-old Melin was training to be an electrical engineer—a métier that had now brought him to the United States. Melin spent his days working in South Plainfield, New Jersey, for a company called AGA, which manufactured heat-storage cooking ranges. But the young Swede's true calling was the Mercedes-Benz—specifically, the great supercharged eight-cylinder sedans of the 1930s.

The bug had bitten early. As a child, Melin had stared in wide-eyed wonder as a friend's eccentric father drove home with Prince Albert Gustaf's 1938 Mercedes-Benz 320, its royal coat of arms still on the door. One look was all it took. Melin plunged into a withering curriculum of Mercedes study. When he married, Melin decided to take his honeymoon in Stuttgart, West Germany, so he could visit the Daimler-Benz archives. His new wife accompanied him to the file rooms, where she read off chassis numbers from the musty ledgers as Melin copied them down.[63]

Now Jan Melin pushed down on the chrome handle and pulled open the 770K's heavy door, slipping into the driver's seat. "I looked along one of the most impressive bonnets [read: hoods] imaginable," he would later write. The Grosser, he could see, was already missing quite a few of its original parts. Still, it was "quite an experience to see the car."[64]

It surely would have been. Though Melin felt his pulse quicken for all supercharged Mercedes-Benzes, Mannerheim's 770K in particular had gripped him for half of his life. "I saw the car for the first time when I was 11 years old," Melin told me. "It happened in June 1948 when the car stopped for a pause in the town of Alingsås, 50 km east of Göteborg [Gothenburg] on its way to be shipped to New York." Even then, people were whispering that the car had been Hitler's—a story that Melin appears to have discounted pretty quickly. "The myths [had] started already in Swedish newspapers," Melin recalls. By his analysis, the reason for that was simple enough: Hitler headlines grabbed more eyeballs and sold more newspapers.[65]

On the day in 1965 that Jan Melin scooched behind the enormous steering wheel of the Mannerheim Mercedes, his research into the car's background had only just begun, and it would continue well into the next decade. In the years ahead, Melin himself would become a critical part of this car's story. For now, though, he simply savored the moment, eyeing the radiator cap that seemed a mile distant from his vantage in the front seat.

7

RUNNING OFF TO CANADA

Aberdeen Proving Ground, nestled in Maryland's northern-most crook, where the Susquehanna waters the Chesapeake. The military base's 72,516 restricted acres consisted of dense and deserted forests, pockmarked artillery fields, and clearings of white-washed government clapboard. On these grounds, the Göring Special—Sgt. Joe Azara's giant WWII souvenir limousine—languished for months and then years.

Today, the United States Army says it has no record of the car ever having been on the base.[1] But it had been there—somewhere. After 1946, one account put the limousine in Building 314, the ordnance museum, where the giant Mercedes supposedly invited public gazing, complete with a bronze plaque recounting Sgt. Joe Azara's heroics.[2] Yet it's just as likely that the mysterious limousine simply took its place in the base's accumulated heap of German plunder, possibly in Building 456, the cavernous hangar where cap-tured cars and trucks lined up below the bow trusses.

About this period, in fact, only two things are certain. The Göring Special moldered at Aberdeen for the better part of a decade. And sometime toward the end of that decade, a directive transferred the car to the army's Property Disposal Division. Uncle Sam had scheduled a surplus auction for 1956. The limousine of Hermann Göring (or whomever the thing had belonged to) had to go.

At this point, what *should* have happened was a letter to Joe Azara, informing him that the army no longer wanted the big Mercedes he had risked his life to capture. "It's mine," Azara had told the newspapers a decade before, and after the United States government was finished with it, he wanted it back.[3]

By now, Azara was forty-four years old, a family man living in Cleveland. Always mechanically gifted, Azara was working on wind-turbine drives for NACA, the National Advisory Committee for Aeronautics, an independent agency that would soon change its name to NASA. Though the war had been over for eleven years, Azara had never forgotten the five-ton souvenir that the army had shipped across an ocean but would not let him keep. "I know he would have liked to have the car," Joseph Andrew Azara, the sergeant's son, says now. "That's a no-brainer."[4]

But the army never told Azara that the car had been designated as surplus or that it would soon be auctioned off. "When he came back with the car after the war ended, he asked for the car and they told him that it was the property of the U.S. government," recalls Debra Weidrick, Azara's daughter. "He said, 'If you ever get rid of it, would you please contact me?' And obviously, they never did. They never contacted him."[5]

On October 19, 1956, a Montreal man named Herbert J. O'Connell noticed a tiny Associated Press story buried on page 29 of *The New York Times*. Its headline read "Goering's Cars at Auction." The item was only nine lines long, but what few details it had were enough to apprise O'Connell, a collector of antique automobiles, of a rare opportunity. Two Mercedes-Benz cars, one of them a "convertible with a bullet-resistant top," were to be sold by the U.S. Army.[6] Aberdeen,

Maryland, was 435 miles away from Quebec, and the auction was only six days off. If he wanted a piece of this action, O'Connell would need to act quickly.

O'Connell called on a friend, one R. J. Rumble, whose somewhat theatrical name suited him well to his profession: Rumble sold cars for a living. Rumble Pontiac Buick anchored the corner of Bayview and Broadway in Toronto's northern suburb of Leaside. A spry man with a trim mustache and a porkpie hat, R. J. Rumble knew his cars, and he certainly knew the value of customers. For O'Connell, Rumble agreed to head down to Maryland and bid on Göring's old Mercedes-Benz.

Legion are the stories of the incredible things the United States government has dumped in one of its many surplus auctions. It is true, for example, that the submarine in Frank Sinatra's 1966 movie *Assault on a Queen* came from such a sale.[7] So did "Lil' Margaret," a P-51 Mustang that later turned up in a garage in Missouri.[8] When one of the U.S. Marine color-guard horses injured its foot in 1979, the corps off-loaded the unfortunate Palomino in a surplus auction. And when a man named Dick Textor bought a used safe from the Secret Service at a government clearance sale in the 1980s, he was more than a little surprised to find blueprints to the White House, which an agent had accidentally left inside.[9]

The reasons why the government sells off its holdings are mysterious and many. But a common one is lack of room, and this was what evicted the Göring Special. By the time WWII ended, the army had shipped home so many of the enemy's captured vehicles and field artillery pieces that Aberdeen's collection had swelled by five hundred "specimens"—everything from King Tiger tanks to V2 rockets. But now, facing a "lack of adequate covered space," the Aberdeen brass decided that all equipment that did not furnish a "background for the study of ordnance materiel" (everything, in other words, that didn't explode) would be deep-sixed.[10]

When Rumble arrived in Aberdeen, he looked over the assemblage of military surplus for sale. Even for a man whose life revolved around motorcars, the Aberdeen sale must have been an exciting thing. One of the vehicles on offer was the "Blue Goose," the powder-blue Mercedes 540K roadster that had participated in the Victory Loan Drive.[11] Its lusty, swaggering lines easily trumped the ponderous profile of the Grosser 770K, but Rumble's instructions were clear: He'd come to get the giant Mercedes only. The auction was closed-bid, so Rumble submitted his price—$2,725—and waited. It's not clear if there were other bidders.

Rumble got the car.

The Buick dealer made arrangements to put the 770K onto an open carrier trailer for the long haul to Toronto. A surviving photo shows the massive Mercedes loaded up just prior to its departure, nose down on a ramp with its fat rump sticking in the air. Not for the first time, the Göring Special did a fine job of suggesting Göring himself. Not that there was any proof that Göring had ever had anything to do with the car.

The week before Christmas of 1956, the mechanics at Rumble Motors came outside to have a look at the infamous limousine that had just trundled in from the road. Perceiving a momentous occasion, R. J. Rumble assembled a group of men (probably a mix of his grease monkeys and his customers, judging from the assortment of coveralls and dress coats) to pose for a group shot with the limousine near the garage bay doors. Though twenty grown men stood shoulder to shoulder around the trophy from Aberdeen, the Grosser Mercedes still dwarfed them.

The mammoth bore many wounds. Cobwebs of cracks in the glass trapped the glint of gray winter sunlight. The odometer's broken gear train still displayed 13,900 kilometers. Not only had the car's front license plate disappeared, so had the entire front-end fog-lamp assembly, stripped away as though an invisible hand had clawed it off.[12] Though he'd paid less than three thousand dollars for the car, O'Connell shelled out another five thousand for bodywork and paint: a fresh coat of glossy black to cover the army-issue gray. With the exception of the splintered window glass—an authentic feature he wanted kept—the new owner ordered a complete exterior overhaul. "Mr. O'Connell required everything to be restored to its original condition," Rumble later recalled.[13]

But there was a problem: Restoring an old automobile to original condition presupposes that the restorers know what the car looked like originally. In the case of this car, nobody did.

Not for the first time, the owner of a Mercedes 770K model W150 would be confounded by a lack of accurate information about his vehicle, plus the even more maddening fact that, to the untrained eye, all of the Grosser limousines appeared to be identical. In fact, small but significant details (the inevitable results of automobiles being built by hand) distinguished one 770K from another—but nobody had noticed them.

This is the problem that had presumably led Christopher Janus to fill his souvenir booklet for the Mannerheim Mercedes with photos of several different Grossers—including images of Hitler riding in a limousine that looked the same but was not the same as the one Janus had imported from Sweden.

This is the same problem that had bewitched the Treasury Department, which had put three captured Mercedes-Benzes on its 1945 Victory Loan Drive (two Grossers and one roadster), but had proven unable to tell any of the vehicles apart. Treasury's confusion had arisen from the U.S. Army's confusion, which was originating, profound, and hopeless: All of the cars that the army had shipped home from Germany were said to have belonged to either Göring or Hitler. But the army's own press department had bungled the attributions, which were all but worthless anyway. The sum total of "evidence" for which Nazi had owned which car was nothing more than a few conversations between Germans who spoke little English and GIs who spoke no German.

And so now, on the eve of 1957, the situation with the two most famous Nazi limousines in North America had arrived at the following state of affairs: Kirkland Gibson was on a national tour with the Mannerheim Mercedes, the car that Christopher Janus had billed as Hitler's personal limousine, even though it wasn't. Meanwhile, in Toronto, R. J. Rumble was preparing to work on a car that he believed had been Hermann Göring's, even though *it* wasn't, either.

What's more, R. J. Rumble was about to confuse the situation even further.

Looking to rebuild the missing fog-lamp cluster on the limousine's front end, but lacking any paperwork that would enable him to research the car, Rumble went looking around for any photo he could find of a 770K Mercedes from the Nazi era.[14] The first photo that Rumble found was apparently the one he used. The car in the picture happened to have a trio of headlamps mounted on an arch-shaped chrome bar attached to the front bumper. Rumble's mechanics copied what they saw in the photo and stuck it on the Grosser in the garage. There. Good enough.[15]

That Rumble was making a historically inaccurate addition to a historically significant automobile—an addition that would make the task of identifying the car's original owner even more challenging than it was already—apparently didn't trouble him.

In late October of 1969, an unusual letter arrived at the curator's office of the Canadian War Museum. The letter was from a man named Claude Pratte, a powerful Quebec attorney who sat on the boards of the Royal Bank of Canada and Canadian Pacific Ltd.[16] Pratte wanted to know if the museum would like to have a limousine that had once belonged to Hermann Göring.

Pratte had acquired the Göring Special sometime in the thirteen years that had elapsed since R. J. Rumble had finished restoring the car for Herbert J. O'Connell. Pratte declared that he would be amenable to loaning or even giving the limousine to the fledgling Ottawa museum, terms to be discussed. Chief curator Lee F. Murray could barely hide his excitement. "I am simply delighted at the prospect that your car with historic military associations will be made available," he wrote back to Pratte.[17]

Left tactfully unsaid was that Pratte's generous gift, valued at $26,850 Canadian, would land him a generous tax credit.[18] No matter. Tax rebates are how museums build their collections, and the Canadian War Museum was urgently trying to do just that.

Though its founding reached back to 1880, Canada's official military museum hadn't actually gained a physical address until 1942. Even then, it found itself quartered at 350 Sussex Drive in a stucco building the size of a toolshed. Not until the Canadian government's old Archives Building next door at number 330 became vacant in 1967 did the little museum finally gain a proper exhibition space. "It is safe to say," admitted *The Ottawa Journal*, "that until this year, Canada had the distinction of possessing the smallest war museum in the world."[19]

The Canadian War Museum's new home was quite a hand-me-down. The resplendent stone building, completed in 1904 as part of Prime Minister Sir Wilfrid Laurier's transformation of Ottawa into a capital befitting the British Empire, joined a procession of Tudor Gothic fortresses along Sussex Drive in the heart of Parliament Hill. The L-shaped building's rusticated face of Nepean sandstone, trimmed by creamy white quoins and lintels, faced the boulevard across a large open courtyard.

Giddy with the prospect of filling up its new Beaux-Arts castle, the museum's curators fell into a fever of acquisition—and weren't terribly picky about what they accepted.[20] Though the museum's mission was to "collect, identify and display artifacts relating to Canada's military history," the truth was that the Mercedes limousine in question had nothing to do with the country's military history.[21] Canada had sent 1.1 million troops to the Second World War, but it was Sgt. Joe Azara of the U.S. Twentieth Armored Division who'd captured this car. Nor had any Canadian divisions gone into Berchtesgaden, the region rich in abandoned Mercedes-Benzes.

Nevertheless, Murray salivated over the chance to exhibit the automobile. "A gentleman in Quebec City has offered to make available to us, either by loan or gift, Field Marshal Goering's Staff car. This is a very valuable historical item," Murray wrote to his superior William E. Taylor, director of Canada's National Museum of Man, a few days after receiving Pratte's offer. The car would make a fine centerpiece for the museum's upcoming V-E Day display, Murray went on to explain, and requested approval to continue negotiations to obtain the big Mercedes.[22]

Murray apparently received his green light. On May 15, 1970, the Canadian War Museum took formal custody of the limousine.[23] Its entry in the acquisitions ledger reads like the birth certificate of a baby Pantagruel: length—eighteen feet, four inches; weight—nine thousand pounds.[24] Engineers had to reinforce the floor to hold the limousine's tonnage. Were it not for the fortuitous addition of the double freight doors belonging to the annex wing added back in 1925, the seven-foot girth of the monster Mercedes wouldn't have fit into the building at all.[25] The curators gave the limousine prime real estate on the third floor, where the car glowered at visitors behind a rope cordon, its pitted chrome glinting below spotlights. Nearby was a placard explaining the fearsome automotive visage: GOERING'S STAFF CAR.[26]

If the acquisition had been a curatorial mistake, the label was a bigger one.[27] The U.S. Army had distanced itself from the Göring attribution back in April of 1945.[28] And yet the groundless story had held. *The New York Times* had carried the auction announcement for the Göring Mercedes, and that is what Herbert J. O'Connell believed he was buying.[29] It was what R. J. Rumble had believed he was restoring. And now it was what the Canadian War Museum believed it was displaying.[30]

8

THE BIG TENT

On June 28, 1971, residents of Rockland County, New York, opened up the pages of *The Journal News* to a startling headline: HITLER'S CAR PARKS IN NYACK.[1] Atop the story was a photo of the Mannerheim Mercedes—the 770K imported by Christopher Janus, traded to George Waterman, put on tour by Kirkland Gibson, and then stashed in the Weld Estate's old carriage house in Brookline, Massachusetts. Now the famous limousine (still erroneously known as Hitler's personal car) had popped up in Nyack, an affluent suburb north of New York City, where it sat in a weedy parking lot two blocks from the Hudson River.[2]

In the photo, a man stands in the well of the 770K's front passenger seat. If he was trying to impersonate Hitler, he was failing: The man had a receding hairline and wore a light summer blazer over an unbuttoned butterfly collar. He was also smiling. Edgar A. Jurist had just acquired the big Mercedes from George Waterman for thirty thousand dollars, and already had a buyer willing to pay him thirty-two thousand for it.[3] And in 1971, two thousand dollars for a quick flip was a nice commission.

Those who knew Edgar Jurist called him Ed—and those who

did were more likely to be movie stars and maharajas than the residents of Nyack. Quiet and secretive, Jurist was always jetting off to some far-flung corner of Europe, South America, or the Middle East, nosing around a barn or wooing a baroness in her castle, all with the aim of extricating rare automobiles.[4] Jurist shipped his finds back home, where the gleaming machines appeared behind the plate glass of an old Cadillac dealership that he'd bought in 1960. He called the place the Vintage Car Store.[5]

"Ed Jurist is a used-car salesman—but he is a drummer with a difference," said a 1967 editorial in *Automobile Quarterly*, calling his store "an emporium whose showroom and lot runneth over with the magnificent likes of Isotta Fraschinis, Rolls-Royces, Bentleys, and Hispano-Suizas. From his lofty vantage he views the world of collecting and collectors."[6] In the first two decades after WWII, if it was a rare automobile you were looking to sell or buy, you went to see Ed Jurist.

It was Jurist who bought Al Jolson's old Mercedes, as well as the Duesenbergs of Greta Garbo and Rudolph Valentino. And when Tony Curtis wanted a Duesenberg and Jack Benny a Maxwell, it was to Jurist they came. Jurist's career finds would include Thomas Fortune Ryan's gold-plated Rolls-Royce, the Maharaja of Johor's 1929 Mercedes SS, and a 1928 Delahaye owned by Emperor Haile Selassie of Ethiopia—the same ruler from whom Christopher Janus had acquired the Abyssinian cats that were kidnapped at the Cairo airport.[7]

Anchoring the base of Nyack's South Broadway shopping district, the Vintage Car Store was an Aladdin's cave of boat-tailed playboy coupes and boxy English limousines. If you happened to require a 1956 Rolls with a wet bar in the backseat, Jurist had one for you. But if you were in the market for a Chevy or a Ford, Jurist would advise you to check the classifieds. "We do not handle unimportant cars here," he declared.[8]

Jurist opened his showroom by invitation only. David A.

Wilkinson, a successful stone contractor in Manhattan, was among those who ventured inside. "He had these marvelous automobiles in there," recalls Wilkinson, who eventually bought a Jaguar XK120 from Jurist. "After the Second World War, there were an awful lot of cars scattered around the world, from India to Europe to behind the Iron Curtain," Wilkinson continues. "Jurist sought them out, found a lot of them, and we'd talk about it. I rather liked the man. He didn't have many friends. He was something of a curmudgeon—but he was terribly knowledgeable about cars."[9]

Jurist's far-ranging reputation was no doubt why George Waterman had chosen him to handle the sale of the Mannerheim Mercedes, which by now had become a very famous automobile.[10] During that summer of 1971, the limousine had arrived on Jurist's property on the back of a truck. The 770K was no longer in running condition. Its many ills included a broken flywheel ring gear on the transmission, a leaky carburetor float, and a generator that wasn't charging. Jurist's mechanic listed fifty-nine components that needed to be checked and, in many cases, replaced. These records also hint at the toll that souvenir hunters had taken on the car, as easy-to-remove parts like the main gas-tank cap and radiator cap had gone missing.[11]

Meanwhile, Jurist explored the titanic Mercedes. Beneath the hood and behind the firewall, he discovered the limousine's original tool chests, the wrenches still snug in their velvet-lined drawers.[12] Elsewhere, Jurist also found blank booking forms that Janus had used for the car, bearing the letterhead of his nonprofit Fight the Dictators Fund. As he rummaged deeper, Jurist uncovered a carton of souvenir brochures, the ones printed up to sell during the car's public tours in the late 1940s and early 1950s.[13]

Jurist flipped through the red booklets, half amused and half disgusted. "The material was interesting, but rather disjointed and with a definite attempt at drum beating and sideshow salesmanship," he later said.[14]

As an authority on antique automobiles, Jurist was right to express skepticism like that. Nevertheless, he also appeared to credit the myth of Hitler's ownership of the car, at least initially. The sales contract from the Vintage Car Store clearly delineates the 770K as "Ex-Hitler/Mannerheim."[15] Jurist also granted an interview to *The Journal News*, which proceeded to reprint all the lore about the big Mercedes—notably, that Hitler had used the vehicle in his "victory parades"—even though all of it was baloney.[16] Jurist also assured the reporter that the Mannerheim car was worth sixty thousand dollars, even though he was paying Waterman precisely half that amount for it. Was Jurist keeping mum about a car whose record he knew wasn't clean? We cannot know. What we do know is that several years later Jurist would dismiss this very limousine as "the so-called 'Hitler Mercedes'" and express anger at the "myths which abound" about the car.[17]

In any case, the car's issues were not Jurist's problem: He wouldn't have to dump the thing on one of his valued clients. A buyer had already come forward, already paid thirty-two thousand dollars—cash.[18] It's unlikely that Jurist liked or trusted his buyer.[19] But Jurist's buyer wasn't the sort of man who gave a damn what anyone thought of him; he was a wealthy real estate baron who knew what he wanted and usually got it.

And what Thomas W. Barrett III wanted more than anything was to get his hands on a car—any car—associated with Adolf Hitler.

The son of a judge on the federal bench, Tom Barrett had grown up in Oak Park, Illinois, west of Chicago. In the eighth grade, his mother gave him a graduation present of forty dollars—money Barrett spent on a 1936 Dodge, whose wheels fell off on the drive home. Undeterred, Barrett successfully bought and sold his first old car, a 1931 Buick Roadmaster, when he was sixteen. Eventually, Barrett became the manager of a car lot in town. Judge Barrett, shaking his head at these events, packed his son off to study law at the University of Illinois. Tom never finished.

In 1960, a thirty-two-year-old Barrett followed the postwar migration to the Sun Belt and moved to Arizona. There, he discovered a nice, dry climate for his growing car collection and a red-hot market in real estate. Land deals soon floated Barrett the cash to buy more old cars, and selling them furnished him with contacts for still more land deals. Before long, Barrett was a wealthy man. "Tom Barrett says only that he's 'in real estate,'" said one publication, "but his friends tell you that he's one of the more successful practitioners of the Arizona land developer's art."[20]

One of the cars Barrett decided to sell soon after his arrival in Scottsdale, Arizona, was a 1933 V16 Cadillac Fleetwood that had been custom-built for Joan Crawford. Answering Barrett's classified ad was a fellow car collector named Russ Jackson, who owned a successful Scottsdale car wash that had helped establish itself in town by giving free suds to the cops.[21] Jackson kicked the tires of Ms. Crawford's Caddy. He didn't buy it. But he and Barrett struck up a friendship, and in 1967 they staged Scottsdale's first classic-car show, the Fiesta de los Autos Elegantes. Planned as little more than a fund-raiser to buy books for the local library, Fiesta was so popular that Barrett and Jackson decided to add an auction to the program in 1971. Their timing could not have been better.

Though there were antique auto clubs in America as early as the 1930s, memberships were small and generally limited to the wealthy and eccentric. Well into the 1960s, most Americans looked upon even the resplendent phaetons of the 1930s as little more than used cars. David Wilkinson, one of Ed Jurist's later customers at the Vintage Car Store, still recalls the day in 1950 that, as a youth living in San Diego, he passed a car lot on the city's auto row and spied a Duesenberg—a car that sells for many millions today—with the asking price of eighteen hundred dollars. And no takers.

But as the postwar years progressed, antique automobile collecting came into its own, fueled by the growing affluence of the middle class and a longing for a "simpler" America lost forever amid the gloom of the Cold War. The Antique Automobile Club of America began its annual meets in Hershey, Pennsylvania, in 1954, the same year that *Hemmings Motor News*—the "bible of the old-car hobby," as the classified monthly dubbed itself—went into print.[22] In 1963, three years after opening the Vintage Car Store, Jurist noticed that "there has been a tremendous surge of interest" in prewar classic automobiles.[23] By 1968, no fewer than eighty thousand Americans had joined vintage and classic auto clubs.[24]

Then, in 1971, not long after Barrett and Jackson had held their first classic-car auction in Scottsdale, the popular Auburn Cord Duesenberg Festival in Auburn, Indiana, decided to hold an auction, too. Taking the microphone that Labor Day was Dean Kruse, whose velvety, rapid-fire baritone and one-line zingers ("Look at your watch, it's time to bid!") would eventually make him a legend in the automotive world.[25] Kruse turned a muddy lot into a field of gold that day, dropping jaws by selling an old Duesenberg—a hulk that would have had trouble fetching five thousand dollars a decade earlier—for sixty-one thousand dollars.

The die had been cast. From 1970 forward, the value of collectible cars would rise steadily by 20 percent a year for the next two decades.[26] That year, syndicated financial columnist Sylvia Porter published a three-part series advising Americans to regard antique cars as an investment. "While tens of thousands of car hobbyists have appeared on the American automotive scene in the past few years," Porter wrote, "there are now also growing numbers investing large amounts in the antique car business strictly for profit."[27]

Tom Barrett didn't need Porter to tell him that. And as he planned his next classic-car extravaganza for Scottsdale, he also didn't need to be told what auctioneer should man the microphone. Dean Kruse agreed to come down to Scottsdale and call the sale.

When it came to antique car auctions, Barrett, Jackson, and Kruse shared a few articles of faith. The first was the importance of turning an auction into a destination. They brought in food and drink, vendors, a town square–like atmosphere—or, as Kruse once put it, "It's like an old car happening, a picnic, a celebration, festival, all rolled up in one."[28] Another belief the men shared was that old cars sold well, but old cars once owned by famous people sold even better.

This, then, was among the reasons Barrett had been willing to travel the 2,140 miles from Scottsdale to the Hudson River town of Nyack in the summer of 1971: Ed Jurist was waiting there with a Mercedes-Benz once regularly driven—or so it was said—by Adolf Hitler.[29]

Jurist's surviving office files contain a photograph of the huge Mercedes loaded up onto a flatbed truck, presumably about to shove off for Arizona. Standing beside the deck, his head about level with the right front hubcap of the Mercedes, is Tom Barrett. His large head, white and round as a baseball, sits atop broad shoulders draped by a well-cut blazer. A receding hairline at his temples have left a peninsula of hair, slicked and combed back. You can almost smell the breath mint. He is grinning like the Cheshire cat.

Today, Barrett-Jackson has a trademark on the slogan "World's Greatest Collector Car Auctions" and stages celebrity-studded events in Scottsdale, Palm Beach, and Las Vegas. Its Scottsdale auction is so big it takes ten days to sell all the cars, and the 1,611 automobiles it auctioned at its 2015 event grossed over $130 million.[30] But the modern spectacle of flashbulbs and red carpeting owes its existence to the first Barrett-Jackson auction of January 6, 1973, which in turn owes its existence to Tom Barrett.

He was flamboyant, autocratic, brilliant, and occasionally terrifying. Barrett stomped around in lizard-skin cowboy boots, swirled Dom Pérignon in his glass, and was known to shoot at flies with his

.45 pistol.[31] He was a man who lived life in fifth gear, steered with one finger, and always seemed to know where all the old cars were hiding.[32] "Half the fun of this business is the chase and the find," Barrett blustered about the autos he bought and sold—and he would buy and sell some twelve thousand of them in his lifetime. "It's like pursuing a beautiful woman," he continued, employing an analogy he did not recognize as distasteful. "You chase 'em, you love 'em, you covet 'em, you parade 'em . . . then go on to the next one."[33]

Watching the big man at one of his car auctions, *Los Angeles Times* correspondent Dean Paul wrote, "With the power and authority of physical bulk, money, rasping directness, sometimes hard-drinking and always audacious damn-it-do-it-my-way Chicago-Irish presence, Thomas William Barrett III showed touches of Farouk and Citizen Kane and Boss Daley and P. T. Barnum."[34] It was hardly the first time that Barrett had been likened to the nineteenth century's consummate promoter, the founder of the Greatest Show on Earth.[35]

If an odor of hucksterism hangs around that metaphor, it is little wonder. The 1973 auction that Tom Barrett was planning for Scottsdale would indeed be a circus, complete with a big top and a center-ring attraction: Adolf Hitler's limousine.

On an outlying stretch of North Scottsdale Road, a moonscape of dry brown earth at the feet of Camelback Mountain, Barrett's men pitched a striped tent for his two-day extravaganza. He charged two dollars a head, which entitled the attendee to the use of the bathrooms at the adjacent Safari Hotel, a postwar pad equipped with arctic air-conditioning and leggy cocktail waitresses.[36]

No motor in Barrett's collection ran smoother than that of his publicity machine, and its pistons started cranking well in advance. The sale to take place on Saturday, January 6, 1973, would be "one of the greatest car auctions ever!"—a "sunny tax-free vacation!" featuring "Adolph Hitler's personally-built parade car!"[37] Scenting a good story, newspaper editors snapped their heads in the direction of Scottsdale. A story headlined HITLER PARADE CAR TO BE AUC-TIONED zipped across the United Press wires, dropping itself into newspapers across the country.[38]

Twenty-four years after Christopher Janus had introduced the Mannerheim car's Hitler mythology into the American imagination, leading newspapers like *The Washington Post* and the *Los Angeles Times* now repeated it almost verbatim: that Hitler had used the car years before "De Fuhrer [*sic*] finally gave it to Mannerheim," or that Hitler had ridden in the car with his Axis chums Mussolini and Mannerheim "as millions heiled."[39] Neither statement was true.[40]

As the auction date approached, rumors began to swirl. A secret consortium of Germans planned to buy the car and ship it home. Another from Japan was planning the same thing. Someone was flying over from Israel. A man had mortgaged his house for $150,000 to have funds for the bidding—and was sending a mysterious woman to do it. Formula 1 driver Phil Hill was coming. Terry Drinkwater from CBS was coming. Hell, *everyone* was coming: From East Coast millionaires to locals from down the road, attendees were en route.[41] In the end, three thousand people rolled like tumbleweed into Tom Barrett's circus tent in Scottsdale.

Among them was a man named Charles Wood, builder of amusement parks in the Catskill Mountains region of Upstate New York. Wood held the standing world record for the most money paid for an automobile at auction: ninety thousand dollars, which he'd plunked down in 1972 to get his hands on Greta Garbo's 1933 Duesenberg. Could the Hitler car break that record? Pre-auction estimates put the price that Barrett's car might fetch at fifty thousand dollars—even one hundred thousand. A reporter asked Dean Kruse if such stratospheric amounts were possible. "That depends entirely upon how bad some museum or collector wants it," he said, neatly dodging the question.[42]

The fact that such a conversation was happening at all signaled that the Mannerheim car had motored past yet another milestone.

After twenty-five years of drawing enormous crowds, the dubious Hitler limousine was about to draw an enormous price. Even if Barrett realized only the low estimate on the sale, it would still represent a profit of eighteen thousand dollars. Barrett had, in fact, already realized a return on his investment. During the year and a half he'd owned the limousine, Barrett had used it to ferry around his prospective real estate clients.[43]

Nobody knew it then, but Barrett had already received offers for up to one hundred thousand dollars for the car. He turned them down. He felt good about this one. The car was going to be a smash.[44]

"Oh, this is going to be beautiful," Dean Kruse said on the night before the big day. "We're going to set a record tomorrow."[45]

Saturday, January 6, 1973, was a clear, sunny day in Scottsdale, with temperatures hovering at a dry sixty degrees. The two banks of bleachers inside Barrett's circus tent were full. Some fifty cars would go under the gavel that day—a 1915 Mercer, a 1925 Locomobile Sportif Special—but everyone, really, came to see just one car.

At noon, they heard what sounded like a large truck approaching from outside.

With his tresses of dark hair, his French cuffs, and a well-cut blazer, Dean Kruse cut a confident profile. On this day, standing at a podium flanked by urns of gladiolas, he was a classic-car evangelist. Kruse told the guards to move the people clear from the tent opening. A charge of excitement crackled in the air.

"All right," Kruse's barrel-deep voice echoed on the PA. "Bring it in there, Governor Barrett, bring it in."[46]

From out of the desert, the chrome prow of the titanic automobile nosed through the tent flap. The car was all hood, hood, hood, until suddenly a smiling Barrett appeared at the wheel. He wore a slate-blue suit with a red carnation tucked into the lapel. Even for those who'd seen pictures of the limousine in the papers, the sight of it was still mesmerizing: twenty shimmering feet of chrome and steel, its mohair top buttoned back to reveal an interior of buttery black leather big enough for eight men.

The car was beautiful. The car was obscene. The car was for sale. Twenty-seven years, seven months, and twenty-nine days after the fall of Hitler's Reich, the limousine associated with the peak of its pageantry had surrendered none of its chilling powers. And was it not this spell that thousands had come to experience, after all? Years later, looking back on this unusual afternoon, one automotive historian would say that the car had raised "goose bumps of delighted horror among the auction goers."[47]

Inside the big top, below the lightbulbs strung between timber poles, the leviathan lurched to a halt.

Barrett had fixed signs to the 770K explaining its features, the way the used-car guy on a lot would patter about low mileage and a clean interior. A placard near the front read STEERING WHEEL IS ADJUSTABLE TO SUIT DRIVER. Another perched beside the retractable bulletproof shield behind the backseat: LEATHER-COVERED METAL SHIELD DROPS OUT OF SIGHT—CONTROLLED BY CRANK BEHIND CUSHION.[48]

"All right then," Kruse boomed over the crowd. "Who wants to be the first bidder here today, ladies and gentlemen? Anybody want to bid two hundred thousand dollars?"[49]

Kruse was joking—or was he? Nobody was sure, so nobody moved. Then, somewhere in the crowd, Charles Wood stirred. He offered forty thousand. Kruse took it, and the thing was on.

"I have forty thousand dollars, Mr. Wood of New York," Kruse trilled into the PA system. Then he shifted into high gear and didn't look back: "Who'll give me fifty? Fifty, got it up here, now sixty, got it, now seventy, now eighty . . ."[50]

Louis Beltrami owned the Lucky Strike Coal Company in Hazleton, Pennsylvania. He had come prepared to spend eighty thousand dollars on the Mannerheim car. As he saw the opening coming he jumped in. But then the price hit ninety thousand and Beltrami was out again just as fast.

Some had whispered about shills dropped into the crowd to goose the price. But the bidding seemed to need no help: With the auction only minutes old, Kruse was already driving toward the six-figure mark. As it approached, a murmur rose from the bleachers. Camera crews from three TV networks bathed the limousine in their klieg lights.

A quiet man named Earl Clark had been eyeing the bidding since it started. He'd come a long way to do it—2,010 miles to be exact, from distant Lancaster, Pennsylvania. Clark was the owner of Dutch Wonderland, a fairy-tale-themed park on the old Lincoln Highway, about an hour's drive west of Philadelphia. With his neatly combed hair and large-frame glasses, Clark still looked like the potato salesman he used to be. But dismissing him would have been a mistake. Clark was a serious businessman. He had the resources to make his presence felt, and now he did: Clark bid one hundred thousand dollars on the car.

It was a new world record. The auctioneer announced this fact from the podium, and the tent erupted in cheers. Even those with no money for bidding, those whose two bucks had paid for a spot on a wooden bench and admission to the Safari's restrooms, instantly got their entertainment's worth. Somewhere in the audience, an old man shook his head in a mixture of perplexity and disgust. "I ain't never seen nothin' like this," he muttered. His trusty old Studebaker, he explained, ran like a top, so "why in tarnation does someone need Hitler's car for?"[51]

The reporter who jotted down that pearl of a quote was Tom Miller, dispatched by the adult magazine *Oui* to cover the auction. Miller still remembers that afternoon in the circus tent, still remembers how the feel of the thing hovered somewhere between unsavory and surreal. Miller had arrived just in time to catch the pre-auction parade of cars and recalls how some of Barrett's lackeys were dressed up like Al Capone's boys—slick suits, flashy ties, fur collars, and fedoras. Miller wondered, *Why would someone do that?* He took one of the men aside to ask about the Mafioso getup. "It's called a *show*," the man whispered, and then stepped back into character.[52]

It sure was a show. And it had just moved into six-figure territory, no place for the undercapitalized.

Back inside, Dick Randall watched the bids fly. If he was sweating, it wasn't just from the hot air in the tent. Randall had come to Scottsdale from Wyckoff, New Jersey, hoping that Tom Barrett's Hitler car, if he could snag it, would solve a problem of his. Randall and his wife operated a midway stand, and their star attraction, Big John the Giant Horse, had been stricken with cancer. The cobalt treatments were not working, and the Randalls worried that the 6½-foot-tall equine wouldn't make it through another season of slogging up and down the East Coast. To Dick Randall's thinking, the only attraction that might suitably replace Big John the Giant Horse was Big Hitler the Giant Mercedes. He decided to go for it.

Randall signaled the podium. He was in for $110,000.

Lounging in the limousine, Barrett felt the pulse of the crowd, which is why his left hand felt for a switch on the Grosser's dashboard.

Barrett had once explained to a reporter that his business was not selling cars so much as making buyers desire them. "I'm really a want creator," he'd said. "I'll take a car, hype it, create a want, and then sell it."[53]

Presently, Barrett decided to demonstrate some of that flair, his talent for notching up the tension and excitement. He flicked the switch, and the siren bolted to the limousine's front bumper filled the tent with a chromium scream.

Yes, there was nothing quite like a little fascist-style fright to keep things moving.

About that siren, it bears noting, once again, that its caterwaul had never once been heard inside Nazi Germany, or even during the Second World War; that it was a Swedish brewery owner who'd installed it two years after Hitler's death, bolted it onto a car that Hitler, with two exceptions, had never ridden in, much less considered his own. But what of it? The entire auction was a fantasy realm whose price of admission wasn't just two dollars, but the suspension of disbelief. Tom Barrett had done his work well: The audience was stunned, and the automobile beneath his ample bottom was suddenly the most expensive used car in the world.

They were all on terra incognita, now, at least for a car auction. One hundred and ten thousand dollars. In 1973, $110,000 was Johnny Bench's record salary with the Cincinnati Reds. It was the amount Nixon allotted to his "dirty tricks" fund (not including the cost of breaking into the Watergate).[54] It was nearly ten times the average yearly income of a family in the United States.[55]

Up at the podium, Dean Kruse decided he'd better spoon a few ice cubes into the coffee. The crowd was too hot. They had all forgotten, perhaps, what the big black and blue limousine represented to some people.

"This car has got its place in history," Kruse intoned. "Adolph Hitler was probably the worst criminal that ever lived, and there is no one that ever wants to say a good word for him. But there's a lot of people, when they look at this vehicle, it brings back memories of the way *not* to be, and makes us all realize that we must live the kind of lives that preserve the freedom that we have here in America."[56] From the bleachers came a round of applause.

It wasn't a terrible speech, exactly. The problem was that no speech, no rhetorical swapping of the evils of Hitler with the blessings of America, could quite sponge off the film that coated the whole undertaking.[57]

If the Mannerheim car's earlier tours had been of questionable taste, at least some local charity had gotten to pocket the change in the goldfish bowl. If Janus's souvenir brochure had been filled with histrionics and errors of fact, at the very least it spoke of Hitler's tyranny. But the Barrett auction was solely about showmanship and profit, and it co-opted the travesty of Nazism to boost that profit. Don Oliver's report for *NBC Nightly News* aired footage of Barrett pulling the big Mercedes around with an enormous swastika flag draped across the backseat.[58] Beside one of the grandstands, the Tumbleweed Trading Post was doing a brisk business selling photos of WWII vehicles—autographed by Erwin Rommel and Adolf Hitler themselves. The sellers assured all comers that, yes, of course, the signatures were genuine.[59]

Given the darkness and weight of what the car represented, did the circuslike trappings of the auction strike any enlightened attendees—say, like journalist Tom Miller—as tacky or insensitive?

"Oh, gosh, yes," Miller says. "The entire operation was a P. T. Barnum thing. Everyone was keeping a straight face, but nobody was going in the one direction I was looking for—which was the Nazi Germany aspect." Miller means that nobody was acknowledging the elephant in this tent. To most of the attendees, the car did not appear to be a signifier of fascism, oppression, or genocide so much as a five-ton German convertible whose presence in Arizona was a reassuring talisman of American military and moral eminence. "Everyone was going for the P. T. Barnum angle," Miller continues, "as you can see from the people who made bids on the car—they were showmen, people in the carny circuit."[60]

He was right. Earl Clark and Dick Randall, the two heavy hitters, were both amusement operators, as was Wood, who'd opened the bidding. Also at the auction was a man named Peter Stranges. He wore dark glasses and a white safari jacket, and ran a tourist museum up in Niagara Falls. "I'm here to try to pick up Mr. Hitler's car," he'd said.[61]

As for Barrett, Miller recalls him as "an oily Scottsdale businessman." And the audience, clearly, was made up largely of people who did not appear to have been pursued by the Nazis. "Let me put it this way," Miller says. "I doubt there was a minion at the auction."[62]

But if the Scottsdale auction was light on Jewish attendance (nobody asked, and nobody will ever know), it was certainly heavy in the condemnation it generated. Many were the voices that had made it clear that they didn't think highly of auctioning off Hitler's Mercedes—or of its existence in general.

The persistent rumor that some wealthy man from Israel planned to buy the car and blow it up turned out, incredibly enough, to be partially true.[63] The man was Louis Beltrami, the coal-mine owner from Pennsylvania, who didn't just want the car, he wanted it destroyed, and he had vowed publicly to do so. "Hitler doesn't deserve any honors," Beltrami had announced.[64] If the bidding hadn't surpassed his budget, Beltrami assured the press he'd have made good on his pledge. "I wanted to bid," he explained, ". . . for the purpose of taking the car and blowing it up to show the leaders of the earth that if they don't use their powers the right way, there will be nothing left of them after they die."[65]

And there were many people far angrier than Beltrami.

Tom Barrett didn't admit publicly that his Hitler car had caused his family to fear for their safety—but his wife did. "People call and say that they'd like to come and burn the car because they had relatives at Dachau or Buchenwald or something. We've had people walking around the driveway at all hours of the night," Bonnie Barrett said. "Oh, gee . . . this thing's gotten out of hand."[66]

Things would get further out of hand come auction day itself. "I remember we had thirty to forty death threats and bomb threats," recalls Dan Kruse, auctioneer Dean's younger brother, who was on hand that day to help out. "It was a big deal. We called the state police and the local police, and I think we had ten to twelve guards from three or four [security] companies." Kruse also recalls that "we were very careful in how we displayed the car, because people were really offended back then."[67] The war, he adds, was still fresh in people's minds.

No doubt it was. But the war's relative freshness was probably not why the sale of the limousine triggered such a discordant response—far more aggressive, certainly, than anything that Janus or Gibson had seen in their days with the car, when memories of the war were, if anything, fresher still. (Asked if he recalls a negative reaction to the limousine during his father's tours, Kirk Gibson says, "If so, I never saw that."[68])

So what had changed? During the 1940s and 1950s, in the afterglow of victory, Americans had regarded the Mannerheim car (Hitler's "personal" car, as it was billed) largely as a war trophy, the symbol of a defeated country and ideology. But more recent events on the global stage—most notably, the 1961 trial of Nazi fugitive Adolf Eichmann—had begun to frame the Holocaust (a term that did not even appear in *The New York Times* until 1959[69]) as more than one of the many horrors of the Hitler regime, but increasingly as *the* horror of the twentieth century, a conflagration of deliberative mass murder unparalleled in history or memory.[70] Around the same time Tom Barrett was selling his Hitler car in Scottsdale, the eminent historian Raul Hilberg began teaching a course on Holocaust history at the University of Vermont. Hilberg was surprised at the large number of students (Jewish and non-Jewish) signing up for his class, and he explained it this way: "After the disorientation of Vietnam, they wanted to know the difference between good and evil. The Holocaust is the benchmark," Hilberg wrote, "the defining moment in the drama of good and evil."[71] As more and more Americans came to understand the Holocaust as the manifestation of evil, was it a surprise that the Mannerheim car—its ownership ascribed to the mastermind of the Holocaust—was now generating the response that it was?

"I don't think you can take out on a car what an individual did," Bonnie Barrett said.[72] Perhaps she was right. But when a historical relic like an old car becomes inextricably associated with an individual such as Hitler, the bets were clearly off.

The reflective mood created by Kruse's oratory lasted only until Barrett reached for the horn toggle again. Get on with it, he seemed to say, and so they did.

Clark upped the bid to $115,000. In an instant, Charles Wood was out. Greta Garbo's Duesenberg would remain the only star of his garage. Dick Randall held on. He had to. When the price reached the doorstep of $120,000, the crowd divided. Boosters yelled, "Higher!" but of course they had nothing to lose. The more cautious contingent had had enough. "Freeze!" they hissed. The bids continued to come in, but they inched forward $1,000 at a time. Even the high rollers were reaching their limit.

Suddenly it was all down to Clark and Randall. They wrestled each other up to $131,000, at which point Kruse dangled just one more carrot. "If you spend $150,000 today," he said, "this car will someday be worth $1 million."[73]

The incentive worked. Clark upped the ante to $133,000, breaking his own personal pledge to spend no more than $125,000 on the Hitler machine. Perhaps he tasted victory, for it was close: Randall raised, too, but there was a hesitance to the way he signalled. This auction was nearing the end of the road.

By now Barrett has started the engine, revving its eight enormous cylinders, summoning its 155 horses nearly as though he were reminding Randall of his dying star attraction back in New Jersey. Randall responded, and the bidding staggered ahead, to $140,000, then past it. Shaken that he violated his pledge to stop bidding at $125,000, Clark vowed to himself that he'd stop at $150,000.[74]

Moments later, he bid $151,000.

Randall was running on fumes, but his son, seated beside him, nudged him on to $152,000. Other than Randall's son and wife, nobody knew the man had finally gone as far as he could. Clark held steady, but his knees were weak, too. Beside him, a friend whispered that he should hang on, that it couldn't go much higher. It was counsel that Clark decided to take: He raised his bid to $153,000 and then . . .

Silence. Kruse's eyes darted around the audience in search of movement. There was none.

"We have a new world's record!" Kruse barked from the podium. "Earl Clark of Lancaster, Pennsylvania, gets the car!"[75]

Many of the other cars at the Barrett-Jackson auction sold for serious money: a 1931 Isotta Fraschini dual-cowl phaeton for $57,000 and a 1932 Rolls-Royce Phantom II Henley roadster for $68,000. On any other day, these cars might have garnered newspaper ink of their own, but not this time. The $153,000 sale price of the Mannerheim car was $63,000 more than anyone had ever paid for an antique car at auction before. A world record gets a story in the paper. So, frequently, does Hitler.

In theory, Tom Barrett could have sold the Mannerheim car with a busted flywheel and the many other problems Ed Jurist's mechanic had discovered. Few of the serious bidders planned to drive the car anyway. But Barrett was no fool, and the three thousand dollars he'd sunk into mechanical work was money well spent. Not only could a running car fetch a higher price, this one permitted Barrett to enjoy a moment he'd obviously been planning. Scottsdale's own P. T. Barnum would drive the car's new owner out of the tent.

Barrett dropped the idling machine into gear as Earl Clark, its new owner, walked around and climbed into the passenger seat. Clark smiled but was clearly uncomfortable.[76] Asked about his fearless bidding, Clark answered with the most utilitarian reason imaginable. "I came here to buy it," he said. "It was a long flight and I didn't want to go back empty-handed."[77]

Chauffeuring his winning bidder out of the tent proved not so easy to do. The moment that Kruse's hammer fell, the bleachers drained their ragtag occupants onto the lot: graybeards in blazers, middle-aged men with muttonchops, a smattering of boys. They followed the car like buzzards, eager for a chance to get closer, to see if a $153,000 Mercedes felt any different from the Chevy at home.

"Hey, John, ya gonna touch it?" one bystander said to his friend.

"I already did."

"Which hand?"

"My right one," said John. "The one I pick my nose with."[78]

Still in their rumrunner attire, Barrett's gang of security men shepherded the 770K through the open tent flap, walking alongside its bulbous fenders as the tires slowly crunched their way through the dust. One of the guards, a freckled young buck in a double-breasted suit, was busy shooing bystanders from the limousine's path when a UPI photographer stuck his lens beneath the young man's chin and snapped a photo. It ran in the next morning's *New York Times*.

For all the images of the Grosser Mercedes that had appeared in the papers over the years, none had conveyed the automobile's sheer enormity like this one. Never had the car's grille and headlamps more resembled teeth and eyes. Never had the car looked more capable of pouncing, gnawing, and chewing. The photo captured the security guards in their Mafioso suits, the gawking crowds, and the striped big top in the background. In short, it was a picture of one of the strangest events in automotive history—and American history, too. Nobody had seen anything quite like Tom Barrett's big Hitler-car auction, a surreal confabulation of rich men and poor taste, national TV and local yokels, swastika flags and polyester slacks—all thrown together in a circus tent pitched beside a desert motor lodge famed for its cocktail waitresses attired like French nannies. "What is America but beauty queens, millionaires, stupid records, and Hollywood?" Hitler himself had asked in 1940.[79] A visitor to Barrett's big top on North Scottsdale Road might well have asked the same question.

Seven days after the auction, STT, the Finnish news agency, released a statement in response to the news—now global—that $153,000 had bought Hitler's personal Mercedes-Benz. In point of fact, said the Finns, the car had belonged only to Field Marshal Mannerheim, not to Adolf Hitler.

The announcement was ignored.[80]

9

SUSPICIONS

The Mannerheim Mercedes drew spectators out of the tent like the pied piper, but the show wasn't over. "Stick around, folks," auctioneer Kruse's voice crackled over the PA, "in a little while we'll be selling the only other car Mr. Hitler had built for him."[1]

Indeed, no sooner had Barrett's Hitler car disappeared than the tent flap lifted again and—miracle of miracles—a second Hitler car appeared, every bit as long and dark and intimidating as the first one had been. *The New York Times* described it as "another Hitler vehicle almost identical to the car that sold for $153,000 except that it was used much more sparingly by the Nazi leader."[2]

Used . . . "*more sparingly*"? And how exactly would someone in an Arizona circus tent have been privy to such a detail?

In fact, the second 770K Mercedes had initially been identified in press reports as having belonged to Field Marshal Erwin Rommel.[3] But Tom Barrett had a way of making history simple. He forgot about Rommel and just dubbed the two cars "Hit 1" and "Hit 2."[4] Barrett claimed this car was purportedly among the captured limousines that the 101st Airborne hauled back from their occupation of Berchtesgaden. It wasn't. Nearly every other detail about the 770K felt slippery, too. For a time, it was said the car had been brought to South Africa, and yet Barrett claimed to have found it moldering under a tarpaulin at a Ferrari dealership in New York City.[5] One thing is sure: There was no proof Hitler had ever been in the car.[6]

"This is the only other car that Hitler owned!" shouted Dennis Kruse, younger brother to Dean, who'd taken over the podium to begin the second auction.[7]

Just before the bidding started, a reporter for *The New York Times* overheard Dean Kruse order another of his brothers, Daniel, to convince Big John the horse's owner, Dick Randall, who'd been shut out of the first auction, that he had another shot at Hitler automotive fame. "Tell him to buy the other car," the elder Kruse barked, "Hurry up and get over there."[8]

But Randall wasn't in the tent. He and his wife had fled to the Safari Hotel's coffee shop. "Right now, we're in a state of shock," Dorothy Randall said.[9] Her husband added that, had he stayed in the bidding for the first car, the limousine might have gone for two hundred thousand dollars. No: Sick horse notwithstanding, Randall would be bidding on no more Hitler cars on this day.

Neither would anyone else—or at least anyone with serious money. Though Barrett had shocked the crowd by producing another Hitler limousine, he'd also made a major miscalculation. The big fish didn't want to nibble a second time. Something smelled rotten, and for once it wasn't just Hitler. What were the odds that the only two cars Hitler had supposedly ever owned would both wind up in the Arizona desert? How did anyone know this 770K was, as Kruse said, just "a second car for Hitler"—or, as Miller wryly put it, "Like a station wagon—to be used for weekly grocery shopping, or to pick up the kids at the day-care center; you know, a second family car."[10]

When the bidding on the second 770K limousine looked unlikely to stumble past seventy-five thousand dollars, a frustrated Barrett grabbed the mic himself. "This car that we're auctioning off was the car that Hitler used between Berlin and Berchtesgarten [*sic*]," he proclaimed. "It has been driven less than 32,000 miles since new."[11] Those in the audience probably didn't know that Hitler would almost certainly have made such a journey by rail or air, not by automobile.[12] Spectators also probably didn't know that the odometer reading Barrett gave included the mileage that he'd put on the car himself.[13]

With a depleted audience and only a handful of bidders, the second auction was a plebian affair that soon turned into a fiasco. Placing the winning bid of ninety-three thousand dollars was an Alabama man named Bill Tanner, who drew plenty of attention when he identified himself as the campaign manager for George Wallace, the pro-segregation governor who'd run for president in 1972.[14] "It's a wonder they [the Nazis] didn't conquer the world," Tanner told reporters, adding, "I really admire their workmanship."[15] Presumably, he was referring only to the Mercedes.

The following morning, over a breakfast of Coors beer on ice, Tanner tried to get himself booked on Johnny Carson's show, then moved on to an untidy piece of business: Tanner didn't actually *have* the ninety-three thousand dollars he had bid on the second Hitler car. Ten days following the auction, after an infuriated Tom Barrett called Tanner "a flake with no money," Tanner sold his position to Don Tidwell, a mobile-home manufacturer from Haleyville, Alabama—who gave Tanner a trailer home for his troubles.[16]

For his part, Clark seemed pleased that he'd won the first auction and steered safely clear of the second. "I wanted the first Hitler car," Clark said, "because it is the only car of its type."[17] But what exactly did that mean? Barrett's second auction had already demonstrated that the first alleged Hitler Mercedes *wasn't* the only car of its type. And to anyone in the crowd who may have recalled the army's Victory Loan Drives of 1945, a realization was slowly dawning: There were a suspiciously large number of Mercedes-Benz 770K Grosser limousines prowling around the United States for *all* of them to have been Adolf Hitler's.

It is here, finally, where the mythos of Hitler's "personal" limousine began to crack. Had Barrett been content to sell only the Mannerheim Mercedes, the story might have escaped scrutiny. Even the niggling details that cast doubt on that car's being specially built for Hitler (including the presence of a cigarette lighter, when it was well known that Hitler did not tolerate smoking anywhere near his person) might have stayed put.[18] But the showman's audacity, trotting out a second Hitler car, then insisting these were the only two ever built for him—that was too much.

Things began to unravel quickly. Curious about the Mannerheim car's provenance, a Finnish automotive expert named Aulis Pakula got his hands on the Mannerheim car's "production serial numbers" and "found out the car was never used by Hitler."[19] The Associated Press broke that news on January 18, less than two weeks after the Scottsdale auction. Immediately, Tidwell began to get cold feet about buying "Hit 2," given the news that "Hit 1" had never belonged to "Hit" in the first place.

Before putting its story on the wire, an AP reporter phoned Earl Clark for a comment. It couldn't have been an easy moment for the Dutch Wonderland owner, who was essentially being told he'd been bilked. But Clark held firm. "I wouldn't have gone [to] that price without checking it out," he said, adding that he had a "wire from Finland" himself, showing that "the car was used personally by Hitler for two months."[20] There was simply no way that could have been true. But not enough was known about the Mannerheim car's past—yet—to entirely dismiss Clark's faith. So he held on to it.

But others did not. One of the publications that had covered the Scottsdale auction was *Motor Trend,* a leading voice in automotive journalism. *Motor Trend* had heard Barrett's claim that his two Grossers were the only two cars ever built for Hitler and, before running the story in its June 1973 issue, fact-checked it by contacting Daimler-Benz. The company responded in short order. "Mercedes says they [the Grosser 770K limousines] were just part of the government car pool," the magazine reported.[21]

No doubt aware of the authority its copy represented to automotive enthusiasts, *Motor Trend* put further mentions of Barrett's automobiles in quotes: the "Hitler cars," it said, ". . . even if they weren't really Hitler's."[22]

The difficulties with proving that any of the surviving Grosser 770K limousines had "belonged" to Hitler in any meaningful sense were many and complicated. The problems began with the Nazis' motorpool system: All of the official cars were shared. A limousine that had carried one Nazi henchman on a given day carried another the next.[23] And while the armor-plated 770Ks had obviously been built with Hitler in mind, Hitler was not the only official to use these cars—and some of them he used rarely or never.[24] Therefore, the closest thing to Adolf Hitler's "personal automobile" was an automobile that Hitler had used routinely, over a period of months or years.

But how was one to prove that? For one thing, official records were not as helpful as they might seem.

Daimler-Benz's original order forms—the *Kommissionsbuch*, massive ledgers kept in Stuttgart—did identify the *besteller*, the official who had placed the order for a car. This information appeared on the left side of the factory purchase order. But the name Adolf Hitler would not have appeared in this space, which instead commonly identified an office, such as Adjutantur des Führers, Berlin ("Führer's Adjutancy, Berlin"). Moreover, the fact that a car had been ordered by the Berlin adjutancy was not by itself proof that Hitler had actually made use of that car.[25]

German military files were also of little help. Surviving paperwork that dealt with the details of Hitler's travel arrangements spoke only of "*Führer*" cars; they listed no vehicles specifically. Other documents that may have linked a particular Grosser limousine in the fleet to Hitler personally—specifically, letters kept by the *Fahrbereitschaft*, the motor pool of the Reich Chancellery— were destroyed in the fighting that engulfed Berlin in April of 1945.[26] Similarly, any files at Daimler-Benz's Sindelfingen plant that might possibly have shed light on the limousines' service life were also lost; Allied bombers had largely laid waste to the plant by 1945.[27]

Proof could, of course, be found in photographs. Yet, here again, it was tricky business. Some American owners of the Mannerheim car (notably Janus, Gibson, and Clark) had used old photos of *der Führer*'s motorcades as "proof" that Hitler had used this particular car—yet these images had, in fact, showed altogether different cars. In defense of these men, the mix-up was easy to make: The Grosser 770K *Offener Tourenwagens* (the convertibles that Hitler favored) were all nearly identical, and the tiny differences that distinguished one from another were often impossible to discern in a photograph.[28] One solution to this problem was to locate an image that showed Hitler in a limousine with a readable license plate. But license plates were easily switched or lost, and few Grossers made it out of Germany with their original plates still on the bumper.

It all came down to this: While it was theoretically possible to prove that Hitler had used a specific 770K, it was extremely difficult. And, in fact, it had yet to be done.

In time, this evidentiary impasse produced a paradoxical consequence: Any American who came into possession of one of the surviving Grosser limousines after the war could safely claim that

Hitler had used it, simply because it was so hard to prove that he *hadn't* used it.

Finding an old 770K in the postwar years wasn't terribly challenging.[29] According to the best estimates, the total production run for the Grosser stood at 207 automobiles.[30] Mercedes had built 44 Grossers for the Reich leadership between 1929 and 1942 and armored a good many of the W150 series.[31] While many of these cars did not survive the destruction of WWII, enough of them did.[32] By one estimate, between 25 and 30 of the model W150 Grossers emerged from the ruins of Europe.[33]

And before long, a pack of them were prowling the main streets and midways of America, billed as Hitler's personal car.

In February of 1949, Detective Sergeant Arthur Casey of the Syracuse, New York, Police Department paid a visit to Ryan Brothers Storage at 811 North Alvord Street. Hidden in the shadows at the back of the warehouse, Casey discovered a twenty-foot-long, jet-black limousine surrounded by crates of refrigerators and washing machines. Peering through a window of the hardtop, the detective must have gotten quite a start: Seated within were a uniformed chauffeur, Hermann Göring, and Adolf Hitler. All of them were wax dummies.

Casey had acted on the tip of a local attorney named Bradley, who represented an Englishman acting as a broker for a French orphan's charity. For seven months, the charity had been unable to locate the 1943 Mercedes-Benz armored limousine it had sent to the United States—a most distressing development, since the fifty-thousand-dollar automobile had, the charity insisted, belonged to Adolf Hitler.[34] It turned out that the American booking agents had stowed the car in Ryan's warehouse on July 12, 1948, but had lost the receipt and forgot where the warehouse was.

Soldiers of the Free French Forces had captured the 9,500-pound limousine in Berchtesgaden on May 7, 1945, after which their commander, General Leclerc, presented it to Charles de Gaulle. For the next two years, the French shuttled the monster automobile between Paris and Lyon, where it raised money for charities.[35] After the car had wowed enough audiences in France, its owners sent it to America. Beginning in the summer of 1947, the limousine toured the country as "Hitler's favorite vehicle"—an odd claim, given that Hitler didn't care for hardtops.[36] Promoters also claimed the Pullman limousine was "the car which was actually used by Hitler, not one that he rode in just a few miles."[37] The importance of that distinction wasn't clear, nor was proof anywhere in evidence.[38]

Following its discovery by Detective Casey, the French Pullman hit the road again, where it became one of several Hitler cars plying the American carnival circuit in the early 1950s.[39] A perusal of the classifieds in the trade paper *Billboard* from those years shows promoters eager to book their vehicles.[40] One of those operators was a man named Pete Sevich, who'd operated a "freak and animal zoo" at the World of Mirth (the "Largest Midway on Earth") before going big with "Hitler's $35,000 Armored Limousine" in 1957. Sevich toured with his Hitler car well into the 1960s, when the car disappeared, having been established as a fraud.[41]

As far as anyone knows, Sevich may not have even been exhibiting a Grosser 770K limousine. But as other examples have demonstrated, owning the top-of-the-line Mercedes automobile wasn't a requirement in this game. In 1947, when a V12 racing car billed as the "Mystery Mercedes" surfaced in Los Angeles, its owners claimed it, too, had been built for Hitler.[42] So did a woman named Hilda Onofrey, who toured the shopping malls of America in the early 1970s with a shiny gold Mercedes 540K—a car, she insisted, that Adolf Hitler had given to his mistress, Eva Braun.[43] The mother of a disabled child, Onofrey said, "I take pleasure in the fact that now Hitler is helping all the crippled children he would have destroyed." The sentiment was genuine; the car was not.[44] As recently as 2012, a repair shop in Edgewater, New Jersey, discovered a 1942 Mercedes-Benz 320 Cabriolet D on an eBay auction and, in a subsequent *New York Times* story, intimated it had been made for Hitler—a highly unlikely prospect, given that the Mercedes 320 was a stubby, workingman's sedan.[45]

Indeed, with the American public (then and now) willing to credit nearly any bizarre story about Hitler—including, clearly, what he kept in his garage—the opportunist bent on claiming he owns Hitler's car not only doesn't need a 770K Mercedes, he doesn't even need a Mercedes. *Long Beach Independent* columnist Charles Sutton once recalled a huckster who toured the country after the war charging twenty-five cents for a peek at Hitler's Duesenberg.[46] Hitler never owned a Duesenberg. In 1984, a Texas car collector announced he was in possession of a 1937 Rolls-Royce that was Hitler's "favorite touring car."[47] Coincidentally or not, a tourist trap along Arizona's Interstate 10 called "The Thing" also harbors a blue 1937 Rolls-Royce touted as Hitler's. The same car, perhaps? It doesn't matter. A letter to the librarian of the U.K. Rolls-Royce Enthusiasts' Club yields the following response: "I can confirm that Hitler never owned a Rolls-Royce motor car."[48]

In September of 1974, a Detroit theater-chain owner named Hyram "Marty" Shafer snapped up an armor-plated 770K Grosser W150 limousine at a Fort Lauderdale auction for eighty-one thousand dollars.[49] The car—which would eventually acquire the sobriquet the "Beast"—had spent the preceding three decades in the United Kingdom, where British RAF forces had shipped the heavy convertible after discovering it abandoned in a Lentforden brewery in April of 1945. The Brits said the limousine had belonged to Hermann Göring (a claim for which there was no proof), and the car's new American owner was happy to do the same as he displayed the menacing Mercedes outside his movie theaters. Shafer even added a cinematic touch by playing a recording of Göring pleading his innocence at the Nuremberg trials.[50] Sometimes the theater man found himself visiting the Beast in the garage of his home in Grosse Ile, Michigan, where he'd "sit for a long time and just look at [the car] and think of the history it represented."[51]

But for Shafer, the gasoline-swilling 770K also represented an unpalatable fuel bill, as OPEC's repeated embargoes spiked prices at American service stations. When Marty Shafer decided to part with the car in 1976, it was none other than Tom Barrett who tried, unsuccessfully, to sell it in his striped tent in Scottsdale. Seeking better luck in California, Shafer took the Beast to Anaheim, where he found a buyer at the Disneyland Hotel.[52]

The Shafer car was a textbook example of how the absence of proof that Hitler hadn't used a given 770K limousine became a reasonable stand-in for proof that he had. During one of the Grosser's public exhibitions, spectators received a flyer printed to look like U.S. currency. It bore the message: "$10,000 reward to anyone who can prove that this car on display at this event was not used by Hermann Göring or Adolph Hitler."[53]

By the early 1980s, the car had wound up in the collection of Las Vegas's Imperial Palace.[54] The casino-hotel excelled at drawing mid-level gamblers to its slot machines and, apparently, sprinkling a little stardust on its 770K Mercedes: By the time the Grosser rolled onto the casino's carpet, it had completely shed its Göring identity in favor of billing as a limousine "manufactured for Adolph Hitler by Mercedes-Benz."[55] It was a neat rhetorical two-step that established a bureaucratic link to Hitler without supplying proof that Hitler had ever used the car.[56]

In addition to acquiring *der Führer* as its original owner, another fascinating fact related to the limousine materialized around this time: Hitler's secret suicide switch.[57] "Oh, yes," pronounced the Imperial Palace brochure, "at the time that this automobile was ordered, Hitler specified that Mercedes-Benz install a self-destruct mechanism that was to operate by the turn of a separate key on the dashboard. When activated it would send a spark to the 66-gallon fuel capacity, blowing the car and its occupants to kingdom come. By the way, it is still there and it still works."[58]

Except that it wasn't, and it didn't. The story was a myth. The tale had gotten started some years earlier, when a Boston mechanic decided to do something about the car's complicated and bug-ridden dual-ignition system. To simplify the start-up procedure, Hugh H. Cook of Antique Automobiles Ltd. simplified it by wiring the battery/magneto to the coil ignition button, a shortcut that left him with a disconnected ignition switch just to the left of the odometer.

"As a joke," Cook later explained, he stuck a SELF-DESTRUCT label below the inoperative switch, "thinking that will puzzle these brash Americans."[59]

And it did.

In 1976, Joe Ogden and Steve Munson, two young hardware wholesalers from Pewee Valley, Kentucky, finagled their way into a crumbling garage behind VFW Post 1990 in Greeneville, Tennessee. Digging down through a heap of rusty plumbing fixtures, old pots and pans, blankets, and discarded Christmas trees, Ogden and Munson laid their hands on a rusting Mercedes-Benz, so large and heavy it had sunk axle-deep into the garage's dirt floor.[60]

The pair knew enough about old cars to realize that this was not a typical barn find for Tennessee—or anywhere, for that matter. The Mercedes was a fully armored Grosser 770K open touring car built in 1938, roughly the time that Hitler's chauffeur Erich Kempka had first commissioned a bulletproof limousine for his boss. Ogden and Munson probably didn't know that particular detail about Kempka, but they did know they'd discovered a remarkable automobile. "We had figured that this one had belonged to someone in the Nazi hierarchy," Ogden said.[61]

The car had been rotting in the garage for nearly three decades. An oft-told story held that a local tobacco scion named Tom Austin had bought the limousine in Belgium after the war for eighteen hundred dollars (possibly paid in cigarettes), shipping it out of the country in pieces.[62] In 1949, after a few years of using the big car in parades to carry American Gold Star Mothers, the Tennessee vets relegated their Mercedes to the garage out back, gradually entombing it in junk as the years passed.

After paying the VFW fifty thousand dollars for the car, Ogden and Munson sent tracings of its serial number plates to Mercedes corporate archives in Stuttgart. Early reports (ones based on no apparent evidence) said the car had belonged to Reichsführer SS Heinrich Himmler. Then Mercedes sent back a factory order showing that the car had been ordered by *"Der Führer und Reichskanzler"*—a fairly standard entry for a car ordered for service in the chancellery motor pool. But *der Führer's* name in the ledgers was as close as anyone had come thus far to linking a specific limousine to Hitler personally, and that was enough for them. Ogden and Munson sunk another fifty thousand dollars into a restoration and, by 1977, the limousine was on the market in Illinois, billed as—what else?—Hitler's personal car. Asking price: one million dollars.[63]

Following the tracks of Marty Shafer's limousine, Ogden and Munson's 770K also found its way to Las Vegas, the one place in America where tackiness is a virtue and nobody raises an eyebrow at anything.[64] In those days, the Imperial Palace Auto Collection was among the largest antique-car museums in the country. Located on the fifth floor of the hotel's parking garage, the sixty-five-thousand-square-foot museum displayed two hundred glistening chrome machines "in a plush, gallery-like setting."[65] The goods always varied, since everything was for sale.

Yet even by the standards of the Imperial Palace—whose "Duesenberg Room" claimed to have the largest assemblage of Model Js in the world—a twenty-foot-long, 11,960-pound Hitlermobile had a way of standing out, especially the way that management had staged it. Unlike the other cars arranged behind velvet ropes, the Ogden/Munson 770K brooded within a high glass enclosure, a gigantic *Blutfahne* (the swastika banner) serving as a hanging backdrop. Occupying the Grosser were four Nazi mannequins, including Hitler clad in a brown tunic, giving the salute from the standing position in the front passenger seat.[66]

These perhaps *too*-realistic touches were the work of Imperial Palace owner Ralph Engelstad, a real estate wizard who'd snapped up the threadbare Flamingo Capri Motel in 1971, realizing that a location across the Strip from Caesar's Palace might be worth owning. Engelstad landed a gambling license, added rooms, and reopened the property as the Imperial Palace. By the end of the 1970s, his personal fortune hovered around three hundred million. The acquisition of the Ogden/Munson 770K (one of several Nazi limousines that would eventually roll through Engelstad's air-conditioned kingdom[67]) was a singular moment in a colorful career; it would also be his unmasking.

Visitors to Engelstad's car museum were unaware that, just on the other side of the parking garage wall, the casino mogul had also built something called the "war room," a three-thousand-square-foot chamber adorned with Hitler murals and stuffed with Nazi relics (uniforms, daggers, swastika flags) and vehicles believed to have belonged to Göring and Himmler. On two occasions, Engelstad would use the room for employee parties—thrown on Hitler's birthday—that allegedly included German marching music, a swastika cake, and bartenders wearing T-shirts reading ADOLF HITLER—EUROPEAN TOUR 1939–45.[68]

It would take a lawsuit filed by an ex-employee in the 1980s to make public these and other sordid details that, once they leaked into the media, exploded into a national story. As *People* magazine put it, "even jaded Vegas is outraged."[69] Irv Rubin, regional director of the Jewish Defense League, called Engelstad "a classic Nazi."[70]

Golden Nugget owner Steve Wynn, who would go on to build the Mirage, the Bellagio, and the Wynn Las Vegas, announced that he'd "like to punch the guy in the mouth."[71]

Engelstad's odd amalgam of denials and apologies only made matters worse. ("I don't hate Jews," he said. "I think of all people the same way—Poles, blacks, Orientals."[72]) In the end, Engelstad wound up paying a $1.5 million fine levied by the state gaming control board, which also required him to hang a sign on his 770K Mercedes limousine announcing that the car's exhibition had no intent of "glorifying or honoring Hitler, the Third Reich, or Nazi Germany."[73]

It's anyone's guess how many Hitler cars were "discovered" in the years after the war, but there were enough of them out there that suspicions about their authenticity appeared pretty early. In 1951, for example, the Kansas *Abilene Reporter-News* got the facts straighter than its editors probably realized when it announced the arrival in town of "Hitler's personal automobile—or one of his automobiles."[74] And despite the fact that there were already more Hitler cars rolling around than Hitler could ever have reasonably used, more were somehow always turning up. In 1968, a Mercedes said to be Hitler's failed to sell for the $45,000 minimum at a U.S. auction, and then wound up in the hands of an unnamed "German nobleman," who paid $47,500 and spirited the car back to Munich.[75] In the early 1970s, an American located a Grosser 770K limousine in Greece— one that the German magazine *Auto Motor und Sport* soon declared to be (yes, indeed) Hitler's personal limousine.[76]

And while the American appetite for gawking at beat-up old Mercedes-Benzes at carnival midways or out front of five-and-dime stores clearly peaked in the years immediately following the war, at least one of these shadowy vehicles remained on the circuit well into the 1970s.

Late on a summer afternoon, in a county fair in Upstate New York, a young boy pleaded with his reluctant mother to part with the fifty cents required for entry to a battered trailer whose painted flanks promised a glimpse at the automobile that had belonged to the century's most evil man. A high-stepped climb up a run of metal stairs led to the trailer's stuffy interior, a narrow catwalk skirting the right-hand side. Assailed by the August sun, the trailer smelled of baking metal, axle grease, and unconquerable mold. Nevertheless, two quarters delivered what the sign outside had promised, or seemed to: behind a wall of chain link, a long black Mercedes limousine brooding in the must. And it was utterly massive. One of the limousine's windows had been left rolled partway down to permit the curious to reach through a slot in the partition and feel the bulletproof slab of glass for himself. The boy, barely able to reach, did exactly that. Then, realizing he was entirely alone with the most fearsome car he'd ever seen, he quickly left the trailer.

I was that boy. [77]

10

DUTCH WONDERLAND

The moment they heard that a local son had just bought Adolf Hitler's car, newspapers in Lancaster, Pennsylvania, pounced on the year's strangest story. LANCASTRIAN BUYS HITLER'S AUTO FOR RECORD $153,000, announced the *Sunday News*. HITLER'S AUTO EN ROUTE HERE, proclaimed the *Intelligencer Journal*.[1] Earl Clark's flight from Scottsdale had landed near midnight the day after the auction. Exhausted when he reached his home, he'd stayed up another four hours taking calls from reporters. Everyone wanted to know the same thing: What use could a local businessman possibly have for Hitler's limousine?

Clark explained that the Mercedes would become the latest attraction at Dutch Wonderland, the amusement park he'd opened in 1963. Earl Clark's folksy fiefdom included a 240-acre camping ground, a cinema, a one-room schoolhouse, and the National Wax Museum of Lancaster County Heritage. As a Mason and a Rotarian who gave generously to local charities, Clark believed his civic duties included educating the public about history. There would actually be two automobiles on exhibit, he explained. The other car on its way back from the Scottsdale auction was F. W. Woolworth's

1914 Brewster, which Clark had snapped up for $10,500. It was in Lancaster that the five-and-dime king had opened his first discount store in 1879, and Earl Clark believed that the man's car belonged on exhibit locally.[2]

But why did Hitler's? That question was harder to answer. "We don't want to glorify Hitler," Clark told the *Lancaster New Era*. "We want to use the vehicle as a remembrance of somebody we never want to have repeated."[3] The Grosser Mercedes, he told the *Sunday News*, "is part of history," and the exhibit would stress as much.[4] Like the owners who'd preceded him, Clark was in the knotty position of having to explain that his planned Hitler attraction wouldn't spotlight Hitler *as* the attraction, just the limousine—whose attractiveness as an attraction was, of course, that it spotlighted Hitler. And around and around it went.

Naturally, a hint of skepticism crept into some of the local coverage of Clark's plans to exhibit the 770K. A bulletproof limousine for Hitler—parked at the gates of a family amusement park? Wouldn't there be criticism? "There's always criticism," Clark said, shrugging off the notion. "I was criticized for building a white castle in the Pennsylvania Dutchland."[5]

That was true. A decade earlier, the *New Era*'s editorial page had condemned Clark's property as a "tourist trap."[6] Clearly, the editors hadn't shared his vision for the future of northeastern Pennsylvania. In fact, few did. Earl Clark was a pioneer, which is another way of saying that his contemporaries thought he was crazy.[7]

One day in 1962, Clark waved his hand over acres of Lancaster's rolling farm country and proclaimed to his wife, Molly, that he would build a castle there.[8] She might have thought he was crazy, too, but she knew better than to doubt him. Clark had left his job as a traveling potato salesman four years earlier, buying a tract of land and building the Congress Inn, a large motel that rose straight out of the corn and barley fields. Clark was among the first to realize that Lancaster County was evolving as a destination. Since the 1930s, the area had drawn vacationers from New York and Philadelphia taken by the region's sylvan charms. Among the sights were the Amish, descendants of the Swiss Anabaptists, who wore boater hats and prairie dresses, eschewed electricity, and clopped around in horse-drawn buggies.[9] But there wasn't much to actually do in Lancaster, and most doubted that Clark would ever fill his fifty-two-room hotel. Just nine months later, however, Clark was grafting another thirty rooms onto the place to meet demand. A fellow Lancaster businessman would later say that Earl Clark "had an ability to see things others couldn't see."[10]

The next thing Clark saw was that children, towed through the area by their sightseeing parents, had nothing to occupy them. So Clark decided he would build an amusement park—"a place where families could bring their kids and not worry about them," he said.[11] The former potato broker bought the Brinkman farm, fourteen acres on the old Lincoln Highway, and broke ground in late 1962. In the manner of an Amish barn raising, Clark did much of the construction by himself, relying on local laborers (many of whom actually *were* Amish) to help out. He finished in May of 1963. The park had all of four attractions—a steam train, two boat rides, and the "Turnpike"—a paved road for track-driven, miniature antique cars. The area had nothing else like it.

Clark appropriated the regional nomenclature for the park's name. The Pennsylvania "Dutch" were, in fact, Pennsylvania Germans—or *Deutsch*, which had sounded similar to local ears. Almost overnight, Dutch Wonderland became the most popular tourist attraction in the county.

Clark would later say that the decision to buy the Mannerheim Mercedes had come to him in a dream. He had known about Tom

Barrett's Scottsdale auction from a newspaper story but had forgotten about it until he'd fallen asleep one night. In his slumber, Clark saw a gauzy vision of himself bidding on the armored limousine and winning it. "I woke up that morning," he later said, "and knew I had to buy the car."[12]

Now he had. But buying the notorious Mercedes had been more complicated than Clark had bargained for, and this realization had broadsided him minutes after the auction's end. For one thing, Clark was on the hook for $153,000. "He *didn't* plan on paying that much," recalls Clark's son, Murl, who today buys and rents residential properties in Lancaster. "He was hoping to get it for $70,000 or $80,000."[13] Clark also realized, to his chagrin, that he'd become instantly famous. As he sat up in the front seat beside Barrett, Clark wore a taut smile that could not conceal his obvious unease with the cameras, the microphones, and the pressing crowds. Earl Clark was a modest man who avoided the spotlight. But what else but a spotlight can a man who buys Hitler's car expect?

One of the men in the crowd that day was Robert Pass, who owned the rig that would be hauling the 770K to Pennsylvania for Earl Clark. Pass understood the value of antique cars better than many of their owners did, since his St. Louis company, Passport Transportation, was responsible for insuring and moving the costly toys around. "When you back the car out of the truck, you can hit the guy's wife, but don't hurt the car," Pass would tell his drivers.[14] He was joking—a little. Robert Pass had actually been aware of the notorious Hitler limousine for some time. He'd even harbored secret hopes of owning the monster machine one day, though that didn't appear very likely now.[15]

The roads and highways that stretched between Scottsdale, Arizona, and Lancaster, Pennsylvania, stretched 2,263 miles. The trailer took several days to get the limousine back to the East Coast. The day the Hitler car arrived in the driveway of the Clark family home happened to be the birthday of Clark's wife, Molly. "Here's your birthday present, sweetheart," Clark joked.[16]

To house Woolworth's Brewster and Hitler's Mercedes, Clark began construction of a wooden building on the Dutch Wonderland property. He chose a spot right in front of his castle. A two-story rectangle of cement block, the castle would have looked more like a car wash had Clark not fitted it out with medieval-style battlements and turrets. Just like his decision to buy the Hitler car, Clark's idea to build the castle had come to him in a dream. Molly Clark would later recall how her husband had awoken in the middle of the night, pulled out a sheet of paper, and begun sketching a castle on it.[17]

Shortly after the car arrived, Clark had some photographs taken for posterity. Pulling the limousine up to the castle's entryway, Clark sat in the front seat with his wife, who wore a white fur stole. Clark's daughter, Julie, stood up in the back, an obliging smile on her young face. The photo is like that of any other American family piled into a new car—except this car was bulletproof and had a swastika flag draped across the backseat.[18]

Missing from the photographs was son Murl, by then twenty-one years old and away at college. The Clark children had grown up at Dutch Wonderland—Julie operating the rides and Murl emptying trash pails and watering the flowerbeds. Once Murl returned home, his park duties resumed and grew considerably more interesting. Clark gave his son the task of driving the Hitler car around, a periodic but necessary task to keep the engine seals lubricated.

Clark had registered the 770K in Pennsylvania. But while the car was legal on local roads, it was so massive as to be impractical. "It was a long, heavy car," Murl Clark says. "I mean, it *wasn't* fun to drive." Instead, young Clark tooled the Hitler machine around in the Dutch Wonderland parking lot and through the adjacent campgrounds. One can only imagine the response of vacationers wiggling out of their sleeping bags at dawn to see a Nazi Mercedes-Benz rumbling through.

Earl Clark was already a collector of antique automobiles. His garage housed a 1929 Rolls-Royce and a white Lincoln Continental that had reportedly belonged to John F. Kennedy.[19] But those were hobby cars. The Hitler limousine—at the time the most expensive used car on planet Earth—would have to earn its keep. Inside its new quarters, the Grosser sat on a raised platform, its chrome glinting in spotlight beams while a recorded narration crackled on a loop of tape. Before putting the car on display, Clark removed the *Führer* Standards from the stanchions on either side of the front grille.[20] Six weeks after the car arrived at Dutch Wonderland, Earl Clark opened the new exhibit to the public.

It was a disaster from the start. Thanks to its central location, everyone heading for the park gates would have to walk right past the exhibition building holding the big limousine—and, indeed, walk right past it was exactly what everyone did. Earl Clark, a man who'd been successful in every venture he'd tried his hand at, watched in dismay as customers paid the regular admission but refused to cough up the extra dollar to see his Hitler Mercedes. "It didn't help attendance in any way," Murl Clark recalls. "And to be blunt, we were very disappointed in how many people weren't interested."[21]

Was the extra admission the problem? Maybe. But over time, Murl Clark realized that his father had made a far more elemental mistake. Dutch Wonderland's bread-and-butter customers were families with children under thirteen. And their parents, it became clear, had zero desire to explain a genocidal butcher to kids clamoring to ride the pedal boats.

But the bad news for the Clark family would not be limited to the dearth of ticket sales nor even the nagging talk that the Grosser Mercedes had never belonged to Hitler in the first place.[22] The pub-

lic anger and disapproval that had reared its head during the Scottsdale auction followed the car to Lancaster. Soon, the Clarks began
to receive threatening phone calls and letters from people who
believed that the park was preserving Hitler's memory.[23] Earl Clark
had intended no such thing. The car, he'd told *The Baltimore Sun*,
was "a magnificent feat of engineering and—good or bad—it's a
piece of history. I hope people can look at it and see the craftsmanship in it. I also hope they can look at it and be reminded of what
can happen when a man like Hitler gets control of things."[24]

It was wishful thinking. Clark would learn the hard way that
when members of the public saw Hitler's car on display, they didn't
see history—they saw only Hitler. The tidy and wishful distinctions
between man and machine, past and present, murderous ideology
and the lessons of hindsight, were lost. Perhaps Clark was naïve to
think he could teach those distinctions. Or perhaps the problem was
that Clark was using an amusement park to do a job better left to a
museum. But one thing was clear: The car was nothing but trouble.[25]

As a seasoned businessman, Clark must have understood the
risk of a backlash on some level. But the vehemence of it took him
by surprise. "It was so unexpected," Murl Clark says. "But it did
bother [my father]. He wasn't comfortable having people think that
he was promoting Hitler."[26]

In the end, Clark saw only one way out: Just 275 days after buying the Mannerheim Mercedes, he would stage an auction to get rid
of it.

Fortunately for Clark, his amusement park lay just twenty-five
miles south of Hershey, Pennsylvania, where the eastern division of
the Antique Automobile Club of America held its autumn rally.
The event drew a million gearheads, many of whom skinned their
knuckles restoring their cars, plus an affluent few who believed that
the best tool for such a job was a checkbook. By choosing Columbus

Day, 1973, for his auction, Clark would time his event to Hershey and guarantee a good turnout. He also picked up the phone and asked auctioneer Dean Kruse to come to Pennsylvania and man the microphone. Clark's purchase of the Mannerheim car might have been a mistake, but he wasn't about to make a second one.

Kruse's involvement meant that little would be left to chance. The Grosser Mercedes would serve as the auction's "lead car," a headliner that would help sell the hundred or so lesser specimens on the block—a 1956 DeSoto, a 1941 Chrysler, and so on.[27] Also on offer was a 1939 Horch said to have belonged to Field Marshal Erwin Rommel of the Wehrmacht.[28] In fact, with its evil-car trappings and three big tents pitched on the grounds, the Dutch Wonderland auction would have many of the same features that Tom Barrett's auction did—including Tom Barrett, who boarded a plane for Pennsylvania to attend Clark's sale. Barrett most likely knew what Clark could only hope: The Hitler limousine, now a juggernaut of dark energy, was going to set another world's record under the gavel.

The stratospheric price that Clark had paid for the Mannerheim Mercedes in January of 1973 had already been surpassed with the sale of the Bonnie and Clyde "Death Car," the Ford V8 that state troopers sprayed with bullets on a Louisiana back road in 1934, reducing its pair of bank-robbing occupants to bloody viscera in the front seat. That car, a wreck riddled with holes, had sold for $175,000—proof, as the Hitler Mercedes had been, that a gruesome past never hurt the resale value of a classic car one bit.[29]

Well in advance of his auction, Clark received inquiries from all over the world—5,783 letters to be exact, with forty firm offers among them.[30] He turned them all down. Clark preferred, he said, to "give anyone interested an opportunity to bid their price for this unusual and important car."[31] Obviously, an auction would give Clark the best price possible on his notorious automobile. "I really don't care who buys [it]," he said—"not as long as they pay for it."[32]

The Dutch Wonderland auction kicked off at 10:00 A.M. on

October 8, 1973. The nibblets went first, and by the time the Mannerheim Mercedes rolled into the main tent at 1:10 P.M., the stands were packed. In signature Kruse style, men in white dinner jackets with carnations in the lapels prowled the audience, eyes peeled for possible bidders. Given the phoned-in threats they'd faced in Scottsdale, the Kruse brothers took no chances on security. The 770K waited its turn in a small side tent, cordoned off and under police guard.

The Scottsdale auction influenced the proceedings in Lancaster in another significant way. By now the talk that Hitler's big Mercedes might not have been Hitler's after all had clearly reached the auction's organizers, who delivered this disclaimer before the bidding got off the ground: "We are not responsible for any statement as to the condition or the authenticity of any car. We are only relaying information that has been provided to us by the owner. We assume it is accurate. If you plan on bidding on a car, please look it over first for your own protection. Once the sale is consummated the car is yours."[33]

Caveat emptor.

But if Earl Clark had worried that he wouldn't recover his $153,000, he needn't have. The sale would be consummated quickly and expensively. Charles Wood, outbid in Scottsdale, was outbid again in Lancaster. Tom Barrett bid the car up to $170,000 before bailing out. It wasn't clear if he actually wanted the big Mercedes back in his garage or was simply testing his hypothesis once more, proving that hype creates want—or was it the other way around?[34] When Dean Kruse brought the hammer down, the Mannerheim Mercedes had a new owner. He'd bid a record-shattering price of $176,000.[35]

He was none other than Robert Pass, the man who owned the trucking company that had hauled the car from Arizona nine months earlier. Far from being dizzy over the sack of money he'd spent, Pass said he'd been willing to take the bidding up to a quarter of a million dollars if necessary. He wanted the car that badly. Earl Clark shook his head. "I didn't even know he was interested," he said.[36]

After the Hitler car left Dutch Wonderland behind, Clark turned its display building into a fudge stand. Today it houses the Breyers Ice Cream & Coffee Shoppe. Murl Clark looks back on his father's brief ownership of the notorious Hitler Mercedes as "a unique experience."[37] It is a diplomatic way of characterizing a close brush with disaster. Clark was lucky: He'd managed to rid himself of the Nazi limousine before it was too late.

Meanwhile, for the custodians of the Göring Special in Canada, it already was.

11

STALEMATE IN OTTAWA

Since January of 1971, The Twentieth Armored Division's old Göring Special—captured and claimed by Sergeant Joe Azara but never returned to him, then owned by two wealthy Canadian collectors—had been sitting under spotlights on the third floor of the Canadian War Museum in Ottawa, identified as "Goering's Staff Car."[1] Only the hypervigilant visitor would have noticed a very subtle qualifier nested deep in the explanatory text. The car, it read, was "said to have been issued to Reichsmarschall Hermann Goering."[2]

There was a world of apprehension contained in those two little words "said to." Unknown to the public was a sticky problem that had been unfolding in the museum's offices for many months. The problem was this: The Canadian War Museum, distinguished state custodian of Göring's 770K bulletproof limousine, had found no documentation whatsoever proving that their Mercedes had ever been used by—much less belonged to—Hermann Göring.

It wasn't for want of trying. In 1969, within days of learning about Pratte's interest in giving the 770K to the museum, chief curator Lee F. Murray quietly attempted to establish the limousine's provenance. In this effort, he was in possession of a rare piece of information—the original license plate number issued in 1940. The plate that had once been on the limousine's front bumper had vanished long before. But in the back of the car, below the trunk and between the taillights, the letters and numbers of the vehicle's original registration were still discernable: IAᵛ148697.

Unfortunately, it did him no good. Murray pecked out a flurry of letters, sending them to any place that might know anything about a 770K Mercedes. He wrote to Aberdeen Proving Ground, to the Smithsonian, to Harrah's Automobile Museum in Las Vegas, and to Daimler-Benz headquarters in Stuttgart. "Any help that you can give us on our problem would be very much appreciated," he said.[3] But license plate or no license plate, nobody had any information on the museum's mysterious car.

Murray also tracked down R. J. Rumble, who'd bought the 770K at the Aberdeen Proving Ground auction and returned to Toronto with it in the winter of 1956. Rumble was adamant about the Grosser's past: "This particular car was . . . issued to Goering," the Pontiac dealer wrote back. "[It] was used as his personal staff car."[4] But Rumble could offer no documentary proof of his contention.

For Murray, the exchange was another dead end. Still, Rumble's letter did include a valuable nugget of information the curator had been missing. It was the car's factory number—429334—taken from the builder's tag just behind the engine firewall. Murray cabled this information to Mercedes in Stuttgart, which had thus far ignored his plea for help. It was a snub that escaped neither the curator's awareness nor his wit. "I have noticed a reluctance in many Germans to admit they were around at all during the Second World War," he said, "and have a feeling that the same is true for this company."[5]

As 1970 dawned, an increasingly anxious Murray began casting his lines still farther in hopes of snaring some detail of the car's murky past. Somehow, Murray heard about the unique expertise of

Ed Jurist at the Vintage Car Store in Nyack, New York, and wrote him a letter on January 21. Meanwhile, Murray reached out to the German consulate in Ottawa to ask Ambassador Joachim Friedrich Ritter if he could coax some cooperation out of Daimler-Benz in Stuttgart. To the ambassador, Murray made his dire predicament plain: "The car would seem to be a most interesting historical relic," he wrote, "but it is comparatively valueless unless something authentic can be learned about its background."[6]

It was Jurist who wrote back first. "There is no question whatsoever that we can be of definite assistance to you with regard to the Mercedes-Benz 770K carrying serial number 429334," Jurist wrote. "As a matter of fact, I am personally familiar with this vehicle."[7] And how was that? As it turned out, O'Connell, who'd hired R. J. Rumble to bid on the car at the U.S. Army's surplus auction at Aberdeen, had tried to sell the car to Ed Jurist at some point long before finding a buyer in Claude Pratte, the man who'd eventually decide to donate the Mercedes to the Canadian War Museum. The family of antique automobile collectors was, in those early days, as close-knit as the mafia.[8]

At least Jurist was familiar with the car. He even remembered that the Canadian War Museum's Grosser 770K had spent many years in storage down at the U.S. Army's base at Aberdeen. The letter must have sent Murray's heart leaping—for a moment, anyway. Jurist wasted little time before dashing his hopes. If the curator was looking to establish that the car in his possession had belonged to Göring, Jurist indicated, he might as well save himself the grief.

A "mistaken impression which has gained considerable publicity is that each of the high-ranking members of the military and political staff of the Third Reich was assigned a particular 770K," Jurist told Murray. "Nothing could be further from the truth."[9] Jurist went on to explain the Nazi's motor-pool setup, and how no official had his own car. The only exception to this system, Jurist noted, was Hitler himself, who availed himself of a number of Grossers set aside for his use. But the Reichsmarschall? He had to share like everyone else.[10]

Suddenly, the odds of verifying the old Göring Special as Göring's went from being a long shot to hopeless. Had the car carried Göring even once? Had he even *seen* the thing? The best-case answer was maybe. And indeed, maybe was the answer that finally came from Daimler-Benz headquarters in Stuttgart.

The company took its time—nearly seven months since Murray's first letter—but by June had forwarded a reply. Of sorts. The limousine, relayed Ambassador Ritter, had been delivered factory-new to Hitler's adjutancy on July 8, 1940. But that tidbit of information proved little more than that chauffeur Kempka would have taken custody of the giant Mercedes and added it to the motor pool. "It could not be found out whether the car had been used by Hermann Göring himself," said Mercedes, "but it is possible."[11]

Murray and his staff now faced a nightmare: Not only were they keepers of an artifact without a provenance—a Göring Special with no documented link to Göring—it was one they were stuck with. As the staff knew all too well, the Nazi automobile had drawn big crowds to the museum. Questioned about what they remembered from their trip to the museum, many visitors were able to recall only the giant Mercedes.[12] Word of the exhibit had made the news in the United States.[13] Problematic as the 770K was, the Canadian War Museum had no choice but to keep it.

What was to be done? For now, the museum decided to leave the matter in limbo.[14] Meanwhile, it commenced a dubious "restoration" that, for unfathomable reasons, involved taking a critical link to the car's past—license plate IA^{v}148697 in the back of the car—and painting it over. As if that obfuscatory misdeed weren't bad enough, the staff decided next to fabricate a new set of license plates, replacing the "IA^v" prefix with a "WL." The new prefix stood for

Wehrmacht Luftwaffe and reflected the belief, despite all evidence to the contrary, that the car had been Göring's, since Göring had commanded the Luftwaffe.[15] More confusing still, the car's new ersatz plates were of a decidedly British design (white characters on a black background), which bore zero resemblance to the license plates the car would have worn in Germany. As things stood, curator Murray could not link the car to Göring, but these modifications made it less and less likely that anyone ever would.

Murray kept up his detective work, sporadically writing letters in the coming years, though he appears to have largely given up after Mercedes headquarters had left him dangling. In September of 1971, the museum's deputy chief curator, Ralph Manning, wrote a rather stern letter to Murray about the Canadian War Museum's problematic centerpiece attraction: "You know my feelings on the so-called 'Goering' car we have," Manning fumed. "We have nothing to link it to him."[16]

Nor would they ever. By 1972, Murray referred to Göring's ownership of the 770K limousine as nothing more than "well established legend."[17]

Joe Azara's old Göring Special had already moldered unwanted in a U.S. Army warehouse for the decade between 1946 and 1956. Now, mislabeled with the name of a Nazi henchman it had never belonged to, the giant limousine would sit on a museum floor in Canada for the decade between 1970 and 1980.

What had initially seemed like the museum's most important donation had become its secret shame.

12

LIKE MARRYING
A MOVIE STAR

The newspaper accounts made it seem as though Robert Pass was a bidder out of the blue. To the public, he was: Nobody in the auction tent had known of his long-standing interest in the Mannerheim Mercedes, nor about the financial apparatus he'd quietly set up to purchase it. But in fact, Pass had had his eye on the 770K for several years.[1] And because Earl Clark had been his client, Pass had been privy to the park owner's eagerness—indeed, his near desperation—to sell. "He'd gotten no end of grief over that car," Pass recalls.[2]

Robert Pass also understood that, as the 770K's new owner, he'd be lining himself up for a share of that grief. Like several of the Mannerheim car's previous custodians, Pass planned to put the car on a national tour and donate the proceeds to charities. But there was a difference this time out—a big one. "As a Jew," Pass told the assembled reporters, "I am buying this car to show everyone what can be done to make money for the Jewish Federation."[3]

The media had been bleating about the Hitler limousine off and on for a quarter of a century already, but the paradox of a Jewish businessman owning it was something new. It was a detail the newspapers jumped on (some of them crudely: HITLER CAR FEES TO GO TO JEWS announced the *Charleston Daily Mail* of West Virginia[4]).

As is so often the case, the truth bore a finer grain than the news reports. Pass, in fact, sought to assist both Jewish and Christian charities, not the former to the exclusion of the latter. "My goal was to offer the car to state fairs around the country, which I would haul it to," recalls Pass, who sold his business in 2000 but still buys and sells antique cars in St. Louis. "My proceeds would go to the charity of their choice—not necessarily [just] Jewish charities, because there were lots of Christians killed in the camps."[5] Born in 1940, Pass had been too young to fight in WWII. But by 1973, in his early thirties, he was disturbed by a lack of Holocaust awareness among the postwar generation. He would set out, with *der Führer*'s car, to teach them.

It is no small measure of Pass's principles that he was willing to climb into debt to accomplish his goal. Though Passport Transportation was prospering, Pass's fleet of three or four trucks did not yield enough revenue to swing the acquisition of the six-figure limousine. So Pass solicited the help of his friend and insurance agent, a man named Walter Klein, and together the pair lined up bank financing to buy the Mannerheim Mercedes. "I thought it would be appropriate to do something good with the car," Pass explains.[6] He would not be the first owner to cherish such notions—nor, as things would turn out, the first to regret them.

Amid the postauction hubbub, the predictable crush of reporters and photographers, Pass and Klein made their way toward the enormous limousine and slid into the front seat. In one photo, a triumphant Klein holds up a card (possibly the vehicle's registration card), while, next to him and behind the enormous steering wheel, Robert Pass rests his hands on his plaid slacks and wears a satisfied smile.

It was a harbinger, perhaps, that when the Grosser's new owners tried to take their five-ton charge for a spin, the engine would not start.

The Dutch Wonderland auction had awakened the media to the enormous prices that old cars were fetching regularly. Robert Pass hadn't just purchased a famous Mercedes-Benz, he'd broken a world record to the tune of "176 big ones," as the specialty newspaper *Old Cars* reported.[7] Pass's winning bid validated the grousing heard at swap meets across America: Collecting antique cars, once an affordable hobby for weekend mechanics, was quickly becoming a rich man's sport.

Three months before Robert Pass bought the Mannerheim Mercedes, *The Washington Post* News Service syndicated a feature about the record demand for antique automobiles. Onetime junkyard cars, the paper reported, were now hailed as paragons of culture and put on display at the Metropolitan Museum of Art and the Rhode Island School of Design. A New York firm calling itself Carriage House Motor Cars Ltd. was selling a pair of "his" and "hers" Rolls-Royces for a quarter of a million dollars. Michael Lamm, then the editor of *Special-Interest Autos* magazine, recalled how the 1932 Cadillac he'd bought in 1950 for just $90 and sold in 1954 for $450 had appeared in a classified ad in 1970—priced at $10,000.[8]

Across the country, demand for old cars had driven the prices beyond the reach of the ordinary hobbyist. Even prices for workaday makes like Ford and Nash had exploded. And the sources were drying up. "There are no dumb farmers left," said *Hemmings Motor News* publisher Terry Ehrich, referring to the hallowed practice (one pioneered and perfected by teen collectors Waterman and Gibson) of trolling barns and back lots in hopes of snaring a prewar treasure. No more. "You can't drive up to Bearton [Vermont]," Ehrich said, "and haul away a Model A for 25 dollars."[9]

Nor would any bargains go on the block at Earl Clark's classic-car auction at Dutch Wonderland. On that fall afternoon of 1973, the hammer prices—a 1933 Ford for $2,600; a 1952 Bentley for $3,750, $14,000, and over $20,000 respectively, in today's dollars—made it clear just how restricted the playing field had become. "Those who really would have liked to acquire a collector's car of their own but lacked the means to do so must have found the last few days frustrating," said one local paper.[10]

Little wonder Robert Pass's $176,000 purchase price created such a stir. But it was more than the high price of the Mannerheim Mercedes that put it into the newspapers. Despite the credible voices (including that of Mercedes-Benz itself) saying that the car had not really belonged to Hitler, newspapers had continued to print all the tall tales that dated back to Janus's ownership: that the limousine had cost Hitler $2.5 million, that it had taken four years to build, that "Hitler used the car . . . to review his Nazi troops"—none of which was true.[11] For some in the automotive community, the only thing more distressing than a car that could command six figures was a car that commanded such a sum based on a fallacy. And within that community, nobody was more distressed than Ed Jurist.

The owner of the Vintage Car Store was more aware than anyone of how embroidered the provenance of the Mannerheim Mercedes had become. He'd watched as Tom Barrett sold the 770K to Earl Clark for $153,000 in January, only to be shocked again nine months later when Earl Clark flipped it for $176,000 to Robert Pass. So when a *New York Times* reporter called him for a comment on the impressive value of rare automobiles, Edgar Jurist blew a gasket.

"Suckers are buying from sharpies every day," he said. "Cars that aren't worth the powder to blow them to hell are being foisted off on people who want to jump into the market, and we've watched this plunge toward instant disaster by the nouveau collector trying to get into a market that has already peaked out."[12]

To hammer home his point, Jurist outed himself as the one who'd originally sold the "Hitler car"—the *Times* put it in quotes—to Tom Barrett prior to the Scottsdale auction, and the price had been thirty-five thousand dollars.[13] The conclusions to be drawn were obvious: An old limousine with a trumped-up reputation had sold for markups of 337 percent and 403 percent of Jurist's original price.[14]

Robert Pass trucked the big Mercedes eight hundred miles back to St. Louis, where he put it in his garage. Prior to the auction in Lancaster, someone had reattached the *Führer* Standards to the limousine's chrome stanchions. Now they hung there, gaudy insignias of yellow eagles and black swastikas. Pass took them off. He didn't want to drive around with those things wagging in the breeze. He stepped up into the car. As he picked his way around the expanse of black leather upholstery, Pass discovered secret compartments—and in those compartments, Nazi Iron Cross medals. Pass gathered these in his fist and tossed them into a desk drawer. The limousine's tires were bad, but the engine turned over, eight fat cylinders punching beneath the hood. Pass pulled hard on the wheel and steered the grumbling monster outside. "It was built like a tank," he remembers. "It drove like a big old Pierce-Arrow."[15]

In time, Pass had an educational exhibit constructed for the car. He hired a commercial voice-over man to narrate a 45 record that crackled to life as spectators entered. Kicked off by a trumpet fanfare and a hair-raising recording of Hitler shrieking into a microphone, the narrator's silky baritone recounted the car's mechanical specs before winding down the garden path of folklore. Errors aside, however, Pass's curatorial approach was—at least for a carnival setting—restrained and thoughtful. The narrator explained how badly Hitler had needed Mannerheim's military cooperation, and how the gift of the limousine had played a part in securing it. Pass's script also pointed out that the 770K, for years "exhibited as Hitler's car," had in fact never been registered in Hitler's name. Finally, lest visitors fail to understand the context that Pass tried to create, the recording closed with a reminder that the car was "not on display to glorify Adolph Hitler," and how the titanic automobile "represents the genius and craftsmanship of a clever people, many of whom were slaves at the time it was built." Instead of dwelling on Hitler's supposed ownership, Pass's exhibit stressed that the car was a "symbol."[16]

Pass invested his own time in the tour. He remembers a perilous moment in Nashville when, as he backed the Mercedes out of its trailer, the automobile's brakes gave out. With Pass at the wheel, the ten-thousand-pound limousine sailed down the ramp like a runaway train. The car was out of control for only a few yards—but "it felt like five miles," he says. "I finally got it in gear before it hit a tree."[17]

By late November of 1974, the big Mercedes had joined thirty-three other antique vehicles at the Chicago Antique Auto Museum, a cement-block box squatting beneath the power lines along Skokie Valley Road in the northern suburb of Highland Park.[18] Other featured guest cars were the Batmobile and the Black Beauty, superhero Green Hornet's 1966 Chrysler Imperial, tricked out by customizer Dean Jeffries and driven in the short-lived TV series. Judging from the reactions of visitors, it was clear that Batman had become a bigger draw than Hitler. "The younger generation glances at the five-ton limousine as though they don't know what it represents," lamented museum proprietor J. J. Born, "and then they start drooling over our more exotic machines."[19]

The lack of response was no doubt frustrating for Robert Pass, but by now he had bigger problems.[20] On the road and in the papers, the big Mercedes was not educating the public so much as inflaming it. An irate response from the Jewish community was perhaps not surprising, but the backlash came from everywhere. Some of it was vicious.

Pass recounts, with rueful humor now, how the callers mistakenly apportioned their threats. They assumed Walter Klein was Jewish and Robert Pass was a Christian, when in fact it was the other way around. "Walter is Catholic and *I'm* Jewish," Pass told me. "But the Jewish hate calls went to Walter and I got them both." The angry callers even included the same charities that Pass had been trying to help, and told him, "If you can spend that kind of money for a car, then you can spend money on our charity instead."[21] The threats were the presumptive reason why, when reporters asked who owned the Hitler limousine on his display floor, J. J. Born would not budge. "The owner insists on anonymity," he said. "He doesn't want to be pestered by people writing or phoning him."[22] Frightened for his family's safety, Pass bought an unlisted phone number—one that remains unlisted to this day, more than four decades later, because of the big Mercedes-Benz.[23]

In the flush of his auction victory, Pass had vowed that he'd never sell the car.[24] One year and four months after acquiring it, Pass decided that selling was his only option.

Pass had learned the same lesson that many of his predecessors had. It is no simple thing to own an automobile affiliated with the twentieth century's most famous mass murderer, altruistic ends notwithstanding. Having gone into debt in an effort to use the car to instruct the public on the evils of Nazism, Pass's motives were as noble as they came. But the weight of the car's notoriety had crushed him nevertheless. Pass had understood that he'd purchased both a relic and a symbol. But he'd underestimated the power of the symbol he possessed. If the car did educate the public to a degree, it fomented the furious, fanatical, and deranged in its ranks far more. In the end, it was not the car that was terrifying; it was the people who heard the car whispering to them who were terrifying. They had been too much for Earl Clark and for Bonnie Barrett. Ultimately, they had even been too much for Christopher Janus, who hadn't been open about his harassment until this time. Reached for comment in November of 1974, shortly before Pass put the car on the block, Janus explained, "I had to get rid of it. I was being bothered all the time by nuts."[25]

"We were scared—Wally and I were scared," says Pass, referring to his co-owner Walter Klein. "We'd have kept the car, but it got crazy. I was intimidated, and we got rid of it."[26]

For the third time, the brothers Kruse left Auburn, Indiana, to auction the Mannerheim Mercedes. On this occasion, they set up their podium and candy-striped tent in Dunedin, Florida, at a place called Josey's Horseless Carriage Shop. The antique car showroom had some three hundred other vehicles on the block that early February weekend in 1975. But, as with every other auction that had included the big Mercedes, only Hitler made the headlines.

The auction's organizers were confident: The Mannerheim car— billed, of course, as Hitler's car—was "expected to [b]ring some $200,000."[27] But it didn't. Not even close.

The auction topped out at $141,000, a price far below the record set the year before. $35,000 LOSS DECLARED IN SALE OF HITLER'S CAR was *The New York Times* headline in its Monday-morning edition.[28] Said *The Hartford Courant*, "Cars of the famous do not always keep going up in price."[29] It was little wonder the car's value had suddenly dropped by 20 percent. Newspaper reports had made it obvious that the limousine was a hot potato: Within months of buying it, the car's last two owners had dumped it.

"Owning this car is like being married to a movie star," auctioneer Dean Kruse would later say. "It takes a certain kind of person."[30] The man who dared take title to the Hitler limousine could expect to "find himself barraged with every type of reaction," Kruse said, including "people who will call in the middle of the night" and those who "may even want to destroy the car."[31]

Who would bid a small fortune for that kind of grief? The car's new owner was one A. J. Frascona, a Buick dealer from Wauwatosa, Wisconsin. And from his first interview with the press, Frascona made one thing clear about his new purchase: He didn't want it.

A. J. Frascona started his career after the war as a buyer for Montgomery Ward, but a sideline of fixing up used automobiles and selling them did so well that he decided to get into the car business full time. At Chicago's West Side Buick in the early 1950s, Frascona proved himself so adept at selling cars that he became something of a legend at General Motors headquarters. He once sold 452 Buicks in a single year—an average of nearly two cars per day, every business day. Only a highly skilled and highly likable guy could sustain numbers like that, and Frascona was both.

In 1956, Frascona struck out on his own, buying a franchise in Wauwatosa and eventually opening a sprawling lot at 112th and Burleigh. Wauwatosa is a suburb of Milwaukee. But when it came time for a new Buick, it wasn't unusual for old customers to drive the ninety-seven miles down from Chicago to buy one from A. J. Frascona.

Don Brill hired on with Frascona in 1968 when Brill was nineteen, and stayed for thirty-seven years. Frascona, who died in 2012, did his own radio spots, and Brill can still hear them in his head. "He used to sing, 'On the road again! I have to get more Buicks on the road again!'" Brill says. "He was the singing car dealer of Milwaukee."[32]

And as of February 9, 1975, Frascona was also the latest owner of the infamous Hitler 770K Grosser limousine. Brill remembers that, too.

"He called me the next day and said, 'Holy Cow.' I said, 'A. J., I can't believe you bought that car,' and he said, 'I can't believe that I bought it.'"[33]

As Frascona later explained, he'd placed his bid "as a joke," and never expected he'd win the auction. But the moment that Frascona's bid was in, the other bidders mysteriously put their paddles down.[34] To this day, Brill believes that Frascona got taken by shills.[35]

An AP photographer and a curious crowd were on hand when the car arrived in Wauwatosa. Frascona turned up in a dark fedora and a double-breasted suit, a glum look on his face. *The Daily Tribune* of Wisconsin Rapids made the car's arrival its page-one story.[36]

Out back of the Buick showroom was an aluminum shed where Frascona kept a collection of old cars, sometimes selling one of them off if the price was good. Frascona stashed the Hitler car in there. Brill recalls taking a ride in the limousine a few times, just around the neighborhood. As befits a lifelong, successful car salesman, Brill remembers that the limousine ran smoothly and also that its weight made it impossible to get the thing up on the lift.

With the 770K stowed away and out of public view, Frascona seems to have escaped the scrutiny and criticism that had bewitched the car's previous owners. The exception was a reporter from *The Wisconsin Jewish Chronicle* who called to ask why a respected member of the Wauwatosa business community had Hitler's car in the garage. "I'm not that proud that I have it," was Frascona's reply. He said he'd called around to a few museums to see if they wanted to display the car, but, he admitted, "I'm not one that has much use for it."[37]

Clearly not. The Mannerheim Mercedes would sit inside the aluminum shed in the back lot of Frascona Buick for five years—longer than most of the car's previous owners had held on to it. Then, in the summer of 1980, a buyer appeared. His name was Axel Ward, though he transacted his business under a corporation named Zulu Ltd. out of San Diego.[38] From here, the story disappears into the mists. It's possible that the car was brought to Mexico.[39] It might have been moved to Southern California. In any case, Ward paid Frascona two hundred thousand dollars, handing him a handsome fifty-nine-thousand-dollar profit on the Hitler limousine Frascona had never wanted to own in the first place.[40]

Then the car disappeared.

For thirty-two years, Americans had been captivated by the story of a sinister limousine, one that had drawn crowds, raised money, and sold papers even though the car's actual contact with Hitler had been fleeting. If so potent a remnant of a terror regime was to endure as a reminder of the evils of the authoritarian state, of Fascism and racism, surely it would have served that purpose better had it been Hitler's *actual* limousine—a Mercedes he had used routinely, a true instrument of power and demagoguery, one that really had borne the hateful little man with the toothbrush mustache past all those demented crowds.

Alas, the Mannerheim Mercedes-Benz was not that car. Nor, apparently, was the old Göring Special, sitting behind the ropes at the Canadian War Museum. But unbeknownst to the curators in Ottawa, a newcomer to the museum staff had been eyeing that car with increasing curiosity. He was an ordinary librarian, defensive and reclusive. And he was about to blow the case wide open.

13

THE SLEUTH

L ate in 1979, the curators at the Canadian War Museum decided to consolidate all of the museum's WWII artifacts on the
second floor. One result of the reorganization was that the five-ton
Göring Special would be moving downstairs.

The old Mercedes had not received much official attention since
chief curator Lee F. Murray had given up trying to identify it in the
summer of 1970. But plans to relocate the car appear to have torn
open an old wound. At the time, deputy chief curator Ralph Manning restated an obvious fact that his staff would rather have forgotten: "We have been unable to come up with one tittle of evidence
that our German staff car had any particular relationship to the
Field Marshal."[1]

Not that this fact ever reached the general public. A museum
press release issued in May of 1980 once more referred to the limousine as "Goering's Staff Car" despite an utter lack of evidence that
was, no doubt, by that time, unnerving and embarrassing to the museum's upper ranks.[2] But by the spring of 1980, the car had drawn
the attention of someone in the lower ranks.

He worked on the museum's second floor, where all of the WWII artifacts were now finding new spots. He was a librarian by the name of Ludwig Kosche. And for reasons that will never be known, the sinister car with the mysterious past seemed to call out in a voice that only Kosche could hear.

Ludwig Kosche would have been more than justified had he plugged his ears. The Nazis had nearly killed him, and he was lucky to be alive, well, and living on Canadian soil.

Born in Bremen in 1929, Kosche was barely four years old when Hitler seized the chancellorship in 1933. He was too young to fight in the war but not too young to slip from the grasp of the Hitler Youth, which bred the Reich's future foot soldiers by applying a program of "struggle and victory" to instill "the conviction of superiority over others."[3] In 1939, a law called the Jugend-Dienst-Gesetz instituted compulsory state service for all German boys ages ten and up. Kosche turned ten in 1939.

In the spring of 1945, as Germany lurched toward its fiery collapse, the Wehrmacht summoned Ludwig Kosche to duty. He was a few months shy of his sixteenth birthday. Reduced to conscripting elderly men and adolescent boys to defend the doomed Reich, Hitler succeeded in doing little more than feeding German males to the meat grinder. Kosche would have known as much but reported for duty regardless. He had no real choice. It was then that a commanding officer looked Kosche over, informed him the war was as good as finished, and advised him to return home.[4] That officer, whoever he was, could have been shot for letting Kosche go. He'd also saved the boy's life.[5]

In 1950, at twenty-one years of age, Kosche left Germany for Ottawa, Ontario. Though the war had doubtless interrupted his education, Kosche made up for it, earning a BA and MA in history, and finally an MLS from the University of Toronto. After completing his studies in 1973, Kosche found a job with the National Museums of Canada, which posted him to the library at the Canadian War Museum.

Kosche was by all accounts a cultivated gentleman. He was frighteningly well read, kept an enormous library of classical music, played chess, smoked a pipe, and knew his way around fine wines. But for all his intellectual gifts, Kosche lacked in a single, serious, regard: He possessed none of the social graces that would have permitted him to make friends, to get along in the museum's bureaucracy, to advance professionally. In the boxes of letters Kosche left behind, his tone changes from formal to furious as quickly as a cold front rolling across Canada's prairie provinces. He was stiff, distant, and impatient, which is largely how he is remembered today.

"He was sort of gruff—not a friendly guy," says Canadian War Museum historian Cameron Pulsifer, now retired, who was acquainted with Kosche in the librarian's final years.[6] "When I met him to use the library for the first time, he didn't want me there," recalls Carol Reid, today a collections specialist in the museum's archives. "If you weren't [a] professional, you weren't worth his time. Students, I'm sure, just maddened him. He was a product of Europe in the 1930s and '40s—very German, with that very precise German attitude."[7] "As a librarian, he was helpful beyond measure," recalls Hugh Halliday, also retired, who joined the museum's curatorial staff in 1974 and knew Kosche as an acquaintance. To his work, Kosche brought an "impatience—even intolerance—of bullshit," Halliday says.

Kosche's precision and intolerance for bullshit may not have helped his social life (he lived alone and had few friends). But these qualities were about to stand the Canadian War Museum very well. Once Kosche's interest fastened on a particular historical question, he was known to devote himself to a relentless pursuit of its secrets. And one day in 1980, the librarian's inquisitive eye fell on the Mercedes-Benz limousine that had rolled to a stop on his floor.

As a museum employee, Kosche would have known about the central problem of the car as a display artifact—that the attribution to Göring was based on hearsay, and that no evidence linking the car to any particular Nazi high official had ever been found. Such a glaring omission in the record of a leading cultural institution would have offended Kosche. It would also have engaged him. And if his interest was casual at first, something happened in February of 1980 that immediately deepened it.

That month, in the course of relocating the car, the museum staff stripped away the layer of black paint that had covered its rear license plate since the limousine had first gone on exhibit in 1971. The numbers were faded, but as Kosche got close enough he could make them out.[8] There was an "IA," denoting a vehicle registered in Berlin, followed by a raised red "v"—a letter indicating a civilian automobile with official permission to operate during the war.[9] After that came the six numbers of the registration itself: 148697. There was little doubt that the plate was genuine: Plainly visible on the white enamel was a stamp issued by the Berlin Polizei: an eagle, its wings outstretched, grasping a swastika wreath in its talons.

This was most likely the clue that hooked Kosche, the one that started him on his quest, as he later put it, "to find out, if possible, what the facts are, and what the mythology is."[10]

Kosche began to keep notes, ones he typed up and then filed in folders and, later on, in ever-thickening binders. "Sometime after the capture of the car, this [license] plate was painted over," reads one of his entries. "With the over-painting now removed, the original inscription, although clearly legible, is somewhat faint."[11]

Being a librarian, Kosche delved into the museum's files first.[12] He'd have been surprised, no doubt, to find how little the museum actually knew about the Nazi limousine it had accepted as a gift from Claude Pratte in 1969. The records would have reflected that, before Pratte took ownership, one R. J. Rumble of Toronto had restored the car for Herbert J. O'Connell after purchasing it from a U.S. Army surplus auction in 1956 in Aberdeen, Maryland.

In the archives, Kosche found the limousine's original factory order number that the German embassy in Ottawa had sent to curator Lee Murray in June of 1970.[13] He'd also have seen that this was the furthest that Murray had gotten. The car was believed to have been captured in Berchtesgaden by the 101st Airborne Division after the war. It was believed to have been Göring's. All sorts of things were believed about the ominous limousine, but beliefs are not evidence. The single most popular WWII artifact on Canadian soil was a five-ton mystery waiting to be solved.

On February 21, 1980, Kosche sent a departmental memo to Murray, informing him of his intention to take on the research about the mysterious Nazi Mercedes. Realizing, as he no doubt did, that Murray had already devoted considerable time to this same effort a decade before, Kosche would have done well to proceed with deference. He didn't. His memo was haughty and didactic.[14]

"I have the obvious advantage of language," Kosche boasted, referring to his fluent German, "and, I think without a word of exaggeration, I know more about it."[15] Having firmly stepped on his curator's ego in an official communiqué, Kosche received a prompt response to his request for museum funding: no.

It didn't matter. Kosche was already off and running, though he hit little but dead ends at first. After contacting the U.S. Army Military History Institute for any leads on the 101st Airborne Division and the 36th Infantry Division, two forces he knew had been in Berchtesgaden in the final days of the war, Kosche eventually located General Maxwell Taylor, who'd commanded the 101st. By letter, Kosche asked the general if he recalled finding any Mercedes-Benz limousines in the vicinity of Hitler's alpine lair. Yes, Taylor answered—lots of them. "Upon entering Berchtesgaden in May 1945, we 'liberated' a number of fine MB's which had allegedly been used by Hitler and his senior associates," Taylor responded. As best the general could recall, all were black, armor-plated touring cars, and they all looked the same to him.[16]

Closer to home, the leads were just as cold. By now, Herbert J. O'Connell, who'd commissioned R. J. Rumble to buy the Mercedes, was dead, and his son knew nothing about the car. When Kosche reached Rumble, still running his Buick dealership in Toronto, the salesman once again related the story that the limousine had been "issued to Goering," but admitted he was merely repeating what he'd been told, presumably at the army surplus auction down in Aberdeen, Maryland.[17]

The Buick dealer did share one new detail, however. Rumble recounted that when he first got his hands on the car in 1956, the fog-lamp assembly on the front bumper was missing. Rumble explained how his mechanics had improvised a U-shaped tubular bar and mounted three new lamps on it. For Kosche, this was an important, early piece of intelligence: It meant that the old Göring Special had looked different during its years of use by the Nazis.[18]

The first few weeks of Kosche's inquiry were devoted to writing. Kosche was a tireless correspondent, sending scores of letters to every lead he could think up—the U.S. Army, WWII veterans, newspaper morgues, museum curators, and antique-automobile experts in the United States and Europe. All of them would unfold a sheet of onionskin paper from the librarian in Ottawa and read Kosche's elaborate and precise account of his project. "The question of ownership, or perhaps more accurately, the historical background of this car has never been satisfactorily answered," Kosche explained to the curator of the West Point Museum in May of 1980, "and I am having a go at it."[19]

But having a go at it also drew Kosche to the car itself, which was his to explore after hours, when the museum emptied of visitors.[20] Kosche sensed, correctly, that the 770K's battle scars would be instrumental in identifying the limousine. Popping black-and-white film into the back of his camera, Kosche took detailed photographs of the shattered window on the right front side, and also the damage to the windshield. Nosing around the car, Kosche also found nine bullet holes—two more than Sergeant Azara had seen in 1945. There were three in the armor plate that rolled up behind the backseat, and two more each in the driver's compartment, in the dashboard, and on the passenger's side. He photographed all of this, too. At some point, Kosche also hefted the enormous weight of the limousine's hood, stuck his head inside, and noted the engine's serial number.[21]

As Kosche spent more time with the big Mercedes, another realization dawned on him. The librarian had located as many photos as he could find of the model W150 Grosser 770Ks, all of which were believed to be identical. But as he compared photos of the other cars to the one on the museum's second floor, Kosche discovered that there were subtle differences among the Grosser fleet. A casual observer would never notice them, but Kosche did.

The limousine on the Canadian War Museum's second floor possessed five features that, taken together, were missing from the other Grossers of the series built after 1938. The museum's car sported ventilation slits lining both panels of the folding hood, and above these were four defroster vents. While several other limousines had three hinges holding the heavy passenger doors to the frame, the museum's car had only two. Kosche had also discovered a small, ornamental crank hole sat at the base of the car's front grille, and, finally, in the back he saw that the rear passenger window was unusually narrow, compact as a pie slice. Of all the other Grosser W150 770Ks that Kosche had found photos of, no other car possessed all of these details.

This fact would be critical to Kosche's work, since he was quickly realizing the limitations of documentary evidence. Kosche knew that senior Nazi administrators drew their cars from a common pool. There would be no smoking-gun certificate that would prove whose car this had been—or, more accurately, who had ridden in the car most frequently. The only proof of who had used the 770K would be found in photographs taken in Germany before the war.[22] As Kosche himself put it, researching the limousine "does not only involve documentary, but more difficult, pictorial work."[23]

In May of 1980, Kosche made his first major pictorial breakthrough.

Armed with the car's license plate number, Kosche wrote to Mercedes expert Jan Melin at the Automobilhistoriska Klubben, the Swedish automobile club. Melin responded on June 30, 1980, and enclosed a photograph from his collection. The grainy newsreel image showed a motorcade passing through the Brandenburg Gate on March 26, 1941. Heading a long procession of limousines was a lead car with plate number IA^{v}148697. In the backseat of the car, seated beside the Reich's diplomat Joachim von Ribbentrop, was the Japanese foreign minister Yosuke Matsuoka, on his way to a meeting with Hitler.[24]

Armed with this information, Kosche dug up a photo feature in *Life* magazine, covering Matsuoka's "grand tour through the Axis"—one, it bears noting, for which the six hundred thousand German spectators had been ordered to turn up and cheer.[25] Together, the images showed the car from many angles, including its distinct features, such as the vents on the hood and the short rear passenger window. The Grosser 770K in the Canadian War Museum, Kosche now knew, had at least been used to take the Japanese foreign minister to a personal meeting with Hitler.

Which proved one thing: This car was clearly not Göring's private limousine.[26]

Since Kosche was reasonably sure that the car had been shipped to the United States by the 101st Airborne Division, he turned his attention back toward that portion of the story. By the summer of 1980, he'd made another breakthrough. Through army channels,

Kosche had begun to correspond with the former driver of Generals John E. Dahlquist and Robert I. Stack of the 36th Infantry division. On August 4, 1980, the man sent Kosche a wartime snapshot of a captured Nazi limousine with a broken passenger window on the right side. Kosche compared the image to the shatter pattern on the museum's limousine: The match was perfect. The driver told Kosche that the car in question had not been captured by the 101st Airborne, but by the 20th Armored Division.

Kosche had not even heard of the 20th Armored Division up until this point, but the implications of the discovery were enormous: "I have been barking up the wrong tree all this time," he said.[27]

With a new lead to pursue, Kosche pounced. At his request, the U.S. Army's Military History Institute dug up the 20th Armored Division's official history and sent it to him. And in that book, on a page titled "Captured," Kosche first laid eyes on the Canadian War Museum's car as it had looked at the war's end, in the hands of American soldiers who'd dubbed it the Göring Special. The photo showed the car packed with soldiers, idling in front of the Hotel Gablerbräu in Salzburg, Austria.[28]

One distinct advantage Kosche had was his native German, which he used to obtain the limousine's original ledger entry from the Daimler-Benz archives in Stuttgart. In the years following the war, automotive researchers had been stymied by the company's unwillingness to discuss the cars it had built for the Nazi government. "Mercedes-Benz wishes to forget this whole unfortunate historic episode as it relates to the production of these enormous juggernauts," is how Ed Jurist of the Vintage Car store appraised the situation.[29]

The recalcitrance shown by Mercedes was just one symptom of a greater German exhaustion over the man—an elected man—who'd led the country into ruin and left it in an enduring state of shame.

Germans simply did not want to talk about Hitler anymore. Writing in the newspaper *Die Zeit* in 1978, Karl-Heinz Janssen summed up the national mood this way: "There we sit after more than thirty years—the Empire in ruins, the East German homeland lost, Berlin divided, Prussia abolished, the old society with all its values destroyed, the new still without contours, the world filled with the rattling of weapons, hearts filled with secret fears, of atomic catastrophe, of inflation and unemployment, of terrorists—and, despite all that, ever again Hitler, Hitler, Hitler—one can't stand it!"[30]

No, the hopeful researcher petitioning the Mercedes archives for information on a limousine built for *der Führer*'s government could not reasonably expect a prompt response, or perhaps any response. But Kosche got one. Not only did he speak flawless German, his letters glowed with the respectful formality that would have charmed any bureaucrat's heart.[31] "My own experience with Daimler-Benz has been very good, albeit a bit slow," Kosche later said. "I at times suspect that people ask more of them than they can give."[32]

Daimler-Benz gave freely to Kosche, which is how he was able to determine that the Canadian War Museum's car had been vehicle no. 429334 and had left the factory on July 8, 1940, bound for the chancellery garage in Berlin. As Kosche had expected, this information from Mercedes did not reveal the identity of the official who'd used the car, but it did establish the beginning of its story. It also gave Kosche a problem: The serial number of the engine as it appeared in the Daimler-Benz records did not match the one he'd found on the engine inside the Canadian War Museum's car. It would take time, and a considerable stroke of luck, to solve that riddle.

By February of 1981, Kosche decided that he'd accomplished all that he reasonably could by writing letters from Ottawa. Requesting leave from his library post, he purchased a five-hundred-dollar round-trip ticket on Eastern Airlines to Washington, D.C., where he would spend the two weeks between March 30 and April 10.

It was quite a time to be in the U.S. capital. Only a few hours after Kosche's plane landed, would-be assassin John Hinckley Jr. shot President Ronald Reagan just outside the T Street entrance to the ballroom of the Washington Hilton, seven blocks north of Dupont Circle. One imagines Kosche amid the tumult of the city that rainy Monday, dressed in his customary gray, carrying a black briefcase, a fifty-one-year-old librarian with a heavy German accent on his own secret mission to the capital city's musty archives. "I sport a rather whitish goatee," the balding, plumpish Kosche would say of his appearance around this time. "On top it is rather thin, and the middle shows up as not exactly slim."[33]

Kosche would strike gold on that trip. At the Library of Congress, he picked his way through no fewer than fifty photo albums that had belonged to Hermann Göring, documenting nearly every aspect of the late aviation minister's decadent and lethal career. The albums "have all sorts of photos of his cars, but not one of [them is] ours," Kosche later wrote, finally able to conclude the obvious: "The car in the Canadian War Museum has nothing to do with Göring."[34]

After reviewing Göring's photo albums, Kosche sat through interminable German, Japanese, and Italian newsreels from the war years. Then he repaired a few blocks west to the National Archives, where he sifted through the photographic files of Heinrich Hoffmann, personal photographer to Hitler. The whole endeavor took days. For Kosche, however, the time must have floated past in a pulse-quickening warp, because only the rare and peculiar few who heed the call of the researcher's vocation can truly know the euphoria of the payoff that comes from days or weeks of toil in the library stacks. And undoubtedly, Kosche knew it: Hunkered somewhere in those granite and limestone fortresses, the cantankerous Canadian librarian solved a mystery that had persisted for nearly four decades.

In a newsreel shot on July 19, 1940, Kosche spotted a 770K limousine with the plate IA^{v}148697 pulled up to the front of Berlin's Kroll Opera House. Visible behind the wheel was the handsome thuggish driver Erich Kempka. And disembarking from the front seat was none other than Adolf Hitler.[35]

Another photo bore the date of March 15, 1942—Heroes' Memorial Day on the Nazi calendar—showing the 770K with plate number IA^{v}148697 idling in front of the Zeughaus (Berlin's old armory) on the Unter den Linden. Looming behind the bulletproof windshield is the unmistakable visage of the dark little man with the toothbrush mustache.[36]

The car popped up again and again—in front of a Berlin flower shop and in a wooded drive of what was probably Berchtesgaden—and each time Hitler was with it. Even in photographs where Hitler was not physically present in the vehicle (such as the March 1941 state visit of the Japanese foreign minister, or Hungarian regent Miklós Horthy's visit to Hitler in Marienburg, East Prussia, on September 10, 1941), Kosche established the car's link to *der Führer* by spotting his personal standard flying from one of the chrome stanchions: Only a limousine in use by Hitler would have carried it.[37]

In addition to reading the numerals "697" on the license plate, Kosche was able to confirm the car's identity through several or all of the distinct features he'd found on it: the slotted hood, the two door hinges, short rear window, the four windshield vents, and the ornamental hole in the radiator grille.[38]

In the coming days, Kosche would locate still more photographs of Hitler riding in the Canadian War Museum's car. The Ullstein archives in Germany would produce a photograph of the car in a parade held July 19, 1940, with Hitler riding in the front seat. In a book by the German historian Max Domarus, Kosche would find a photo of Hitler stepping from the limousine as he left the birthday party for Foreign Minister Joachim von Ribbentrop on April 30, 1941. Jan Melin sent a still from the Swedish State Television Archives

showing the November 28, 1941, funeral of Luftwaffe ace Werner
Mölders, with Hitler walking toward the open door of Mercedes
IA^{v}148697.

Once Kosche was able to list all of the photos chronologically, he
concluded that the Canadian War Museum's car had served Hitler
personally for nearly a year and eight months. "The car is a genuine
Hitler car," Kosche concluded. "There are various photos, together
with other evidence, to remove all doubt."[39]

Kosche's trip to Washington was an unmitigated victory, though
proving that the car had been used by Hitler did not get Kosche any
closer to understanding how it had fallen into American hands.

The photograph Kosche had found of the Göring Special in the
Twentieth Armored Division's scrapbook had furnished him with
a small but important detail: Wearing its new coat of olive drab,
the limousine in the photo bore the letters "CCA"—short for
Combat Command A—on its fenders. Since September of 1980,
Kosche had been stymied in his efforts to locate a veteran of that
command.[40]

But now that he had Washington's colossal library system at his
disposal, Kosche was able to locate a 1945 clipping from *The Washington Post* announcing a public exhibition of the Göring Special
downtown as part of the Victory Loan Drive. Appearing with the
car, the story read, "will be Sargt. Joe Azara of Cleveland, Ohio,
who captured it on a railroad siding."[41]

Kosche's heart must have skipped a beat. Here was the man he'd
been trying to find for the last nine months.

Two days before he was due to fly home, Kosche—who clearly
had lugged his typewriter down to D.C. with him—pecked out a
letter to the Joe Azara he'd found listed at 9110 Orchard Avenue in
Cleveland: "Dear Mr. Azara, Please forgive a complete stranger for
intruding on your time, but if you . . . served in World War II with

either the 101st U.S. Airborne Division, or the 20th U.S. Armored Division . . . then I would very much appreciate if you would get in touch with me as soon as possible."[42]

What Kosche had no way of knowing was that Sgt. Joe Azara had died fourteen years earlier, in 1966. It was his son, Joseph Andrew Azara, who was listed in the directory. Kosche apparently received no response to his letter, but he'd scribbled the family's Ohio telephone number down in blue ballpoint ink in the upper right corner of his notes. Some days later, the telephone in the Azara home rang. "My mother answered the phone and handed it to me," Joseph Andrew Azara recalls. "She said, 'He's asking about daddy.'"

Kosche's voice was tentative. "Are you," he asked, "the Joe Azara who captured Hermann Göring's car?"

"No," Azara responded, "—but my father captured the car."

It was then that Kosche's voice faltered. The stiff, dispassionate German had finally come upon the moment that softened him. He could not speak for several moments. "You don't understand. . . ." Kosche stammered over the phone, he'd been waiting for this moment to come for nearly a year.[43]

A combination of old newspaper articles and conversations with the Azara family filled Kosche in on the story of how Sergeant Joe Azara had found the car abandoned on a railroad siding in Laufen in 1945. It was never determined what had happened to the car between Hitler's last documented use of it in March of 1942 and Azara's discovery of it in May of 1945: Why had a car that had been based at the chancellery garage in Berlin made its way to Berchtesgaden, which had its own garage of automobiles? Or why had the limousine been lashed to a flatbed railroad car, bound for a destination unknown?

That unsolved mystery aside, Kosche pieced everything else together. He located the May 24, 1945, issue of *The Dispatch,* the Twentieth Armored Division's newspaper, which had run a story about the Göring Special on its front page. The article described the bullet holes found in the limousine's interior and on the rear slab of retractable armor plate. It was the precise damage—right down to the locations of the bullet scars—that Kosche had discovered inside of the museum's 770K.

Later, as Kosche examined newspaper photos and snapshots of the limousine taken by the soldiers of the Twentieth Armored, he noticed the cracks in the heavy glass of the windshield and the right front passenger window. These also matched those on the museum's car. An article that covered the Mercedes's arrival at Boston's Castle Island noted that the car's odometer was broken. From his talk with Rumble, Kosche knew that the Toronto restorer had not repaired it. When the limousine had arrived in Boston in 1945, the odometer's tumblers stood frozen at 13,900 kilometers. Peering through the gauge's dusty glass on the second floor of the Canadian War Museum, Kosche discovered this same number.[44]

One of the things that had long confused Kosche was why the limousine's engine number as recorded on the Daimler-Benz factory ledger did not match the number he found on the engine sitting inside the car. The Azaras were able to explain how Sergeant Joe threw a rod on the original motor and later salvaged a spare engine from another 770K captured by the 101st Airborne in Berchtesgaden. One night in late April of 1981, Joseph Azara called Kosche to tell him he'd discovered a metal builder's plate among his father's things. This turned out to be the tag that Sgt. Azara had pried off the 770K from which he'd lifted the replacement engine in Berchtesgaden in 1945. The number on the metal tag in the Azara home in Cleveland, Ohio, was a perfect match to the number on the engine sitting in the Canadian War Museum in Ottawa, Ontario.

"This is rather conclusive evidence," Kosche noted in his files.[45]

It was. In fact, it essentially closed the case, even though Kosche would continue to run down leads on the car for a couple more years. "All evidence flatly contradicts that legend that the armored Grosser Mercedes in the Canadian War Museum was 'Goering's staff car,'" Kosche would later write. "It is in fact one of the cars which Hitler used during the heyday of his devastating career."[46]

What had motivated Kosche? It would be easy to read into the librarian's motives, to presume that some kind of emotional wound from the past, an unresolved piece of business with the Nazis, was the thing that caused him to throw himself into the search for the limousine's true provenance. But there's no evidence of this. Kosche was unemotional about his past and took a clinical approach to his present. Still, what he did was rare and remarkable.

"Quite frankly, I don't know what motivated him," former war art curator Hugh Halliday says. "Doing the kind of in-depth research that he did wasn't fashionable in the museum."[47] At the time Kosche worked in the library, his old colleague explains, the pay was poor, the academic standards low, and the staffing chronically inadequate. Yet, according to the expense tally left behind in Kosche's papers, he spent a total of $2,652 Canadian on his efforts to research the War Museum's Mercedes. It is a considerable sum for a low-level civil servant today, let alone in 1981.

The only explanation left is the elemental one Kosche himself might have sanctioned: The Grosser Mercedes was an artifact that required research, and he was in a position to do that research. Unlike the rest of the Canadian War Museum staff, Kosche understood the German bureaucratic culture, knew the language, and was possessed of the discipline required, including an essential trait: He was simply interested. His interest in the automobile was borne of no immediate personal experience—Ludwig Kosche neither owned nor drove an automobile—but it seems, rather, to have arisen from the man's career-long hunger for amassing and ordering facts, which were a kind of currency in his solitary life. "I think," Halliday concludes, "it was basically curiosity."[48]

Kosche was proud of his work and began preparing an account

of it—one he sold to the British war magazine *After the Battle*, which published it in February of 1982. The article gave him a degree of recognition among military and automobile aficionados and, much later on, the museum's curators.

"This is without question the most concise and properly documented treatise on the subject that has ever been printed," Edgar Jurist told Kosche after reading his article.[49] "Kosche's study is thorough, meticulous, and indisputable, and it transformed the significance of the artifact," the Canadian War Museum's Cameron Pulsifer wrote in 1999. If the mysterious and sinister Mercedes-Benz was initially "an object of moderate interest when associated with the second-ranking Nazi leader," Pulsifer continued, after Kosche's revelation "it became one of intense fascination when associated with the arch-villain behind the whole Nazi enterprise, the *Führer* himself."[50]

But if Kosche hoped his work would place him in better standing within the museum establishment, he was to be disappointed. The problem was not that his scholarship was lacking, but rather that the chilly, tone-deaf side of his personality once again offended the authorities whose recognition he expected. Five months after his story appeared in print, Kosche submitted a two-page memorandum to curator Lee Murray, proposing that the museum produce a book about the librarian's investigation. Kosche insisted that he do the writing, select the photos, retain the rights, and receive a two-thousand-dollar flat fee in addition to all royalties. In his munificence, Kosche allowed that the Canadian War Museum could have the job of paying all of the book's production costs.[51]

The response from the head office was swift: "Totally unacceptable."[52]

By the fall of 1983, realizing that his book would not materialize, Kosche appealed to the museum to reimburse him for the fees he incurred in proving that the Göring Special had, in fact, been Hitler's car. He argued that he had stepped in to solve a mystery

that the museum had failed to solve, that the institution had bene-
fitted from his work, and that the mammoth Mercedes 770K on the
second floor would appreciate in value as a consequence.[53]

All of these contentions were clearly true. But Kosche had overlooked a foundational truth: He had undertaken his research wholly
on his own initiative and with no blessings from the upper ranks.
He had acted outside his official duties.[54] And as spectacularly successful as he'd been, did success alone make the case for a check to
be cut after the fact? The museum thought not, and never parted with
a cent.[55]

The denial of payment turned an already surly librarian into a
bitter man. Even three years later, Kosche was still smoldering over
how he'd been treated. "All the research expenses, and these were
very substantial, were borne by myself," he railed—again in another
memo. Reimbursement? "I received none," Kosche said, "though I
had asked for it."[56]

Kosche's anger at the museum might have led to the mutinous
move he made next. Kosche was aware that Ralph Engelstad, the
owner of the Imperial Palace Auto Collection in Las Vegas, had a
taste for 770K Grossers with a Nazi provenance. Engelstad was the
collector who'd acquired Detroit theater king Marty Shafer's Grosser
limousine and also the armored 770K that Joe Ogden and Steve
Munson had pulled out of a VFW garage in Greeneville, Tennessee. In fact, it was Kosche, moonlighting as a freelance researcher,
who would establish the provenance of the latter vehicle—including
the photographic proof that Hitler had actually used the Ogden/
Munson car on several public occasions between 1939 and 1941.
Aware of Engelstad's appetite for Grossers, Kosche began working
behind the scenes to help Engelstad buy—"repatriate" was the term
he preferred—the Canadian War Museum's car.[57]

It didn't work. In April of 1985, a letter on the Imperial Palace's
blue-and-gold-foil letterhead arrived at the office of Leo Dorais,
secretary general of the National Museums of Canada, offering

US$250,000 for the hulk of a Mercedes sitting below spotlights at the Canadian War Museum.[58] Dorais didn't bite. The car would remain in Canada.[59]

Ludwig Kosche retired in September of 1985. The loss of his skills at the library desk was, obviously, a great one. But Kosche's arrogance and abrasive personality had obviously won him few allies among the higher ranks: A year after he left the museum, when the curator's office finally got around to issuing a press release announcing that the 770K in the museum was in fact "Adolph Hitler's personal staff car," it attributed the groundbreaking research only to "a former museum librarian."[60]

There remained one nagging mystery that Kosche had failed to solve before his retirement, and this was the fate of the limousine's front license plate. It was present in photographs Kosche had found of the car in Austria, serving as the Twentieth Armored Division's Göring Special. But the plate had vanished by the time the limousine emerged from the bowels of the Liberty ship *George Shiras* in Boston Harbor.

Then, in January of 1987, a memorabilia collector from Quincy, Illinois, named Darrell Williams sent the Canadian War Museum a color photograph of a Berlin license plate from the war years. Williams revealed that he'd obtained the plate three months earlier from a retired postal worker named Marlyn L. Olson. In 1945, Olson had been a Technician Fifth Grade in the United States Army, and had served in Germany as the driver for Major General Orlando Ward, commander of the Twentieth Armored Division. Olson had removed the plate from the Göring Special as a war souvenir and taken it home with him to Kellogg, Iowa, where the relic—rusty, dirty, but entirely genuine—had spent the preceding forty-one years. In his letter, the collector, Williams—"a WWII historian first and a WWII collector second"—stated that he would be willing to part with the license plate for the price of four thousand U.S. dollars.[61]

The museum declined, but the color photograph Williams had taken of the plate was, in a sense, more valuable than the thing itself. Dirty and rusted, the artifact was a precise match to the plate that had remained bolted to the rear of the gigantic Mercedes: IA^{v}148697. Williams's handwritten letter, which the museum forwarded to Kosche, would serve as a final piece of validation for a remarkable piece of detective work.

Kosche lived in the seclusion of his books and records in his apartment at 255 Metcalfe Street in Ottawa until the end of his life on May 17, 2000. At Kosche's own request, there was no memorial service.

14

THE CULT OF A CAR

For all the courtesies that the Azara family had shown to Ludwig Kosche in the course of his months of research, the librarian failed to reciprocate in the one way that would have mattered most. Once Kosche had positively identified the Canadian War Museum's limousine as having been Hitler's, he neglected to tell the family of the man who'd captured it. Joseph Andrew Azara continued to assume that the big car—a car that arguably should have been in the family garage in Ohio instead of a museum in Canada—had originally been made for Hermann Göring.

Still, the younger Azara was grateful to at least know where his father's giant limousine had ended up and, a few years after communicating with Kosche, he decided to drive up to Ottawa to see it. Azara might have made the trip sooner, but he decided to wait for his three boys to grow old enough to appreciate the experience. Shortly before he piled his family into the car, Azara called one of the senior curators to say he'd like to show his family the 770K. "You come up here anytime," Azara was told, "and I'll give you a tour."[1]

Ottawa is a long way from Cleveland—coincidentally, about 770 miles by road. With Lakes Erie and Ontario standing in the path of a straight-line drive, the trip takes a good twelve hours. When the family finally arrived, Azara walked up the steps of the gothic stone building at 330 Sussex Drive and presented himself at the front desk. He still recalls the exchange vividly.

"I'm Joe Azara," he said, "and we're here to see Göring's car." The desk attendant gave him a puzzled look, considered, then responded, "Hermann Göring's car is not here."

At this, Azara had a moderate and understandable fit. "You have to bring over the director," he shot back. "There's been some kind of mistake. I just drove all the way from Cleveland!"

Within a few minutes, the curator presented himself and straightened Azara out about the details. "No, that's not Göring's car," the official told his visitor. "We found out that it's Hitler's."

Azara was stunned. Yet in an instant, a daylong drive in an automobile with three young boys assumed an even greater monumentality than it had had just moments before. Because, while most every family with a relative who fought in the Second World War reveres those keepsakes that remain behind—a cap, discharge papers, perhaps a dog-eared photo album—few indeed are the families who can count a Mercedes-Benz as proof of one man's service, let alone a Mercedes-Benz limousine that carried the megalomaniacal racist who'd started the war itself.

Sgt. Joe Azara's son and grandsons made their way to the museum's second floor, where the black beast crouched in the corner. The creased and cracked leather seats still sagged from the weight of long-vanished passengers, notorious and humble, dead and living, and a stranger roster of these would be difficult to imagine: Americans who'd bought war bonds in the summer of 1945, Brig. Gen. Cornelius Daly, Sgt. Joe Azara and his buddies, Goo Goo the duck, the Japanese foreign minister Yosuke Matsuoka, Third Reich diplomat Joachim von Ribbentrop, chauffeur Erich Kempka, and, of course, no less than Adolf Hitler himself, who had used the limousine as his personal automobile for a period of at least one year, seven months, and twenty-four days.[2]

And what did Joseph Andrew Azara feel as he gazed at the twenty-foot-long limousine his father had managed to haul from the ruins of the greatest conflict in history? "I was just looking at it and I was . . ."—Azara's voice breaks here—"I was really proud of my dad."

Though Ludwig Kosche's identification of the museum's 770K with Adolf Hitler did not change the way the car looked, it radically changed how spectators looked at it. The limousine's link to Hitler "not only greatly increased its monetary value, but transformed its significance, both for the museum itself and for the visiting public," Cameron Pulsifer has written. "Its positive identification as a car that had been used by the Führer himself imputed to it new meanings and levels of significance that transcended its status as a car, even one with a known Nazi provenance. This, of course, takes us beyond material history as we know it, and closer perhaps to the world of the personality cult."[3]

It did get close—too close.

The Canadian War Museum did not get around to updating the limousine's caption until some two years after Kosche's article appeared, finally attributing the car to Hitler in April of 1984.[4]

Shortly afterward, staffers began work on a new backdrop for the prize limousine. When they finished in 1986, the display was a jaw-dropper: The sleek Grosser limousine now sat on ersatz cobblestone in front of a half-timbered house flying a huge swastika banner.

For a car already known to have been Hitler's, the setup seemed a needlessly extravagant way of hitting the public over the head with the fact. The Bavarian streetscape was also alarmingly myopic, devoid of any references to the fact that Hitler's regime hadn't just staged impressive rallies in Nuremberg—it had systematically murdered over six million people.[5] Some time later, amid the heat of criticism, the museum hastily tacked a Holocaust photograph onto the placard mounted in front of the Grosser, but the addition failed to add balance or dimension to a presentation that many saw as thoughtless and offensive.

"The German streetscape was pretty tacky," Pulsifer says today, looking back on the period that predated his tenure. At the time, he explains, the museum staffers were "good, honest citizens interested in our military past, but they weren't clued into the intellectual issues that museums give rise to. They just put the car on display, thinking, *This is great. People will come and look at it.*"[6]

As always, people did come and look—but those people included individuals that the museum had no intention of attracting. The curators began to notice that neo-Nazis had chosen the Hitler limousine display as a place to congregate.[7] Many years before this, the owners of the Mannerheim Mercedes had learned of the machine's treacherous dual personality—how the limousine could be displayed as a means of informing and even benefiting the public, but now it also was a magnet for those who heard the sound of jackboots in their heads. The Canadian War Museum had come to the same realization: A big, fancy limousine associated with Hitler wasn't just a significant artifact; it was a socially radioactive one.

Nobody understood and feared this dichotomy better than Jack Granatstein, who became the museum's CEO and director in 1998. A noted author and historian, Granatstein was under no illusions about the dark, residual power that still swirled around the old car. But in his efforts to free the museum from that power, Granatstein would also fall prey to it.

In February of 2000, the director announced that the time had come for the museum to unburden itself of the car completely. Charging that the big black limousine "glorifies the evils of Nazism and sends the wrong message to visitors" (that is how the *Ottawa*

Citizen phrased it), Granatstein declared that the car's proper place was the auction block, where it might fetch as much as twenty million dollars—money that the cash-strapped institution could put to better uses. The intellectual grounding for Granatstein's argument was simple: An artifact with no direct connection to Canadian military history had no business in its war museum. Meanwhile, the director warned that the public's ignorance of WWII history, coupled with the museum's idyllic, Bavarian-flavored backdrop for the car was a toxic combination. "If you look at the car, the instinct is to say, 'Hitler must have been a real cool guy to have such a sharp car,'" Granatstein said. "People come away with a sense of the power and glamour of that regime rather than its horror."[8]

The *Ottawa Citizen*'s headline: DUMP HITLER'S CAR, MUSEUM BOSS SAYS.[9]

The response was explosive. Canadians barraged the museum with so many e-mails and phone calls—an average of one every two minutes—that the public-affairs office posted five staffers to man the lines. Two days into the rumpus, the *Ottawa Citizen* devoted a full page to reader mail under the banner: SHOULD WAR MUSEUM SELL THIS ARTIFACT?[10]

Surprisingly or not, the overwhelming answer was no. "This vehicle is part of history," wrote Thor Palsson of Stonewall, New Brunswick, "—good or bad, it is still history." From the Ontario district of Malton, Brad Fallon warned that sanitizing history is not how one learns from it. "I should think that the museum would be grateful to have such a rare and interesting piece," Fallon said, adding that the next time he was in Ottawa, he would "make certain to stop by" the museum and see the car. Richard Cyrenne, writing from the Ottawa neighborhood of Orléans, believed that the Canadian War Museum was fortunate to own an artifact this important in the first place: "Most visitors to the museum probably wonder how did we ever get our hands on this car," he said. "This Mercedes should be used to generate interest in the museum. Nobody comes away impressed by the Nazis." And from Zephyrhills, Florida, Charles Tapp pointed out that no museum would hesitate to display the shield of the barbarian ruler Attila, and no museum that did so would be said to have been glorifying the butchery of the Huns.

Countering Granatstein's notion that the opulent limousine encouraged a slick view of the Nazis, several readers pointed out that the car's slickness—or, rather, the dangerous appeal of it—was the point. "Hitler was a man who seduced an entire nation," Paul Griffin wrote from San Rafael, California. "This car was part of that seduction."

Indeed, some visitors (ones far more sophisticated about their history than Granatstein had reckoned) had apparently contemplated this very argument. "When I visited the museum and saw the Hitler car, I closed my eyes and could almost imagine what it would be like to visit 1930s Germany," wrote Michael Kroitor of North Gower, a small town twenty miles south of Ottawa. "It brought shivers of fear into my heart."

Less than a week after the news of the car's possible sale broke, the story was over. "The people have spoken," announced the *Ottawa Citizen*. Hitler's Mercedes would "stay parked in Ottawa."[11]

Granatstein's failure to sell off Hitler's Mercedes exposed another of its many complications: Not only was getting rid of the monster limousine not so easy as some had supposed, selling it would carry risks of its own. "If we put it up at auction, we can't control who buys it," Granatstein explained. "This car would be such a powerful icon for a neo-Nazi or extreme group. If it fell into the wrong hands, we would feel very foolish, and worse. The possible consequences are frightening."[12]

Now, perhaps for the first time, the full implications of owning the dazzling and wretched machine came into sharp focus. It was as though the museum, by accepting Claude Pratte's gift in 1969, had made an unwitting pact with the devil, and everyone knows how that deal works out. The Devil's Mercedes had delivered renown and admission receipts to the museum, but it had also conjured a dark cloud whose presence over the institution would be permanent. The Canadian War Museum would always be known, despite its countless other holdings, despite its broad base of archival study, as the home of Hitler's Mercedes-Benz.

Once it became clear that the museum would be keeping the 770K, the fact led to a reconsideration of how to display it. If the museum staff could not hope to completely contain the car's negative energy, then at least they could, perhaps, encourage visitors to contemplate where that energy had come from. At the very least, the curators would get rid of the idyllic Bavarian display that had helped to draw a new, and unwanted, generation of brownshirts. "When Granatstein brought in more university-trained people, we spent a lot of time debating how we would exhibit this Hitler car with these concerns in mind," Pulsifer recalls. "It was a big issue."[13]

It became an even bigger issue as the millennium turned and the museum began preparations to leave 330 Sussex Drive and take up new quarters a mile and a half west of Parliament Hill in the old LeBreton Flats industrial district. The museum's new home, a Raymond Moriyama–designed building to rise at 1 Vimy Place, would be a soaring edifice of concrete, copper, and glass, a majestic but challenging space whose pockmarked walls evoke the terror of a bomb shelter, even as the windy sway of native grasses planted on the roof and grounds whisper of deliverance and rebirth. In a structure already weighted with symbolism, no single artifact would be as emotionally charged or closely scrutinized as Hitler's armored limousine. So as Pulsifer and his colleagues debated how to display their notorious holding, no detail, no nuance was too small to ponder. "You have to be careful with an artifact loaded with [as much] historical baggage as the Hitler car," Pulsifer recalls. "We spent a lot of time on how we'd exhibit it."[14]

Today, a visitor to the museum pays his admission, moves past a set of doors and a uniformed attendant, and disappears into a haunting realm of darkened passageways, galleries, and dioramas devoted to documenting and re-creating the violent conflicts that stain the fabric of Canadian history. One can stare down the barrel of a cannon from the Boer War, walk the muddy wastes of Belgium's Passchendaele trenches and contemplate a chunk of the Berlin Wall. The low light and curvilinear arrangement of the galleries is deliberate: It succeeds in re-creating the fear, foreboding, and uncertainty of warfare. And since the labyrinthine layout also manages to conceal many of the displays until one turns a corner and encounters them, the visitor who comes in search of Hitler's limousine may conclude, after enough nervous wandering, that things are the other way around: Hitler's car is instead in search of him. The car has this way of sneaking up on people. Walking the passageway skirting the Hall of Honour, one makes a casual turn into Gallery 4, glances to the left, and suddenly there it is.

In its splendor, in its horror.

It crouches on the bare concrete floor, its paint and pitted chrome flashing like obsidian below floodlights. Suspended from the ceiling to drape behind the car is an immense, photo-imprinted canvas. It is a well-known image depicting the 1936 Nazi Party rally at Nuremberg's Luitpold Arena—capacity 150,000—every acre packed with columns of helmeted storm troopers. The backdrop is realistic enough to make the car appear as though it has actually drawn up into the rally, that Hitler has stepped from the running board and made for the distant rostrum—and that the visitor has arrived just in time to hear his shrieking.[15]

The backdrop is a logical historic reference, but its simplicity belies its allegorical power. The spectacle of so many turned backs (not a single soldier in the photo shows his face) testifies to mindless adherence. Red is the sole color in the mammoth black-and-white photograph, skillfully daubed onto the trio of swastika banners, and stands out like an open wound. And there is of course the car itself. With its black body and black tires and black empty seats, it is hearselike, a chariot of death. Even the shattered front window— transformed into a glistening spectacle under spotlights—becomes a kind of metaphor: to the violence of war, to shattered lives. None of these interpretations are official, but the fact that they are plausible is proof of the display's thematic depth.

This is the exhibit that Pulsifer and his colleagues labored so long and hard on in the years leading up to the museum's reopening at 1 Vimy Place in May of 2005. And it succeeds not only for what it includes—those perceptive enough will notice a Nazi flag buried in masonry debris behind the limousine's left rear tire—but also for what it leaves out.[16] There are no wax figures in uniform and no narrated loop of audiotape. And though the museum would have been within the bounds of historical accuracy to return the *Führer* Standards to the car's stanchions, it has not done so. The car alone is enough.[17]

"The vehicle itself is a very powerful symbol," says museum historian Andrew Burtch over a cup of coffee in the museum cafeteria. Burtch hastens to add, however, that the 770K is more than a symbol of the despot who motored around in it. By pairing the car with the Nuremberg photomural, he says, the museum sought to conjure the limousine's "propaganda power as an expression of political power." In other words, the sleek and muscular limousine embodies not only the hypnotic sway of Hitler's stagecraft but testifies to the result of placing the power of state in the hands of such a man. "The immediate consequences of [Hitler's] power," Burtch says, "led to world catastrophe."[18]

Do visitors—and the war museum gets half a million of those every year—absorb all of these layers of symbolism? The answer seems to be that some do and some do not.

On two late-summer afternoons, I spent a few hours in the shadow of Hitler's Mercedes-Benz, watching the various ways that visitors respond to it. Many are visibly daunted. A middle-aged woman and her son enter the limousine's realm and pause in front of the placard by the running board. "*La voiture d'Hitler*," she whispers to him ominously, and they take their leave.[19] Some parents who arrive with children attempt to use the car as a teachable moment. A father reads the placard's caption aloud to his two school-age sons: ". . . one of history's most brutal and murderous dictatorships," he announces. Nearby, a mother with a curious child in tow struggles through an exchange that has doubtless taken place here countless times:

> "Hitler—this was his car," the mother begins. "Hitler was the man who started the war."
>
> "Why did he start the war?" the child wants to know.
>
> "Well . . ." There is a long pause, then a sigh. "He wanted to get rid of a lot of people."[20]

As these responses unfold, another set of reactions is taking place as though on a different reality plane occupying the same space. Unlike their counterparts who moved into the space as though reluctantly drawn by an ominous current, this second group doesn't look upon the limousine warily at all. They do not read the car's symbolism but instead see only a rakish Mercedes-Benz limo, one made wickedly alluring by virtue of its original owner.

"That's Hitler's *actual* car?" crackles an adolescent male voice. "That's amazing. I wonder if it still works." Another teen saunters in and immediately recognizes a photo op. Taking his place in front of the car, he smiles and flashes crossed peace signs. His friend snaps the photo, and they amble out. Minutes later, two more teenage boys wander in with their father. It takes them a few seconds to size up what they're looking at. "Is this the actual car?" asks one of the boys. "This is *the* car," his father answers. To which the youth responds: "Wow—cool!"

That the smitten, enthusiastic reactions to the vehicle belong almost exclusively to adolescent boys is not happenstance. In 2009, Sara Matthews, an associate professor at Wilfrid Laurier University, published an entire academic paper exploring this very response. Many schoolteachers were "most disturbed by the ways in which adolescents responded to the car," Matthews wrote, because "instead of expressing moral outrage towards a material object that . . . held so much symbolic evil, the young visitors were in awe of the display. Many posed for pictures beside it while uttering phrases such as 'awesome!' and 'cool!'"[21]

Perhaps expecting deep reflection on a historic artifact is too much to ask of a bunch of ordinary teenage boys, especially when the object of attention is a powerful and dangerous-looking car. But instead of descending into an either-or debate about how spectators should interpret the limousine, Matthews focuses on the fact of the dichotomy as a kind of meaning in itself. The Hitler car awakens in its viewers certain "psychical dynamics of desire and resistance," an "interplay between fascination and revulsion"—the knowledge, if you will, that while the car represents a force of evil, it remains a frustratingly alluring object. A beautiful automobile once owned by the ugliest of humans—it is not an easy duality to reconcile.[22]

And perhaps one simply cannot. After all, a closer look at the exhibit shows that it is a compendium of unresolvable contradictions. A car that has nothing to do with Canadian military history has nonetheless become its military museum's most famous artifact. Its non-Canadian provenance could provide a solid academic reason to dispose of the car, yet the museum's sole attempt to do so met with the Canadian public's demand to keep it.[23] And there is a further incongruity: The car so purportedly valued by the public must also be kept a safe distance from it. One cannot help but notice the Plexiglas barriers (there is an invisible alarm, too) that enforce a perimeter around the limousine. The official reason for this measure is to impede those who'd try to pry a souvenir off the body.[24] But the barrier is there to protect the car, as well, because visitors might try to deface it. And have they tried? "Absolutely," says Carol Reid, the archive's collections specialist. "People think we shouldn't have it. There have been people who have come and spat on it. It does engender wild emotions in people."[25]

In the end, how one will regard the 770K Mercedes at the war museum probably has a lot to do with who one is before he or she walks in. As Burtch puts it, "People attach meaning to objects, and they do so largely on the basis of personal experience."[26] The car may be dazzling as a gem, or vivid as a nightmare (or perhaps some mixture of both) in keeping with one's expectations. Part of this perception is no doubt the influence of the museum setting. But much of it is the very real emotional pull that objects salvaged from the past—souvenirs, and in this case Joe Azara's souvenir—have on all of us. "While a souvenir may share the mystical value of a religious relic, its power as a historical relic accrues from the extraction of the real," Smithsonian curator William L. Bird Jr. has observed. "The souvenir's most memorable qualities are derived from a connection with an actual person, place, or event—in short, it is an association object."[27]

Given the imposing presence of a twenty-foot-long bulletproof limousine, it is not difficult to make an association between the car and Hitler. The grab handle behind the windshield that Hitler used to steady himself as he stood in the front-seat well is still there. The boot scraper on the passenger side is visibly worn from use. These are real and chilling things. And by harnessing them, a visitor can, with a little mental conjuring, actually feel, if perhaps only for a moment, some of the danger and fear that was Europe during the reign of the National Socialists. And if the visitor can indeed bring him- or herself to feel this much, then therein lays the reason not just for seeking the car out, but for the museum keeping it on display. Because the Grosser 770K in Ottawa is an important, rare, and powerful object to the extent that it acts as a window to its own past and is possessed—in ways that books or photographs perhaps are not—of a kind of alchemy: It furnishes many who look upon it with a uniquely experiential glimpse, immediate and haunting, into the black depths of Nazi Germany. This is the service, if you will, that Hitler's limousine performs. This is its value.

That window of reflection also closes quickly. For as much as one tries to retain some deeper sense of meaning of Hitler's Mercedes, there's also no denying that the thing before you is, physically, still just a 1940 Mercedes. And upon closer inspection, one sees that it is falling to pieces.

Hydraulic jacks tucked beneath the car's axles now relieve the rotting tires of their five-ton burden. The mohair ragtop, now faded into tatters, hangs limp, draping the trunk and touching the floor.[28] Blisters cluster along the once-smooth chrome strips lining the limousine's flanks, stretching back along a hood that no longer closes snug, its vents crushed inward. Atop the radiator is a sheared shaft of pot metal where the hood ornament used to be. Rust reddens the hubcaps, and a yellowed headlight stares ahead like a sightless eye. Spend enough time crouched down near the dented front grille, and the trace odor of engine oil meets your nose as it wafts low over the floor.

I related this anecdote of actually *smelling* Hitler's car—the way that the leaking oil was a kind of olfactory proof that the machine was falling apart—and Burtch told me a story.

Ten or more years earlier, working then as an ordinary research assistant, Burtch found himself completely alone with the car. The move to the new Moriyama-designed building at 1 Vimy Place, he explained, had been a long and complicated one, and so the curators made use of a former streetcar barn down on Champagne Avenue to store some artifacts. The Hitler Mercedes was one of them. Burtch had seen the limousine many times before, of course, but it had always been in the "hushed environment" of awed visitors and low lighting. But here it sat in an old warehouse amid machinery and stacks of wooden pallets. "I remember walking up to [the limousine]," Burtch recounted, "and just saying, 'Wow, this is an old wreck.'"[29]

"We're consciously using the car as a symbol," he added. "But, in the end, it's [just] a car."

15

CALIFORNIA

Bill Lyon was only eight years old in 1984, and this is why the door did not open for him. The door stood at 211 West G Street, a few blocks in from downtown San Diego's dingy and neglected waterfront. In the boom years after the war, before the interstates came, the building had been a roller rink called Skateland. But the place had gone bust by 1967, as the waterfront—a district catering to the needs of carousing sailors even in its best days—descended deeper into its already murky repute.

Now the former Skateland was a warehouse, and a place that looked abandoned to the young Bill Lyon. The proprietor had taken to using an eye-level viewing slot in the door, a sardonic touch in a neighborhood notorious for its peep shows.[1] The boy heard the slot open, far above his head. But since the man on the inside could not see him, the door stayed closed. "It was like a speakeasy," Bill Lyon recalls. "When my dad knocked, they let us in."[2]

Dad was Major General William Lyon, a venerable figure in Southern California—in the country overall, actually. The senior Lyon had already notched a heroic career in the United States Air

Force, training pilots and delivering planes to Europe and North Africa during WWII, flying in combat over Korea, and finally serving as chief of the Air Force Reserve. Lyon's sharp eye and steady hand had served him outside the cockpit, too: In the postwar years, he'd noticed the gaping need for houses that returning GIs could afford to buy, and so Lyon began to build them. As the Golden State swelled with starter families, its orange groves ceding their sandy loam to earthmovers, Lyon's company prospered. The "General," as people addressed him, was a highly respected, highly successful man, and by the early 1980s he was two decades into building a fine collection of antique automobiles.[3]

As a boy in West Hollywood during the Great Depression, General Lyon had regularly seen movie stars motoring down the palm-shaded boulevards in their Cadillacs, Packards, and Duesenbergs. By age ten, Lyon had resolved to own one of these elegant machines. His start was not auspicious. In 1941, a teenage Lyon climbed a steep hill to inspect a Model T that a high school friend was selling. The General can still recite what he was told: "Here—it runs great. If you really get into trouble, shove this thing in the middle and it'll lock the wheels." A prudent man would have turned and run, but "when you're young, you're not afraid," Lyon explains. He handed over the asking price—eight dollars—and the Ford was his. "I took this thing home and drove it all over the place until it finally disintegrated."[4]

The prospering of Lyon's real estate business allowed him to start buying automobiles—nice ones, this time—in the early 1960s. The passage of years affirmed his good taste: By the time he knocked on the door of the abandoned roller rink, the General was well on his way to amassing a thirty-five-car collection valued at twenty-six million dollars.[5] Unlike many collectors of antique automobiles, General Lyon was not flashy. He tucked his finds into a pair of warehouses in Costa Mesa, where they awaited a new home on an estate that Lyon was building up in the mountains of Coto de Caza.

Hitler inspects the gift car soon to be shipped to Field Marshal Gustaf Mannerheim of Finland. This image was taken in November 1941 at the Wolfschanze ("Wolf's Lair"), Kętrzyn, Poland. Hitler's young chauffeur Erich Kempka is standing by the opened hood. (Canadian War Museum)

Mannerheim (center, in fur cap) inspects his gift from Hitler outside of Finnish Army headquarters in Mikkeli on December 16, 1941. Kempka stands on the far left. (Finnish Armed Forces)

With the hoods opened, Kempka explains the features of the supercharged, 8-cylinder monster to Mannerheim. In time, the Finnish field marshal would enjoy encouraging his own chauffeur to press the 770K to its top speed. (Finnish Armed Forces)

At the time of the car's delivery to Finland, it wore SS license plates and swastika flags (one is partially visible on the right stanchion) put on in Germany. The Finns removed these after the Germans departed. (Finnish Armed Forces)

On June 4, 1942, Hitler paid a surprise visit to Mannerheim for his seventy-fifth birthday. After touching down at the Immola airfield in Southeastern Finland, Hitler stepped aboard the 770K he'd given to Mannerheim five months earlier. Finnish president Risto Ryti (wearing fedora in backseat) escorted Hitler to Lake Saimaa, where Mannerheim waited in his military train. (Finnish Armed Forces)

Because the Mercedes' enormous weight would have lodged the car in the mud, Hitler continued on foot to his trackside meeting with Mannerheim. (Finnish Armed Forces)

His lunch with his reluctant war partner finished, Hitler reboards the 770K for the return to the airport. This will be the third—and last—contact that Hitler has with the Mannerheim Mercedes. (Finnish Armed Forces)

A bit of a gearhead, Field Marshal Mannerheim added the Grosser to his collection of cars at home, which included a 1938 Packard 8 limousine, shown in the rear of this July 1942 photograph. (Finnish Armed Forces)

Accepting the 770K in lieu of payment on a ball-bearing deal, Chicago importer Christopher Janus takes delivery of the colossus on the *M.S. Stockholm*, Pier 97, New York City, on June 28, 1948. Janus has been assured by his Swedish agent that the car had belonged to Hitler. (Courtesy of K. H. Gibson III)

When Janus put "Hitler's Car" on display in Rockefeller Center, it drew enormous crowds. Among the visitors was no less a figure than Howdy Doody. (Courtesy of K. H. Gibson III)

Janus leased his car to 20th Century–Fox for its 1951 film *The Desert Fox*. Here, James Mason (as Rommel) poses with the limousine, probably on the set in Borrego Springs, California. (Courtesy of K. H. Gibson III)

A young George Waterman (center) and Kirkland Gibson (right), the pioneering Yankee car collectors who'd later add the Mannerheim Mercedes to their automotive caboodle. (At the wheel of the DeDion Bouton is Samuel Eliot, who'd go on to invent the Cricket III, a car that ran on compressed air.) (Reprinted with permission from *The Bulb Horn Magazine*, published by the Veteran Motor Car Club of America)

The Mannerheim Mercedes, by now showing signs of wear, parked in front of George Waterman's Rhode Island Garage, sometime in the early 1950s. (Courtesy of K. H. Gibson III)

In 1953, Kirkland Gibson commissioned the Trailmobile Corporation to build this custom rig to carry the Mercedes to carnivals and fairs. "Gibson was a bit of an eccentric," George Waterman III says today. "He had off-the-wall ideas." (Courtesy of K. H. Gibson III)

Kirkland Gibson sets up his Hitler car exhibit in September 1958. "Oh, it was popular," his son Kirk recalls. "There would be a line formed. It's not like this was the bearded lady." (Courtesy of K. H. Gibson III)

In 1973, Arizona developer Tom Barrett (at the wheel) sold the Mannerheim Mercedes for a record $153,000. The auction, complete with attendants dressed like gangsters, became a media spectacle. In the passenger's seat is the luckless winner Earl Clark. (AP Wirephoto)

Earl Clark took the car home to his amusement park in Lancaster, Pennsylvania. "Here's your birthday present, sweetheart," Clark joked to his wife, Molly (shown here in the front seat, with daughter Julie in back.) Frightened by threatening phone calls and letters, Clark sold the car less than a year later. (Courtesy of Murl Clark, former owner of Dutch Wonderland)

General William Lyon quietly purchased the Mannerheim car in 1984. Its restoration would take twenty years to complete. Today, the car resides in the family's private auto museum in Southern California. (Photo by Robert Klara)

Passing through the Bavarian town of Laufen in the war's final days, Sgt. Joe Azara got into a firefight and snared himself a Mercedes 770K. The limousine looked, he later said, like "some big shot's job." Indeed, it was. (Courtesy of the children of Joseph Azara)

"Most GIs overseas confined their souvenir collections to something that could be packed in a barracks bag," said a newspaper back in the states. "But not so with Tech. Third Grade Joseph Azara." The mud-splattered fenders suggest that the sergeant had quite a time with his new Mercedes. (Courtesy of the Canadian War Museum)

A Berchtesgaden mechanic attested that the limousine had belonged to Hermann Göring, and Azara took him at his word. When the 20th Armored Division repainted the Mercedes, shown here in Salzburg, the men dubbed it "The Göring Special," and it became Brig. Gen. Cornelius Daly's regular ride. (Canadian War Museum)

At Boston's Castle Island, a crane hoists "The Göring Special" from the hold of the liberty ship *George Shiras* on August 8, 1945. A reporter for *Newsweek* called the car a "battered trophy of war." Azara called it his souvenir. (Canadian War Museum)

Herman Goering's Auto

Captured at Laufen, Germany by Sgt. Joe Azara

WILL BE EXHIBITED AT
TOWSON ARMORY
Monday Night - Nov., 19 - 8:30 p. m.
. *FREE* .
NO ADMISSION CHARGE

Brought to the United States by the Treasury Department for use in the VICTORY LOAN campaign, this official personal car of the former Reich Marshal Herman Goering will be on exhibit at the Towson Armory at 8:30 on Monday night, November 19th. Accompanying this car will be Sgt. Joe Azara of the American 20th Armored Forces who captured it at Laufen, Germany . . . about 60 miles from Berchtesgarden. An added feature of this occasion will be the special close-order and arms drill contest of Company B, Maryland State Guard for the Towson Post 22 American Legion Trophy.

Baltimore County War Finance Committee

For the rest of 1945, Azara and his buddies took the limousine on tour up and down the Eastern Seaboard as part of the Treasury Department's final Victory Loan Drive. The trip turned "G.I. Joe" Azara into a minor celebrity. Note the poster heading and the usage of the American spelling for the Nazi leader's last name, *Goering*, as opposed to the German *Göring*. (Courtesy of the children of Joseph Azara)

Azara showing off the 770K on Flatbush Avenue in Brooklyn, New York. The car raised record sums to pay American war debt. "For a certain amount of money, you could sit in the car with my dad," Azara's daughter Debra Weidrick recalls. "And for more money, he'd drive you around the block." (Courtesy of the children of Joseph Azara)

Azara was happy to let the Treasury Department use his souvenir, but he made no bones about the 770K being his. "When it sells a big quota of bonds," he said, "I'll still be there fighting to get a clear certificate of title." In the end, however, the United States government never relinquished the automobile. (Courtesy of the children of Joseph Azara)

Former Reichsmarshall

Hermann Goering's

PERSONAL CAR

(MERCEDES—BENZ)

450 Horsepower ∗ ∗ Weight 9,000 Lbs.

ARMORED SIDES, FRONT and REAR

DUAL SUPERCHARGER

This car was formerly publicized as belonging to Hermann Goering, made a bond tour throughout the United States under that publication. However since that time there is some doubt as to the authenticity of that statement. There is a commission in Germany at the present time investigating the facts.

Loaned through the courtesy of

U.S. ARMY RECRUITING SERVICE

403 10TH ST, N.W.

230484

By the spring of 1946, the Army—here displaying the captured limousine at a Chevrolet dealership in Washington, D.C.—had begun to doubt the car's Göring lineage. Its solution was to stash the Mercedes in a warehouse at the Aberdeen Proving Ground for the next decade, then sell it as surplus. (National Archives [111-SC-230484])

Finding itself in possession of the old "Göring Special," the Canadian War Museum failed to find any connection to Göring. In the summer of 1980, librarian Ludwig Kosche got involved. "The historical background of this car has never been satisfactorily answered," he said, "and I am having a go at it." (Canadian War Museum)

Kosche scoured the National Archives and the Library of Congress for photos showing a 770K with plates IAv148697. This photo, taken at the Kroll Opera House on July 19, 1940, instantly discredited the notion that the car had been Göring's. The man stepping from the running board is Hitler. (Canadian War Museum)

In addition to the plates matching up, the Grosser in this photo—showing Hitler aboard and Hitler's standard flying from the stanchion—shared unique characteristics of the Grosser in Canada, including the hood and defroster vents, the crank hole in the grille, and the pie slice–shaped rear window. (Canadian War Museum)

In the end, Kosche found enough photographs—including this one, taken on March 15, 1942, at the old Berlin Arsenal—to prove that the Canadian War Museum's limousine had been used by der Führer exclusively for nearly two years. "The car is a genuine Hitler car," Kosche concluded. "There are various photos, together with other evidence, to remove all doubt." (Canadian War Museum)

Nearly fifty years after its arrival, the ex-"Göring Special," firmly identified as Hitler's limousine, continues to be one of the biggest draws for the Canadian War Museum. (Photo by Robert Klara)

The bullet damage sustained by the limousine's passenger-side window (very possibly during Sgt. Joe Azara's firefight with the Wehrmacht in 1945) testifies to the car's authenticity. It also contributes to its haunting quality. (Photo by Robert Klara)

Still true to his military discipline, the General was a private man. He didn't talk about his cars.

"Most people don't know what he has," Randy Ema told the *Los Angeles Times*. Ema, something of a secretive man himself, ran a shop in Anaheim that specialized in restoring Duesenbergs for wealthy clients who'd soon come to include comedian Jay Leno. "Other collectors have parties to show off their cars," Ema said. "[General Lyon] doesn't."[6]

It was a tip that had brought the Lyons to this rundown district in San Diego, and the source of that tip had been none other Tom Barrett, the automotive impresario of Arizona. Since first auctioning the Mannerheim Mercedes to Dutch Wonderland owner Earl Clark in 1973, Barrett had never let go of his fascination with the famous limousine he'd insisted had belonged to Hitler. Barrett had a special kind of radar (or perhaps it was just his Rolodex) and always seemed to know where Grosser 770K limousines were hiding. The homing device in Barrett's head also knew where potential customers were, too, and he'd fashioned a relationship with the General some years earlier.

General Lyon knew that Barrett's boasting blew hotter than jet exhaust—"He talked mumbo jumbo," the General believed—and held him at arm's length. Nevertheless, Lyon liked Barrett and recognized the value of knowing him. "He did have connections all over the states," said Lyon. "He knew where the cars were."[7] Bill Lyon recalls how Barrett used to send truckloads of antique cars to the Lyon home, hoping to sell or trade all of them, or just a few of them: "He'd say, 'Check them out, see what you think.' He was always trying to work out some kind of deal."[8]

Sometimes that deal was a raw one. Barrett once tried to push a 540K roadster on the General, using his proven tactic of touting a car's famous prior owners, real or imagined. "It was supposed to be Stalin's car," Bill Lyon said, "and it had nothing to do with Stalin." On the promise of some hot prospect, sometimes Barrett persuaded the elder Lyon to hop over the Santa Rosa Mountains (a reasonable enough errand, as the General loved to fly the airplanes he collected, too) to visit Barrett in his desert kingdom. "We'd fly in, and he'd have a huge truck with some grand car in the back," General Lyon recalls. "It was usually nothing."[9]

So it was that the Lyons weren't quite sure what to expect when Barrett led them to the abandoned roller-skating rink in San Diego. The car in question might be a true find or just another of Barrett's fantasies. But the Scottsdale auctioneer had dangled a big carrot this time: The old rink on G Street held a 770K armored limousine.

Barrett was acting only as a broker for the big Mercedes, and he turned up at the tail end of a four-year period where the car's whereabouts remain a mystery. In 1980, the wealthy collector Axel Ward had taken the Mannerheim Mercedes off the hands of A. J. Frascona, who'd kept the car behind his Buick dealership in Wauwatosa, Wisconsin, never having wanted it in the first place.[10] About the mysterious Axel Ward, this writer was able to discover precisely nothing, apart from what the Lyons recalled of him, and that is not much, either. What is clear is that Ward, who may have been a Mexican national, had a great deal of money and liked to spend it on automobiles. It's anyone's guess why Ward felt the need to be so secretive. The business under which he'd transact the purchase of the Mannerheim Mercedes—Zulu Ltd., the company was called— listed its headquarters as 211 West G Street in San Diego: the abandoned roller-skating rink.[11]

The door opened, and the General and his boy stepped through. Even today, over thirty years after the visit, Bill Lyon still recalls the spectacle inside that old roller rink, whose date with the wrecking ball was not far off. "On the outside, it looked like nobody had been there in years," he said, but "inside, it was all clean."[12] Inside, in fact, it still was a roller rink, a kind of time capsule. The lacquered hardwood floors, smooth enough for the hard rubber wheels beneath the feet of skaters, still gleamed in the rays of cone lanterns hanging from the ceiling. Wooden pilasters divided the walls into sections fitted with glass-block windows. Nobody looking in from the outside would ever guess what was in there.[13]

Axel Ward had filled the cavernous room with scores of antique automobiles—about a hundred, from the looks of the surviving photos, but easily more than that. He'd parked them in four long rows, a veritable Whitman's Sampler of cars. There was a 1952 Oldsmobile Rocket 88, and a 1941 Cadillac Series 61 woody—sold as an "Estate Wagon" before the war—and a late-model Rolls-Royce, too.[14] "He had hot rods. He had a special roadster, and a few big Mercedes," Bill Lyon recalls. Adds the General, "He had five or six Cadillacs, all brand-new—the stickers were all there." Amid the glint chrome and paint, Axel Ward himself stepped forward. General Lyon recalls that the man spoke perfect, unaccented English and was obviously well-to-do. He took the Lyons to lunch, and applied no pressure. "Ward was very helpful," the General says. "He kept the cars serviced well. He knew what he was talking about. He wasn't overplaying us."[15]

Barrett, of course, was a different story: The man thrived on doing deals, and this one must have felt ripe. Barrett knew, after all, that as impressive as Ward's collection was, the Lyons had not come to San Diego to kick the tires of a '52 Olds. They were there for the 770K, which sat on its own, cordoned off behind the sort of red velvet ropes one might see in a movie palace.

It was a grim colossus, wearing a few more dents, perhaps, but still every bit as overwhelming as it was the moment it had emerged from the murky hold of the MS *Stockholm* before the wide eyes of Christopher Janus, 2,426 miles away in New York and nearly thirty-six years earlier. The newspapers with reporters present on Pier 97 on that June Monday of 1948 had all printed what Janus had told them: that this was the personal automobile of Adolf Hitler. And for all of the ensuing years, through the ownership of Waterman and Gibson, of Tom Barrett, of Earl Clark, of Robert Pass and Walter Klein, of A. J. Frascona of Wisconsin, and Axel Ward of the southwest borderlands, that is what the car had stayed: Hitler's. Even though it technically wasn't, even though it had been Mannerheim's car, even though Hitler had ridden in the back of it but twice. Myths are powerful things, and though we may doubt them, we tend to repeat them—and that is apparently what Tom Barrett proceeded to do.

Eleven years earlier, Barrett had sold this very same car as "Adolph Hitler's personally built parade car."[16] He'd traveled across the country—to Pennsylvania, and then to Florida—to bid on it when its subsequent owners had thrown in the towel. Whether or not Barrett actually believed the car had been Hitler's, he was clearly invested in the story. He was, after all, a "want creator"—as he had once said—"I'll take a car, hype it, create a want, and then sell it."[17] Now here he was, making the sale again. Neither Bill Lyon nor General Lyon recalls the pitch, but the former is pretty clear on how it went down. "Knowing Barrett," Bill Lyon says, "my dad probably thought it was supposed to be Hitler's car."[18]

General Lyon was by no means a naïve buyer. To the contrary: He was among the most sophisticated automotive collectors in the United States. Perhaps it was a lot to expect paperwork for a car that had made it out of history's greatest war. And did this car have any? "No," General Lyon says. "We had nothing." But the lack of documentation posed no hindrance. The simple truth was that the General understood the rarity of a W150 series 770K *Offener Tourenwagen*, regardless of who had owned it. And critically, Ward was not driving a hard bargain. He wanted to sell the car. "He wasn't coming up with crazy prices," the General recalls.[19]

And this was how, inside an abandoned roller-skating rink on the rundown side of San Diego, Hitler's *Geschenkwagen*, the limousine he had given to the field marshal of Finland in a bid to keep a reluctant ally in a losing war, passed to its last owner.

Agreeing to Ward's asking price (one that the Lyons prefer not to reveal), the General had the car moved to his storage facility. It would remain there for the next decade. In the meantime, a fateful encounter awaited Bill Lyon.

In 1985, Jan Melin—the Swedish electrical engineer and self-taught Mercedes-Benz historian, the man who'd traveled to Boston twenty years earlier to see the Mannerheim car for himself—completed his life's work. Actually, it was only the first volume of his life's work, but the fact made the effort no less remarkable. The book's workmanlike title—*Mercedes-Benz: The Supercharged 8-Cylinder Cars of the 1930s*—belied its monumentality: After thirty-five years of research, Melin had cataloged the Mercedes prewar monsters down to their bolts and washers. His book plodded through every model—the 380, the Nürburg 460, the 500N, 540K, and so on—distilling every tedious hour he'd logged at the Daimler-Benz archives into the sort of concentrated intelligence that the company itself did not possess. Melin detailed how each model was designed and built. He published tables of chassis and body numbers, of car weights, and even paint colors and their most common two-tone combinations.[20] He'd also amassed hundreds of original photographs of the cars, and these he published, too.

Heavy as a yearbook and encumbered by formal, almost academic, prose, Melin's book slid off the presses of a Swedish publisher called Nordbok. It was not the sort of volume one happened across at a mall bookstore in America. But collectors recognized Melin's work as definitive and eagerly sought the book out (one reason why, as of this writing, a single new copy of Melin's first volume commands prices as high as $970). Sometime after the book's appearance, a copy made its way into the hands of Bill Lyon, for whom a surprise was waiting inside.

The book contained an entire chapter devoted to the Mannerheim 770K.

Having monitored the car's American exploits from across the Atlantic, Melin was incredulous about the trumped-up Hitler claims used to flout the automobile. He blamed the media, "who built up an atmosphere of hysteria about the car," and looked on with surprise and dismay as the car fetched mind-boggling prices at auction. "At each of these sales," he wrote, "the car was claimed to have been Hitler's."[21] Melin also decried the Americans' practice of hanging *Führer* Standards on the fender stanchions—"pennants that were stupidly added to the car in the United States"—since the car had in fact never flown Hitler's personal insignia.[22] Lest there be any remaining doubt about the matter, Melin pronounced the belief that the 770K had been Hitler's automobile as "completely spurious."[23]

The Mercedes master had spoken. And while doubts about the Mannerheim car having belonged to Hitler had surfaced as early as Tom Barrett's 1973 auction in Scottsdale, Melin's was the voice that finally settled the matter.

Were the Lyons disappointed by the news in Melin's book? "I don't think so," Bill Lyon says. "We're car guys first, and this historic aspect was secondary. It was exciting to have a whole chapter in the definitive 770 book that dated that car."[24]

Perhaps, in retrospect, the younger Lyon is applying some balm to the bruise of his father having purchased an object whose past did not measure up to Barrett's hype. But that is not the same thing as saying that General Lyon had wasted his money. By any measure, he did not. As Bill Lyon points out, the car is significant from an engineering perspective alone, having arguably once been the most sophisticated automobile on the road. And, exaggerated as its link to Hitler might have been, the links were there nevertheless:

the Mannerheim car was genuinely historic. "It is to be hoped that the next time it surfaces, it will be owned by someone who appreciates it for what it is," Melin wrote, "namely a magnificent automobile, and not for what it is erroneously claimed to be, the car owned by Hitler."[25] These were, in fact, the last words in Melin's book.

The Swedish researcher was more prescient than he could have known: The car was indeed now in the hands of someone who appreciated it for what it was.[26] But it would be many years before the car would surface in any public sense.

In the spring of 1994, a Mission Viejo man named Richard Martin rolled up his sleeves and began the enormous task of restoring the Mannerheim Mercedes. An accomplished technician, "Marty" Martin was known and respected in automotive circles for his meticulous attention to historic detail. He'd been restoring cars professionally since 1967 and had worked for General Lyon since the mid-1970s.

Martin had inspected the Mannerheim car shortly after Lyon had bought it, and quickly spotted some of the many headaches he'd be in for. Sun visors, switches, knobs, rearview mirrors—all were missing in whole or part. Someone had attached the bumper guards backward. Parts of the car were clearly not original, including the plastic spare-tire covers and the huge chrome siren on the front bumper. (Mercedes had originally mounted a blackout light there.)[27] Martin also discovered that the German limousine had been rolling around on American rims. It turned out that Christopher Janus had—probably sometime after all the blowouts he'd suffered on his disastrous drive to Chicago in 1948—ordered safety-ring rims put on the car to allow for the easy change-out of American truck tires.[28]

But by far the biggest challenge facing Martin was the 770K's sheer immensity. The Mercedes was too heavy for any conventional lift, and so Martin had to devise a number of jury-rigged contraptions just to begin the disassembly process. As the Lyons would discover, the limousine's armor plating was integral to the body panels—it could not simply be separated and lifted away—which left Martin to contend with (among other things) doors that weighed twice what a grown man did.

The Lyons' restoration man preferred to work alone. This was not such a wise idea when it came to a Grosser Mercedes—a fact Martin himself conceded. "I'm 56 years old and seem to be diminishing in physical size," he lamented, "while the cars I take on appear to be getting bigger and heavier."[29] But appearances were only too real in this case. Martin made reasonable progress breaking down the car and commissioning the fabrication of the missing parts, but by 1997 he was still pecking away at the hulk.[30] "This was a mammoth task for one person, obviously," Bill Lyon remembers.[31]

In all, Martin toiled on the Mannerheim car for some six years.[32] He was woefully outmatched. But other factors conspired to slow down the work, too. When the economy cooled, the Lyons downsized their automotive operations, and work on the Mannerheim car stopped completely. By the time the General decided to resume the restoration in or around 2005, Martin had retired. "We had to get a new team," Bill Lyon says.

The new team would be headed by Randy Ema, who practiced his automotive wizardry inside an unmarked warehouse in Orange, California. It took Ema several years to finish the job, and some parts took even longer. The Lyons would spend a total of fifteen years hunting for a tire strong enough to carry the weight of a ten-thousand-pound automobile.[33] By 2008, Ema's team had rebuilt enough of the limousine that the General could finally have the car repainted. Martin had pointed out early on that previous repaintings of the car had obliterated the original deep blue of the hood and body panels. Fortunately, he'd discovered four small areas along the bottom inside ridge of the fold-down hoods that retained the original shade—just enough surface area to permit a color match.[34]

There was one shop in California—one shop in America—to which the top collectors entrusted the painting of their cars. That was Junior's House of Color, which sat on an industrial strip in Bell Gardens, a few miles south of downtown L.A. The shop was the domain of Herschel "Junior" Conway, who'd learned his trade in the 1950s as a sand boy for legendary car customizer George Barris, the man who'd go on to build the original Batmobile in 1965.[35] It was Conway who sprayed the electric blue onto Chili Catallo's chopped-up 1932 Ford, the Little Deuce Coupe that showed up on the cover of the Beach Boys' fourth album in 1963.[36] A paint job at Junior's could run seventy-five thousand dollars—even two hundred thousand—yet the waiting list for the "Degas of the Driveway" stretched into years.[37] Conway mixed and applied his paints by hand—sometimes using Q-tips and toothbrushes in advance of his spray gun. You did not rush the man. In turn, Junior did not disappoint.

The Mannerheim Mercedes restoration would not be fully complete until 2014, two decades after it had begun.

Mark, my driver, seldom gets passengers destined for Coto de Caza. Those who live in the gated community tucked into the mountains above Mission Viejo have their own cars, of course, and these tend to run to the Jaguar and Mercedes end of things. As it turns out, I am up here to see a Mercedes, though it is nothing like the low-slung sedans prowling these roads carved through the California scrub. It is July of 2015, and General Lyon has extended an invitation to his estate to let me see the limousine that Adolf Hitler gave to Field Marshal Mannerheim.

As Mark taps the brakes and squints for the street address, I ponder how unlikely it is that this car is not only still around at all, but has found a home in a setting so unlike the one that produced it. The Sago palms and hibiscus, the Eden-like warmth of California, the polo-shirt prosperity that feels so undeniably American—all of it stands in sharp contrast to the fascist forges that belched out this machine for Hitler, seventy-three years ago and 5,880 miles from here.

The SUV rumbles off the road and pauses before an enormous pair of wrought-iron gates. With a few words exchanged over the intercom, they glide open. Mark wheels the car into a storybook kingdom—onto a redbrick bridge built over a waterfall, then up a steep and winding drive hemmed by white fencing and rosebushes. To the left, rows of orange trees, their branches heavy with fruit, rise from hillocks of dun-colored dirt. A Federal-style mansion of white brick comes into view at the hill's crest. The road skirts beneath its portico and bends to the left, leading to a circular drive in the back. Mark stops, pops the door lock, and accepts a clump of bills I press into his palm. My blue Topsiders land on pristine white gravel, and my ride is gone.

I am early—impolitely so—but it is of no consequence: Ever the military man, General Lyon is a habitual early riser, has in fact been up for hours, and is standing on the bricks of the breezeway, fixing me with a contemplative gaze. The General is tall and lean, sporting chinos and a lavender dress shirt. He wears his white hair brushed back. He looks two decades younger than his ninety-two years. An Alaskan malamute named Lobo wanders out on a lazy reconnaissance. Meanwhile, Jeff McCann, one of General Lyon's two full-time mechanics, has also appeared. McCann, who bears a striking resemblance to Jay Leno, does the courtesy of introducing me to the General. (And "General" is how everyone *still* addresses him.) We exchange niceties. His handshake is dry and firm.

He shows me down a brick path to the garage. It is an inadequate term for a twenty-three-thousand-square-foot building with columned porticos and a border of box hedge. Inside, just beyond the vestibule, a pair of Chesterfield sofas sit atop a Persian rug. I slide into one of them and the General settles into the couch opposite. Unsure of how many of my e-mails to his son and his assistant have reached my host, or whether he remembers our telephone interview of nearly a year before, I remind the General of my project, that I've come from New York to see the 770K. He nods, remembering.

As it turns out, the Mannerheim car has been occupying as much of the General's attention as mine of late. It is not just because a restoration that took the Lyons the better part of two decades had finally been completed. And it is more than the fact that they finished in time to bring the car up to the 2014 Pebble Beach Concours d'Elegance, where it won first place in the Mercedes-Benz prewar category.[38] The General regards the car as a kind of apogee to a lifetime of collecting: It is an eight-cylinder beast he is pleased to have finally added to his menagerie. "Before I pass on," he tells me, "I wanted to do this car."[39]

As he says this, we sit surrounded by seventy or so other cars the General has "done"—so many beautiful machines that even those oblivious to the allure of old cars would be impressed. Cadillacs, Chryslers, Lincolns, and Rolls-Royces, most of them from the 1920s and 1930s, rest their treads on the glazed brick floor. Their chrome grilles and candy-colored bodies reflect the glow of neon dealership signs bolted to the walls. Their headlamps glisten like punch bowls. Their backseats are dark and velvety like the linings of expensive coats.

I am taken with this spectacle, but General Lyon's bearing is, naturally, more removed: He is used to having these prizes around. And though the General is a man of few words, the ones he chooses make clear that he regards the restoration of his automobiles as closer to a responsibility than a hobby. In the case of the 770K, he was willing to spend years ferreting out the limousine's missing parts, fabricating new ones from historic photos, matching paint and upholstery, and assuring that not a single thing that wasn't on the car in 1941 would be put on it now. "I'm not out to make the car better," he tells me. "The point is to make it what it was."[40]

Without realizing it, the General is slowly settling a difficult question I'd lugged out here with me, and one I'd raised with his son many months before on the phone, when I'd first traced the Mannerheim Mercedes to the Lyons. It was one thing to restore an old car, yet quite another to restore *this* old car. Given its weighty history, why would someone want such a vehicle in his garage?

"I think it's more an issue now than it was for my father's generation," Bill Lyon had told me. "Separating the historical significance from the evil side of what the Nazis were about may be harder for the younger generation. They ask, 'Why would you want anything to do with the car?' But it's an important piece of history, and there's a reason to respect it."[41]

Bill Lyon was referring, I believe, to the spirit in which Christopher Janus had first imported Mannerheim's Mercedes and also the one that prompted Joe Azara to coax the 101st Airborne to ship back the one he'd captured in Bavaria. From the perspective of these men, the enormous cars were relics of a war long fought and hard won. Their immensity and engineering were as much the tangible proof of the Nazi menace as they were of the American determination to defeat it. To these men, WWII had been a personal event. To the General, it still is.[42]

He rises from the Chesterfield and leads me through a doorway. We enter another wing of the garage. Here, the brick floor turns to marble and light descends from chandeliers. And in the center of the room, parked on a turntable, is Field Marshal Mannerheim's old Mercedes-Benz.

It looks a great deal like the 770K in Ottawa, but with a key difference: This car has been restored to factory specs. Its gleaming paint and flashing chrome are precisely what Hitler would have seen when chauffeur Erich Kempka brought the car to the Wolf's Lair in November of 1941, just before escorting it to Finland. Because of its pristine condition, the car's details are more pronounced and, somehow, more sinister. Its fender lines sweep back down the body with the fearsome grace of an ocean swell. The V-shaped grille, rising to sternum height, resembles nothing so much as an ax blade. The car is a sumptuous, frightening visage.

General Lyon grasps a chrome handle and turns it. The front door of the Mercedes swings open, heavy as a submarine hatch. Inside is the enormous steering wheel that Kempka had held. To its right is the tilt-up seat concealing a platform for standing during motor rallies—a feature that Hitler never used on this car, though its presence would be seen as "proof" that this limousine had been *der Führer*'s personal vehicle.

I wander around the car in silence for several minutes, trying to take in the size of it and the fact of it. General Lyon stands aside, hands clasped behind his back, watching me watch his car.

"Would you like to see the engine?" he asks. I would.

McCann has reappeared, this time with one of the General's assistants in tow, and there is a reason for this: The hood is so heavy that it requires two men to raise it. This they do, after first laying a beach towel across the fender. One glance from a belt buckle will nick Junior Conway's paint job. "It's such a beautiful car, but you have to treat it with kid gloves," McCann tells me. "I don't want to be the one to put a scratch in it."[43]

With effort, the men stow the hood in the upright position. Below it is the cast-en-bloc eight-cylinder motor, a glistening assemblage of gray steel, black enamel, and chromed exhaust hoses. Just behind the damascened firewall, McCann pops open a hidden compartment, where a set of wrenches rests in velvet-lined drawers. He tells me there is no detail on this car that Mercedes overlooked. I believe him.

The General asks his men to show me the medical kit. McCann wanders to the back of the limousine and opens the bulbous trunk that joshing observers (though probably none in Nazi Germany) once likened to Hermann Göring's backside. McCann lugs out a black leather box, rests it on the floor, and lifts its lid. Inside, in stacked trays, is a full complement of bandages, splints, and antiseptics, virtually untouched since 1941. McCann fishes around and, beneath a cotton arm sling, produces a tiny bottle of valerian tincture. It is still full, its ground-glass stopper wrapped in paper and string. The bottle's blue label bears the name of the Hof Pharmacy in Stuttgart, as well as its address: on the Schlossplatz at Adolf-Hitler-Strasse.[44]

By itself, that little bottle places this Mercedes outside the realm of any mere collector car. Its presence in the trunk brings the reality of Hitler home, as it were, and that is an uncomfortable place to have him. In fact, knowing this car's history makes it impossible not to see the devil in every detail, and the tincture bottle isn't the only one of those. The doors feature hidden compartments for Luger pistols, the make that Hitler always carried. The grab handles inside are woven and thick as hippopotamus whips. Hitler was partial to those, too.

I noticed the grab handles when, after a few minutes, I finally ventured into the limousine's backseat. Based on photos that survive in the Finnish government archives, it is indisputable that Hitler rode back here during his visit to Mannerheim in June of 1942. He rode here twice, on the drive to and from the Immola Airfield. He sat on the right side.

The backseat is quiet; of course it is quiet. And there is nothing particular to be felt here, except for the emptiness of the space. Perhaps that is fitting.

During my trip to California, I had it in mind that I was going to visit the lesser of the two notorious 770Ks that had come to America and caused so much excitement and trouble. The Mannerheim Mercedes was one I had heard myself refer to as "bogus," since it had been billed as Hitler's personal car, though it was actually not. But now, climbing out of the backseat, I realize I've changed my mind. If the significance of a relic is to be determined by the hands through which it has passed, then that significance—at least in the case of Hitler—must be a kind of absolute. And if the 770K at the Canadian War Museum is the more important car (whatever that distinction means) for having sat in Hitler's garage, for having carried Hitler more frequently, or motored him to more decisive events, I leave it to others to argue the point. The Mannerheim car possesses the same dark, residual power—and also the same capacity to be instructive—by dint of a tragic and undeniable association.[45] Once upon a time, this automobile carried the worst man the twentieth century produced. That seems enough.

The Pebble Beach Concours includes an event called the Concours d'Elegance, a rally that allows competition entrants a chance to show their cars in action, and gives them an advantage in the judging.[46] In 2014, some 150 cars made the eighty-mile loop. The Mannerheim Mercedes, with General Lyon at the wheel, was one of them.

The course is not an easy one. It makes hairpin turns through the cypress valleys east of Monterey, climbs into the Carmel Highlands, and skirts the high Pacific cliffs all the way to Big Sur. The 770K performed flawlessly.[47] "This is going to sound silly, but it's easy to drive," General Lyon told me. "I wouldn't have believed it the first time. But the car just responds in every way. It runs, sounds good, and everything works. It's a *job* to drive—it's a big car. And you're rolling a lot of steel around. So I had to watch what I was doing."[48]

Hundreds of fellow motorists and spectators were, meanwhile, watching General Lyon. It was the first—and possibly the final—time that Hitler's *Geschenkwagen* for the field marshal of Finland made an appearance at a golf club in California.

Did anyone, I asked the General, know the historical significance of the car they were looking at? No. "People went by and tooted their horns," he said, pausing. "I don't think anyone who sees it would know what it was."

EPILOGUE

Great thinkers whom I dare not argue with—Ralph Waldo Emerson, Jane Addams, and Eleanor Roosevelt among them—have counseled on the merits of doing things that frighten us. I have not quite lived up to that fine piece of character-building advice, though the volume you hold in your hands may be my best attempt. It took a little over two years to research and write this book, and the project frightened me most every day that I worked on it.

The reason was not so much the complexity of the undertaking, even though running down the stories of a bunch of old cars is not, I discovered, as straightforward an undertaking as researching presidents of the United States, as I had done in my first two books. Nor was it the unpleasant business, exactly, of dealing with Adolf Hitler—a man whose evil was so complex and confounding that scholars continue, seven decades after his death, grappling with explanations for it.

Instead, for me, the problem lay with presenting a figure like Hitler through the lens of an automobile: With all the horrors and human tragedy for which the man was responsible, would it seem flippant to devote an entire book to the vehicle that happened to cart him around? Why was I bothering with such bizarre ephemera? If a writer worries about one thing more than angering his audience, it's confusing them. This topic, I feared, stood a good chance of doing that.

But I went ahead anyway, clinging to a belief that helped to germinate this idea and one that I hope this work has borne out. Nearly any personal possession can tell us something about its owner, but automobiles have more to reveal for the simple reason that they are not like other possessions. Ostensibly purchased and driven for the purpose of getting from one point to another, cars actually satisfy other needs that, while less apparent, may be even more important. Automobiles are manifestations of their owners' psyches, expressions of their achievements, and sometimes they are windows onto their delusions.

In most instances, the examples—particularly in American culture—are harmless and amusing. The dynamic that drives the successful L.A. plastic surgeon to buy a Bentley is the same one, presumably, that explains why the young men in my Brooklyn neighborhood attach racing spoilers to their Hondas. In other instances, outsize personalities and their outsize rides furnish material for deeper contemplation: Al Capone's opulent 1928 Cadillac Town Sedan sported a green-and-black paint job that closely resembled the livery of Chicago police cars. Evangelical cult leader Father Major Jealous Divine (the "Messenger," and "Dean of the Universe") boasted of having no earthy possessions, yet he was chauffeured around in a 1937 Duesenberg Landaulet "Throne Car" with its own PA system.

In Hitler's case, however, his motor vehicle of choice expressed far more than grandiosity. It was a machine designed not just to elevate its owner but also to subjugate and intimidate his subjects, and the 770K accomplished this work with the same steely efficiency with which it whisked Hitler and his henchmen up the steep roads of Berchtesgaden. The 770K was a frightening car suited to a frightening man, and was also his perfect, mechanical surrogate. The limousine wasn't just from Hitler, it was *of* him, too. It accentuated his megalomania, punctuated his arrogance. It functioned—especially after it reached North American shores—as a stand-in for the man himself.

I wrestled to explore and explain these layers of symbolism as I wrote these pages, yet even my best arguments were not enough to dispel a nagging feeling that I had devoted myself to a story too obscure to be relevant. Fortunately, I would discover that those fears were unfounded.

Shortly after returning to New York from my visit with General William Lyon in Southern California, I was having coffee with my friend and colleague Sam Thielman, who'd recently landed a gig at *The Guardian*. After I regaled him with the tale of getting to see one of the notorious Hitler cars tucked away in a marble-floored garage in the mountains over Mission Viejo, my friend insisted that I frame the story as a feature and pitch it to his editor. I did so, and the piece appeared online on September 13, 2015.[1]

I'd harbored reservations about writing the article, since it's seldom a great idea to go public with a book you're working on—to reveal a topic that someone else might grab out from under you so far in advance of a release date. My editor was gracious enough to let me do the story, seeing some strategic advantages in it. His hope—one that I shared—was to generate a little advance publicity.

But more than anything else, the feature represented a chance to plumb a global readership to see if anyone cared about the story of the Hitler cars. And, as it turned out, people did care—they cared a great deal.

The comments section below the story stretched for pages. Some readers expressed admiration for the Mercedes engineers, while another condemned German industry's complicity in the Reich's war crimes. Some dismissed the "fetishistic" spotlighting of the limousine, though others seemed fascinated that it still existed. "Regardless of its provenance," said one, "it's a beautiful car."

Some called for the car's preservation and public display, several for its immediate destruction, and still others argued that if the car signified something unpleasant, it was nevertheless notable for that fact alone: "Like removing the Confederate flag," offered one, "destroying this car would symbolize the wish of some people to change history." Though I do not condone the flying of the Confederate flag over state houses, I do understand the analogy.

For other readers, the car invited speculation about everything from Hitler's physical shortcomings ("Did you ever see such a sinister machine? It must have been inspired by terrible sexual problems") to conspiracy theory ("I've always wondered whether people who buy stuff like this end up on INTERPOL and FBI watch lists)."

Of course, there was also the predictable backlash against me. One writer derided my "flowery imagination" for suggesting that there was still a sort of aura about the car. I was taken to task for my puns. Another charged that the "author wishes for past glories of the Reich." (It is a sentiment that, as a gay man of Polish descent, I can assure you I do not possess.) But even as various readers derided me—and *The Guardian* for publishing me—it was clear that the topic had stirred people, or at least stirred them up. One sentiment I did not detect was indifference.

"A book on Hitler's limousines?" wrote one reader. "Surely we would rather hear about his toothbrushes." To which another retorted, "To be honest I'm interested in the book."

Well, sir, here you are.

Going public with my intent to write this book also spurred some people to write to me directly—not to complain, fortunately, but to ask for help in identifying Mercedes-Benz limousines of purported Nazi provenance that had, by virtue of a relative or friend who'd fought in the war, become part of family lore. "I am trying to track down a car of Hitler's that my grandfather helped transport while in Germany during his time in the Army," a man named Brenden wrote to me. "The car should have initials under the hood, 'L.L.H.'" Regrettably, none of my research files (and these filled two drawers of my filing cabinet) contained a mention of initials under the hood.

Another man—Michael from Arizona—wrote to me about one Brooks Belton Boman, a private from Vernon, Alabama. Private Boman, a school friend of the writer's recently deceased mother, appeared in a yellowing photograph that the man had plucked from a family photo album. In the photograph—scanned and sent to me—was a strapping young man in dress uniform, sitting behind the wheel of a 770K Cabriolet D (or was it an F?) somewhere in Germany. The limousine showed the classic signs of confiscation and use by the U.S. Army: a missing spare tire and white lettering painted down the length of the hood. It read, USA 1838691. On the back of the German-made Agfa-Lupex photographic paper, a few lines of faded fountain pen ink, written in Private Boman's hand, read, *Me in Hitler's touring car. This is the car Hitler used for tport* [*sic*: transport] *use and parades so he could stand up.*"

Michael had written in the hope that I could identify the 770K limousine in the photograph. Alas, I regretfully told him that I could not, just as I had no idea which of the Grosser limousines might conceal an "L.L.H." beneath its hood.

Now might be a good time to state that it was never my intent to author a definitive history of the automobiles that motored the Nazis around. There were, no doubt, hundreds of such vehicles. Tracking them all down to determine what had become of them would be a decades-long effort and not the sort of work I am interested in or qualified to perform. I am a storyteller, nothing more or less. My aim was to recount two chronologically intertwining tales—ones now forgotten almost entirely—because the stories raised compelling questions about this country's relationship to its greatest war, and also because, well, these stories are strange, unsettling, and fascinating.

When the two limousines that make up the backbone of this narrative came to the United States in the years after the war, they cast a troubling but undeniable spell over the public. As my article receded into the distance and I finished the last chapters of this book, I at least worked with the assurance that that spell, all these decades later, had not been entirely broken. I might even venture that the Mannerheim Mercedes—and certainly the one in the Canadian War Museum—are both still doing some of the disagreeable work they were built to do: They are still drawing attention, still triggering a mixture of awe, fear, and revulsion.

A few weeks after I finished this manuscript, I took a walk to the western end of Fifty-seventh Street in Manhattan, to where the great liners once nudged their prows up to the Hudson River piers—specifically, to where Christopher Janus appeared on a June day in 1948 to fetch his Hitler car from the forward hold of the MS *Stockholm*. Nearly seventy years had passed since that unusual episode that made the newspapers, and I'm not sure what I expected to find.

As the pricey, chintzy condominiums rising on the far west side attest, New York is no longer a shipping town. It is no longer a city "filled with a river light," as the short story writer John Cheever so beautifully sketched it, a gritty and magical world where "you heard the Benny Goodman quartets from a radio in the corner stationery store," a city where "almost everybody wore a hat."[2] I was only a little surprised, then, that when I arrived at the pier where the tires of the Mannerheim Mercedes first touched New York cobblestone, there was nothing left.

The West Side Elevated Highway—an engineering marvel when completed in 1936 and only twelve years old when Christopher

Janus passed below it on his way to pick up his prized limousine—has vanished without a trace. A salt-corroded hazard by the late 1960s, the highway partially collapsed in 1973 and closed for good. The last section came down in the fall of 1989. Gone, too, is the great brick headhouse of the Swedish American Line, along with its moss-green shed that once stretched 750 feet behind it into the Hudson River. SAL halted all passenger operations in March of 1975. In the ensuing years, its once-magnificent terminal, relegated to a roost for pigeons, began to collapse. The city's Department of Sanitation razed what was left in 1988 and then used the pier deck as a parking lot for its garbage trucks.[3] Most recently, Pier 97 has become part of Hudson River Park, a waterfront preserve of grass and trees stretching from Fifty-ninth Street to the Battery, whose 550 acres include thirteen piers rebuilt for public recreation.

The pier's renovation was, at the time of my visit, listed as ongoing—the presumable reason for a high chain-link fence standing at the water's edge, fitted with a red NO TRESPASSING sign. Beyond the fence, the pier stretched its neck out into the river, a plinth of bare concrete as immovable and anonymous as an airport runway.

I wandered south a ways to a triangular patch of green now called Clinton Cove. There, set into the rise of a hill, I found a cluster of weathered granite slabs, their flat surfaces and rounded edges clear signs of a long-ago mason's attention. They'd been coping stones, pulled from the shoreline's original bulkhead and then given to MKW, the architectural landscaping firm that built this park a few years earlier. The architects, I later read, intended these slabs to function as "informal seating."[4] They suited that purpose well.

On my walk over there, I'd daydreamed of what a fine thing it would be to find if not a remnant of the old Swedish American pier, then something that would tie up my work in some crisp, poetic way. (An abandoned Mercedes hubcap, for instance, would have been nice.) But such are the fantasies of the aging English major: I should have known better. Tidy endings seldom wait for you at the end of any historical tale. And how naïve had I been to expect such a convenient denouement for this one? The entire undertaking had been fraught with unanswerable questions, briar patches of moral ambiguity, and always the feeling—pulling from beneath my feet like sand drawn by a receding wave—that the condition of being interested in an automobile that had belonged to such a destructive and vicious man was somehow tantamount to an endorsement of that man himself.

And so, as I stared at where Pier 97 had once stood, at the spot where the fabled Hitler Mercedes had so long ago descended from one of the MS *Stockholm*'s powerful winches, I understood that the red metal sign affixed to the fence, rattling in the river wind, was perhaps as fitting a coda as any. Many times, this project had felt like something akin to trespassing—a venturing into territory better left alone. But I had gone anyway. And what I'd found on the other side of that barrier was neither punishment nor reward—only open space that waited, like an empty pier stretching into the river, to be filled.

ACKNOWLEDGMENTS

Very late in the production process of this book—indeed, past both my original deadline and then a generous extension of that deadline—a yellow DHL packet from Finland appeared in the lobby of my Brooklyn apartment building.

The contents of the padded pouch consisted of a slim volume of fifty-eight pages, bearing the title *Marsalkka Mannerheimin Mercedes 770*. As the title suggests, the work—overnighted to me by the Mannerheim Museum in Helsinki—concerned the late field marshal's wartime limousine. As the title might also suggest, the book was entirely in Finnish, a lush and complex language of which I understand not a single word.

The time I spent looking for this booklet, waiting for it, and then having pertinent parts of it translated into English tinged the last of my writing days with the unmistakable flavor of panic. It was also a reminder of a truth no responsible author can deny: The writing of a book, and a historical one especially, requires the assistance of many people.

A great number of individuals expended an effort, ranging from a quick e-mail to many hours of personal time, to help me unravel the two unusual stories at the heart of this narrative. I wish to thank as many of them as I can by name, with apologies that I cannot mention all of them.

My deepest gratitude goes to General William H. Lyon and his son Bill Lyon, not only for sharing with me their recollections of acquiring and restoring the Mannerheim Mercedes but also for inviting me to the family home in Southern California to see the limousine in person. To staff mechanic Jeff McCann, thank you for lifting the hood and explaining the workings of a supercharged Mercedes to a layman. To Kim Cantrell, General Lyon's assistant, thank you for seeing to every detail that made that visit possible. It is not every day that a writer has a chance to eat cheeseburgers with a genuine hero of WWII and a leading citizen of this country; General Lyon, I quickly understood, is both of those.

An equal measure of gratitude goes to the many custodians, past and present, of the Grosser 770K in the Canadian War Museum in Ottawa, Ontario. To Hugh Halliday, Andrew Burtch, and Cameron Pulsifer, your insights were essential to this work. I am especially indebted to collections specialist Carol Reid, who tolerated my needy presence in her archive and responded to my endless requests with unfailing expertise and humor.

Given that the bulk of people who figure prominently in this story are deceased, I relied upon—and was extremely fortunate to locate—both descendants and friends of many of those people, without whose help I could never have reconstructed these events in the detail they warranted. In particular I wish to thank Murl Clark (son of Dutch Wonderland founder Earl Clark) and George H. Waterman III (son of famed automobile collector George H. Waterman), who had nothing to gain by humoring my requests for their time but who were exceedingly generous with it regardless. To K. H. Gibson III, I am indebted not only for some of the richest anecdotes that appear in this volume but for many stunning photographs—all of which he would not accept a cent of payment for my using. Thank you, Kirk.

I am extremely fortunate that there are not many Azaras listed in the Cleveland, Ohio, telephone directory, and also because the Azara I did find wasn't only the right one, but a man willing to talk to me about his father, Sergeant Joe Azara, who captured himself a genuine Hitler Mercedes in the closing days of the war and had the gumption to get it shipped back to the United States. To Joseph Jerome Azara and his sister Debra Weidrick, I am flattered by your interest, grateful for your memories, and hopeful that I have made good on the promise to give your father a measure of the credit he is due.

Though I have loved antique automobiles since I was a kid, my residency in the city of New York—one of the places in America where motor vehicles are not necessary to sustain life—means that I still had much to learn about cars, old cars, and the buying and selling of same. Thanks are due, then, to David Wilkinson, who shared his memories of the late Edgar Jurist of the Vintage Car Store, and to veteran automotive journalist Michael Lamm, who informed me on the world of collecting. Additional thanks are due to Philip Hall of the Rolls-Royce Enthusiasts' Club and to Barbara D. Fox of the Veteran Motor Car Club of America.

A few years ago, a Gallup survey revealed that the job of car salesman is among the least respected in America. (Note: That of journalist was not too much better.) Those who hold that view have obviously never met Don Brill. A salesman since 1969, Brill spent most of his career in the employ of Frascona Buick (where the Mannerheim Mercedes spent a few years holed up in the garage.) Brill is a man with a million stories, and I am thankful for those he shared with me.

A special note of thanks goes to Robert Pass, who, as one of the owners of the Mannerheim Mercedes during the height of its fame and controversy in the early 1970s, was a treasured source and a perfect gentleman. I am also grateful to Tom Miller, who covered Tom Barrett's surreal auction in Scottsdale, and to Daniel J. Kruse, who staffed it.

Though I have long boasted about doing my own research, the truth of the matter is that this work cannot be done well (or done at all) without the help of an increasingly rare species known as librarians and archivists. I am indebted to many of them, including Samantha Mills of the San Diego Historical Society, Carol Weiss of the Nyack Library, John Beekman of the Jersey City Free Public Library, and Philip Crnkovich of the Lancaster Public Library. Thank you, also, to Tom Fitch of the Illinois State Fair Museum Foundation and Jeff Thompson, archivist at 20th Century–Fox. My special thanks to Christine Roussel, who presides over the Rocke-feller Center Archives and made it worth my visit for the conversation alone.

I would be remiss in not thanking David Smith, now retired from the New York Public Library but still a friend and champion of my work in every sense.

I also wish to thank Michael Swanson of the University of North Dakota's Special Collections Department, Professor Peter Lev of Towson University, and Professor Edward Portnoy of Rutgers University's Department of Jewish Studies for their help.

Generous assistance came my way from overseas, as well, from Göran Flank of the Swedish Federation Motorhistoriska Riksför-bundet, who connected me to the redoubtable Mercedes expert Jan Melin. My thanks to Toni Piipponen of the Mannerheim Museum in Helsinki, Finland, for express-mailing that booklet to me, and to Sari Kokkola, for translating its contents.

The idea for this book started over coffee at French Roast on West Eleventh Street in New York, and it never would have left the table were it not for the unfailing support of my agent, Gary Heidt. I am also obliged to Peter Wolverton of Thomas Dunne Books for the funding and the time necessary for me to research and write this book, and to his former assistant, Emma Stein, for extinguishing the brush fires that inevitably ignite during that process.

To my family—my mother and father, my sister, Maria, and my brother-in-law, Pete—thank you for enduring my enthusiasm for this often unsettling topic. And if your own enthusiasm wasn't in fact up to the level of mine, thank you for not letting on.

To David, my companion of many years, thank you for telling me that you're proud of me and for telling me that often enough to keep me working.

Finally, I'd like to express my gratitude to someone who will never read any of these words, the late Ludwig Kosche. He was the librarian who, thirty-five years ago, working alone and at his own expense, cracked the case of the mystery Mercedes whose presence had utterly stymied his Canadian War Museum superiors. His was a Holmesian bit of sleuthing—and it went almost wholly unrecognized.

Having spoken with a few of Kosche's old colleagues, I am confident that the man would not have liked me. To be sure, he would have kept his files from me, and it was only his death—and the subsequent bequeathing of his personal papers to the Canadian government—that permitted me to peruse his research and appreciate its depth. I am probably kidding myself, too, in fancying that Kosche might have acknowledged me as a writer had I approached him at his reference desk. But it doesn't matter. The simple truth is that were it not for the cantankerous, German-born librarian, nobody would have known that a terrifying wreck of a black limousine sitting in Ottawa had once carried Hitler. Which is also to say that were it not for him, this book would not exist, either. *Danke für die hervorragende Leistung*, Herr Kosche.

—Robert Klara
Brooklyn, New York
May 9, 2016

NOTES

1. The Stockholm Deal

1. June is the closest time reference that can be put on this conversation, since the car—which arrived in the United States on June 28, 1948—took three weeks from the phone call to do so, according to Janus's subsequent interviews.
2. "People and Events," *Chicago Tribune,* February 26, 1946, 25.
3. This figure varies by account and ranges from a low of $27,000 to a high of $40,000. The author has chosen a middle figure. "Hitler's Car Part of Antique Display," *Lubbock* [TX] *Avalanche-Journal,* November 29, 1974, 8.
4. This quoted exchange is assembled from Janus's memoirs and also his recollections in a 1974 Associated Press story. Ibid., 8. Christopher G. Janus, *Angel on My Shoulder: Remembrances at Eighty* (Charleston: West Virginia Library Commission Foundation, 1993), 115.
5. Janus, *Angel on My Shoulder,* 115.
6. "Hitler's Car Part of Antique Display," 8.
7. It was J. R. Short who'd wanted the young couple to move to Chicago from New York, where Janus had worked briefly as a reporter for *The New York Times,* and Short who'd made the introductions that landed Janus his job at J. Walter Thompson in Chicago. The couple purchased a large home in the affluent suburb of Winnetka on Chicago's Gold Coast. Janus, *Angel on*

My Shoulder, 78. Chuck Neubauer, "He Loses $635,000 Bet on Peking Man," *Chicago Tribune*, January 18, 1981, 3.

8. Janus, *Angel on My Shoulder*, 115.

9. Damon Runyon, "Spyros Skouras," *Evening Review* (East Liverpool, OH), April 21, 1942, 4.

10. Skouras also had an office in Los Angeles and a large estate in Rye, New York. Jeffrey Thompson, archivist, 20th Century–Fox, telephone conversation with author, December 2, 2014.

11. This description is drawn from a photo of Skouras seated at his desk in May of 1942, six years before this incident took place. A subsequent photo taken in 1957 shows no apparent change in the furnishings. Peter Lev, *Twentieth Century-Fox: The Zanuck-Skouras Years, 1935–1965* (Austin: University of Texas Press, 2014), 51, 179.

12. Andrew Sarris, trans., *Notes of Spyros Skouras*, Stanford University Library Department of Special Collections, Skouras Papers, box 1, Biographical Material folder, 6.

13. Arthur Miller recounted a hilarious and terrifying visit to Skouras's office in 1951, in which Skouras accused President Roosevelt, dead six years, of being an agent of Stalin's and, a few moments later, saving Americans from starvation during the Great Depression. Arthur Miller, *Timebends: A Life* (New York: HarperCollins, 1988), 401.

14. Jim Bishop, "Big Man in Films Begins New Career," *Pottstown* [PA] *Mercury*, August 26, 1970, 6.

15. Janus, *Angel on My Shoulder*, 116.

16. Miller, *Timebends*, 399.

17. Janus, *Angel on My Shoulder*, 116.

2. The Screwball of Winnetka

1. Janus, *Angel on My Shoulder*, 116.

2. Ibid.

3. Descriptions of the ship's layout and the position of the Mercedes therein are drawn from the original 1948 newspaper photos of the car being unloaded in New York and from copies of plans for MS *Stockholm*, "M/S 611, Aktiebolaget Svenska America Linien," n.d., Associazione Navimodellisti Bolognesi, Italy; both sources in author's collection.

4. "Hitler's Car Booed and Hissed as It Reaches New York," *Chicago Tribune*, June 29, 1948, 10.

5. According to Jeff McCann, one of the personal mechanics for Gen. Wil-

liam Lyon, who owns the former Christopher Janus Mercedes as of this writing, the steps for starting up the 770K are, in order: Turn battery switch (located below and to the right of the driver's seat) clockwise to "on," push key in ignition switch, turn on fuel pumps to fill the reserve tank, turn fuel value clockwise to "Reserve," turn choke knob clockwise, put spark control in *nach* position (to the right), and then push the starter button. The automobile's current owners said nothing about a secret switch hidden below the dashboard, though nearly seventy years and the hands of many mechanics have passed over the car since it arrived in New York. The detail about the hidden switch appeared in Douglas Danford, Daniel Lang, and Brendan Gill, "Deal," *New Yorker*, July 10, 1948, 14.

6. The Zumbach mechanics arguably knew more about Mercedes-Benz cars than anyone in the country, but even they puzzled over the car for four hours before figuring out how to start it up. "Hitler's Car Gets 7 Miles per Gallon, Crisscrossing Country on Exhibit," *Daily Herald* (Chicago), December 17, 1948, 19.

7. "Hitler's Armored Car Soon to Pound Chicago's Streets," *Chicago Tribune*, June 26, 1948, 9.

8. "Hitler's Bullet-Proof Auto Coming to U.S.," *Los Angeles Times*, June 28, 1948, 1.

9. Danford, Lang, and Gill, "Deal," 14.

10. Ibid.

11. "Hitler's Car Booed and Hissed as It Reaches New York," 10.

12. Janus, *Angel on My Shoulder*, 116–17.

13. Bob Considine, "Bob's Nose Burned by Hitler's Mercedes," *Long Beach Independent*, July 6, 1948, 21.

14. Danford, Lang, and Gill, "Deal," 14.

15. "A Full Day's Entertainment in Rockefeller Center and Radio City," tourist booklet, n.d., N.Y. Museum of Science & Industry folder, Rockefeller Center Archives, New York.

16. "New York Museum of Science and Industry," untitled typed document, N.Y. Museum of Science & Industry folder, Rockefeller Center Archives, New York.

17. Paul Mandel, "Lament for a Lost Sport," *Sports Illustrated*, March 19, 1962, E5.

18. "New York Museum of Science & Industry—Bubble Gum Contest," memorandum of May 24, 1948. N.Y. Museum of Science & Industry folder, Rockefeller Center Archives, New York.

19. "Hitler's Mercedes-Benz Armored Automobile," press release, n.d., N.Y. Museum of Science & Industry folder, Rockefeller Center Archives, New York.

20. Which of the Rockefellers the memo was addressed to—Winthrop, David, Nelson, John, or Laurance—is unspecified. "Memorandum to Mr. Rockefeller from R. P. Shaw," June 7, 1951, N.Y. Museum of Science & Industry folder, Rockefeller Center Archives, New York, 7.

21. In 1945, Rockefeller Center hiked the museum's rent from $50,000 per annum to $85,000 and continued to increase it each year thereafter. Unable to sustain itself, the museum would be forced to move out of Rockefeller Center by May of 1949.

22. "Hitler's Mercedes-Benz Armored Automobile."

23. Ruth Constad, "Symbol of Hitler Glory Piques Curious 'Foes,'" *Dayton*, [OH] *Journal*, July 19, 1948, 4. All visitor quotes in this section come from this newspaper article.

24. Roland Young appears in a photo on page 8 of *Hitler's Armored Car Souvenir Book*. The undated photo of Howdy Doody, part of the collection made available to the author by K. H. Gibson III, bears the caption "Howdy Doody and his pals in the Hitler Car." The four children were probably members of the famous Peanut Gallery, the kids-only audience that played a key role in the show's success.

25. According to the booklet that would later be sold during the car's many public tours, the engine could develop 155 horsepower without the supercharger and 230 with the supercharger engaged. *Hitler's Armored Car Souvenir Book*, 4. These figures are somewhat at variance with others that appear in connection with the W150 series 770K Grosser, which will be discussed later.

26. Craig Fitzgerald, "1948–1953 Jaguar XK120: In 1948, Production Cars Didn't Come Any Faster," *Hemmings Motor News*, January 2007, www.hemmings.com/hmn/stories/2007/01/01/hmn_feature16.html, retrieved December 24, 2014.

27. "Stevedores Land 9,500-Pound Hitler Car on Dock Here to a Chorus of Boos, Hisses," *New York Times*, June 29, 1948, 25. "Hitler's Bullet-Proof Auto Coming to U.S.," *Los Angeles Times*, June 28, 1948, 1.

28. According to Mercedes author Peter Vann, "The maximum horsepower, 230 bhp [brake horsepower] with supercharger from 7.7 liters, could only be utilized up to a speed of 80 kph [50 mph] before—understandably—initiating a tire alarm." Only the nonarmored version of the Grosser could

go modestly fast, about 105 mph. Peter Vann, *Fantastic Mercedes-Benz Automobiles* (Minneapolis, MN: Motorbooks, 1995), 100.

29. This quote is the newspaper's, not Janus's, though the information about the car would have come from him. "Adolph's Big Car to Be Displayed on Local Streets," *Bakersfield Californian*, March 28, 1950, 19.

30. Janus, *Angel on My Shoulder*, 115.

31. Ibid.

32. "Hitler's Armored Car Soon to Pound Chicago's Streets," 9. "Stevedores Land 9,500-Pound Hitler Car on Dock Here," 25.

33. Roy J. Harris, "A Guide to Illinois' History of Scandal," *St. Louis Beacon*, December 14, 2008, www.stlbeacon.org/#!/content/13821/a_guide_to _illinois_history_of_scandal, retrieved December 25, 2014.

34. This quote is Janus's and is a paraphrase of what the public relations director told him. Janus, *Angel on My Shoulder*, 117–18.

35. In his memoirs, Janus clearly states that the governor had these plates made up before Janus made the drive from New York to Illinois, though a photo taken in Pennsylvania midroute shows ordinary license plates on the car. Nevertheless, Janus clearly had the vanity plates by early 1949, since he posed with them for at least two photographs. The author has given Janus's chronology the benefit of the doubt. Janus, *Angel on My Shoulder*, 118. "This Must Be Der Tag," *Dunkirk* [NY] *Evening Observer*, February 8, 1949, 1.

36. Clip from *Billboard*, July 24, 1948, no headline. *Hitler's Armored Car Souvenir Book*, 7.

37. "Hitler's Armored Car Made Recruiting Steed, Heads for Illinois Fair," *Milwaukee Journal*, final edition, August 10, 1948, 1.

38. *Hitler's Armored Car Souvenir Book*, 8.

39. Jack Mabley, "Driver Has No Angle—He's Just Friendly," *Chicago Tribune*, November 14, 1974, 4.

40. "Hitler Auto Gets Official City Welcome Before Starting Air Force Recruiting Drive," *New York Times*, August 11, 1948, 6.

41. "Hitler's Armored Car Made Recruiting Steed" 1.

42. Mabley, "Driver Has No Angle," 4.

43. John H. Thompson, "Disabled Vets at Vaughan See Hitler's Big Car," *Chicago Tribune*, August 24, 1948, 9.

44. Schneider was aboard because he had been chosen "most typical Air Force recruit," a distinction that apparently made him the ideal candidate for chaperoning an electric torch for a three-day drive. "Hitler's Car to Carry Torch of Freedom," *Illinois State Journal*, August 11, 1948, 22. The torch

was, at least by one account, meant to symbolize New York City's Golden Jubilee. It had been fifty years since the boroughs of Manhattan, Brooklyn, Queens, the Bronx, and Staten Island were officially consolidated as the city of New York in 1898. "Hitler Auto Gets Official City Welcome Before Starting Air Force Recruiting Drive," 6.

45. Jack Mabley, "Giant Hitler Car Heads for Chicago," *Chicago Daily News*, August 10, 1948, 6.

46. Ibid.

47. A reasonable estimate for the car's top speed was 140 km per hour—about 87 mph. And though the car could reach that speed and slightly higher in the right conditions, the drum brakes were not up to the task of stopping it. James Taylor, *Supercharged Mercedes in Detail* (Beaworthy, Devon, UK: Herridge & Sons, 2014), 197.

48. The fun ended there, however. "When I drove the Adolf Hitler Mercedes, or, more properly, the Christopher Janus Mercedes," Purdy said, "the power-boosted brakes were out of adjustment and stopping the car was a matter of standing on everything and then just sitting there waiting for something to happen." Five tons rolling at any speed, he added, "take a lot of stopping." Ken W. Purdy, "The Big White Cars," *True: The Man's Magazine*, July 1949, 46.

49. Ralph Stein, *The Great Cars* (New York: Ridge Press, 1967), 140.

50. This speeding incident was one Janus later admitted to *Chicago Tribune* reporter John Thompson, who wrote, "Janus said he's had it up to 95 on a New York turnpike." The road trip to Chicago was the only occasion on which this bit of derring-do could have taken place. "Disabled Vets at Vaughan See Hitler's Big Car," 9.

51. It would take another forty-six years before California restorer Richard Martin, working for Gen. William Lyon, would discover that Janus had ordered safety-ring rims to be put on the wheels so they could take American truck tires. But it remains unclear whether Janus had this work done before or after his ill-starred drive from New York to Chicago. See Letter from Richard J. Martin to Jan Melin, June 23, 1994, Kosche Papers, Canadian War Museum, 58A 3, box 4, folder: "To Mr. Jan Melin." Jeff McCann, one of the mechanics who cares for the Mannerheim Mercedes as of this writing, opined that the blowouts that Janus suffered were possibly because the Americans did not know how to handle the inner tubes because of the Schrader valve, which pokes out through the rim at a pronounced angle. That, along with the sheer weight of the car, tends to make the inner

tube pop. Interview with Jeff McCann, mechanic to Gen. William Lyon, July 14, 2015.

52. As it turned out, tire problems with the Grosser had beset Hitler, too. As built to factory specifications, the limousine came with chambered, bulletproof tires. But during driving these caused a severe vibration that upset Hitler's sensitive stomach. Instead, ordinary tires inflated to low pressure were used. Peter Hoffmann, *Hitler's Personal Security* (Boston: Da Capo Press, 2000), 64.

53. Jack Mabley, "Our Country Cousins Appear to be Nicer," *Chicago Tribune,* October 2, 1977, 4.

54. Ibid.

55. Jack Mabley, "Hitler Auto Drives Like a Jet Plane," *Chicago Daily News,* August 11, 1948, 9.

56. "Hitler's Former Private Auto Seen by Many on Turnpike, Illinois and New Role as Display for Charity," *Bedford* [PA] *Gazette,* August 26, 1948, 1.

57. Mabley, "Hitler Auto Drives Like a Jet Plane," 9.

58. Ibid.

59. "Hitler Auto Due Here Tuesday, But Adolf's Not Making the Trip!" *Evening Review* (East Liverpool, OH), August 7, 1948, 2.

60. Janus, *Angel on My Shoulder,* 118.

61. Jack Mabley, "Hitler's Auto Rumbles On," *Chicago Daily News,* August 12, 1948, 4.

62. "Radiator Cap Gone Off Late A. Hitler's Car," *Illinois State Journal,* August 22, 1948, 36.

63. Shortly before Janus put the Mercedes on display at Rockefeller Center in New York, he'd let the U.S. Marines recruiting office borrow the car. This apparently triggered the call from the man in California, who insisted that the Luger in his possession had been Hitler's "personal" gun. Janus, *Angel on My Shoulder,* 117.

64. "He'll Use Hitler's Car to Buck Traffic in Chicago," *Brownsville* [TX] *Herald,* September 22, 1948, 12. For some reason, it was frequently women who'd warned Janus that Hitler's ghost was still in the car. Many believed it was in the driver's seat, though Hitler rarely drove an automobile. "Hitler's 'Ghost' Car Due Here Next Month," *Chicago Daily News,* July 13, 1948, 6.

65. "Hitler's Car Brings Buyer Strange Life," *Bakersfield Californian,* September 16, 1948, 27.

66. "100 Chips in for Hitler's Car," *Long Beach* [CA] *Independent,* June 30, 1948, 25.

67. Jack Mabley, "Hitler's Auto Rumbles On," *Chicago Daily News,* August 12, 1948, 4.

68. "Hitler's Car Brings Buyer Strange Life," 27.

69. H. I. Phillips, "The Once Over," *Morning Herald* (Hagerstown, MD), July 3, 1948, 10.

70. The total casualty figure used here—more precisely 1,078,594—is the sum of 407,316 killed and 671,278 wounded, and is taken from the data of the National World War II Museum, www.nationalww2museum.org, retrieved December 26, 2014.

71. Broad-scale American awareness of the Holocaust, the historian Peter Novick has argued, would not truly begin until the public trial of Adolf Eichmann in Israel in 1961. Peter Novick, *The Holocaust in American Life* (New York: Houghton Mifflin, 1999), 133.

72. Phillips, "The Once Over," 10.

73. With two exceptions, all of the anecdotes in this paragraph were disclosed by Christopher Janus Jr. to his father's obituary writer. Stephen Miller, "Colorful Chicagoan's Biggest Stunt, Detective Mission to Find Peking Man, Led to Fraud Plea," *Wall Street Journal,* updated February 28, 2009, www.wsj.com/articles/SB123579056359499267. The detail about the grocery-store parking appears in "Christopher George Janus, Sr.," *Evanston Review* obituary, March 5, 2009, B33. Finally, Janus himself went public with his plans to use the car for commuting: "I intend using [the car] to drive between my Winnetka home and my Chicago office." See "He'll Use Hitler's Car to Buck Traffic in Chicago," *Brownsville* [TX] *Herald,* September 22, 1948, 12.

74. Janus, *Angel on My Shoulder,* 125.

75. Ibid., 5–6.

76. Ibid., 74–75.

77. Christopher G. Janus with William Brasher, *The Search for Peking Man* (New York: Macmillan, 1975), 70.

78. Later in his life, when Janus found himself under indictment for bank fraud, one of his associates said that he was a man "for whom money was never a problem." William Crawford, "Janus Pleads Guilty to Fraud in Search for Peking Man," *Chicago Tribune,* May 30, 1981, 3.

79. Janus and Brasher, *The Search for Peking Man,* 70.

80. Chuck Neubauer, "He Loses $635,000 Bet on Peking Man," *Chicago Tribune*, January 18, 1981, 3.

81. William Mullen, "Chicagoan Searching World for China's Lost Peking Man," *Chicago Tribune*, January 21, 1973, 18.

82. "Roosevelt's Bullet Proof Car to Tour," *Rushville* [IN] *Republican*, August 14, 1952, 14.

83. "Hitler's Car Arrives Today," *Nevada State Journal*, April 26, 1950, 16. "Hitler Car Aids Charity; Earns $25,000 on Tour," *Chicago Tribune*, October 15, 1949, A7.

84. Janus, *Angel on My Shoulder*, 118.

85. "Hitler's Car Raises $100,000," *New York Times*, October 15, 1949, 17.

3. The Great Mercedes

1. Victor H. Bernstein, "Unfinished Business," *Gazette and Daily* (York, PA), October 17, 1946, 19. Bernstein's editorial references the hanging of eleven, not ten, war criminals. Bernstein probably filed his story before the news broke that Hermann Göring had committed suicide in his cell just hours before his appointment with the gallows.

2. Herbert Mitgang, "Daimler-Benz and Its Nazi History," *New York Times*, August 23, 1990, C20.

3. Daniel James Brown, *The Boys in the Boat* (New York: Viking, 2013), 311.

4. Hoffmann, *Hitler's Personal Security*, 128.

5. Henrik Eberle and Matthias Uhl, *The Hitler Book: The Secret Dossier Prepared for Stalin* (New York: PublicAffairs, 2006), 39, 200.

6. Andrew Nagorski, *HitlerLand* (New York: Simon & Schuster, 2012), 172.

7. Ernest K. Bramsted, *Goebbels and National Socialist Propaganda: 1925–1945* (East Lansing: Michigan State University Press, 1965), 218.

8. David Welch, *The Third Reich: Politics and Propaganda* (London: Routledge, 1993), 111. For example, Mercedes ads from the war years picture a fighter plane above the caption *"Mercedes-Benz. Zu Lande, zu Wasser und in der Luft!"* ("On land, water and air!"). Another shows the company name below a heroic illustration of two-engine bombers and heavy trucks driven by soldiers. A poster of the period shows a swastika banner unfurled below the Mercedes star within an illustration of a factory complex with workers pouring out of it. The caption: *"Wir dienen der Nation—Daimler Benz Aktiengesellschaft"* ("We serve the nation—Daimler-Benz Corporation").

Bernard P. Bellon, *Mercedes in Peace and War* (New York: Columbia University Press, 1990), photo insert.

9. Thomas Wolfe, *You Can't Go Home Again* (New York: Harper Perennial, 1998), 591–92.

10. Albert Speer, *Inside the Third Reich* (New York: Macmillan, 1970), 48.

11. Nagorski, *HitlerLand*, 175.

12. Michael Berenbaum, *The World Must Know* (Boston: Little, Brown, 1993), 18.

13. Richard J. Evans, *The Third Reich in History and Memory* (New York: Oxford University Press, 2015), 182.

14. Hoffmann, *Hitler's Personal Security*, 61.

15. "Hitler 'Car Loan' Letter Discovered," United Press International dispatch, June 23, 2010, www.upi.com/Top_News/World-News/2010/06/23/Hitler-car-loan-letter-discovered/72461277341405/, retrieved December 12, 2013.

16. Bellon, *Mercedes in Peace and War*, 220.

17. Henry Ashby Turner Jr., ed., *Hitler: Memoirs of a Confidant* (New Haven, CT: Yale University Press, 1985), 73–74.

18. "Car Buff Hitler Couldn't Drive," *Montreal Gazette*, November 13, 1985, G1.

19. Gerald A. Rolph, "The Grosser Mercedes," *Antique Automobile*, November/December 1983, 18. A 1938 brochure from a Park Avenue showroom called the Grosser the "Mercedes Maximum." See "The Mercedes-Benz Automobile Manufacturing Program for 1938," sales brochure from Mitropa Motors, Inc., New York, author's collection.

20. The 152-horsepower figure is a conversion from 150 brake horsepower and represented the W07 series' power output without the supercharger engaged. Graham Robson, *The Magnificent Mercedes* (New York: William Morrow, 1981), 77.

21. Jan Melin, *Mercedes Benz: The Supercharged 8-Cylinder Cars of the 1930s*, vol. 1 (Gothenburg, Sweden: Nordbok International Co-Editions, 1985), 16.

22. Hoffmann, *Hitler's Personal Security*, 62.

23. Hitler's stock in the company was administered by Jakob Werlin. Bellon, *Mercedes in Peace and War*, 221. According to the memoirs of Wulf Schwarzwäller, Hitler said, "I can claim credit for the things that make the Mercedes cars so beautiful today. In drawings and designs, I tried hard

year after year to perfect that shape to the utmost." Wulf Schwarzwäller, *The Unknown Hitler* (Toronto: Stoddart, 1988), 137. There actually seems to be some justification for this boast. When Canadian War Museum librarian Ludwig Kosche traveled to Munich in 1982, he interviewed Fritz Eickenberg, who was Hitler's chauffeur Erich Kempka's number two. Eickenberg said, quoting Kosche's notes, "Hitler influenced the design through J. Werlin, who seems to have been in his entourage, and to whom he passed on his wishes." Kosche's notes from interview of May 8, 1982, Kosche Papers, Canadian War Museum, 58A 3, box 2, folder 15.

24. The story of the development of these two great automakers is far longer and more complex than the abridged account presented here. Fuller particulars can be found in any of the excellent historical materials put forward by Daimler itself. The author has relied on three documents in particular: "Daimler Garden House in Bad Cannstatt," Daimler AG, 2015, www .daimler.com/company/tradition/museums-historical-sites/daimler -memorial.html ; "Benz Patent Motor Car No. 1," DaimlerChrylser AG, n.d., www.andrew.cmu.edu/course/24-681/handouts/mesh-based%20mod-eling/first-car.pdf; and "The History Behind the Mercedes-Benz Brand and the Three-Pointed Star," Daimler AG, April 17, 2008, www.emercedesbenz .com/Apr08/17_001109_The_History_Behind_The_Mercedes_Benz _Brand_And_The_Three_Pointed_Star.html—all documents retrieved January 13, 2014.

25. His father was the renowned Rabbi Adolf Aharon Jellinek of Vienna, a highly respected authority on Midrashic and mystical literature. David B. Green, "This Day in Jewish History: A Luxury Car's Namesake Is Born," *Haeretz,* September 16, 2013, www.haaretz.com/news/features/this-day -in-jewish-history/.premium-1.547246, retrieved January 14, 2015.

26. This figure is the average of the model W150's recorded weights (chassis and body) converted from kilograms to pounds and rounded. Melin, *Mercedes Benz: The Supercharged 8-Cylinder Cars of the 1930s,* 155.

27. Purdy, "The Big White Cars," 46.

28. Robson, *The Magnificent Mercedes,* 78.

29. Daimler-Benz did not publish the prices for the armored 770K W150 touring cars it built for the Reich, listing them only as *Auf Anfrage* ("on request")—but the cost can be approximated roughly. A new W150 Pullman limousine (the hardtop model) for 1938 listed for 44,000RM, which converts to US$17,671 for that year. The *Offener Tourenwagens,* being custom-built,

were costlier than this, but the author has used this figure simply for comparison. (See: Taylor, *Supercharged Mercedes in Detail*, 197.) The American car showroom prices used here are as follows: A 1938 Packard four-door sedan, $2,995; 1938 Cadillac V8 60 Special, $2,399; and 1938 Ford four-door sedan, $685.

30. The more common induction path on cars equipped with a Roots-type supercharger has the air passing through the carburetor first, then into the supercharger. But the Mercedes 770 and 540 types of this period allowed the air to enter the supercharger first. When the supercharger was not engaged, air flowed directly into the carburetor. Bill H. Lyon, e-mail message to author, February 2, 2014. See also Stein, *The Great Cars*, 140.

31. As noted earlier, the horsepower outputs of the 770K W150 vary by source. According to the souvenir booklet published for the limousine that Christopher Janus put on public tour, the engine could develop 155 horsepower without the supercharger and 230 with it. *Hitler's Armored Car Souvenir Book*, 4. In 1983, the Antique Automobile Club of America published ratings in *brake* horsepower, a unit of measurement that takes into account frictional losses during power delivery to the wheels. The club's BHP (brake horsepower) figures given for the W150 series 770K were 150 without the supercharger and 280 with the supercharger engaged. Converted to horsepower, these figures become 152 and 284. Rolph, "The Grosser Mercedes," 18. In his book, automotive historian Graham Robson published figures of 155/230 BHP (or 157/233 HP) for the W150 series. Robson, *The Magnificent Mercedes*, 77.

32. "Germany's Car on Parade," *Motor Sport*, March 1938, 110.

33. Speer, *Inside the Third Reich*, 35–36.

34. A. N. Wilson, *Hitler* (New York: Basic Books, 2012), 57.

35. "Germany's Car on Parade," 110.

36. Melin, *Mercedes Benz: The Supercharged 8-Cylinder Cars of the 1930s*, 208.

37. Ernst Hanfstaengl, *The Unknown Hitler: Notes from the Young Nazi Party* (London: Gibson Square, 2005), 233. Hanfstaengl also recalled that when Captain Hans Streck "tried to bring some order into the motor pool by sacking drivers who turned up late for duty, he found Hitler insisting that they should be reinstated because they were old Party Members" (p. 82).

38. James P. O'Donnell, *The Bunker: The History of the Reich Chancellery Group* (Boston: Da Capo Press, 2001), 80.

39. Erich Kempka, *I Was Hitler's Chauffeur* (London: Frontline Books, 2010), 19.

40. Ibid., 21.

41. O'Donnell, *The Bunker*, 227. O'Donnell, who served with the U.S. Army Signal Corps during the war and went on to become *Newsweek*'s first bureau chief in Germany, uses many words to describe the character of Erich Kempka, none of them kind: "vulgar," "primitive," "crude," "vainglorious," and "thoroughly unpleasant" (pp. 227, 235).

42. Kempka, *I Was Hitler's Chauffeur*, 24. That the car was armored on four sides and on the undercarriage would have made little difference had anyone lobbed an explosive *into* the sedan—a simple enough thing to do, given Hitler's penchant not just for riding around in an open-top car but often standing up in one.

43. The more detailed, original specifications are as follows. The under-body armor plating was armored steel 18mm thick, and the glass of the windshield and side windows measured 40mm thick. The windows were not a solid casting but consisted instead of five fused layers: a 13mm thick central pane, sandwiched on either side by 9mm panes, in turn bookended by 4.5mm panes. Taylor, *Supercharged Mercedes in Detail*, 196.

44. Johannes Steinhoff, Peter Pechel, and Dennis Showalter, eds., *Voices from the Third Reich: An Oral History* (Cambridge, MA: Da Capo Press, 1994) 19–21.

45. O'Donnell, *The Bunker*, 317.

46. It should be noted that these automobiles were not necessarily 770Ks, though they were large and imposing government Mercedes-Benzes nevertheless. Richard Bessel, *Germany 1945* (New York: Harper Perennial, 2009), 62.

47. One of these cars was the bulletproof limousine that Hitler had given to Goebbels in 1941. The other was, presumably, one of the older, unarmored Grossers. The propaganda minister rode alone in the armored car, consigning his family to the Mercedes with no protection. O'Donnell, *The Bunker*, 115.

48. The opportunistic Fegelein had married Eva Braun's sister Gretl the year before, but in this case being family was no help to him. Ian Kershaw, *Hitler 1936–1945: Nemesis* (New York, W. W. Norton, 2000), 816. In his memoirs, Kempka noted that the two cars Fegelein borrowed were "the last survivors to remain serviceable from my once great vehicle fleet." These cars were returned to the chancellery garage just half an hour later, but without Fegelein, who'd left on the pretext of visiting Himmler's headquarters in Hohenlychen. Instead, Fegelein was found in his apartment, preparing to flee the city. Kempka, *I Was Hitler's Chauffeur*, 65.

49. David Stafford, *Endgame 1945* (London: Abacus, 2008), 173. Pétain received his death sentence on August 14, 1945. Owing to Pétain's advanced age, General Charles de Gaulle, acting as the provisional leader of France, commuted the sentence to life imprisonment. Pétain would live in solitary confinement until 1951, dying at age ninety-five in the Atlantic fortress of Île d'Yeu.

50. Kempka continues, "[Hitler] did not speak. This was to be the last time he sat beside me in a car." Kempka, *I Was Hitler's Chauffeur*, 55.

51. The exact amount of gasoline specified was two hundred liters, which equates to approximately fifty-two gallons.

52. The street's name would be returned to the original—Ebertstrasse—in 1947. See www.luise-berlin.de/strassen/bez02h/h491.htm, retrieved February 13, 2015.

53. Kempka, *I Was Hitler's Chauffeur*, 76–77.

54. Joachim Fest, *Inside Hitler's Bunker* (New York: Farrar, Straus and Giroux, 2004), 110; Kempka, *I Was Hitler's Chauffeur*, 76.

55. In Kempka's version of this event, he lights a cloth with the match and starts the pyre that way. Another account has valet Heinz Linge lighting a torch using some papers he had on him, and tossing it onto the bodies. Still another account maintains that Otto Günsche lit a rag and tossed it onto the bodies. The exact circumstances will, of course, never be known. Kempka, *I Was Hitler's Chauffeur*, 78–80. Fest, *Inside Hitler's Bunker*, 118. Ada Petrova and Peter Watson, *The Death of Hitler* (London: Richard Cohen Books, 1995), 40.

4. The Göring Special

1. *20th Armored Division in World War II* (Atlanta: Albert Love Enterprises, 1946), 128.

2. As several historians have written, a concentration camp was so beyond the moral imagination of most American GIs that the experience of discovering one rewrote their psyches and, frequently, their behavioral codes. "Liberating soldiers, shocked by the visual evidence of German depravity, were less attached to the rules of due legal process," writes the historian Ian Buruma. "At Dachau, American soldiers stood by as SS guards were lynched, drowned, cut up, strangled, or battered to death with spades, and at least in one case beheaded with a bayonet leant by a GI to a former inmate for this purpose. Sometimes the GIs took it upon themselves to shoot

the German guards." Ian Buruma, *Year Zero: A History of 1945* (New York: Penguin Press, 2013), 76.

3. Petrova and Watson, *The Death of Hitler*, 10–11.

4. "Crowds View Goering Car on Exhibition in City," *The News* [Frederick, MD], November 21, 1945, 8.

5. Ibid.

6. Ibid.

7. The Twentieth Armored Division's newspaper, *The Dispatch*, referred to the bullet holes as an "unexplainable feature" of the car. Perhaps. In an interview he gave to the Frederick, Maryland, *News* when he was on tour with the car in November of 1945, Azara stated that while he was fighting the German soldiers, "My first shot nicked the window where you can still see the mark." ("Crowds View Goering Car on Exhibition in City," 8.) It seems quite likely that at least some of the other bullet holes came from this firefight. Given the fighting in the area, the car could easily have sustained hits prior to Azara's discovering it, too. The scenario of a GI deciding to "test" the bulletproof glass by firing at it after Azara's appropriating the vehicle is also a possibility, though a remote one. Azara was highly protective of his souvenir, and given that his Mercedes would soon be serving as an American general's transportation, the idea of an ordinary American soldier taking a potshot at such a prize seems implausible. In any event, the damage to the car—and especially to its glass—would prove pivotal in the years to come, as it would be one of the unimpeachable pieces of evidence that would help to positively identify the automobile. See Ludwig Kosche, "The Story of a Car," *After the Battle*, no. 35 (January 1982), 5, 7, 8, 9. "Goering's Armored Car Transformed into Staff Service for CG of CC 'A,' " *The Dispatch*, May 24, 1945, 1.

8. This is yet another knotty detail of the story. By Azara's account, it was the German "brutes" he'd captured the car from who'd told him that they'd run out of gasoline. "Crowds View Goering Car on Exhibition in City," 8. Yet in the version of the story published in the Twentieth Armored's newspaper, it was a Dutch displaced worker "in a German garage near where the car was found" who told Azara that there was no more petrol to be had in the area. See "Goering's Armored Car Transformed into Staff Service for CG of CC 'A,' " 1. Azara would also later mention his having spoken to a mechanic—this one at the "Hitler garage" in Berchtesgaden. "Goering's Car on Display Dec. 5th," *Aiken Standard* (SC), November 30, 1945, 1. This

was the man who'd told him the car had been Göring's, but apparently didn't mention any problems with a lack of gasoline. It's possible, perhaps even likely, that that these two mechanics Azara encountered were actually the same person, their identities split and confused in the course of storytelling.

9. Russell A. Gugeler, *Major General Orlando Ward: Life of a Leader* (Oakland, OR: Red Anvil Press, 2009), 394.

10. "Crowds View Goering Car on Exhibition in City," 8.

11. James Charlton, ed., *The Military Quotation Book* (New York: Thomas Dunne Books, 2002), 128.

12. Thomas Childers, *Soldier from the War Returning* (Boston: Mariner Books, 2009), 109, 120.

13. Sidney D. Kirkpatrick, *Hitler's Holy Relics* (New York: Simon & Schuster, 2010), 18.

14. J. Glenn Gray, *The Warriors: Reflections on Men in Battle* (New York: Harcourt, Brace, 1959), 82.

15. Michael McAfee, Curator of History, West Point Museum, telephone interview with author, April 11, 2013.

16. Rick Atkinson, *The Guns at Last Light* (New York: Picador, 2014), 544–45; "December 2–8 is 'Victory Week,'" *Aiken Standard* (Aiken, SC), December 5, 1945, 1.

17. Colin MacInnes, *To the Victors the Spoils* (Middlesex, UK: Penguin, 1966), 201.

18. Generally speaking, soldiers "requisitioned" motor vehicles and "liberated" consumer goods. Frederick Taylor, *Exorcising Hitler* (New York: Bloomsbury, 2011), 131. See also William H. Honan, *Treasure Hunt* (New York: Delta, 1997), 65.

19. Douglas Botting, *From the Ruins of the Reich* (New York: Crown, 1985), 32–33.

20. Ibid., 210–11.

21. "Goering's Car on Display Dec. 5th," 1.

22. Wilson, *Hitler,* 61.

23. Leonard Rapport and Arthur Northwood Jr., *Rendezvous with Destiny: A History of the 101st Airborne Division* (Greenville, TX: 101st Airborne Division Association, 1948), 751.

24. Kenneth D. Alford, *Nazi Plunder: Great Treasure Stories of World War II* (Boston: Da Capo Press, 2000), 61.

25. David Kenyon Webster, *Parachute Infantry* (New York: Bantam Dell, 2002), 293.

26. Ibid.

27. According to Webster, Taylor's "four-ton armored Mercedes-Benz touring car" had belonged to Hitler, but of course he'd have had no way of knowing the car's provenance with any certainty. Meanwhile, Colonel Sink was also said to have availed himself of a Mercedes roadster, purportedly Göring's. This was, most likely, the 540K roadster that participated in the Victory Loan Drives in America several months later. Again, however, at this stage, positive identification of any Mercedes found in Berchtesgaden—and especially claiming ownership by specific Nazi officials—was heresay. Rapport and Northwood, *Rendezvous With Destiny*, 749, 751–52.

28. Webster recounts, "Captain Spiers, who could be ferociously vindictive when he was crossed, said to his audience, 'We'll see just how goddamn indestructible these cars are.' He started the motor, drove up the road to a cliff, and slid out of the driver's seat just before the car plunged into the abyss." Webster, *Parachute Infantry*, 294.

29. According to Webster, the 101st parking area for captured German vehicles was "beside the P. W. [prisoner of war] enclosure . . . on the main road from Berchtesgaden to Munich." Webster, *Parachute Infantry*, 295–96.

30. "Goering's Car on Display Dec. 5th," 1. The account of his adventures that Azara gave to the *Standard* places him in Berchtesgaden at the time he claimed his new engine, though it's not certain whether he did so at the 101st park for captured autos, though that would appear to be the most likely place. The car from which the engine was harvested was another Grosser 770K limousine—one that the Twentieth Armored's newspaper claimed was "Hitler's personal car, discovered at Berchtesgaden." See "Goering's Armored Car Transformed into Staff Service for CG of CC 'A,'" 1. Discovered at Berchtesgaden, the car surely was—but it hadn't belonged to Hitler. The car from which Azara took his spare engine had been ordered in December of 1942 by Major General Hans Rattenhuber (Daimler-Benz order no. 399902). Rattenhuber headed up Hitler's SS security detail, though this link proves nothing more than the possibility that Hitler might have ridden in the car. Mercedes delivered this car to Berlin on April 17, 1944. Kosche, "The Story of a Car," 4–5.

31. Azara's quote appeared in "Goering's Car on Display Dec. 5th," 1. A detailed topographical map showing the Obersalzberg complex, including

the huge garages Bormann had erected near the Berghof, can be found in Hoffmann, *Hitler's Personal Security*, 184–85.

32. The way Azara explained this exchange, the mechanic apparently showed him "the special orders checking my souvenir as having been built for and assigned to the Reichmarshall [*sic*]." It is impossible to know, now, exactly what papers Azara had been shown—or if they indeed did demonstrate such a link. Some critical information was certainly lost owing to the language barrier, and it's highly unlikely that Azara could read the German on whatever paperwork it was that he was shown. In any case, subsequent events would cast grave doubts on the veracity of this purported evidence. See "Crowds View Goering Car on Exhibition in City," 8. The mechanic also told Azara that the Mercedes was on the flat car because it had been on its way from Berchtesgaden to Munich, but the invasion of the Americans had interrupted the transport. "Goering's Car on Display Dec. 5th," 1.

33. The details are thin for this part of the story. While the Grosser Mercedes from which Azara got his new engine had been discovered by the 101st in Berchtesgaden, it's unclear how or why the car was sent to Trostberg. Probably it was for Azara's convenience, since his own car was nearby. Kosche, "The Story of a Car," 4–5.

34. For a time, Azara's wife Jackie put Hitler's lace runner over her organ at home. As of this writing, these objects remain in the possession of Azara's children. At some point, Joe Azara also mailed home a machine gun he'd captured somewhere in southern Germany, but his wife was too afraid to keep the thing in the house. The gun wound up as a loaner piece of decor in a local bar. Telephone interview with Joseph Andrew Azara and Debra Weidrick (née Azara), March 25, 2015.

35. Ibid.

36. Some sources have suggested that the Mercedes was given a white star to denote its being used as a brigadier general's car. In fact, the army had adopted the white star as a badge for its vehicles two years earlier, simply because it was the one symbol that could be most easily identified from a distance. See Rick Atkinson, *The Guns at Last Light* (New York: Henry Holt, 2014), 142.

37. The Twentieth Armored Division had been assigned to the Seventh Army as of April 23, 1945. Twentieth Armored Division page, U.S. Army Center of Military History site, www.history.army.mil/html/forcestruc/cbtchron/cc/020ad.htm, retrieved March 3, 2014.

38. "Goering's Armored Car Transformed into Staff Service for CG of CC 'A,'" 1.

39. Kosche, "The Story of a Car," 6.

40. "Goering's Car on Display Dec. 5th," 1.

41. Some guessing is necessary here. Lasko said that General Daly didn't want him to drive faster than 35 mph, but it's not clear how the sergeant arrived at that number. The Mercedes speedometer would have measured kilometers per hour, so if the needle hit 35 it means they were only making 22 mph. It's possible, of course, that Lasko was simply using his internal sense of velocity when he gave that figure. "December 2–8 is 'Victory Week,'" 1.

42. Ibid.

43. To quote Azara: "I checked at Berchtesgaden, [and] found Goering's personal mechanic," and: "I talked with a mechanic in the Hitler garage." See "Crowds View Goering Car on Exhibition in City," 8; "Goering's Car on Display Dec. 5th," 1.

44. Webster, *Parachute Infantry*, 293.

45. According to the account published in the Twentieth Armored Division's newspaper, "a Dutch displaced person, who worked in a German garage near where the car was found, said the car was being transported by flat car from Berchtesgaden to Munich because it was out of gas, and even Goering could get no more." See "Goering's Armored Car Transformed into Staff Service for CG of CC 'A,'" 1.

46. Webster, *Parachute Infantry*, 299,

47. Göring stepped from his car "pudgy and immaculate," wearing a green coat and riding breeches. The quote about the dusty ride is also from the newspaper account of the event. A. I. Goldberg, "Goering, No. 2 Nazi, Gives Up to 7th Army," *Fresno Bee*, May 9, 1945, 1.

48. "Crowds View Goering Car on Exhibition in City," 8.

49. According to the general's biographer, "An exception to the divisional policy against appropriating German vehicles was a huge bullet-proof Mercedes convertible sedan that one of Ward's combat commands captured." This was unquestionably Azara's car, for Combat Command A had no other. "Ward had the car shipped to the U.S. where it was used in bond drives." Gugeler, *Major General Orlando Ward*, 396.

50. Telephone interview with Joseph Andrew Azara and Debra Weidrick (née Azara), March 25, 2015.

51. Standing by to do the honors of driving the car onto the U.S. mainland was seventy-year-old car aficionado George Crittenden, the "original automobile

man of Boston," as he was locally known. "Not many people know the workings of the foreign made cars," wrote one reporter on the scene, "so Mr. Crittenden, or 'Crit,' as he likes to be called, did the honors." Crittenden's role in the chronology isn't entirely clear. He was said to have driven the car off the ship—but the *George Shiras* hoisted the Mercedes off. Perhaps Crittenden drove the car off the lighter instead. "Ancient Autos Pause Enroute [*sic*] to Greenfield," *Fitchburg* [MA] *Sentinel*, September 15, 1945, 7.

52. "Goering's Gear," *Newsweek*, August 20, 1945, 52.

53. "Detour for Goering's Chariot," *Brooklyn Eagle*, August 9, 1945, 3.

54. "Goering's Auto Bullet-Proof to Protect Fat Marshal's Hide," *Boston Daily Globe*, August 8, 1945, 2.

55. Letter from Ludwig Kosche to Herbert O'Connell Jr., January 11, 1980, Kosche Papers, Canadian War Museum, 58A 3, box 4.

56. "Crowds View Goering Car on Exhibition in City," 8.

57. Michael McAfee, Curator of History, West Point Museum, telephone interview with author, April 11, 2013. The West Point Museum's collection includes several war trophies fitting this description, including Hitler's pearl-handled, gold-plated pistol, and Göring's jeweled field baton.

58. "Detour for Goering's Chariot," 3.

59. "The Victory Loan Drive and Its Setting," *Monthly Review of the Federal Reserve Bank of Atlanta*, September 30, 1945, 101.

60. Allan M. Winkler, *Home Front U.S.A.: America During World War II* (Wheeling, IL: Harlan Davison, 2000), 36.

61. The Treasury Department "hoped that it would be able to give rides to at least a few bond buyers" and, indeed, did so. "Bond Buyers May Ride in Hitler's Car," *Miami News*, October 21, 1945, 1.

62. Telephone interview with Joseph Andrew Azara and Debra Weidrick (née Azara) March 25, 2015.

63. The army had given the returning Twentieth Armored a thirty-day leave first. Gugeler, *Major General Orlando Ward*, 397–98.

64. "Goering's Auto Put on Display to Aid D.C. Victory Loan Drive," *Washington Post*, November 2, 1945, 4. The location was the pie-slice intersection where H Street crosses New York Avenue. The limousine was wearing a new license plate up front: W-169290. Fortunately, the car still kept its original German tag in the back, a piece of evidence that would prove critical in the years to come.

65. Rapport and Northwood, *Rendezvous With Destiny*, 749, 751–52; Webster, *Parachute Infantry*, 293.

66. Göring appeared in "a Mercedes Benz with servants and a great load of luggage," reported the *Brooklyn Eagle*. That car had accompanied Frau Göring to her house arrest at Fischhorn Castle, until the Ninetieth Infantry Division took it away from her. See "Nazi Arrogance Stirs U.S., Shows Need of Stern Justice," *Brooklyn Eagle*, May 15, 1945, 8. Initially, the AP reported that this car "disappeared" (Howard Cowan, "No Curtains for Frau Goering," *Bradford* [PA] *Daily Record*, June 27, 1945, 6) but it was Lieutenant Hubert J. Tyrrell of the Ninetieth Infantry Division who'd had the car confiscated. Alford, *Nazi Plunder*, 53–54.

67. Bob Hope, "It Says Here," *Harrisburg* [PA] *Telegraph*, July 20, 1945, 11.

68. The car Azara found arrived in Boston on August 8, 1945. On September 21, an item in the *Chicago Tribune* noted that another armored Mercedes-Benz captured by the 101st was on its way to the United States for use in a war-bond tour. This car was given no other identifying details in the article, which also carried no photo. The story stated that the car had been Hitler's, but without further information, that claim is impossible to substantiate. "Black Horse Troop of Chicago Ready to Sail for Home," *Chicago Tribune*, September 21, 1948, 1. Indeed, the 101st Airborne apparently kept no identifying information on the two cars it had sent to New York. A movement order from the Headquarters U.S. Forces European Theater specifies "two (2) captured German motor vehicles." Kosche, "The Story of a Car," 9.

69. "A group of Aberdeen Proving Ground maintenance and repair experts put the Goering car back into top-notch shape." See "Goering Auto's Visit Will Spur Local Bond Campaign," *Morning Herald* (Hagerstown, MD), November 17, 1945, 21.

70. The Grosser Mercedes in the Signal Corps photograph shows a grille with no ornamental crank hole at the base (a feature Azara's car had) and also features a blackout lamp mounted above the center of the front fender (a feature that Azara's car lacked). Kosche, "The Story of a Car," 10.

71. Examples of the confusion fostered by the newspaper coverage include but are not limited to: Harrisburg, Pennsylvania's *Evening News* referring to a "19-foot Mercedes-Benz roadster" (the roadster was a little over seventeen feet), and a paper in Zanesville, Ohio, running a photo of a 770K Grosser limousine but describing a "blue sports-model car" (which was clearly the roadster, not the limousine) instead. "Hitler's Auto is Shown Here," *Evening News* (Harrisburg, PA), November 10, 1945, 24; "Fuehrer's Automobile Pays Armistice Day Visit Here," *Sunday Times* (Zanesville, OH), November 11,

1945, 1. Newspapers, no doubt taking their cues from the sloppy information supplied by the Signal Corps, also said that the roadster was bulletproof (it wasn't) and that it had belonged to Hitler (it hadn't). A story out of Syracuse, New York, correctly stated that the roadster was Göring's even through the paper ran a photo of Sergeant Azara and his buddies, who'd captured one of the limousines and had nothing to do with the roadster. "Four Who Seized Goering's Huge Car to Bring it Here," uncited clip, Kosche Papers, Canadian War Museum, 58A, box 3, folder 2.15. While Azara and his buddies' car had reached North Carolina on the Victory Loan Tour by the end of November 1945, a newspaper in Lumberton featured a description of the Grosser captured by the 101st Airborne (see note 68), not the one captured by Azara—unless the two cars were traveling together, which the paper does not mention, in any case. "Men Who Captured Goering's Car to Show it Thursday," *The Robesonian* (Lumberton, NC), November 26, 1945, 1.

72. "Treasury to Exhibit Hitler, Goering Autos," *New York Times*, October 20, 1945, 16.

73. The other Grosser limousine—the one used in Germany by General Maxwell Taylor of the 101st Airborne—would be in Kansas City on November 27, around the same time that Azara and his buddies were heading toward South Carolina in their car. This automobile had been captured by four men of the 506th Parachute Infantry of the 101st Airborne Division (Lieutenant Jack G. Holland of Rocky Mount, Virginia; Technical Sergeant Thomas F. Meggs of Union County, North Carolina; Corporal Roderick D. Smith of Toccoa, Georgia; and Staff Sergeant Frank J. Malik of Detroit), who managed to get the car away from German soldiers in Berchtesgaden who were trying to destroy it. "Car as Bond Drive Aid," *Kansas City Star*, November 25, 1945, 16. After Kansas City, the car paused in Lawrence, Kansas, where the paper noted that it had come via Colorado, having started out in Washington, D.C., on November 1. "See Goering Car," *Lawrence Journal-World*, November 26, 1945, 1. The men traveling with the car were all eligible for discharge but had volunteered for the arduous tour, which ran seven days a week, featured two stops a day, and involved driving at night. "Hitler Car Display Here Thursday," *Mason City Globe-Gazette* (Mason City, IA) December 3, 1945, 11. This 770K would be taken to President Truman's home at 219 North Delaware Street, Independence, Missouri, for a photo op on or about November 30. *Marion Star* (Marion, OH), November 30, 1945, 1.

74. Letter from Karl F. Kempf, curator, Aberdeen Proving Ground, to Lee Murray, curator, Canadian War Museum, November 24, 1969, Kosche Papers, Canadian War Museum, 58A, box 3, folder 2.15.

75. "The Things We Escaped . . ." *Statesville* [NC] *Record & Landmark*, October 25, 1945, 6.

76. "Brief History of World War Two Advertising Campaigns, War Loans and Bonds," Duke University Libraries, http://library.duke.edu/digital collections/adaccess/guide/wwii/bonds-loans/, retrieved March 7, 2015.

77. "'Fatso's' Captured Car Here Tomorrow," *Jersey Journal*, November 7, 1945, 2.

78. "Hundreds Inspect Goering's Auto," *Jersey Observer*, November 9, 1945, 6.

79. "Goering's Car Gives Victory Loan a Push!" *Trenton Evening Times*, November 6, 1945, 1.

80. "Nazis Used to Heil Thug Who Owned This Car," *Elmira Advertiser*, uncited clip, Kosche Papers, Canadian War Museum, 58A, box 3, folder 2.15.

81. "Crowds View Goering Car on Exhibition in City," 8.

82. "Goering's Auto Aids Fund Drive," uncited clip, Kosche Papers, Canadian War Museum, 58A, box 3, folder 2.15.

83. Telephone interview with Joseph Andrew Azara and Debra Weidrick (née Azara), March 25, 2015.

84. "Crowds View Goering Car on Exhibition in City," 8.

85. Ticket stub, Kosche Papers, Canadian War Museum, 58A, box 3, folder 2.15.

86. "Goering's Car on Display Dec. 5th," 1. At least Aiken residents were merely goaded into buying bonds. In Danville, Virginia, the rules were clear: "Only those who agree to buy another bond in the current drive will be admitted." Untitled item, *The Bee*, November 27, 1945, 8.

87. The tour neared its end on November 31, when the Mercedes reached Lumberton, where the American Legion planned a Saturday-night barn dance featuring the Lone Star Quintet, Looney Luke, Cousin Nimrod, and the "Added Attraction . . . Hermann Goering's Mercedes Automobile." Ad for radio station WPTF's Carolina Barn Dance, *The Robesonian* (Lumberton, NC), November 30, 1945, 5.

88. "Men Who Captured Goering's Car to Show it Thursday," 1.

89. At this time, the Proving Ground contained 3,289 pieces of foreign military equipment that, since 1919, had been stored and exhibited for study. The installation's official history makes no mention of the captured Nazi

automobiles but given the stupendous size of its collection, plus the fact that its curatorial mission focused on ordnance, the fact is not especially surprising. Karl F. Kempf, *Aberdeen Proving Ground Museum, 1919–1960* (Aberdeen, MD: Aberdeen Proving Ground, 1961), 4, 36, 38.

90. "Crowds View Goering Car on Exhibition in City," 8.

91. "German Mercedes Benz," ad for Capitol Motors, *Evening News* (Harrisburg, PA), April 20, 1945, 15.

92. This allegation—one of many—was among those that became part of Ludwig Kosche's exhaustive research into this Mercedes. Kosche, "The Story of a Car," 7.

93. The newspaper accounts do not offer details sufficient to determine beyond a shadow of a doubt which of the two Göring-attributed 770K Grosser limousines at Aberdeen had been involved in this theft/accident. However, given that Azara's car had license plates, was street-legal and fully operational, it is the more likely candidate. Also, one report noted that the "flasher siren" bolted to the car's front bumper had been damaged in the accident. Only Azara's car had such a fixture up front (attached, apparently, as part of its overhaul at Aberdeen); the other Grosser was equipped with a blackout lamp. "Goering Mercedes Automobile Recovered After Disappearance," *Pottstown Mercury* (Pottstown, PA), June 10, 1946, 1; "Crack-Up Here was First for Goering Car," *Pottstown Mercury*, June 11, 1946, 1.

94. The only other media mention of a Mercedes referable to Göring, at least that the author was able to locate, was an automobile show held in Syracuse, New York, in May of 1948. But here, it's truly impossible to verify whether or not it was Azara's car that made the appearance, since the ad for the Centennial Automobile Show lists only "Hermann Goering's Bulletproof Mercedes (Courtesy of the U.S. War Department.)" *Post-Standard* (Syracuse, NY), May 3, 1948, 7.

5. The Finnish Connection

1. Janus and Brasher, *The Search for Peking Man*, 70.
2. Danford, Lang, and Gill, "Deal," 14.
3. Janus, *Angel on My Shoulder*, 114–15.
4. "Adolph's Big Car to Be Displayed on Local Streets," 19.
5. Ibid.
6. "Hitler's Own Car Arrives in U.S.," *Daily Courier* (Connellsville, PA), July 1, 1948, 1.

7. "Hitler's Car Due in Salem," *Oregon Statesman*, June 11, 1951, 1.

8. "Famous Car of Hitler Will Be in Kennewick," *Tri-City Herald* (Pasco, WA), July 9, 1951, 5.

9. Ibid.

10. "Hitler's Car Booed and Hissed as It Reaches New York," 10.

11. Mabley, "Hitler Auto Drives Like a Jet Plane," 9. The author has found no evidence that Hitler ever personally drove one of his 770K limousines, though he did in fact know how to drive (see note 15).

12. Thompson, "Disabled Vets at Vaughan See Hitler's Big Car," 9.

13. "Hitler's Car Gets 7 Miles Per Gallon, Crisscrossing Country on Exhibit," 19.

14. "Famous Car of Hitler Will Be in Kennewick," 5.

15. While Goebbels could be obsequious toward Hitler himself, to everyone else he was invariably an iron-willed monster—a "vicious, satanically gifted dwarf," Ernst Hanfstaengl wrote, the "pilot-fish of the Hitler shark"—and sufficiently fearless (if that is the term) to ultimately murder his entire family and then kill himself. Peter Conradi, *Hitler's Piano Player* (New York: Carroll & Graf, 2004), 134. Contrary to popular myth, Hitler did indeed know how to operate an automobile, but rarely did. In his memoirs, Wulf Schwarzwäller noted "print shop owner Adolf Mueller had taught Hitler how to drive the more recent car models. Hitler passed his driving test, but drove rarely." Wulf Schwarzwäller, *The Unknown Hitler* (Toronto: Stoddart, 1988), 129. While Eva Braun could have easily attempted to have Hitler do her personal bidding, Albert Speer said she never did. "Eva Braun had no interest in politics," Speer wrote. "She scarcely ever attempted to influence Hitler"—this despite "the cynicism with which Hitler had treated her." Speer, *Inside the Third Reich*, 93. And finally, while Hitler did have several opportunities to escape from Berlin as Soviet forces approached, he refused all of them. "Gentlemen, if you believe that I will leave Berlin, you are sorely mistaken!" he screamed at his subordinates in the bunker on April 22, 1945. "I'd rather put a bullet through my head." Eight days later, still in the bunker, he did just that. Joachim Fest, *Inside Hitler's Bunker*, 63.

16. It was during the car's trip through Central Park in the summer of 1948 that the first mention of this photo appears: "[Janus] has pictures of Hitler riding in it in a victory parade in Berlin in 1941. Hitler is shown standing up in the front seat, giving the big salute." While none of the newspapers of the period reproduced this photo (at least none that the author has been

able to locate), it's likely that the image is the same one that later appeared on the front cover of the brochure used during the car's public tours—a photo that does indeed show Hitler standing in front, giving the salute, during what appears to be a city parade. The hood of the car in his photograph has a perfectly smooth hood, whereas the hood of Janus's car featured two sets of very prominent ventilation slits—twenty on either side of the center hinge. This feature, one of several that later allowed Ludwig Kosche to conduct his groundbreaking work on the Göring Special, is physically prominent and cannot be discarded: The car in the photograph and the car in Janus's possession were two different cars. Danford, Lang, and Gill, "Deal," 14. Another photo that Janus may have regarded as "proof" of his car's validity—which later appeared on page 2 of his souvenir booklet—shows Hitler in another Grosser 770K, this time at the Berlin Olympic Stadium during a May Day rally, probably in 1938. But this event predates the construction of the Mannerheim car, which was ordered in June of 1941, so it could not be the same car. The Grosser limousine in this photo also had a smooth hood with no ventilation slits, which the Mannerheim car did have. For some reason, the license plate on this car in Janus's souvenir booklet has been doctored to read "A-1." The car's original license plate number was IA^{v}148485. *Hitler's Armored Car Souvenir Book*, 6. See also: "$2.6 Million to Build: Hitler's Car Brought $153,000 at Auction," *Baltimore Sun*, March 11, 1973, WHS34. Finally, it is worth quoting the analysis of Kosche who, after determining the identity of the Göring Special, took an interest in the Mannerheim car: "All this car has got to do with Hitler is that it was a gift from him to Marshal Baron Mannerheim of Finland, and that he inspected it around late November, early December 1941, after which it was delivered by his personal driver Erich Kempka. It was Christopher Janus who got the whole thing mixed up, and anybody with a little brain could have seen that there was a good deal amiss, given the year of construction which was 1941, so that it could not have been used before the war as some of the photographs seem to indicate." Letter from Ludwig Kosche to Ed Jurist, September 28, 1982, Kosche Papers, Canadian War Museum, 58A 3, box 6, folder 17.

17. Jan Melin, the unimpeachable authority on the supercharged Mercedes-Benz cars of the 1930s, refers to this part of the plant as the "department for special cars." Melin, *Mercedes Benz: The Supercharged 8-Cylinder Cars of the 1930s*, 27, 230.

18. The purchase order for the Mannerheim car shows that the Untertürkheim

factory took the initial order, but the car was assembled and finished at Sindelfingen. Ibid., 12, 13, 230.

19. A curious detail about this purchase order—entered on July 2, 1941—is that Mannerheim was not yet a field marshal. Finland's President Ryti would bestow that honor on Mannerheim on June 4, 1942. It's possible that the Mercedes clerk added this detail to the ledger subsequent to the fact. See ibid., 230.

20. Jonathan Clements, *Mannerheim: President, Soldier, Spy* (London: Haus Publishing, 2009), 248.

21. Winston Churchill, "House of Many Mansions" speech, broadcast from London, January 20, 1940.

22. Nazi Germany had signed a nonaggression pact with the Soviets a year prior to this time, on August 23, 1939. To Hitler's thinking, the agreement merely cleared his path to the invasion of Poland; the treaty with Stalin was temporary. In his memoirs, Albert Speer writes of overhearing a snippet of conversation between Hitler and General Wilhelm Keitel on June 28, 1940, in which Hitler likened invading the Soviet Union to "a child's game in a sandbox." Speer, *Inside the Third Reich*, 173. On December 18, 1940, Hitler put his name to Directive 21 ("Operation Barbarossa"), which would lead to Germany's attacking the Soviet Union on June 22, 1941.

23. Heinrich Himmler, who would carry out Hitler's Final Solution, paid two visits to Finland—one, if not both, of which were occasions that found the *Reichsführer* SS riding in Mannerheim's Grosser 770K Mercedes. But Himmler failed to convince the Finns to deport their Jewish population. Only in a single case did the country extradite eight Jews who were not Finnish citizens. The Nazis immediately killed seven of the eight. In 1944, Mannerheim himself would order 160 Jewish refugees sent to Sweden, a move that unquestionably saved their lives. Rachel Bayvel, "While Jews serve in my army I will not allow their deportation," *Jewish Quarterly*, Summer 2006, http://jewishquarterly.org/issuearchive/article8d14 .html?articleid=194, retrieved March 15, 2015.

24. Clements, *Mannerheim: President, Soldier, Spy*, 261.

25. Hitler almost certainly did not pay for the Mannerheim car with his personal earnings. He had use of a private slush fund—their coffers eagerly filled by the captains of German industry to the tune of 100 million marks a year—from which to draw for, among other expenses, his art collections and gifts. Administered by the Union of German Employers Associations and the Reich Association of German Industry, the funds represented a

.5 percent wage tax imposed on all workers employed in German industry. Wolfgang Benz, *A Concise History of the Third Reich* (Berkeley: University of California Press, 2007), 106–7. The captains of Germany industry viewed Hitler as "a gift from god," and accordingly were happy to make quarterly contributions to his private fund. Schwarzwäller, *The Unknown Hitler*, 193–94.

26. Kempka, *I Was Hitler's Chauffeur*, 23.

27. Hoffmann, *Hitler's Personal Security*, 3. It was here that Hitler would stay until Stalin's advancing armies forced him to flee in November of 1944, and it was here that the famous (and, unfortunately, failed) plot by Colonel Claus von Stauffenberg to kill Hitler with explosives packed in a briefcase took place. Stauffenberg, chief of staff of the Replacement Army, was a member of a sizable underground group of young, pedigreed officers who'd come to realize (if too late) that Hitler's total-war agenda would inevitably lead to the complete destruction of their country. A war hero and a monarchist, Stauffenberg was the brains behind the assassination plot known as Operation Valkyrie, which called for Stauffenberg to place a briefcase packed with two pounds of timed plastic explosives below Hitler's conference table. Regrettably for Stauffenberg, the bomb blew Hitler's trousers off, but failed to kill him. Indeed, the plot probably wound up doing more harm than good, for it only more firmly anchored Hitler in his psychosis. "Having now escaped death," he told Mussolini, "I am more than ever convinced that the great cause which I serve will be brought through its present perils and that everything will be brought to a good end." Of course, Hitler's end was not good—and neither was Stauffenberg's: He was executed that same evening. Matthew Hughes and Chris Mann, *Inside Hitler's Germany* (New York: MJF Books, 2000), 188–89.

28. Photos of this event are available at the Finnish government's Wartime Photograph Archive, http://sa-kuva.fi/webneologineng.html. Kempka's memories here are brief ones, but they place him squarely at the center of things: "In December 1941 I handed over to Baron von Mannerheim, the Finnish leader, an armored open Daimler-Benz 150 touring car." Kempka, *I Was Hitler's Chauffeur*, 24.

29. The German plates—SS-02047—would later be replicated and put back on the car by Gen. William Lyon, who devoted considerable resources to returning the car to exactly how it looked when it left the factory. Author's visit with Gen. William Lyon, Coto de Caza, California, July 14, 2015.

30. Vann, *Fantastic Mercedes-Benz Automobiles*, 101.

31. Ibid.

32. Melin, *Mercedes Benz: The Supercharged 8-Cylinder Cars of the 1930s*, 234. The presence of the platform would later make it all too easy to conclude that the car had been Hitler's.

33. Vann, *Fantastic Mercedes-Benz Automobiles*, 101; Melin, *Mercedes Benz: The Supercharged 8-Cylinder Cars of the 1930s*, 234.

34. Hitler's airplane—full name Focke-Wulf 200 Condor C-4—featured a wingback, parachute-equipped ejector seat just for Hitler. This remarkable feature demonstrated the preposterous lengths that Hitler's handlers went to protect his life. The upholstered chair looked like ordinary living-room furniture but was encased in an armored shell. If the plane encountered trouble, Hitler need only to have pulled a red lever, which caused the entire seat to drop through a trap door at the bottom of the fuselage. The parachute opened automatically, and tests with crash dummies demonstrated that the contraption stood a good chance of working. Hoffmann, *Hitler's Personal Security*, 76.

35. The Finnish government retains an extensive collection of photographs of this event. Hitler can clearly be seen with Ryti in the Grosser's backseat in images 89624 and 89625. Finnish Wartime Photograph Archive, http://sa -kuva.fi/neo?tem=webneoeng, retrieved August 1, 2015.

36. Though there are plenty of right arms held aloft in the German newsreel footage of his meeting, Mannerheim acknowledges Hitler and the German contingent simply by touching his hand to his side cap. "Hitler meets Mannerheim in Finland, 4 June 1942," www.youtube.com/watch?v=6fyRYvw _ilc, retrieved March 21, 2015. Similarly, in the Finnish government's Wartime Photograph Archive, image no. 89604 shows Mannerheim seeing Hitler off at Immola with a traditional military salute. (See: http://sa-kuva .fi/webneologineng.html)

37. Unbeknownst to Hitler, Yleisradio, the Finnish Broadcasting Company, was secretly recording this meeting, hiding a microphone on a hat rack and running the cables outside the railroad car's windows. The eleven minutes of recorded conversation—the only known recording of Hitler speaking informally—was lost for many years and surfaced only in 1992. Kirsikka Moring, "Conversation Secretly Recorded in Finland Helped German Actor Prepare for Hitler Role," *Helsinki Times*, September 15, 2004, www .fpp.co.uk/Hitler/docs/Mannerheim/recording_040642.html, retrieved March 21, 2015.

38. General Wilhelm Mohnke, who'd been awarded the Knight's Cross for

leading the SS Panzergrenadier Regiment 26 in Normandy, later recalled how "Hitler . . . had a whole carton filled with these medals." O'Donnell, *The Bunker*, 272.

39. "Hitler meets Mannerheim in Finland, 4 June 1942."

40. Melin, *Mercedes Benz: The Supercharged 8-Cylinder Cars of the 1930s*, 235, 236. Jan Melin and Sven Hernström, *Mercedes Benz: The Supercharged 8-Cylinder Cars of the 1930s*, vol. 2 (Sparreholm, Sweden: Gamla Bilsalongen, 2003), 177. The informational booklet sold at Finland's Mannerheim Museum also clearly states that Hitler rode in Mannerheim's car on both the trip out and back to the Immola Airfield. Juutilainen Anssi and Juha Koivulahti, *Marsalkka Mannerheimin Mercedes 770* (Lahti, Finland: Geisir Oy, 2014), 39.

41. "Special Topics: Cars," C.G.E. Mannerheim site, Ministry for Foreign Affairs of Finland, www.mannerheim.fi/13_erity/e_auto2.htm, retrieved November 27, 2013.

42. Anssi and Koivulahti, *Marsalkka Mannerheimin Mercedes 770*, 41.

43. On paper, the buyer was one Jordan-Benson & Co. at 68 West Washington Street, Chicago. But the actual recipient was Janus. Melin, *Mercedes Benz: The Supercharged 8-Cylinder Cars of the 1930s*, 239

44. Jan Melin recalls that, as early as 1948, before the 770K left Gothenburg for New York, the myth of Hitler's ownership of the car had already sprouted in local newspapers in Sweden. Jan Melin, e-mail message to author, May 3, 2016.

45. "Hitler's Car Part of Antique Display," 8.

46. Rommel had uttered these words in the teeth of the El Alamein crisis. David Fraser, *Knight's Cross: A Life of Field Marshal Erwin Rommel* (New York: Harper Perennial, 1994) 382.

47. "20th Near Deal to Acquire 'Rommel,'" *Hollywood Reporter*, February 14, 1950, 10.

48. "Zanuck Replies to Complaints on 'Fox,'" *Hollywood Reporter*, November 16, 1951, 2.

49. Zanuck also attempted to point out what he believed was Rommel's redeeming moral character with a voiceover recording of Winston Churchill: "His ardor and daring inflicted grievous disasters upon us, but he deserves . . . our respect because, although a loyal German solider, he came to hate Hitler and all his works, and took part in the conspiracy to rescue Germany by displacing the maniac and tyrant." See "The Desert Fox," American Film Institute Catalog of Feature Films, www.afi.com

/members/catalog/DetailView.aspx?s=&Movie=50076, retrieved February 3, 2014.

50. *The Illustrated London News* reported, "Frau Rommel, widow of the German Field Marshal, gave her permission for the film to be made." See "Rommel—Desert Fox, His Defeat and Death," *Illustrated London News*, September 8, 1951, 354.

51. Janus, *Angel on My Shoulder*, 118. This $2,500 weekly rate is at variance with the one Janus quoted in a 1974 interview with the Associated Press: "Skouras' studio paid me $1,000 a week for its use in the James Mason Film," Janus said. Even if the lower figure was the correct one, it was still a dear price. "Batmobile Overshadows Hitler's Car in Museum," *San Bernardino County Sun* (CA), November 28, 1974, 86. Unfortunately, none of these facts can be checked with Fox, which discarded the house files on most of its pre-1955 films, according to studio archivist Jeff Thompson, with whom the author spoke in February of 2014.

52. "Use Hitler's Own Automobile for New Rommel Film," *The Desert Fox Exhibitor's Campaign Book*, 20th Century–Fox, n.d., 9, author's collection.

53. The degree of Rommel's role in the assassination plot against Hitler has been the subject of much debate. It was clear that, at the very least, Rommel possessed knowledge of a conspiracy, and this was sufficient grounds for the charge of treason against him. But the larger and understandable questions for the film's critics seem to have been where Rommel fit in the broader picture of Nazi evil and whether his late-stage opposition to Hitler—however brave it may have been—was redeeming enough to cast him as the moral hero that the film portrays him as being. The historian David Fraser has argued that Rommel "was blind to moral issues . . . which transcended strategy and politics." Moreover, Rommel clearly possessed some knowledge of the atrocities committed against the Jews, in the East as well as Germany itself. In this context, the real-life field marshal's decision to concern himself only with matters of military strategy clearly falls short of establishing him as the sort of principled paragon on view in *The Desert Fox*. Fraser, *Knight's Cross*, 536.

54. Gynter C. Quill, "'Desert Fox' Great Though Controversial," *Waco Tribune-Herald*, December 23, 1951, 38.

55. "Six Congressmen Seek to Keep 'Fox' Out of Germany," *Variety*, November 21, 1951, 1. "Glorifying Rommel?" *Variety*, October 17, 1951, 4.

56. "Squawks Vs. 'Fox' in 2 Countries but Biz Socko," *Variety*, March 12, 1952, 2.

57. Janus, *Angel on My Shoulder*, 118.

6. Men with Cars

1. Janus, *Angel on My Shoulder*, 125.
2. The characterization belongs to Michael Lamm, in "Cars I've Loved and Hated," *Hemmings Motor News* blog, May 21, 2012, http://blog.hemmings.com/index.php/2012/05/21/cars-ive-loved-and-hated-michael-lamms-unauthorized-auto-biography-chapter-15-special-interest-autos/, retrieved December 26, 2013.
3. Telephone interview with Michael Lamm, January 2, 2014.
4. Letter to Miss P. Waterman and Miss L. Waterman from George Waterman, November 23, 1926, furnished via e-mail between author and George H. Waterman III, May 10, 2015.
5. Telephone interview with K. H. Gibson III, January 8, 2014.
6. Though Waterman and Gibson had united their respective auto collections for several years, they would split them again by the late 1930s. Telephone interview with George H. Waterman III, May 10, 2015.
7. Waterman and Gibson's solicitation postcard, courtesy of K. H. Gibson III, telephone interview, January 8, 2014.
8. According to RM Sotheby's, probably the world's most prestigious collector car auction house, "both Gibson and his collecting colleague and partner George Waterman . . . could, and in fact did, own just about anything they wanted in the late 1930s and 1940s, when these classics were simply older cars in barns and carriage houses of New England." This background appeared as part of a catalog listing for a 1924 Mercedes 28/95 Sport Phaeton, body by Sindelfingen, a car that was once in Waterman and Gibson's collection, and one the youths would have obtained for a very modest (if indeed any) price. If it's an indication of the pair's keen eye for cars, in 2011 this Mercedes sold at RM Sotheby's auction in Monterey, California, for $1,017,500. RM Sotheby's auction catalog, August 19–20, 2011, 478, 480.
9. When the owner of Noyes Buick in Boston decided to move his dealership up to the suburb of Arlington, he told the boys they could keep some of their cars in his vacant storefront. "I've got a picture of one hundred or so very old cars lined up in the dealership showroom," Gibson says. "These boys were *into* cars." Telephone interview with K. H. Gibson III, January 8, 2014.
10. At some point—when, exactly, remains unclear—the boys combined their respective collections into one. It certainly made sense from a storage standpoint. Telephone interview with George H. Waterman III, February 8, 2014.

11. In 1981, Gibson donated this vehicle to the Smithsonian in Washington, D.C. Dudgeon Steam Wagon, National Museum of American History, http://amhistory.si.edu/onthemove/collection/object_1324.html, retrieved April 19, 2015.

12. Telephone interview with George H. Waterman III, February 8, 2014. Waterman's interest in former presidential wheels did not end here. In time he would also pick up the 1953 Cadillac Eldorado that President Eisenhower used in his inaugural parade—the car that popularized the wraparound windshield.

13. "Putting famous automobiles on cross-country tours has become a hobby since Janus got Adolph Hitler's bullet proof automobile in 1948," said the Associated Press. "Roosevelt's Bullet Proof Car to Tour," *Rushville* [IN] *Republican*, August 14, 1952, 14.

14. Telephone interview with George H. Waterman III, February 8, 2014.

15. Ibid.

16. "Trades Hitler's Car," *News-Herald* (Franklin, PA), March 21, 1952, 1. "Roosevelt's Bullet Proof Car to Tour," 14.

17. According to George H. Waterman III, Gibson and Waterman split their collections in the late 1930s, though they remained close friends. Waterman, with his wife, continued to hunt throughout New England. The Mannerheim Mercedes seems to have been a car that Waterman and Gibson owned together ("jointly bought," Waterman speculates). Telephone interview with George H. Waterman III, May 9, 2015.

18. Janus, *Angel on My Shoulder*, 125.

19. Telephone interview with K. H. Gibson III, January 16, 2014.

20. It would be overstating the case to say that Gibson needed money, though he certainly lacked the deep pockets of his friend Waterman. Gibson was descended from a prosperous family of piano makers. But the death of his father in 1924 led to his mother's selling the business to Ivers & Pond. The proceeds were enough to see the family though the Great Depression and pay Gibson's college tuition, but it wasn't enough to leave him an inheritance. Looking back on the road show with the car, Kirk Gibson says, "it probably had something to do with money, maybe to drive up the selling price." After all, he adds, "they *did* buy and sell cars." Ibid.

21. Telephone interview with George H. Waterman III, February 8, 2014.

22. Marilyn M. Slade, "Auto Museum's Strange Companions," *Boston Globe*, August 2, 1970, A66. In his collection, the author has an undated color postcard of the car from the Antique Auto Museum, where Waterman

would eventually put the 770K on display. The photograph shows the Mannerheim car outdoors. In direct sunlight, the hood's dark blue contrasts clearly with the black fenders. The gleam on the paint makes it reasonably certain that this image was taken after Waterman and Gibson's repainting, which in turn indicates that the men replicated the car's original paint scheme.

23. "Burke Fixes Hitler Car Feb. Opener," *Billboard*, January 22, 1955, 48. The Ripley franchise mounted its first touring "Odditorium" between 1933 and 1934. The second tour took place after Robert Ripley's death in 1949, when a showman named John Arthur purchased most of the collection and placed it back on the road between 1950 to 1955. Electronic correspondence between author and Edward Meyer, Vice President of Exhibits & Archives, Ripley Entertainment, Inc., April 28 and 29, 2015.

24. Want ads, *Billboard*, March 17, 1956, 67, and April 27, 1957, 78.

25. As early as August of 1952 (after Waterman and Gibson's acquiring the car but before Gibson's purchase of the trailer for it), the big Mercedes spent three days parked on Purchase Street at the intersection of Williams Street in the Massachusetts town of New Bedford—in front of S. S. Kresge. Another photo shows the car (this time in its trailer) at a Kress five-and-ten. Exhibition permission letter from John W. Davies, New Bedford chief of police, July 21, 1952; photographs courtesy of K. H. Gibson III.

26. "People would walk in and *ooh* and *aah*," he adds. Telephone interview with K. H. Gibson III, January 16, 2014.

27. Many of the visitors were, to quote the booklet, "mechanical-minded men," whose interest purportedly lay in the size and complexity of the vehicle. But it's a good bet that most spectators clomped up those metal stairs not so much to inspect an automobile, but to simply to get a look at something that had supposedly been the property of Adolf Hitler. *Hitler's Armored Car Souvenir Book*, 3.

28. Telephone interview with K. H. Gibson III, January 16, 2014.

29. "I slept under the trailer in my sleeping bag," Gibson recalls. "I *wish* I'd have slept in the Hitler car—I'd have a story to tell." But of course, he does have a story to tell. Ibid.

30. *Hitler's Armored Car Souvenir Book*, 2, 3. Hitler could not have used the Mannerheim car as a "getaway vehicle" because he saw it only once before its delivery to Mannerheim. And while it's not an impossibility that Hitler paid a visit to Daimler-Benz, it's also not very likely. It was chauffeur

Kempka, by his own account, who made repeated visits to the Stuttgart factory, and he who was tasked with keeping Hitler apprised on the progress of the *Geschenkwagens*. Erich Kempka, *I Was Hitler's Chauffeur*, 23.

31. For example, the booklet's inside cover showed Hitler riding his big Mercedes into a packed Olympic stadium. The trouble is, the Berlin Olympics were held in 1936, a year the Mercedes model W150 Grosser limousines (of which the Mannerheim car was one) were still on the drawing boards. According to the Daimler-Benz ledger, the completed Mannerheim car was ready for its delivery to Berlin on November 13, 1941. See Melin, *Mercedes Benz: The Supercharged 8-Cylinder Cars of the 1930s*, 27, 230. Another photograph shows Hitler standing in his Grosser as the car prowls the narrow streets of "Memel, Germany" (which should have read Memel, Lithuania). Yet this event, which took place March 22, 1939, was well over two years before the Mannerheim Mercedes was built. A photo on page 22 shows Hitler snug in a 770K limousine's backseat beside Mussolini. But Il Duce began his state visit to Germany on September 25, 1937, and, here again, this event unfolded well before Daimler-Benz finished building the Mannerheim car—four years, one month, and nineteen days before, to be precise. The United States Holocaust Memorial Museum has footage of this visit that contains the motor parade. In it, Hitler and Mussolini are clearly riding in a W07 Grosser, the model that precedes the W150, www.ushmm.org/wlc/en/media_fi.php?MediaId=200. As will be explored in greater detail, the Mannerheim 770K eventually found its way into the collection of Maj. Gen. William Lyon, who owns the car as of this writing. At or around the time the General purchased the limousine in 1984, one of the old souvenir booklets used during the postwar publicity tours found its way into the hands of Lyon's son, Bill, who realized as he paged through it that the booklet's purported photographs of the Mannerheim car were, in fact, images of several different cars. "I could point out five or six differences between the cars pictured and the physical characteristics of this car," Lyon said. Telephone interview with Bill H. Lyon and Maj. Gen. William Lyon, January 20, 2015.

32. In October of 1949, during Janus's period of ownership, the car made a stop in Joplin, Missouri, on one of its many "victory parades." An account in *The Joplin Globe* mentioned the corresponding sale of souvenir booklets. Each booklet featured three articles: "The Story of Hitler's Armored Car," "Secrets of Hitler's Personal Life," and "Is Hitler Alive or Dead?" Such

features are all but identical to those in the booklets sold during the Waterman and Gibson period: "Hitler's Victory Parade Car," "Hitler's Love Life Photos," and "Is Hitler Alive or Dead?" See "Hitler's Armored Car Here this Week," *Joplin Globe,* October 9, 1949, 31.

33. For example, "This armor-plated Mercedes-Benz automobile was once owned by the World's worst criminal, Adolph Hitler," intones one passage. "He never dreamed that, in a few years, it would be touring a free country, as a symbol of his tyranny, the like of which we hope the world will never see again." *Hitler's Armored Car Souvenir Book,* 1. The sensational tone rings similar to that of the statement Janus prepared for the press during the Grosser's 1948 exhibit at Rockefeller Center: "This armored automobile is more than a vehicle owned and used by the most wicked and infamous tyrant of all time. . . . Hitler and his evil henchmen had the mistaken idea that, just because you make an individual groggy with propaganda, you can knock him out. We, in a free democracy, know that the individual is unconquerable. . . . Hitler forgot that. Other tyrants should remember it." See "Hitler's Mercedes-Benz Armored Automobile," undated press release, New York Museum of Science & Industry folder, Rockefeller Center Archives, New York.

34. *Hitler's Armored Car Souvenir Book,* 3.

35. Constad, "Symbol of Hitler Glory Piques Curious 'Foes,'" 4.

36. The casualty figure is taken from American War and Military Operations Casualties: Lists and Statistics, Congressional Research Service, www.fas.org/sgp/crs/natsec/RL32492.pdf, retrieved May 7, 2015.

37. "Hitler's Auto Grosses Much for Charity," *Daily Journal-Gazette* (Mattoon, IL), October 15, 1949, 8.

38. Though sixteen million men and women would serve in World War II, that number represented only about 9 percent of the population. And while the conflict obviously restructured domestic life in manifold ways—rationing, shortages, factory jobs for women, and so on—"many areas and communities in the United States experienced relatively little direct impact of war," the historian John W. Jeffries has written, adding that many Americans suffered from "a lack of any real ideological or principled understanding of the war's purpose." John W. Jeffries, *Wartime America: The World War II Home Front* (Chicago: Ivan R. Dee, 1996), 6, 12.

39. Paul Fussell, *Wartime* (New York: Oxford University Press, 1989), 145.

40. Thomas Doherty, *Projections of War: Hollywood, American Culture, and World War II* (New York: Columbia University Press, 1999), 238.

41. George H. Roeder Jr., *The Censored War* (New Haven, CT: Yale University Press, 1993), 13, 17.

42. Doherty, *Projections of War*, 261.

43. Peter Braestrup, *Battle Lines: Report of the Twentieth Century Fund Task Force on the Military and the Media* (New York: Priority Press, 1985) 44–45.

44. Brooke Hindle, "How Much Is a Piece of the True Cross Worth?" in *Material Culture and the Study of American Life*, ed. Ian M. G. Quimby (New York: W. W. Norton, 1978) 5–7.

45. "Who Was Hitler? Kids Ask While Viewing Car," *Abilene* [TX] *Reporter-News*, December 23, 1951, 7A.

46. Wilson, *Hitler*, 1; Kershaw, *Hitler, 1936–1945*, xvii.

47. "Hitler's 'Escape Car,'" *Jewish Daily Forward*, June 29, 1948, 12.

48. The author is indebted to Professor Edward Portnoy of the Rutgers University Department of Jewish Studies for his perspective on, and assistance with, this question. E-mail correspondence with Edward Portnoy, June 24–July 1, 2015.

49. *Hitler's Armored Car Souvenir Book*, 1.

50. In the years of Hitler's ascendency, Mercedes willingly fell into lockstep with his regime. Daimler-Benz advertised in the National Socialist newspaper, and quietly made arrangements to lend or give Hitler the cars he desired. These friendly gestures to the National Socialists were presumably behind the boast that it was "helping to motorize the movement." Bellon, *Mercedes in Peace and War*, 218–19. Its reasons for doing so were foremost economic ones: Hitler's elimination of the automobile tax in 1933, his dismantling of trade unions, and building of the autobahn all meant black ink on the Mercedes books. As Hitler geared up his machinery for war, Mercedes began filling orders for everything from trucks to aircraft engines. Its military contract work from the decade of 1933 to 1943 rose from 26 percent of production to 91 percent; between 1939 and 1943, its profits more than tripled. Ibid., 220; Neil Gregor, *Daimler-Benz in the Third Reich* (New Haven, CT: Yale University Press, 1998), 85. But clearly Daimler-Benz management had ideological motivations, too. An estimated two-thirds of senior management at Daimler-Benz were members of the Nazi party. "We have no occasion to diminish the attention which we have until now afforded Herr Hitler and his friends," Daimler-Benz chairman Dr. Wilhelm Kissel said in 1932. "He will be able to rely on us in the future, as in the past." Bellon, *Mercedes in Peace and War*, 219. As labor

shortages squeezed the war-production quotas of Mercedes, the company turned increasingly to forced labor, first prisoners of war and then, as the war ground to its apocalyptic end, concentration camp inmates. "Given the lack of suitable skilled labor please supply us with 400 Jews," wrote a manager for Poland's Rzeszow engine plant in June of 1942. Gregor, *Daimler-Benz in the Third Reich*, 176, 194, 210. Mercedes plants used internees from Sachsenhausen, Ravensbrück, and Dachau on its assembly lines—mainly those in Mannheim and Genshagen—housing them in squalid barracks ringed with barbed wire, the SS terrorizing them into productivity with Walther pistols and the ever-present threat of reinternment. "Daimler-Benz's managers collaborated in the exploitation of forced foreign workers primarily because it was in the company's interests to do so," the Yale historian Neil Gregor has written. "It is a mark of the extent of the erosion of moral norms in the Third Reich that the appalling suffering of the victims was not, apparently, discussed once." Ibid., 148–49, 195, 216. While the Sindelfingen plant did use Soviet prisoners of war on its Luftwaffe assembly lines, it seems reasonably clear that no forced labor was used to build the Grosser limousines. Soviet prisoners were working on the Luftwaffe's assembly lines at Sindelfingen as early as 1941. Ibid., 182. Yet it's most unlikely that unskilled labor would have been able to build the Grosser. As the firm's marquee product, the car demanded the most experienced craftsmen Daimler-Benz employed. They built the cars by hand, and photos from the period show them doing it in white lab coats. Melin, *Mercedes Benz: The Supercharged 8-Cylinder Cars of the 1930s*, 14, 23, 27, 148–49.

51. Outsourced parts for the Grosser fleet determine the same associative guilt. Patrick Verkade, a writer and WWII researcher based in the Netherlands city of Gouda, spent fifteen years uncovering the wartime story of his grandfather, Hendrik David Hoogendoorn, whom the Nazis conscripted into forced labor in 1943. The twenty-two-year-old Hoogendoorn, a musician by training, found himself in annexed Poland, working at a glass factory called Sigla Sicherheitsglas G.m.b.H. Sigla provided the bulletproof glass that Mercedes installed in the 770K Grosser that Sgt. Joe Azara discovered, and probably provided the glass for other limousines, too. E-mail correspondence between author and Patrick Verkade, January 19, 2015 and November 8, 2015.

52. David Henderson, "Parade Car for a Madman," *Modern Man*, July 1961, 4.

53. Telephone interviews with K. H. Gibson III, January 8 and 16, 2014.

54. Ibid., January 16, 2014.

55. "He'll Use Hitler's Car to Buck Traffic in Chicago," *Brownsville* [TX] *Herald,* September 22, 1948, 12; "Hitler's 'Ghost' Car Due Here Next Month," *Chicago Daily News,* July 13, 1948, 6; Henderson, "Parade Car for a Madman," 4.

56. Heavy with 545 of the *Doria's* survivors, *Stockholm* limped back to New York, where she tied up at Pier 97, where Christopher Janus had come to retrieve his big Mercedes eight summers before. The collision had telescoped the *Stockholm's* bow section, but she'd stayed afloat. Up and down the West Side wharves, the Swedish ship took on a new name, one that some had also applied to Hitler years before: *Villain.* William H. Miller Jr., *Doomed Ships* (New York: Dover, 2006) vii.

57. Barbara D. Fox, historian, Veteran Motor Car Club of America, e-mail to author, May 4, 2015. Today, the collection's shortened name is the Larz Anderson Auto Musuem.

58. Telephone interview with K. H. Gibson III, January 8, 2014.

59. Anne Wyman, "Dream World of Old Cars," *Boston Globe,* November 10, 1963, A7.

60. "Hitler's Armored Mercedes is 'Car of the Month' at Brookline's Museum of Transportation," press release with photo, March 15, 1968, author's collection.

61. The author's letter to the museum's director, dated December 27, 2013, received no reply. For reasons unknown, Janus would claim in his memoirs that he owned the Mannerheim car for two years "before giving it to a museum in Boston." He makes no mention of Waterman. Janus, *Angel on My Shoulder,* 117. In July of 1968, *The Boston Globe* was back with another human-interest story, assuring its readers that "you can still sit in Adolph Hitler's bulletproof limousine." William A. Davis, "Where Oldest Car in World Still Runs," *Boston Globe,* July 31, 1968, 2. In August 1970, the *Globe* returned yet again. This time the paper did note the car's connection to Mannerheim but nevertheless referred to the car as "Hitler's Mercedes." Strangely enough, this account noted that "a good Yankee trade" had brought the car to America, and that Waterman was "the second American purchaser of the Mercedes." Readers would never learn the name of the first purchaser, who was of course Christopher Janus. Slade, "Auto Museum's Strange Companions," A66.

62. Melin recalls that he saw the Mercedes in Waterman's garage in 1965, though the record makes clear the car had already found a home at the

museum by that time. Even so, Waterman did hold title to the car and could, of course, have moved it anyplace he pleased. Jan Melin, e-mail message to author, May 3, 2016.

63. Vann, *Fantastic Mercedes-Benz Automobiles*, 96.

64. Melin, *Mercedes Benz: The Supercharged 8-Cylinder Cars of the 1930s*, 240.

65. Jan Melin, e-mail message to author, May 3, 2016.

7. Running Off to Canada

1. Amburr Reese, public affairs officer, U.S. Army Garrison, Aberdeen Proving Ground, e-mail to author, February 10, 2015.

2. "Azara Captures Goering's Car," *Wing Tips*, November 1, 1946, 1, carries the only mention of this plaque, which seems quite an extravagance for the U.S. Army. After all, even General George S. Patton's 1938 Cadillac staff car, currently on display at the Patton Museum in Kentucky, does not have a bronze plaque. If such a plaque existed for Azara's car, it appears not to have been with the vehicle when it arrived in Canada following the Aberdeen surplus auction of 1956.

3. "Crowds View Goering Car on Exhibition in City," 8.

4. Telephone interview with Joseph Andrew Azara and Debra Weidrick (née Azara), March 25, 2015.

5. Ibid.

6. "Goering's Cars at Auction," *New York Times*, October 19, 1956, 29. The mohair ragtop of the 770K was not bullet-resistant in any sense of the term.

7. "Rising Star Joins Sinatra," *Florence* [SC] *Morning News*, January 15, 1967, 17.

8. Nicholas A. Veronico, *Hidden Warbirds: The Epic Stories of Finding, Recovering, and Rebuilding WWII's Lost Aircraft* (Minneapolis, MN: Zenith Press, 2013) 166.

9. The gelding's name was Neon Moon. "Palomino Among Base's Surplus Auction Items," *San Bernardino County Sun* (CA), February 18, 1979, 20; "Government Auctions Virtually a Giveaway," *Standard-Speaker* (Hazleton, PA), July 14, 1989, 16.

10. "The Museum maintained a program of selection which was designed to prevent excess items from accumulating," reads the base's official history. "Only those items were kept and placed on display as were needed to show the development of foreign materiel . . . all items not required were salvaged." Kempf, *Aberdeen Proving Ground Museum, 1919–1960*, 4, 38, 70.

11. "Blue Goose" was a nickname applied to the car by the soldiers of the 101st Airborne, which captured it during the division's occupation. Brought back to the United States at the Treasury Department's request, the 540K became one of the three Nazi autos to tour the country as part of the Victory Loan Drive. At the time, this car was erroneously billed as Hitler's personal car, though there is zero evidence that Hitler ever drove it, much less owned it. Powder blue was known to be a favorite color of the flamboyant Göring. The car also carried a coat of arms—another gaudy perk that made a link to Göring logical. Finally, the portly Reichsmarschall was photographed with the car in the summer of 1939. For many years this 540K's whereabouts were a mystery, but its buyer turned out to be one George S. Tunick, an affluent businessman from Stamford, Connecticut, who paid $2,800 for the car. A photograph of Tunick sitting in the car alongside Robert L. Kessler, former head of Aberdeen Proving Ground's Property Disposal Division, appeared in newspapers in 1972. Letter from R. J. Rumble to Lee Murray, November 27, 1969, Kosche Papers, Canadian War Museum, 58A 3, box 1, folder 5. "Used Car Salesman?" *Evening Herald* (Shenandoah, PA), June 20, 1972, 12. "Goering Cars Bring $6,000," *New York Times,* October 27, 1956, 4.

12. The limousine would originally have had a blackout light atop a triangular mount in front of the grille. It appears that some sort of siren had been substituted for it after Azara requisitioned the car in Austria. When the Göring Special arrived at the Aberdeen Proving Ground in Maryland for its August 1945 overhaul, the army attached a large "flasher siren," a bullet-shaped metal fixture with a red-glass lens on the front. This apparatus made the Victory Loan Drive with the vehicle, but was damaged in an accident on June 8, 1946. See "Goering's Mercedes Automobile Recovered After Disappearance," 1. It seems likely that the army then simply removed the entire front assembly, either before or after the limousine's long period of storage. Whatever the order of events, the 770K that Rumble brought up to Toronto was missing all of its fog-lamp hardware up front, including any original pieces of the mount that may have remained. This factor not only made it more difficult for Rumble to identify the car, it also greatly reduced the odds of his restoring it accurately and, indeed, he did not. Kosche, "The Story of a Car," 9.

13. The splintered glass "lent more authenticity to the war action the car had seen," O'Connell felt. Letter from R. J. Rumble to Lee Murray, November 17, 1969, Kosche Papers, Canadian War Museum, 58A 3, box 1, folder 5.

14. The Grosser in Rumble's possession (the car he'd bought at the U.S. Army surplus auction down in Aberdeen) lacked paperwork of any kind. Rumble had no means of learning anything about the Mercedes he was restoring, including the original detailing it had sported when it was new. It's not clear if Rumble had attempted any research with the information that was still on the car: a license number in the back and a serial number on the builder's plate fixed to the car's firewall. Even if he did, there's little chance he would have learned much. Which senior Nazi had used which Grosser was not information that Daimler-Benz kept in its archives, and the company was hardly responsive to such inquiries at this time in any case. So far as license registration goes, those records were almost certainly lost in the chaos and destruction of the final, fiery days of WWII. Kosche, "The Story of a Car," 3.

15. As librarian and researcher Ludwig Kosche has proven, the Grosser limousine whose photograph Rumble found bore the license plate 1A^v148485. It was a Grosser open touring car that had picked up Hitler at Templehof after the signing of the ill-fated Nazi-Soviet nonaggression pact of 1939. Kosche, "The Story of a Car," 10, 13. Strangely enough, this was also the same car that turned up in Christopher Janus's souvenir booklet, presumably as proof of *his* car's link to Hitler, which it was not.

16. Pratte's law firm was LeTourneau, Stein, Marseille, Delisle & La Rue. At this time, he was also two years into a successful association with Canadian media tycoon Paul Desmarais. *The Canadian Who's Who,* vol. 12, 1970–1971, 973; Musée de la Gaspésie, "CHAU-TV au fil du temps," https://museedelagaspesie.wordpress.com/chau-tv-au-fil-du-temps/comment-page-1/, retrieved May 31, 2015.

17. Letter from L. F. Murray to Claude Pratte, October 29, 1969, Kosche Papers, Canadian War Museum, 58A 3, box 1, folder 5.

18. Cameron Pulsifer, "'Hitler's Car' and the Canadian War Museum: Problems of Documentation and Interpretation," *Material History Review,* no. 50 (Fall 1999), 67. Acquisition ledger notes for the Pratte car, Kosche Papers, Canadian War Museum, 58A 3, box 1, folder 5.

19. Len Carter, "A New Look at Old Wars," *Ottawa Journal,* August 26, 1967, 33.

20. At this time, the holdings of the Canadian War Museum were comparatively small, consisting mainly of artifacts culled from the aftermath of battles recent and distant—rifles, shells, trench mortars, and uniforms—

some of those dating back to the eighteenth century. The end of WWII had brought larger items including tanks and artillery pieces, but the collection still hovered around only thirty thousand artifacts, compared to the half million it cares for as of this writing. As the museum's retired staff historian Cameron Pulsifer has written about this heady period, "Inevitably, a large number of items came into the collection in this era that, while they were related to the general theme of warfare in the twentieth century, lacked that specific association with Canada's involvement in this warfare." Pulsifer, "'Hitler's Car' and the Canadian War Museum," 67.

21. *Canadian War Museum* (Ottawa: National Museums of Canada, 1973) 5.

22. Letter from L. F. Murray to W. E. Taylor, November 3, 1969, Kosche Papers, Canadian War Museum, 58A 3, box 1, folder 5.

23. The 770K itself did not arrive until September of 1970. The delay of several months was owing to the Montreal mayor Jean Drapeau's request that the Grosser be put on display at the city's *Man and His World* exhibition, an offshoot of the city's wildly popular Expo 67, which opened in 1968 and would draw twenty million people. When the Mercedes went on display, it was billed, oddly enough, as Hitler's Mercedes—even though there was less proof of that connection at the time than a connection to Göring. The exposition finally closed for good in 1981. "Expo 67, *Man and His World*," Library and Archives Canada, http://www.collectionscanada.gc.ca/05/0533 /0533020602_e.html, retrieved May 19, 2015.

24. There are discrepancies between the weight and dimensional figures given by the museum for the Göring Special and the ones supplied for the Mannerheim Mercedes via its souvenir booklet, with the Canadian War Museum's figures coming in on the shorter side. It's evident that the museum staff was not taking its 770K's bumpers into account for the length and width measurements. As for the weight, the museum's documentation clearly states nine thousand pounds while the Mannerheim souvenir booklet reads ten thousand. Granted, these were two different cars, and the thickness of the armor plate may have accounted for some of the variation. More likely, both parties were simply estimating. Catalog entry for Claude Pratte's donated Göring Mercedes, n.d., Kosche Papers, Canadian War Museum, 58A 3, box 1, folder 5. *Hitler's Armored Car Souvenir Book*, 4.

25. According to Cameron Pulsifer, retired staff historian of the Canadian War Museum, the old archives building needed its floor reinforced to hold the car. Though the museum had tanks in its collection, the floors could

never have accommodated those. "The Mercedes might have been the heaviest thing" in the building, Pulsifer said. Telephone interview with Cameron Pulsifer, September 13, 2014. In August of 2014, the author paid a visit to the old archives building, which is vacant as of this writing, the Canadian War Museum having moved across town to 1 Vimy Place in 2005. Despite the security fencing raised in the rear portion of the property, the old freight doors (one per floor) are visible—and clearly the only means by which a car as big as the Grosser could have gained entry to the building. The author's presumption that there was a freight elevator behind those doors was quickly put to rest by former curator of war art Hugh Halliday: "Freight elevator be damned—you used a crane. I have a vivid memory of Lord Dorchester's coach being hoisted to the second floor." Telephone interview with Hugh Halliday, October 3, 2014.

26. Cameron Pulsifer, "'Hitler's Car' and the Canadian War Museum," 67.
27. Cameron Pulsifer, a retired staff historian at the Canadian War Museum, believes that the staff at the nascent museum was too hasty in putting the Göring Special into the public eye. Telephone interview with Cameron Pulsifer, September 13, 2014.
28. "German Mercedes Benz," ad for Capitol Motors, *Evening News* (Harrisburg, PA), April 20, 1945, 15.
29. "Goering's Cars at Auction," 29.
30. A 1971 story in the *Ottawa Citizen* quoted a museum staff historian named John Swettenham, who told the story of how the limousine "was used by Goering for field inspections and state occasions." See "Goering Car in Canadian War Museum," *Ottawa Citizen*, January 27, 1971, 18. On their way out, visitors to the museum could also buy a postcard photo of the vehicle identifying it as having been Göring's. "Hermann Goering's Car," postcard, ca. 1971, Kosche Papers, Canadian War Museum, 58A 3, box 1, folder 4, and Kosche's photo binder, box 2, folder 15.

8. The Big Tent

1. Louise Steneck, "Hitler's Car Parks in Nyack," *Journal News* (Nyack, NY), June 28, 1971, 1.
2. The newspaper did not refer to the limousine as "Hitler's Personal armored automobile," as had been the case in 1948. See "Hitler's Armored Car Soon to Pound Chicago's Streets," *Chicago Daily Tribune*, June 26, 1948, 9. But the paper did term the car a "Mercedes-Benz commissioned and used by

Adolph Hitler for Nazi victory parades"—a rehash of Janus-era hoopla. Steneck, "Hitler's Car Parks in Nyack," 1.

3. The $30,000 price comes from a bill of sale dated August 25, 1971 between George Waterman and the Vintage Car Store. The $32,000 price appears in a bill of sale dated June 22, 1971 between the Vintage Car Store and Tom Barrett. These documents were among those that Jurist later photocopied as a courtesy to Ludwig Kosche of the Canadian War Museum when the latter was conducting his research on the Göring Special. Kosche Papers, Canadian War Museum, 58A 3, box 6, folder 17.

4. In addition to his prodigious car hunting, Jurist also devoted himself to the salvation of historic aircraft. A pilot with the Eighth Air Force during WWII, Jurist had been shot down, taken prisoner, and escaped. He'd never lost his love for flying airplanes—even dangerous ones. At the stick of a vintage De Haviland Mosquito fighter-bomber he'd bought in England, Jurist lost power over the English Channel en route to France and made an emergency landing on a remote mountain airstrip near Vigo, Spain. It so happened that Aeroclub of Vigo was, that very day, celebrating the feast of the Virgin Loretto, patron saint of pilots. After Jurist sputtered to a stop in his twin-engine plane, his brethren aviators, rejoicing to the heavens, slung a Virgin Loretto metal around his neck. Jurist never took it off. "A Wheel Dealer," *Journal News* (Nyack, NY), November 8, 1987, 12.

5. Ed Jurist had started out selling cars from a Greenwich Village carriage house in 1958. Two years later, he located a faded Cadillac dealership in Nyack and moved his business there. With plate-glass windows on South Broadway and a huge sales floor, the 1927 structure was an ideal roost for automobiles, complete with a garage and adjacent lot. Once Jurist took over, it also became the oldest continuously operating automobile showroom in the United States. Letter from Ed Jurist to Edward R. Acker, vice chairman, Village of Nyack, July 3, 1987, Local History Division, Nyack Library.

6. L. Scott Bailey, "Comments," *Automobile Quarterly*, Winter 1967, 334.

7. "A Wheel Dealer," 12; Mel Heimer, "My New York," *Kane Republican* (Kane, PA), July 10, 1968, 4; Bruce Gruber, "Vintage Car Fancier Combs the World," *Rockland County Journal-News*, November 13, 1963, 19; ". . . for Vintage Cars," uncited clip, vertical file, Local History Division, Nyack Library. The story goes that Jurist also once acquired a Rolls-Royce made of unpainted stainless steel. It had belonged to a maharaja who'd

used it to hunt tigers and wished to avoid scratches to the paint that the car would have sustained in driving through the bush. Michael Spring, "Keeping the Past Alive," *Travel & Leisure*, October 1976, E18b. The kidnapped-cat anecdote appears in Janus, *Angel on My Shoulder*, 114.

8. "... for Vintage Cars," uncited clip.

9. Telephone interview with David Wilkinson, August 26, 2014.

10. Why did Waterman decide to get rid of the car? According to Kirk Gibson, it "didn't really fit the Waterman or Gibson collections." Waterman's tastes ran more to racing cars, not five-ton limousines. Telephone interview with K. H. Gibson III, January 8, 2014.

11. "Mercedes Benz Special Car Ex Hitler," maintenance list of Ed Jurist, Kosche Papers, Canadian War Museum, 58A 3, box 6, folder 17.

12. When Jurist wrote to Waterman to obtain his signature on the bill of sale, he mentioned this gear specifically: "The tool chests and sets received with the car were incredible," he wrote. "Did you ever examine the quick detachable distributor units very closely? The parts which accompanied the car were almost as impressive as the car itself." Letter from E. A. Jurist to George H. Waterman Jr., July 8, 1971, Kosche Papers, Canadian War Museum, 58A 3, box 6, folder 17.

13. Jurist had his secretary write a letter to Barrett advising him that the tool kits and the found paperwork would be included with the car, the latter for his files. Letter from Jacqueline Moffett to Thomas W. Barrett III, June 30, 1971, Kosche Papers, Canadian War Museum, 58A 3, box 6, folder 17.

14. Letter from E. A. Jurist to Ludwig Kosche, May 11, 1981, Kosche Papers, Canadian War Museum, 58A 3, box 6, folder 17.

15. Vintage Car Store, contract of sale for the Mannerheim Mercedes, June 22, 1971, Kosche Papers, Canadian War Museum, 58A 3, box 6, folder 17.

16. Steneck, "Hitler's Car Parks in Nyack," 1.

17. Letter to Ludwig Kosche from Ed Jurist, October 14, 1982, Kosche Papers, Canadian War Museum, 58A A, box 6, folder 17.

18. In fact, Barrett paid for the car weeks before Jurist could get Waterman to sign the car over to him. The sale to Barrett was dated June 22, 1971. Jurist would not close his deal with Waterman until August 25, 1971, when Waterman signed the car over. Bills of Sale for the Mannerheim Mercedes, from files of Ed Jurist, Kosche Papers, Canadian War Museum, 58A 3, box 6, folder 17.

19. In later years, Jurist would refer to Barrett as "the Desert Fink ... plying his trade among the cacti." Letter from Ed Jurist to Ludwig Kosche,

October 1, 1985, Kosche Papers, Canadian War Museum, 58A 3, box 6, folder 17.

20. Dan J. Poshag, "The Spoils of War," *Car and Driver,* August 1973, 77.

21. Larry Edsall and Bill Goldberg, *Barrett-Jackson: The World's Greatest Collector Car Event* (Minneapolis, MN: Motorbooks, 2006) 15.

22. The first issue of *Hemmings* was four pages long; by the early 1970s it would rise above 200 pages. Its May 1973 issue set a record at 215 pages, according to publisher Terry Ehrich. John Henry, "Demand Grows for Antique, Classic Cars," *Lawton* [OK] *Constitution & Morning Press,* July 8, 1973, 42.

23. Gruber, "Vintage Car Fancier Combs the World," 19.

24. Bob Cochnar, "Vintage Cars Like Vintage Wines—They're Rare, Coveted and Costly," *Jackson* [TN] *Sun,* March 12, 1968, 17.

25. Kruse would come to term his style of auctioning cars as "old car revivals." Among his other signature lines: "When the top goes down, the price goes up," and "You have a million-dollar smile—spend some of it." See "Kruse Collector Car Auction," The Auction Network, www.youtube.com/watch ?v=WZh_fjaILHA, retrieved June 20, 2015.

26. Peter W. Frey, "A Driving Passion," *New York Times,* March 18, 1990, SMA74.

27. Sylvia Porter, "Antique Car Boom," *New Castle* [PA] *News,* July 20, 1970, 7.

28. Dave Kurtz, "King of the Auctioneers," www.kpcnews.net/special-sections /cruising1/cruising11.html, retrieved December 23, 2013. This profile has since been removed from the site, but KPC News continues to publish at http://kpcnews.com/.

29. For reasons unknown, it was reported that Barrett had owned the Mannerheim car since 1959 and had bought it for $40,000. He hadn't, and didn't. "Hitler Car Is Sold at Auction for $153,000," *New York Times,* January 8, 1973, 53.

30. "Barrett-Jackson Reaches Historic Highs for Sales, Crowds and Celebrity Appearances in Scottsdale," January 18, 2015 press release, www.barrett -jackson.com/Media/Home/Reader/barrett-jackson-reaches-historic -highs-for-sales-crowds-and-celebrity-appearances-in-scottsdale, retrieved June 20, 2015. Barrett-Jackson celebrated its forty-fifth anniversary at Scottsdale in 2016, ringing up sales of $102 million on 1,469 vehicles.

31. Paul Dean, "It's Life in the Fast Lane for a Flamboyant Car Dealer," *Los Angeles Times,* January 24, 1982, F1.

32. Asked what he recalled about Barrett, Daniel Kruse said, "He drank a lot," then added, "He was a brilliant car trader, buyer, and storyteller. He flew

all over the world, bought cars all over the world. He was the 007 of car collecting. He knew where cars were at, and I think he had a photographic memory. If he saw a car once, he could recall it all the time." Telephone interview with Daniel J. Kruse, January 7, 2014.

33. Dean, "It's Life in the Fast Lane for a Flamboyant Car Dealer," F1.

34. Ibid.

35. The Barrett-Jackson Company's own official history attests to Barrett's being "a showman, a wheeler-dealer who operated in the tradition of P. T. Barnum." Edsall and Goldberg, *Barrett-Jackson: The World's Greatest Collector Car Event*, 20.

36. Opened in 1956, the Safari was a sprawling motor hotel and convention center with swimming pools and palm trees—"12 Garden Acres of Fun and Sun"—a postage stamp of green in the endless Arizona desert. At the time of Barrett's auction, the Safari was still a Scottsdale hotspot. "The Famous Safari Resort Hotel & Convention Center," undated sales brochure, author's collection.

37. Poshag, "The Spoils of War," 77.

38. "Hitler Parade Car to Be Auctioned," *Daily Herald* (Provo, UT), December 29, 1972, 23. For its part, the Associated Press ran a photo of the limousine with the caption "The parade car used by World War II German leader Adolph Hitler will be sold at auction in Scottsdale, Ariz., Saturday." See "Hitler's Car to Be Sold," AP Wirephoto, January 5, 1972, author's collection.

39. "Hitler's Car on the Block," *Washington Post*, December 29, 1972, B2; "Hitler's Auto: Going, Going, but for What?" *Los Angeles Times*, January 2, 1973, 5.

40. The latter statement was not only false, but impossible: Had the papers checked their own morgues, they'd have discovered that Mussolini's motorcade-worthy visits to Germany had taken place in 1937 and again in 1940—two events that clearly predated the completion of a 1941 Mercedes-Benz limousine. Mussolini's state visit to Germany had taken place on September 25–29, 1937, when he rode with Hitler in a motorcade through Munich. He visited again, riding in a Grosser Mercedes, on June 18, 1940. Given that Daimler-Benz did not have the Mannerheim car completed for delivery to Berlin until November 13, 1941, that limousine could not possibly have been used for either of Mussolini's visits. Melin, *Mercedes Benz: The Supercharged 8-Cylinder Cars of the 1930s*, 27, 230.

41. Rumors about the German and Japanese consortia appeared in Tom

Miller, "Adolph's Used Cars," *Oui*, December 1973, 101. By another account, a "German contingent" was prepared to pay $200,000 for the car but had failed to register in time. "Hitler Car Owner Explains Purchase," *Lancaster New Era*, January 8, 1973, 36. The rumors about the man mortgaging his house and sending a woman to bid, along with the attendances of Hill and Drinkwater, appeared in Poshag, "The Spoils of War," 77. The rumor about the Jewish man who wanted the car blown up also appeared in the Miller and Poshag accounts.

42. "Hitler's Auto: Going, Going, but for What?" 5.
43. "Hitler Car Is Sold at Auction for $153,000," 53. Barrett had owned the Mannerheim car from June 22, 1971, until January 6, 1973.
44. Barrett settled on $125,000 as a "minimum price" for the car. If it were met, he planned to bring out a second 770K, which is exactly what wound up happening. "Hitler's Car," UPI photo caption, January 7, 1973, author's collection.
45. Poshag, "The Spoils of War," 77.
46. Ibid.
47. This was the writer Peter Vann, who also noted that the Mannerheim Mercedes had been "grandly if somewhat inaccurately, presented as the 'Führer's car.'" Vann, *Fantastic Mercedes-Benz Automobiles*, 103.
48. Miller, "Adolph's Used Cars," 101.
49. Poshag, "The Spoils of War," 77.
50. Ibid.
51. Miller, "Adolph's Used Cars," 101.
52. Telephone interview with Tom Miller, June 8, 2014.
53. Dean, "It's Life in the Fast Lane for a Flamboyant Car Dealer," F1.
54. "'Dirty Tricks' Costs Set at $110,000," *Daily Herald* (Chicago), November 1, 1973, 3.
55. According to the Bureau of Labor Statistics, in 1973, the average family income in the United States stood at $11,419.
56. Miller, "Adolph's Used Cars," 101.
57. Contacted for this book, Dean Kruse replied via an associate: "Mr. Kruse remembers that his auction company sold the car. Dean could not think of anything unique about the vehicle." E-mail to author from Robert Thomas, curator, National Military History Center and Horsepower Museum, September 5, 2014. The financial chaos caused by the 2008 recession spelled the end for Dean Kruse's once mighty classic-car empire, which came crashing down amid a tangle of legal actions that eventually led to the loss

of Kruse's auction license. Dave Kurtz, "Kruse Soared High, Crashed, Over and Over," http://kpcnews.com/features/special/kpcnews/article _cc0bd224-25ef-5976-9a1b-8d4773fde79e.html, retrieved December 23, 2013.

58. "Earl Clark purchases Adolf Hitler's 1941 Mercedes Benz at an Auction in Arizona," NBC News, aired January 6, 1973, www.nbcuniversalarchives .com/nbcuni/clip/5112499297_006.do, retrieved June 14, 2015.

59. Miller, "Adolph's Used Cars," 101.

60. Telephone interview with Tom Miller, June 8, 2014.

61. Poshag, "The Spoils of War," 77.

62. Telephone interview with Tom Miller, June 8, 2014.

63. "There's a guy coming in from Israel who wants to buy the Hitler car and blow it up," Dean Kruse said. Poshag, "The Spoils of War," 77.

64. David Larsen, "Hitler's 5-Ton Car Goes for $153,000," *Los Angeles Times*, January 7, 1973, 1.

65. Tom Miller, "Adolph's Used Cars," 101; Poshag, "The Spoils of War," 77.

66. Poshag, "The Spoils of War," 77.

67. Telephone interview with Daniel J. Kruse, January 7, 2014.

68. Telephone interview with K. H. Gibson III, January 8, 2014. Questioned about any possible backlash against the car because of its past, George Waterman's son similarly said he had "no recollection" of there having been any problems. Telephone interview with George H. Waterman III, February 8, 2014.

69. According to historian Thomas D. Fallace, "In May 1959, the *New York Times* first printed the term holocaust in reference to the Jewish persecution in its reportage of the dedication of the Yad Vashem memorial." Thomas D. Fallace, *The Emergence of Holocaust Education in American Schools* (New York: Palgrave Macmillan, 2008), 13.

70. Tim Cole, *Selling the Holocaust* (New York: Routledge, 1999), 7–8.

71. Hilberg quoted in Edward T. Linenthal, *Preserving Memory: The Struggle to Create America's Holocaust Museum* (New York: Columbia University Press, 2001) 11.

72. Poshag, "The Spoils of War," 77.

73. Miller, "Adolph's Used Cars," 101.

74. "I intended to go to $125,000 and stop," Clark later said. "But things just seemed to happen." Kelly, "$2.6 Million to Build," WHS34.

75. Miller, "Adolph's Used Cars," 101.

76. According to Murl Clark, his father "definitely thought he would get [the

car] for less than $153,000," which might have accounted for his apparent discomfort, though the modest Earl Clark was known to avoid the spotlight in general. Telephone interview with Murl Clark, January 2, 2014.

77. "Hitler Car Is Sold at Auction for $153,000," 53.
78. Miller, "Adolph's Used Cars," 101.
79. Arthur Herman, *Freedom's Forge: How American Business Produced Victory in World War II* (New York: Random House, 2013), 13.
80. "Special Topics: Cars," C.G.E. Mannerheim site.

9. Suspicions

1. Poshag, "The Spoils of War," 77.
2. "Hitler Car Is Sold at Auction for $153,000," 53.
3. "Cars Used by Rommel, Hitler to be Auctioned," *Hartford* [CT] *Courant,* December 28, 1972, 14.
4. Miller, "Adolph's Used Cars," 101.
5. "Hitler's Car," *Motor Trend,* June 1973, 88. "The guy who owned it was a real nut," Bonnie Barrett added. "He was a diehard, waiting for the Reich to come back." Poshag, "The Spoils of War," 77. The Ferrari importer's name was Luigi Chinetti. Prior to that, the car had been in the possession of a New Jersey horse breeder by the name of Van Geibig. Letter from E. A. Jurist to Ludwig Kosche, February 23, 1981, Kosche Papers, Canadian War Museum, 58A 3, box 6, folder 17.
6. Indeed, Barrett furnished no evidence whatsoever that either car had been owned or used by Hitler. "There was no presentation made of the provenance or credibility or ownership or lineage," recalls Tom Miller who, as a journalist, would naturally have been interested in seeing such documents. Telephone interview with Tom Miller, June 8, 2014. As to the identity of "Hit 2," the author defers to the exhaustive research of Ludwig Kosche, who identified this Grosser 770K as one ordered by Hitler's adjutancy on November 3, 1939. The limousine was originally intended—presumably as a gift car—for Milan Stojadinović, foreign minister of Yugoslavia, though the car instead wound up in the Reich Chancellery motor pool in Berlin. Kosche never located a single photograph or any documentary evidence that Hitler had ever used this limousine. Ludwig Kosche, "Mercedes-Benz Automobiles of the Third Reich in the United States," unpublished manuscript, 1985, 23–25, Kosche Papers, Canadian War Museum, 58A 3, box 4. In 1982, Barrett appeared in an Associated Press photo, standing in the

front passenger seat of "Hit 2" which was "on its way to Belgium and will be displayed at an automobile show in Essen, Germany." "Hitler's Chariot," AP Laserphoto, November 7, 1982, author's collection. However, Motor Show Essen '82 wanted nothing to do with Barrett's limousine, and banned it outright. In an icy statement, the event's organizers said, "the motor show . . . on no account needs a Hitler vehicle to make the show more attractive." "Hitler's Car Banned from German Motor Show," *The Jerusalem Post*, November 29, 1982, 4.

7. Miller, "Adolph's Used Cars," 101.

8. "Hitler Car Is Sold at Auction for $153,000," 53.

9. Ibid.

10. Miller, "Adolph's Used Cars," 101.

11. Ibid.

12. Berlin and Berchtesgaden are nearly 340 miles apart as the crow flies, or 460 road miles. The latter figure is a contemporary one, but the point still suffices: It was too long a trip to be practical by automobile. When he traveled significant distances inside of Germany, Hitler almost always traveled by air or by his private train, the *Führersonderzug*. Automobiles would be waiting for the last leg of the journey only. Hoffmann, *Hitler's Personal Security*, 126.

13. "Hitler Car Is Sold at Auction for $153,000," 53. As auctioneer Dean Kruse himself would later say, Barrett used the car "for chauffeuring real estate clients on tours of Arizona development properties." "Owning Hitler's Car Like Marrying Star," *Ocala Star-Banner* (FL), March 10, 1975, 10A.

14. Queried why he'd bought the second 770K limousine at the auction, Tanner twice blurted "I just like Hitler," that Hitler "fascinated" him, and that he believed "Governor Wallace spellbinds people that way," too. Poshag, "The Spoils of War," 77.

15. Tanner clarified that he was a "behind the scenes" manager for Wallace, and only in northern Alabama at that. "Hitler Car Is Sold at Auction for $153,000," 53.

16. Poshag, "The Spoils of War," 77. Tidwell returned to Alabama with the car and reportedly put it on display at the Atlanta Motor Home Show. Asked what his fellow citizens thought of his purchase, Tidwell said, "I'm sure they're all saying I'm crazy. Most people in this town say that anyway." "Hitler's Car to Be Displayed," unidentified clip, Kosche Papers, Canadian War Museum, 58A 3, box 1, folder 4.

17. Larsen, "Hitler's 5-Ton Car Goes for $153,000," 1.

18. Ludwig Kosche, the librarian sleuth who'd identify the Göring Special at the Canadian War Museum, took a later interest in the Mannerheim car. In December of 1981, his research trail led him to Ed Jurist, through whose hands the Mannerheim car had passed on its way to Tom Barrett before the 1973 Scottsdale auction. In a letter to Jurist, Kosche wryly noted the description of a cigarette lighter in the Mannerheim car, and wrote, "One would imagine that some of these well-heeled car buffs would at long last realize that Hitler did not smoke, and did not tolerate it in his presence, so that the cigar lighter is from the very beginning a give-away." Letter from Ludwig Kosche to Ed Jurist, December 12, 1981, Kosche Papers, Canadian War Museum, 58A 3, box 6, folder 17.

19. It's unclear exactly what sort of research Pakula did. Perhaps he gained access to the Daimler-Benz factory order books, though he did not reveal exactly what he discovered there. "$93,000 Hitler Auto Goes on Sale Again," *Los Angeles Times*, January 18, 1973, A15. Another source states that Pakula conferred with Mercedes expert Jan Melin before leaving for the United States. Pakula's conviction that the car wasn't Hitler's—which was, of course, correct—could well have been grounded in Melin's knowledge. Anssi and Koivulahti, *Marsalkka Mannerheimin Mercedes 770*, 45.

20. "$93,000 Hitler Auto Goes on Sale Again," A15. Clark also used the same backup that Janus had—namely, that he had a photograph of Hitler riding in the Mannerheim car. Odds are, however, that Clark was referring to the same image that Janus had used as "proof" twenty-five years earlier—one showing Hitler riding in a Grosser with a smooth hood. The Mannerheim car had ventilation slits in its hood. Another image that Clark might have had in his possession, also one that had appeared in Janus's souvenir booklet, showed Hitler riding in a 770K W150 Grosser limousine that looked very much like the car he'd bought from Tom Barrett. See photo in Kelly, "$2.6 Million to Build," WHS34. But this image was taken during a May Day rally at the Berlin Olympic Stadium, most likely in 1938. The Mannerheim car would not even be ordered until the summer of 1941.

21. John Pashdag, "Hitler's Car," *Motor Trend*, June 1973, 88.

22. Ibid.

23. As *Car and Driver* relayed the information it received from Daimler-Benz: "Some 770Ks . . . were assigned to the Reich motor pool, but none were reserved for *der Fuehrer*'s personal use." Poshag, "The Spoils of War," 77.

24. Even Jan Melin, who spent his adult life researching the supercharged eight-cylinder cars that Mercedes-Benz built in the 1930s, did not come up with an exact number of the models that were armored; he can say only "some" of the Cabriolet D and F models and "many" of the *Offener Tourenwagens*. In addition, a number of the hardtop limousines were armored, too. Melin, *Mercedes Benz: The Supercharged 8-Cylinder Cars of the 1930s*, 153. What's more, it's clear that Hitler could not have used all of these cars. It's known that Hitler did not care for the hardtop limousines. As the historian Peter Hoffmann has written, Hitler's chauffeur Kempka recalled only one of these four hardtops in the chancellery garage, and "even this was hardly ever used." Hoffmann, *Hitler's Personal Security*, 62. As far as the open touring cars go, it is certain that Hitler made no regular use of Field Marshal Mannerheim's car—the armored 770K that Christopher Janus brought to the United States. To cite another example, the armored 770K that Detroit theater owner Marty Shafer purchased in 1974 (bearing plates WL-461462) had been delivered to the Reich Chancellery but was later returned to Stuttgart. In the hundreds of photographs he examined and cataloged during the many years he spent ferreting out the old Third Reich automobiles that had appeared in the United States, Ludwig Kosche could not find a single image that showed Hitler using this car. Kosche, "Mercedes-Benz Automobiles of the Third Reich in the United States," 24–25.

25. Kosche, "The Story of a Car," 1. As Kosche has also explained at great length, the presence of the word *"Führer"* on the order form is not in itself evidence that Hitler used the car. Roughly a dozen such orders on the Daimler-Benz ledgers contain the term. The only way to be certain that Hitler made use of any particular Mercedes is to locate an image of him in it and, if possible, match up the surviving vehicle's identification numbers with the license plate number in the photo. See Kosche, "Mercedes-Benz Automobiles of the Third Reich in the United States," 27–28.

26. Kosche, "The Story of a Car," 1; Kosche, "Mercedes-Benz Automobiles of the Third Reich in the United States," 2–3.

27. Melin, *Mercedes Benz: The Supercharged 8-Cylinder Cars of the 1930s*, 26.

28. These features include such things are door handles, number of hinges, vents, and other details that will be discussed in further detail. For the sake of the Mercedes aficionado, it should be pointed out that the clunky fender styles of the 770K Cabriolet D and F models were fairly easy to spot, though that assumes a good side view often lacking in many photographs.

Since Hitler's overwhelming preference was for the open touring cars, however, for the purposes of this inquiry it is accurate to say that the W150 series 770Ks, save for small details, all looked about the same.

29. As the British automotive author Graham Robson has written, "Quite a few of these cars [the 770K Grossers] survive, and when one changes hands it is almost to be expected that it is claimed once to have belonged to Hitler or Göring!" Robson, *The Magnificent Mercedes*, 78.

30. This figure is the sum of 88 of the model W150 Grossers and 119 of the earlier W07 series. Taylor, *Supercharged Mercedes in Detail*, 113.

31. The figure of forty-four—the cars built for Administration Obersalzberg and the Reich Chancellery motor pool in Berlin between 1929 and 1942—appears in Hoffmann, *Hitler's Personal Security*, 62. The exact number of W150 Grossers used by Hitler can never be known with certainty, but these figures are as close as will likely ever be found. The total of eighty-eight 770Ks of the model W150 series (forty-six of which were open-top models) is the number given by James Taylor in his book *Supercharged Mercedes in Detail*, 195, 197. Jan Melin furnishes the same figure and probably computed it originally. Melin, *Mercedes-Benz: The Supercharged 8-Cylinder Cars of the 1930s*, 149, 153. The late Canadian War Museum librarian Ludwig Kosche, who devoted years to the study of Hitler's automobiles—and the Grosser 770K W150 in particular—has written that the Reich license plates beginning with the number "148" belonged to the Grossers meant for Hitler's use, though not exclusively his. Of the eight cars that Kosche found with that numerical prefix, all but two are open-top touring sedans. See Kosche, "The Story of a Car," 13. This number agrees with the official count from Daimler on its Web site (which states that "six cars were built for the Reich government")—at least, it did at the time the author retrieved the information on February 2, 2015. Daimler has since revised its history of the 770K, omitting that sentence. The revised page can be found here: http://media.daimler.com/marsMediaSite/instance/ko.xhtml ?oid=9361509&filename=Special-protection-vehicles-from-Mercedes-Benz -up-to-1945, retrieved July 11, 2016.

32. The byzantine underground complex of bunkers in the New Reich Chancellery included two massive garages where Kempka kept his fleet. In the early morning hours of April 24, 1945, a Soviet shell landed and collapsed the ceiling, destroying sixty cars. "As the concrete roofing caved in, everything was reduced to a chaotic tangle of twisted iron and rubble," Kempka remembered. By April 27, Kempka was able to get two vehicles to run, but

these were apparently the only survivors of the large fleet in Berlin. Kempka, *I Was Hitler's Chauffeur*, 60, 65.

33. Taylor, *Supercharged Mercedes in Detail*, 197.

34. "Search for Hitler's Missing Car Ends with Revelation Machine Has Been Stored Here Months," *Post-Standard* (Syracuse, NY), February 4, 1949, 1. The car bore license plate no. Z 96-501, though it's unclear where and when those plates were put on the car.

35. See, for example: "Hitler Car on Exhibition: Bullet-Proof Vehicle Draws Crowds in Paris," *New York Times*, December 2, 1945, 33.

36. "Hitler (in Wax) and His Car on Display in Syracuse," *Post-Standard* (Syracuse, NY), July 9, 1948, 7.

37. "Hitler's Armored Limousine to be Shown at Penndel," *Bristol Daily Courier* (Bristol, PA), October 20, 1949, 10.

38. It was said that this car had taken Hitler and Göring to Stalingrad. Hitler did visit Saporoshje (today Zaporozhye, Ukraine) on February 17, 1943, but there was zero evidence that chauffeur Erich Kempka had used this automobile there. This was the visit during which Hitler was nearly ambushed by a column of Russian tanks from Dnjepropetrovsk. Hoffmann, *Hitler's Personal Security*, 149–50.

39. By the fall of 1949, the French Pullman had toured twelve cities in the United States and was scheduled to visit Cuba. Between July 16 and 20, 1950, the car appeared at Stengers Ford in Dayton, Ohio. By August of 1950, it was in Monongahela, Pennsylvania. In 1952, it turned up in Indiana. While the car's appearances were sponsored by the American Legion, it seems worth noting that between 1949 and 1951, ads in the back pages of *Billboard* magazine listed this Mercedes—"Adolph Hitler's Genuine Personal Armored Limousine . . . World's most talked about car and Greatest Attraction"—as available for booking by Prospect Associates of Souderton, Pennsylvania. See, for example, *Billboard*, June 24, 1950, 70. The magazine writer Edward Morehouse recalls seeing a Pullman limousine advertised as Hitler's at a sideshow in the 1950s. "For a quarter, one got to view this black behemoth—in rather dingy condition—in an enclosed, dimly-lit tractor-trailer," Morehouse wrote. "I still remember the very thick glass of the side windows and a red-lensed spotlight on the driver's side. Perhaps it was genuine after all." Edward Morehouse, "Hitler's Cars: Transportation for a Dictator," *Car Collector*, December 1984, 31.

40. These "Hitler" vehicles were regarded all but interchangeably. For example, in its May 7, 1955, issue (p. 61), *Billboard* notes that Burke, the supervisor

for Gibson's Mannerheim car (referred to as Hitler's car), had hired on booker Clif Wilson "who toured one of the first Hitler cars in 1948." If that was Janus's car, the paper obviously had no idea it was speaking of the same automobile. Later, in its November 5, 1956, issue (p. 61), *Billboard* carried this tiny item: "Jim Stutz reports his Hitler Car show drew 24,756 people at the Tupelo, Miss., fair, with 6,629 of them coming in one day." The author has not been able to establish which car Stutz connected himself to. According to the Web site Sideshow World, the years immediately following WWII saw "a whole slew of Mercedes cars" appear on American midways, "several of which were billed as Hitler's personal limousine." See "Adolf Hitler's Pair of Mercedes-Benzes," http://sideshowworld.com/a/at/atsHitCar.html, retrieved April 19, 2015.

41. Curiously, the value of the Sevich car was the same amount that Christopher Janus had claimed for his own. "WOM Debuts Big, Colorful '57 Show," *Billboard*, June 10, 1957, 73, 78; "Adolf Hitler's Pair of Mercedes-Benzes," http://sideshowworld.com/a/at/atsHitCar.html, retrieved April 19, 2015.

42. "Preparing 'Mystery Car' for 500-Mile Race," *New York Times*, April 29, 1947, 38.

43. An American GI had stumbled on this Mercedes in a barn in Germany during the last days of the war. By the 1950s, the car had surfaced at a Los Angeles body shop, where it began a series of ever-gaudier facelifts that eventually left the car with the fenders of a Jaguar, swastikas adorning the hubcaps, the outsize eagle hood ornament, and a candy-apple red paint job. Other fantasies about this automobile included the belief that its engineering was thirty-five years ahead of its time, that its body was built in one piece with no seams, that it could cruise at 200 mph, and that it was worth $250,000. Joyce Manchester, "She Owns a $250,000 Car," *Ames Daily Tribune* (IA), May 25, 1973, 9.

44. This machine—one of two eventually attributed to Hitler's mistress—suffered from several obvious credibility problems, among them that Eva Braun had never owned a car, let alone the finest sports car that Mercedes-Benz had on the market. Ludwig Kosche, "The Enduring Myth: Eva Braun's Spurious 540K," *Car Collector*, July 1987, 14. Eventually, Tom Barrett got his hands on the car. Before putting it up for auction, Barrett announced that he'd give the car back to Hitler's mistress—whom Barrett apparently believed was still hiding out somewhere in the world—if Braun came to Scottsdale personally to claim the car. It was this PR stunt in particular

that led the *Los Angeles Times* to describe Barrett as a "promoter par excellence, unabashed and controversial, fringing on the vulgar." Eva Braun, dead since 1945, did not appear. But ten women called in from South America, claiming to be her. In the end, the car didn't sell. Dean, "It's Life in the Fast Lane for a Flamboyant Car Dealer," F1. Barrett was still in possession of the car in 1983, when *Life* magazine came to call for a feature about the surprising number of Americans who kept collections of Nazi memorabilia. By then, Barrett still wanted $350,000 for the spurious automobile. The story featured a two-page photograph of Barrett at the wheel of the car, driving through the desert of Scottsdale with his daughter in the front seat. "The Hitler Business," *Life*, July 1983, 83.

45. There is precious little chance that the car had anything to do with Hitler, though it may have been used by a high-ranking military official. "There are photos, which still exist from that era, that show Hitler in a Mercedes-Benz type 770," said Mercedes spokesman Adam Paige. "At the time this was the top of the line. The 320 was considered a middle-class car, and that fact alone puts the Edgewater car claim into very speculative area." Paige also noted that "used-car dealers like to bring cars in a correlation with Hitler in hope [*sic*] to get a better price for their car." James Barron, "Hitler Drove This Mercedes. Or Did He?" *New York Times*, July 8, 2012, http://cityroom.blogs.nytimes.com/2012/07/08/hitler-drove-this-mercedes-or-did-he/?_r=0, retrieved July 10, 2016.

46. Charles Sutton, "On Tour with a Mercedes," *Independent* (Long Beach, CA), November 22, 1974, 24.

47. The Rolls was, according to this piece, apparently shared by Hitler and Eva Braun. Like so many claims about automobiles owned by Hitler, this one is wholly without foundation of any kind. "Antique Car Show Set for May 12–13," *Galveston* [TX] *Daily News*, May 6, 1984, 25.

48. E-mail from Philip Hall, RREC librarian, to author, November 24, 2014.

49. The license plate on this car was WL-461462. The limousine's initial price had been reported as $165,000. See "Goering's Car Sold for $165,000," *New Castle* [PA] *News*, October 29, 1974, 22. But the Shafers themselves later said the cost had been less—most likely $81,000. Esther Billings, "Auto Chit-Chat," *Terre Haute* [IN] *Tribune*, January 4, 1976, 44.

50. Shafer built a display trailer to cart the monster machine around and reportedly made $2,000 a week doing it. "Former Nazi Auto Auctioned for $160,000," *Amarillo* [TX] *Globe-Times*, January 5, 1976, 2.

51. Jack Boettner, "Antique Cars Valued at $3 Million Go on Block," *Los Angeles Times*, January 30, 1976, OC7.

52. The car did garner a winning bid of $160,000—See "Former Nazi Auto Auctioned for $160,000"—but the unidentified buyer apparently couldn't raise the money. The Shafers tried again at the Disneyland Hotel. "Goering's Car Sold for $125,000," *Los Angeles Times*, February 3, 1976, OC2A. See also Boettner, "Antique Cars Valued at $3 Million Go on Block," OC7.

53. Given its flashy, cash-oriented theme, it's possible that this handout had been distributed when the car became part of the Imperial Palace Auto Collection, which was known to occasionally send its cars to various events. But there is no identifying information on the back or front to indicate a date or place. Nevertheless, the plate number—WL-461462—makes it clear that this was Shafer's car, originally the "Göring" car of the British. "Ten Thousand Dollars Reward" leaflet, n.d., author's collection.

54. The "Beast," unidentified clip, Kosche Papers, Canadian War Museum, 58A 3, box 2, folder 5. Prior to its residence at the casino, the car had passed through the hands of Colorado collector Bob Esbenson, the business partner of thriller writer Clive Cussler in an antique-car venture. Clive Cussler and Craig Dirgo, *Clive Cussler and Dirk Pitt Revealed* (New York: Pocket Books, 1998), 88.

55. "1943–44 Mercedes Benz," Imperial Palace Auto Collection brochure, n.d., Kosche Papers, Canadian War Museum, 58A 3, box 2, folder 5.

56. This Mercedes (plate no. WL-461462) was one of five ordered in 1942 by the Reichssicherheitsdienst, or RSD, the Reich Security Service, according to Daimler-Benz's ledgers. (The Grosser limousine that Sgt. Joe Azara discovered near Laufen was also one of the 770Ks in this order.) But here again, the order form information alone does not substantiate use by either Göring or Hitler. As Ludwig Kosche notes, while Göring was indeed sometimes driven around in a Grosser, he was personally fonder—oddly enough, given his considerable girth—of smaller Mercedes models. See Kosche, "Mercedes-Benz Automobiles of the Third Reich in the United States," 33–35.

57. It was the Imperial Palace that publicized the existence of the supposed self-destruct switch, though Shafer had known about it: "They tell me the button still works," he said. "I've got the key but I'm not about to test it." "Goering's Car Sold for $165,000," 22.

58. "1943–44 Mercedes Benz," Imperial Palace Auto Collection brochure.

59. Ludwig Kosche, "The British 'Göring,'" *Wheels and Tracks,* no. 4 (1983), 39.

60. Margaret Carroll, "From Seeds to Mercedes," *Chicago Tribune,* October 14, 1977, A5; "Like the Car? It Was Once Owned by a Little Dictator Who Only Drove it to Wars," *Danville Register* (VA), October 23, 1977, 25.

61. Larry S. Finley, "Car Buffs Hit Pay Dirt: Hitler Mercedes," *Los Angeles Times,* October 20, 1977, C2.

62. It's unclear if this $1,800 figure represented the dollar value in 1945 or in 1984, when this account was published. Morehouse, "Hitler's Cars," 28.

63. "$1 Million Price Tag on Hitler Staff Car," *Chicago Tribune,* October 6, 1977, C16. To *Chicago Daily News* reporter Larry S. Finley (see "Car Buffs Hit Pay Dirt") Ogden explained, "We sent the numbers back to Germany to see who it really belonged to. It came back that it belonged to Hitler." One presumes he meant the numbers of the car's body (200 606) and engine (189 744). Apparently, Mercedes was able to locate the original order for this car (no. 303 305), which is how Ogden and Munson were able to discover that the car had been ordered by or for *"Der Führer und Reichskanzler."* As a later newspaper article stated, "There have been other so-called Hitler cars. But the owners of this Mercedes 770-K Grosser (Grand) have factory records to prove it was made for the Nazi leader and delivered to him." "Like the Car? It Was Once Owned by a Little Dictator Who Only Drove it to Wars," 25. The problem, of course, was that the mere presence of the *"der Führer"* on the order form was not proof that Hitler had actually used the car; only that the car had been ordered for the chancellery garage. In the course of his research on the Canadian War Museum's "Göring Special," and later in articles he'd written, Ludwig Kosche took great pains to make this point. Yet this Grosser would turn out to be among the very rare cases in which Hitler's use would later be substantiated. Kosche's photographic research showed that Hitler had indeed used this car on four public occasions: motoring to the Reichstag on October 6, 1939, to deliver his infamous plea for peace speech; during a meeting with Mussolini on June 18, 1940; during Hitler's triumphant return from a defeated France on July 6, 1940; and on the occasion of another address to the Reichstag on May 4, 1941. Kosche, "Mercedes-Benz Automobiles of the Third Reich in the United States," 27–31.

64. The Imperial Palace appears to have come into possession of the Ogden/ Munson car (license plate IAᵛ148461) in May of 1983. For a fee of $1,000, Ralph Engelstad of the Imperial Palace would hire Ludwig Kosche of the

Canadian War Museum to investigate the background of the Grosser
770K—a car that, Kosche assured them off the bat, was not Himmler's, as
early accounts had claimed. Letter from Ludwig Kosche to Richard Clyne,
June 7, 1983, Kosche Papers, Canadian War Museum, 58A 3, box 6, folder
16. In writing, Engelstad made it clear that he wasn't interested in a detailed history of the car—"but only want to be sure in our minds that what
we purchased is . . . a car used by Adolph Hitler." Letter from Ralph Engelstad to Ludwig Kosche, July 8, 1983, Kosche Papers, Canadian War
Museum, 58A 3, box 6, folder 16. Kosche furnished Engelstad with a detailed account of the car's past upon his return from Germany on October
1, 1983. Kosche also secured photographs of Hitler riding in the car in
question for the Imperial Palace.

65. "Imperial Palace Auto Collection," n.d., author's collection.
66. The Imperial Palace displayed the limousine for many years, then reportedly relegated it to the basement before a brewery tycoon in Munich
purchased it and shipped it back to Germany. This car was considered
"lost" for a time following the beer mogul's death in 2008. Then, in 2009,
the car was suddenly in Moscow, purchased by an unidentified Russian
billionaire for an undisclosed price. According to published reports, the
Russian collector had hired one Michael Fröhlich, a dealer in antique
automobiles, to find the car. Fröhlich did, apparently in a garage in the German town of Bielefeld. "I was of two minds about tracking down the car of
this shit Hitler," Fröhlich told *Der Spiegel*. "Most of my relatives died in the
war and I was saved by the Americans in the Berlin airlift, they supplied
penicillin which I needed because I was suffering from tuberculosis. The vehicle disgusts me, I have to say." Still, business is business: Fröhlich brokered
the deal, which was believed to have been worth between $6 million and $15
million. David Crossland, "Nazi Cars for Sale: Russian Investor to Shell
out Millions for 'Hitler Limousine,'" *Spiegel Online*, November 23, 2009,
www.spiegel.de/international/zeitgeist/nazi-cars-for-sale-russian-investor
-to-shell-out-millions-for-hitler-limousine-a-662876.html, retrieved November 27, 2013. See also "Hitler's Mercedes Tracked Down for Russia
Billionaire," BBC News, November 23, 2009, http://news.bbc.co.uk/2/hi
/europe/8375046.stm, retrieved August 11, 2012.
67. Under Engelstad, the Imperial Palace developed quite the appetite for
Grosser 770K limousines with Nazi pasts, scouring the United States and
going so far as to travel to Germany in search of them. By the mid-1980s,
the hotel had purchased several of the huge limousines. Letters from Ralph

Engelstad to Ludwig Kosche, December 6, 1983, and April 23, 1984; letter from Richie Clyne to Ludwig Kosche, January 20, 1986, both in Kosche Papers, Canadian War Museum, 58A 3, box 6, folder 16.

68. These details appear in the complaint of case no. 88-11 of the Nevada State Gaming Control Board, cited in Jeff Burbank, *License to Steal: Nevada's Gaming Control System in the Megaresort Age* (Reno: University of Nevada Press, 2000), 59. The room also included a life-size Hitler portrait bearing the inscription TO RALPHIE FROM ADOLPH 1939. As Burbank writes, this photo "was from a vehicle broker in Phoenix, Arizona, from whom Engelstad had purchased a rare Mercedes 770K vehicle." Burbank, *License to Steal*, 71. Engelstad himself wrote, "This was sent to me as a joke. I had purchased a number of German vehicles through a broker in Phoenix. As a gag, he had a local artist paint a picture of Hitler and inscribe it 'to Ralphie from Adolph 1938 [*sic*].' I took it as a joke also." Engelstad explained this in a full-page ad he took out in a North Dakota newspaper. Ralph Engelstad, "An Open Letter to the People of Grand Forks and the State of North Dakota," *Grand Forks Herald*, October 8, 1988, 3C. Engelstad had endowed the University of North Dakota with a $5 million gift, which had made him both a local celebrity and figure of shame once the Nazi scandal broke. The name of Tom Barrett does not come up in these documents as the one who commissioned the Hitler portrait, but it appears unlikely that there was a Phoenix-based broker of Nazi-era Mercedes-Benz vehicles other than Barrett.

69. William Plummer and Linda Marx, "Learning of a Casino Owner's Birthday Parties for Hitler, Even Jaded Vegas Is Outraged," *People*, October 24, 1988, 52. The public backlash was, predictably, immediate and furious, not least because the hotel's printing shop had also allegedly produced bumper stickers that read HITLER WAS RIGHT. "Chronology of Events," *Las Vegas Review-Journal*, February 19, 1989, A14. As members of the Jewish Defense League picketed his casino, Engelstad quickly shifted into apology mode. The "war room," he tried to explain, was eventually to become part of the museum proper, hence the need for the Hitler murals and swastika banners. The parties thrown on Hitler's birthday proved harder to explain. "Every year I try to find excuses for get-togethers and I always try to give them a theme to make them more fun," Engelstad said. "I suggested one with Adolph's birthday as a theme. It wasn't meant to honor Hitler." Instead, he said, the gathering was "a silly excuse for a party. I can't tell you

how much I regret my insensitivity on this point. It was innocent, but it was very, very bad judgment and it was in very bad taste." Ralph Engelstad, "An Open Letter to the People of Grand Forks and the State of North Dakota," *Grand Forks Herald*, October 8, 1988, 3C. About the bumper stickers, Engelstad said that someone else (he did not reveal who) had "cause[d] them to be made." When he discovered them, he said, he had them destroyed. There was no law restricting Engelstad, as a private citizen, from collecting Nazi artifacts or having a party of Hitler's birthday. But as an employer and the holder of a gambling license, Engelstad had run afoul of Regulation 5.011 of the Nevada Gaming Control Board, which called for the revocation of an operator's gambling license for "failure to exercise discretion and sound judgment to prevent incidents which might reflect on the repute of the State of Nevada." Burbank, *License to Steal*, 57.

70. Burbank, *License to Steal*, 63.

71. Plummer and Marx, "Learning of a Casino Owner's Birthday Parties for Hitler," 52.

72. Ibid.

73. Some viewed the fine as excessive, while others saw it as little more than a wrist slap. Said Rabbi Mel Hecht, "The message has been sent out that if you have money in this town, you can buy your way out of trouble." Burbank, *License to Steal*, 77. Ralph Engelstad died in 2002. Caesar's Entertainment bought the Imperial Palace in 2005 for $370 million, changing its name to the Quad, and later the Linq. As late as 2000, the hotel's auto collection had a Hitler car for sale. Asking price: $25 million. For this car, a hotel official said, "I've turned down $15 million." Robert Zausner, "First It Carried Ballots; Now, a High Price Tag," *Philadelphia Inquirer*, December 14, 2000, E1.

74. "'Who Was Hitler?' Kids Ask While Viewing Car," 7A.

75. "A Hitler Mercedes Sold for $47,500 to a German," *New York Times*, August 20, 1968, 11.

76. Poshag, "The Spoils of War," 77.

77. A telephone call placed to the corporate offices of New York's Dutchess County Fair on August 3, 2015, yielded assurances that no exhibitor records from those days were available for research purposes and, further, that such an attraction would never have been at the fair. Except—with apologies to the fair's organizers—that it was. I will never forget the thickness of that glass that I pressed in between my thumb and index finger. Memories

fade, of course, and details grow inexact. But whether or not the car had ever carried Hitler, it was clearly a late-1930s Mercedes-Benz with bullet-proof windows—a hardtop, if memory serves. It seems at least plausible that this vehicle may have been one of the Grossers captured by the French and later sent to the United States. At the very least, the chronology makes it possible. In 1985, Dean Kruse tried to auction a 770K captured by the Free French Forces (the car failed to meet its minimum price and was withdrawn from sale), so it's evident that one of the French Grossers was still in the country. One account said the car was owned by a "New Jersey investor," while another attached it to one George Marks of Philadelphia, who claimed to have "two binders packed with documents and photographs tracing the car's connection with Hitler." Those papers would certainly make for interesting reading. "Hitler's Car Up for Auction," *Washington Post*, August 31, 1985, B4. "Car Auction Fails to Sell Hitler's Armored Mercedes," *Bangor* [ME] *Daily News*, September 4, 1985, 11.

10. Dutch Wonderland

1. "Lancastrian Buys Hitler's Auto for Record $153,000," 1; "Hitler's Auto En Route Here," *Intelligencer Journal* (Lancaster, PA), January 8, 1973, back page.
2. Clark explained that he'd bought Woolworth's car for "sentimental reasons." "Lancastrian Buys Hitler's Auto for Record $153,000," *Sunday News* (Lancaster, PA), January 7, 1973, 1.
3. Clark continued, "We're using an adverse figure, but the main part of it is history, regardless of what happened, and history is slipping by the wayside. You can't wipe out history, whether it's good or bad." Jeff Forster, "Hitler Car Owner Explains Purchase," 36.
4. "Lancastrian Buys Hitler's Auto for Record $153,000," 1.
5. Forster, "Hitler Car Owner Explains Purchase," 36.
6. Gil Smart, "Castle Caused a Coup," *Sunday News* (Lancaster, PA), August 2, 1998, A-1.
7. When Dutch Wonderland celebrated its thirty-fifth anniversary in 1998, Lancaster Historical Society president Jack W. W. Loose recalled, "There were a lot of people who thought Clark's idea was nutty." Smart, "Castle Caused a Coup," A-1.
8. Stephen Kopfinger, "50 Years of Fun: Dutch Wonderland Milestone," *Sunday News* (Lancaster, PA), September 1, 2013, E1.
9. The Amish take their name from Jacob Amman, a German reformer who

broke with the Mennonites. Starting in 1698, his followers began to leave Bavaria for the New World, where they settled in Lancaster County, Pennsylvania. It is commonly believed that the term "Pennsylvania Dutch"—who are not Dutch in any sense of the word—resulted from Americans mistaking *Deutsch* ("German") for Dutch.

10. Smart, "Castle Caused a Coup," A-1.

11. "Earl E. Clark, 63, dies; tourism pioneer here," *Lancaster New Era,* June 24, 1993, A1.

12. Kelly, "$2.6 Million to Build," WHS34.

13. Telephone interview with Murl Clark, January 2, 2014.

14. Telephone interview with Robert M. Pass, July 22, 2014. Today, many firms are engaged in the business of transporting collector automobiles, but in the early 1970s, Pass and his St. Louis company, Passport Transportation, had the sector all to himself. "We were the exclusive transporter of antique classic cars in the U.S.," he says. At the time he parked his trailer in Scottsdale, Pass had been trucking pricey automobiles across America for three years. Passport Transportation prospered during the years to come and, in 2000, Pass sold his business to Federal Express.

15. Ken Cooke, "Famous Hitler Car Sold for $176,000," *Intelligencer Journal* (Lancaster, PA), October 9, 1973, 1.

16. Kelly, "$2.6 Million to Build," WHS34.

17. Smart, "Castle Caused a Coup," A-1.

18. Photograph, undated but probably mid-January of 1973, courtesy of Murl Clark. The Blood Standard, or Swastika flag, was almost certainly still in the backseat because Tom Barrett had left it there. Footage of the Scottsdale auction that had aired on NBC on January 6, 1973, showed Barrett preparing the car for its entry into the auction tent, and the flag appears in the backseat. It is in the same position in the Clark family photograph. See www.nbcuniversalarchives.com/nbcuni/clip/5112499297_006.do, retrieved June 14, 2015.

19. Fran Pennock, "Classic Car Buffs Enjoy Love Affair," *Intelligencer Journal* (Lancaster, PA), October 8, 1973, 32. Though one story, laced with typesetting errors, suggested that this Lincoln may have been in the presidential motorcade when JFK was shot on November 22, 1963 ("Hitler Car to Go on Block," *Reading Eagle* [PA], October 1, 1973, 13), that is most unlikely. While there were two 1964 Lincolns in JFK's motorcade in Dallas—car no. 6, carrying Vice President and Lady Bird Johnson, and car no. 15, which served as the third congressmen's car—both were gray and the latter

was a hardtop. Another report—this one doubtless closer to the truth—said that the Lincoln had been the "last personal car used" by Kennedy. "Hitler's Car Set for Tour," *Delaware County* [PA] *Daily Times*, October 9, 1973, 2.

20. Forster, "Hitler's Car Sold for Record $176,000," 1.

21. Telephone interview with Murl Clark, January 2, 2014.

22. Earl Clark had owned the Mannerheim Mercedes for only a few days before local reporters began to question him about the car's authenticity. Shortly after returning home to Lancaster, Earl Clark told a local reporter that he would be "receiving a document in the mail outlining the vehicle's history." Forster, "Hitler Car Owner Explains Purchase," 36. No further details about this document ever surfaced. Clark would be questioned about the car's authenticity once more when Barrett's second alleged Hitler car returned to the auction block on January 17, 1973. A story that appeared the following day stated that Clark still "had no doubts that the car was authentic." See "$93,000 Hitler Auto Goes on Sale Again," A15.

23. The threatening calls and letters were "not a lot" in number, Murl Clark says, "but [they were] enough to make us uncomfortable." Telephone interview with Murl Clark, January 2, 2014.

24. Kelly, "$2.6 Million to Build," WHS34.

25. Clark never commented on the possibility, but there were those who believed that the Mannerheim Mercedes was simply a cursed car, as the seers and sorcerers who'd written to Christopher Janus had suggested. Stories of such cars were not unknown in the collecting world, though their campfire appeal greatly exceeded any evidence of actual ghosts. The Gräf & Stift double phaeton in which Archduke Franz Ferdinand fell to an assassin's bullet in Sarajevo in 1914—the spark that kindled World War I—was said to have killed no fewer than sixteen of its owners in a series of ever-odder and -gorier accidents. That the story was a complete myth, apparently concocted in 1959 by paranormal/thriller author Frank Edwards, has not impeded its popularity. See Frank Edwards, *Stranger Than Science* (Secaucus, NJ: Citadel Press, 1959), 163–66; and Mike Dash, "Curses! Archduke Franz Ferdinand and His Astounding Death Car," April 22, 2013, www .smithsonianmag.com/history/curses-archduke-franz-ferdinand-and-his -astounding-death-car-27381052/, retrieved July 17, 2015. The car remains one of the most popular artifacts in Vienna's Heeresgeschichtliches Museum. At the Vintage Car Store, Ed Jurist would always remember the Rolls-Royce Phantom IV that had belonged to the late Sultan Mahomed

Shah, Aga Khan III, hereditary imam of the world's Shia Imami Ismaili Muslims. Jurist had purchased the nineteen-foot limousine from the sultan's widow in 1961, and misfortune had followed every owner since. When the first buyer's business collapsed, Jurist took the car back and sold it again. The second buyer was dead shortly afterward. "No matter who bought it," Jurist said, "something happened to its owner." See "A Wheel Dealer," 12.

26. Telephone interview with Murl Clark, January 2, 2014.

27. The "lead car," as explained by Leo Gephart of Kruse's auction firm, is the marquee car with the necessary fame and reputation to draw enough bidders to sustain a classic car auction. Pennock, "Classic Car Buffs Enjoy Love Affair," 32.

28. The Horch drew a high bid of only $17,000, below the seller's minimum. Later, after the auction ended, Jim Southland, owner of an Atlanta firm called Classic Car Investments, Inc., bought the car from Tom Kerr of Wyckoff, New Jersey, for $20,000. Cooke, "Famous Hitler Car Sold for $176,000," 1.

29. Bonnie and Clyde's Ford had, according to press releases from Kruse Classic Auction Company, sold for $178,000 originally, a figure that the company subsequently declared erroneous. The price was $175,000, it said, making the $176,000 Pass paid for the Mannerheim Mercedes a new world record. Forster, "Hitler's Car Sold for Record $176,000," 1.

30. Cooke, "Famous Hitler Car Sold for $176,000," 1.

31. "Hitler's Parade Car on Auction Block," *Lebanon* [PA] *Daily News*, October 2, 1973, 13.

32. Clark was actually selling six cars that day, cleaning out his entire collection. In addition to the Mannerheim Mercedes, Clark had also decided to part with F. W. Woolworth's 1914 Brewster. Clark was also selling John F. Kennedy's Lincoln Continental (see note 19), a 1901 Oldsmobile (a replica car), a 1929 Rolls-Royce, and a 1942 Mercer. Pennock, "Classic Car Buffs Enjoy Love Affair," 32.

33. Forster, "Hitler's Car Sold for Record $176,000," 1.

34. To quote Barrett again: "I'm really a want creator. I'll take a car, hype it, create a want, and then sell it." Dean, "It's Life in the Fast Lane for a Flamboyant Car Dealer," F1. Exactly what Barrett was doing at the Lancaster auction, bidding on the same car he'd sold less than a year earlier, is unclear. He surely understood the value of flipping cars, but Barrett wasn't about to reveal his motives to the media. At the Scottsdale auction, when

reporters questioned Barrett as to why he decided to sell the Mannerheim car, he replied, "It's time to get a boat and maybe take a trip around the world." Larsen, "Hitler's 5-Ton Car Goes for $153,000," 1.

35. Though only 55 percent of the cars on the block wound up selling that day, Dean Kruse still considered the event a success, since this auction was the first that Dutch Wonderland had held on its property. Percentages notwithstanding, what had really made the auction a success was the sale of the 770K. Cooke, "Famous Hitler Car Sold for $176,000," 1.

36. Ibid.

37. Telephone interview with Murl Clark, January 2, 2014. Clark added that the brief and troubled tenure of the big Mercedes at Dutch Wonderland— and the auction of it in particular—had an unexpectedly positive outcome. "To be honest, we got so much free publicity for Dutch Wonderland, it was more than worth it for that price," Murl Clark says. "That wasn't the *intention*," he adds, but "we got national TV and radio, all the major networks. You can't buy that kind of advertising."

11. Stalemate in Ottawa

1. Pulsifer, "'Hitler's Car' and the Canadian War Museum," 67.

2. "Goering's Staff Car," typewritten copy of description that accompanied the Mercedes from 1970 to 1980, Kosche Papers, Canadian War Museum, 58A 3, box 2, folder 15.

3. Letter from Lee Murray to Mercedes-Benz Company, Kosche Papers, Canadian War Museum, November 18, 1969, 58A 3, box 2, folder 15.

4. Rumble continued that the car's having been issued to Göring was "substantiated by the serial number, etc.," though the vehicle's registration number would have furnished no link to the car's user, and in fact it didn't. Letter from R. J. Rumble to Lee Murray, November 27, 1969, Kosche Papers, Canadian War Museum, 58A 3, box 1, folder 5.

5. Murray made this comment to Pratte in a letter dated January 29, 1970. Pulsifer, "'Hitler's Car' and the Canadian War Museum," 67.

6. Letter from Lee Murray to Dr. J. R. Ritter, February 11, 1970, Kosche Papers, Canadian War Museum, 58A 3, box 1, folder 5.

7. Letter from Ed Jurist to Lee Murray, February 17, 1970, Kosche Papers, Canadian War Museum, 58A 3, box 2, folder 15.

8. In 1981, Jurist recalled, "I recently unearthed a letter from a Canadian who was offering to us one of these armor-plated behemoths on behalf of a man named McConnell, which we somehow or other failed to buy." Letter from

Ed Jurist to Ludwig Kosche, April 17, 1981, Kosche Papers, Canadian War Museum, 58A 3, box 6, folder 17.

9. Letter from Ed Jurist to Lee Murray, February 17, 1970, Kosche Papers, Canadian War Museum, 58A 3, box 2, folder 15.

10. In his letter to Murray of February 17, 1970, Jurist stated, "several of these cars were indeed assigned for Hitler's use." Jurist went on to mention his belief that the Mannerheim car was one of these. It's impossible to know now whether Jurist meant that Hitler *had* actually used the car or it had originally been *assigned* for his use. In any case, he was mistaken: The Mannerheim car was shown in Daimler-Benz's own ledgers as being ordered as a "gift car" for Mannerheim. However, Jurist would not have had the benefit of such specific knowledge in 1970.

11. Letter from G. E. Stamp, German Embassy, to National Museum of Man, June 12, 1970, Kosche Papers, Canadian War Museum, 58A 3, box 1, folder 5.

12. As Cameron Pulsifer has written, "A visually striking and impressive artifact, it is one that visitors to the museum tend to remember—not infrequently to the exclusion of anything else." This observation was made in 1999, but the Grosser limousine succeeded in generating a great deal of attention from its arrival onward. Pulsifer, " 'Hitler's Car' and the Canadian War Museum," 67.

13. It would take a little time for the story to appear in America, but appear it did: "Goering's Car Put on Display in Museum," *Lebanon* [PA] *Daily News*, June 10, 1971, 7.

14. The museum's materials were evidently inconsistent when it came to identifying Göring as the limousine's original owner. A 1973 booklet published by the museum stated outright that "Hermann Goering's staff car (pictured below) [was] a gift to the museum in 1970." *Canadian War Museum* (Ottawa: National Museums of Canada, 1973), 46. But, in a similar booklet issued a year later, the qualifier appears, referencing the staff car "said to have been used by Reichsmarschall Hermann Göring." D. J. Goodspeed, *Canadian War Museum* (Ottawa: Canadian War Museum, 1974), 40. In the early days, the media appeared unaware of the museum's own doubts regarding the car's provenance. In 1971 the *Ottawa Citizen* splashed the headline GOERING CAR IN CANADIAN WAR MUSEUM across the top of one of its pages, stating unequivocally that the big Mercedes "was used by Goering for field inspections and state occasions," a statement with no factual support whatsoever. "Goering Car in Canadian War Museum," 18. The

caption placed near the limousine itself does appear to have reflected the staff's uncertainty from the beginning, however, using the "said to have been used by" qualifier in the text. "Goering's Staff Car," typewritten copy of description that accompanied the Mercedes from 1970 to 1980, Kosche Papers, Canadian War Museum, 58A 3, box 2, folder 15. Yet this placard also restated a number of myths about the limousine, namely that eighteen coats of paint had been found on it, including some shades of green purportedly put there "for field inspections." Such details stemmed from Rumble's claim that he had discovered green paint—"Luftwaffe green," he said—as he'd stripped down the car. There is no evidence that he actually did, but the presumed existence of this color only fed the popular supposition that the 770K had belonged to Göring, who'd commanded the Luftwaffe. Pulsifer, "'Hitler's Car' and the Canadian War Museum," 67.

15. Pulsifer, "'Hitler's Car' and the Canadian War Museum," 67. Years later, when Kosche looked back on the original plate's being overpainted, he termed it "a most unfortunate tampering of historical evidence." Untitled typewritten statement by Ludwig Kosche ca. 1986, n.d., Kosche Papers, Canadian War Museum, 58A 3, box 1, folder 5.

16. Manning's letter continued: ". . . nor do we have any worthwhile supporting evidence for its having been painted Luftwaffe green. This legend originated with Rumble Motors in Toronto, who did the overhaul in Toronto, and they wouldn't know Luftwaffe green from Wehrmacht green." Pulsifer, "'Hitler's Car' and the Canadian War Museum," 67.

17. In apparent desperation, Murray wrote again to R. J. Rumble in 1972, asking him to furnish what proof he might have. "We haven't ourselves been able to get any substantiation of the well-established legend that it was a car that was issued to Field Marshal Goering on your assurance to us that this was so," Murray wrote. If Rumble replied, the author was unable to locate that piece of correspondence. Letter from Lee Murray to R. J. Rumble, April 14, 1972, Kosche Papers, Canadian War Museum, 58A 3, box 1, folder 5.

12. Like Marrying a Movie Star

1. "I knew the car," Pass explained. "Earl Clark was one of my customers." Telephone interview with Robert M. Pass, July 22, 2014. After the auction, Pass said to a local reporter, "I've been following this car for 10 years." Cooke, "Famous Hitler Car Sold for $176,000," 1. "I don't know if it was *10 years*," Pass told me in 2014, but it was several.

2. Telephone interview with Robert M. Pass, July 22, 2014.

3. Cooke, "Famous Hitler Car Sold for $176,000," 1.

4. "Hitler Car Fees to Go to Jews," *Charleston Daily Mail* (WV), October 10, 1973, 5. Other reports, fortunately, were possessed of more tact. Pass "plans to take the parade car, used by the man whose regime exterminated millions of Jews, on a tour of the country," said one paper. Forster, "Hitler's Car Sold for Record $176,000," 1. Another paper reported, "Two St. Louis men who purchased Adolf Hitler's touring car say they will display it around the nation to raise money for Jewish charities." "Hitler Car Sells for $176,000," *Gettysburg* [PA] *Times*, October 9, 1973, 12.

5. Telephone interview with Robert M. Pass, July 22, 2014.

6. Ibid.

7. Photo caption, *Old Cars*, December 16–31, 1973, 17.

8. John Henry, "Demand Grows for Antique, Classic Cars," *Lawton* [OK] *Constitution & Morning Press*, July 8, 1973, 42.

9. Ibid.

10. Phil Clark, "Hitler's Car Sells for $176,000," *Lebanon Daily News* (PA), October 9, 1973, 14.

11. Another spurious tidbit was that the car "has a specially stuffed seat that made [Hitler] appear taller." There was no such seat. "Hitler Car Sells for $176,000," 12.

12. Iver Peterson, "The Antiques Boom," *New York Times*, October 21, 1973, 597.

13. Ibid. This price is higher than the $32,000 that appeared on the bill of sale dated June 22, 1971, between the Vintage Car Store and Tom Barrett. Kosche Papers, Canadian War Museum, 58A 3, box 6, folder 17. The percentages given here are based on the $35,000 figure.

14. Today at least, Pass understands that the car's connection to Hitler was tenuous. "Hitler never 'owned' anything—these [cars] were all registered to the Reich," he told me. "He might have ridden in it once, that's it." The Grosser's identity as Hitler's personal automobile, Pass adds, was the hocus-pocus of Tom Barrett. "Tom was a real Barnum and Bailey–type promoter," he says. Telephone interview with Robert M. Pass, July 22, 2014.

15. Ibid.

16. Specifically, "a symbol of tyranny that few of us will ever forget." Found on "The Great Mercedes: The Story of Hitler's Armored Car," 45 record, n.d., Rob-Wal Productions, St. Louis, MO, author's collection.

17. Telephone interview with Robert M. Pass, July 22, 2014.

18. "Hitler Car on Display Here," *Chicago Tribune*, November 21, 1974, N_ A15. The auto museum was located at 3160 Skokie Valley Road and was, in fact, only ten miles north of the Chicago suburb of Skokie. Two and a half years later, Skokie—where, at the time, an estimated one in six residents were Holocaust survivors—would make national news when the National Socialist Party of America attempted to hold a march there, an event that Skokie officials used all in their municipal authority to suppress. The dispute wound up in the Supreme Court, which ultimately upheld the First Amendment right of the neo-Nazi group to march. But the scheduled event of June 25, 1978, was canceled at the last minute. See "Chronology of Events: Events Related to the Proposed Nazi March," Skokie Historical Society, http://skokiehistory.org/chrono/nazis.html, retrieved August 29, 2015.

19. Born tried his best to knit the cars together thematically by pointing out that he was displaying the cars of two of the world's greatest (if fictitious) crime fighters, along with the car belonging to "the world's authentic great criminal." See "Batmobile Overshadows Hitler's Car in Museum," 86. This account is not specific, but the odds were that the Batmobile on display was one of the three fiberglass replica cars made from customizer George Barris's original Batmobile, which he created for the TV series from a Ford Futura concept car. The Black Beauty is today part of the Petersen Automotive Museum collection in Los Angeles.

20. Pass's goal of pressing the 770K into noble service wasn't entirely lost on people. The *Chicago Tribune* remarked on the irony that "this symbol of tyranny" was "being used to raise money for charity." See "Der Fuehrer's $2.5 Million Armored Car Alive and Well?" *Chicago Tribune*, November 10, 1974, W10.

21. Telephone interview with Robert M. Pass, July 22, 2014.

22. "Batmobile Overshadows Hitler's Car in Museum," 86.

23. Telephone interview with Robert M. Pass, July 22, 2014.

24. Cooke, "Famous Hitler Car Sold for $176,000," 1.

25. "The most curious thing of all," Janus continued, "was the number of people who warned me that I couldn't keep the car because Hitler's ghost wouldn't let me. I told them I didn't believe in ghosts and anyway ghosts don't bother free men." See "Batmobile Overshadows Hitler's Car in Museum," 86.

26. Asked today if he believes that he was able to accomplish anything good by

displaying the Mannerheim car, Pass responds, "I don't think so," and adds, "We were young—thirty years old. We thought we'd do good and then sell it and make some money." Mainly, Pass remembers the fear that the car brought into his life. Telephone interview with Robert M. Pass, July 22, 2014.

27. "Adolph Hitler's Parade Car," photo by Dave Pierson, *St. Petersburg Times,* February 7, 1975, author's collection.

28. "$35,000 Loss Declared in Sale of Hitler's Car," *New York Times,* February 10, 1975, 55.

29. "Hitler's Car Sells for Less," *Hartford* [CT] *Courant,* February 16, 1975, 33.

30. "Owning Hitler's Car Like Marrying Star," 10A.

31. Ibid.

32. Telephone interview with Don Brill, August 8, 2014.

33. Ibid.

34. Marlene Lerner, "Hitler's Car—'Some Joke,'" *Wisconsin Jewish Chronicle,* February 20, 1975, 2.

35. Brill explains, "This is not a fact, but this is what I think. They shilled him [Frascona] into buying the car. There were a few guys bidding that didn't want the car. And when the hammer went down, they picked him up like he's won the World Series." Telephone interview with Don Brill, August 8, 2014.

36. Pointedly, the paper identified the Grosser 770K as one "said to have been used" by Hitler. "Hitler's Car," *Daily Tribune* (Wisconsin Rapids, WI), February 15, 1975, 1.

37. Lerner, "Hitler's Car—'Some Joke,'" 2.

38. It remains unclear if this gentleman's surname was Ward or Wars. Correspondence from the Imperial Palace, which tried to get its hands on the Mannerheim car in 1984, reference Axel Ward, as does Ludwig Kosche, in the limited research he conducted on this car. The registration certificate lists the buyer in 1980 as "Zulu Ltd. by: Axel Wars," but the "s" is very faint and possibly a misprint. Application for Arizona Certificate of Title and Registration, August 19, 1980, furnished courtesy of Bill H. Lyon.

39. In his account published in 1985, Jan Melin wrote, "A rumor in 1984 said that it had been sold to Mexico, but turned out to be untrue." Melin, *Mercedes Benz: The Supercharged 8-Cylinder Cars of the 1930s,* 240. The car may never have ventured south of the border, but there seems some basis for that rumor, wherever it came from. Maj. Gen. William Lyon, who'd purchase

the Mannerheim car in 1984, recalls that the seller was a Mexican national. Bill H. Lyon, e-mail message to author, December 12, 2014.

40. Don Brill recalls that his boss sold the limousine to Ward for about $200,000. Telephone interview with Don Brill, August 8, 2014.

13. The Sleuth

1. Pulsifer, "'Hitler's Car' and the Canadian War Museum," 67.

2. "Goering's Staff Car," press release, May 9, 1980, Kosche Papers, Canadian War Museum, 58A 3, box 2, folder 15. This press release had been issued as part of the Canadian War Museum's centennial. It not only referred to the mystery Mercedes as "Goering's Staff Car" but as a "roadster." It was neither.

3. H. W. Koch, *The Hitler Youth* (New York: Cooper Square Press, 2000), 115–16.

4. This story was related by the author and historian Hugh Halliday, who joined the curatorial staff of the Canadian War Museum in 1974 and eventually became friendly with Ludwig Kosche. "About his past I knew next to nothing," Halliday relates. "He mentioned (perhaps twice) his 'military record.'" Hugh Halliday, e-mail message to author, September 27, 2014.

5. "Some commanders refused to take on replacements offered by the young Hitler Youth soldiers. The berserk SS commanders were not ashamed to stoop so low," the German historian Jörg Friedrich has written. The ragtag civilian force, young and old, who did fight, "initially managed a ruinous resistance, but was worn away in hundreds of devastating battles in small towns and villages." Jörg Friedrich, *The Fire,* trans. Allison Brown (New York: Columbia University Press, 2006), 142.

6. Telephone interview with Cameron Pulsifer, September 13, 2014.

7. Interview with Carol Reid, Canadian War Museum, Ottawa, July 31, 2014.

8. For reasons unknown, Kosche would claim credit for having discovered this original plate, though the records make it clear that chief curator Lee F. Murray had known about the plate's discernable number since late 1969. Pulsifer, "'Hitler's Car' and the Canadian War Museum," 67.

9. Kosche, "Mercedes-Benz Automobiles of the Third Reich in the United States," 30, 34–35.

10. Letter from Ludwig Kosche to George Collins, July 27, 1980, Kosche Papers, Canadian War Museum, 58A 3, box 4, binder section "M-B 770 IA'148697."

11. "Front number plate, police registration no IA^{v}148697," notes of Ludwig Kosche, Kosche Papers, Canadian War Museum, 58A 3, box 1, folder 5.

12. Because the record of Kosche's work (comprehensive as it is) is incomplete, and because many of his accumulations bear no dates, the author has reconstructed the following account of the librarian's work based on the most logical flow of his factual discoveries, adhering to known chronology as much as possible.

13. Letter from G. E. Stamp, German Embassy, to National Museum of Man, June 12, 1970, Kosche Papers, Canadian War Museum, 58A 3, box 1, folder 5.

14. What particularly irritated Kosche was the museum's manufacturing of new license plates for the Mercedes, which read: WL-148697. As explained in Chapter 11, the museum kept the numeric portion of the license plate number still visible on the back of the limousine, but swapped out the "IA^v" prefix for "WL," meant to stand for *Wehrmacht Luftwaffe*. To complicate matters further, the ersatz plate was white-on-black, the reverse of what Berlin plates would have looked like during the war. It seems the museum manufactured this new plate to conform to the legend that the 770K was Göring's. Instead, it only clouded the research problem further—a fact that Kosche did not hesitate to point out. Memorandum from Ludwig Kosche to Lee Murray, February 21, 1980, Kosche Papers, Canadian War Museum, 58A 3, box 1, folder 5.

15. Ibid.

16. Kosche had sent General Taylor a number of photocopied images of 770K limousines, but his surviving files do not contain copies of the images that he sent. The only car that the general recalled specifically was the 540K roadster known as the "Blue Goose." This car had been one of the vehicles that the 101st shipped back to the U.S. for use in the Victory Loan Drive of 1945. The general told Kosche that he'd seen the car in 1947, at the Indianapolis Motor Speedway, when it was part of a division reunion. This was an interesting bit of ephemera, but it did not help Kosche identify the Grosser limousine at the Canadian War Museum. Letter from Maxwell D. Taylor to Ludwig Kosche, March 4, 1980, Kosche Papers, Canadian War Museum, 58A 3, box 1, folder 7.

17. Letter from Ludwig Kosche to R. J. Rumble, April 6, 1980, Kosche Papers, Canadian War Museum, 58A 3, box 4, binder section "M-B 770 IA^{v}148697."

18. By sending old photographs of various Grosser 770Ks to Rumble, Kosche

established that it was the limousine with plate no. IA-148485 that Rumble had used as a guide for fashioning the new front-end headlight assembly. Rumble also told Kosche that he had removed eighteen layers of paint (alternating black and green) from the limousine before repainting it in black. Ibid.

19. Letter from Ludwig Kosche to Richard E. Kuehne, May 4, 1980, Kosche Papers, Canadian War Museum, 58A 3, box 4, binder section "M-B 770 IAᵛ148697."

20. He'd have had to disable the museum's alarm system that protected the car, in any case. Cameron Pulsifer recalls that it was customary for museum staffers to stay late into the evening, and some even stayed overnight. It's quite probable that Kosche was one of them. Telephone interview with Cameron Pulsifer, September 13, 2014.

21. Typewritten note in Kosche's file noting engine number and bullet damage, October 7, 1980, Kosche Papers, Canadian War Museum, 58A 3, box 2, folder 15.

22. Kosche, "The Story of a Car," 1.

23. Memorandum from Ludwig Kosche to Lee Murray, February 21, 1980, Kosche Papers, Canadian War Museum, 58A 3, box 1, folder 5.

24. Letter from Jan Melin to Ludwig Kosche, June 30, 1980, Kosche Papers, Canadian War Museum, 58A 3, box 1, folder 4. Hitler would attempt to use Matsuoka's visit to convince the Japanese to attack Singapore, a move that Hitler believed would both mortally wound Great Britain and also keep the United States from joining the war. See Kershaw, *Hitler 1936–1945*, 363.

25. "Japan's Foreign Minister," *Life*, May 5, 1941, 40. The order compelling German citizens to show up along the parade route read, in part, "600,000 populace are required to form the lane from Anhalt Station to Bellevue Palace . . . Commercial and industrial enterprises will be informed as to when to give their employees time off without reduction of pay." Hoffmann, *Hitler's Personal Security*, 129.

26. Left out of this narrative are the nagging doubts that Kosche had that the license plate number he found on the car was really original. Rumble had apparently told Kosche that, at the time his men began the restoration in 1956, no such plate was on the car. Rumble, not for the first time, would turn out to be incorrect. See Letter from Ludwig Kosche to E. A. Jurist, February 1, 1981, Kosche Papers, Canadian War Museum, 58A 3, box 6, folder 17.

27. Letter from Ludwig Kosche to John J. Slomaker, August 4, 1980, Kosche Papers, Canadian War Museum, 58A 3, box 4, binder section "M-B 770 IA^{v}148697." In February of 1981, Kosche would write to R. J. Rumble, "Mr. O'Connell made exactly the right decision when he did not have the damaged glass replaced. It would have meant the destruction of evidence." Letter from Ludwig Kosche to R. J. Rumble, February 1, 1981, Kosche Papers, Canadian War Museum, 58A 3, box 4, binder section "M-B 770 IA^{v}148697."

28. *20th Armored Division in World War II* (Atlanta: Albert Love Enterprises, 1946), 157. Letter from John J. Slomaker to Ludwig Kosche, September 2, 1980, Kosche Papers, Canadian War Museum, 58A 3, box 4, binder section "M-B 770 IA^{v}148697."

29. Letter from Ed Jurist to Ludwig Kosche, April 17, 1981, Kosche Papers, Canadian War Museum, 58A 3, box 6, folder 17.

30. Janssen quoted in Gordon A. Craig, *The Germans* (New York, Meridian: 1991), 74.

31. "I think a lot of [Kosche's success with his research] was the fact that he knew the language," Reid ventures. "Having grown up in Germany, he knew how Germans liked to work. He knew their mentality, and the strict order of everything. So I think that put him in a better position than an Anglo, an Englishman." Interview with Carol Reid, Canadian War Museum, Ottawa, July 31, 2014.

32. Kosche continued, "Their archives are naturally restricted to the production end of these cars, and even there not everything may have survived the war. However, they have nothing with respect to the consumption of their products, so to speak." Letter from Ludwig Kosche to E. A. Jurist, March 8, 1981, Kosche Papers, Canadian War Museum, 58A 3, box 6, folder 17.

33. Letter from Ludwig Kosche to Joe Azara, May 6, 1981, Kosche Papers, Canadian War Museum, 58A 3, box 4, binder section "M-B 770 IA^{v}148697."

34. Letter from Ludwig Kosche to Ruth McNicholas, April 6, 1981, Kosche Papers, Canadian War Museum, 58A 3, box 4, binder section "M-B 770 IA^{v}148697."

35. Hitler used the Kroll Opera House as the German Parliament following the Reichstag fire in 1933, though the assembly was little more than a rubber stamp for his policies, since he would eliminate all political opposition. On June 22, 1941—eleven months after this image showing the Canadian War Museum's 770K was taken—Hitler would again motor to the Kroll to

declare war on the Soviet Union. Henrik Eberle and Matthias Uhl, eds., *The Hitler Book* (New York: PublicAffairs, 2006), 73.

36. In terms of chronology, this would be the last documented use of the car by Hitler. Pulsifer, "'Hitler's Car' and the Canadian War Museum," 67.

37. The *Führer* Standard would fly from the right (passenger) side when Hitler was physically in the limousine. It would appear on the driver's side on occasions of the car being used to drive a guest of Hitler's. Kosche, "The Story of a Car," 1.

38. Photo orders of April 2, 1981, Kosche Papers, Canadian War Museum, 58A 3, box 1, folder 4, and Kosche's photo binder, box 2, folder 15. As Kosche would later note, the "IA" portion of the license plate denoted a Berlin registration, and the raised "ᵛ" in red, introduced after the start of the war in 1939, indicated a civilian vehicle necessary for wartime use. As to the numerals, Kosche believed that the "148" prefix, which he subsequently discovered on eight license plates, "appear[s] to be exclusive to Hitler." Kosche also ventured that Christopher Janus "confused" the car he had purchased from the Swedes with the one that later came to the Canadian War Museum, because it was one of three W150 series 770K Grossers that shared features such as the vents in the hood and the pair of heavy door hinges. This theory fails to stand up to scrutiny, however. There's no evidence that Christopher Janus spent any time comparing the physical details of various 770K limousines or, indeed, that he was even aware of the presence of IAᵛ148697—which, in any case, would still have been known as Göring's car at the time Janus imported his Mercedes limousine in 1948. In other words, Kosche appears to have given Janus too much credit. Kosche, "The Story of a Car," 1.

39. Letter from Ludwig Kosche to Ruth McNicholas, April 6, 1981, Kosche Papers, Canadian War Museum, 58A 3, box 4, binder section "M-B 770 IAᵛ148697."

40. Through the army's Office of the Adjutant General, Kosche sent a letter he hoped would be forwarded to Brig. Gen. Cornelius N. Daly, who led Combat Command A in Europe. But the army returned his letter, explaining that no retired officer by that name was in its files. This must have been a major disappointment to Kosche, since Daly would surely have recalled the Göring Special. Kosche would later learn that Daly had died in 1974, though that did not deter him from writing still more letters in search of the general's survivors. Letter from Ludwig Kosche to USAR Components Personnel and Administration Center, November 25, 1980;

letter from Win Curran to Ludwig Kosche, December 3, 1980; letter from Ludwig Kosche to Win Curran, January 17, 1981, all in Kosche Papers, Canadian War Museum, 58A 3, box 4, binder section "M-B 770 IAᵛ148697."

41. "Goering's Auto Put on Display to Aid D.C. Victory Loan Drive," *Washington Post*, November 2, 1945, 4. While in D.C., Kosche initially went to the National Records Center in hopes of finding veterans of the Twentieth Armored Division's Combat Command A, but that trail led nowhere.

42. Letter from Ludwig Kosche to Joe Azara, April 8, 1981, Kosche Papers, Canadian War Museum, 58A 3, box 4, binder section "M-B 770 IAᵛ148697."

43. Telephone interview with Joseph Andrew Azara and Debra Weidrick (née Azara), March 25, 2015. Azara said he was suspicious of Kosche at first, but when it became obvious that the man knew what he was talking about, Azara softened. Eventually, the Azaras invited Kosche to visit their home in Brooklyn, Ohio. Kosche accepted and visited them on May 16, 1981. He borrowed some of the family's mementos of Joe Azara's service in Europe, reproduced them when he returned to Ottawa, and sent them back. Contrary to many people's memories of a gruff and unsociable Ludwig Kosche, Joseph Andrew Azara found him to be "a very pleasant gentleman."

44. Pulsifer, "'Hitler's Car' and the Canadian War Museum," 67.

45. Typewritten notes dated April 24, 1981, Kosche Papers, Canadian War Museum, 58A 3, box 2, folder 15. The Daimler-Benz ledger entry for the Canadian War Museum's car showed an original engine number of 1015000304. The number of the engine that Kosche found inside the vehicle was (and remains) 10150005.0028. This motor was similar in horsepower rating to the original, but it came from a later series that Mercedes had built for the 770Ks.

46. Kosche, "The Story of a Car," 1.

47. Telephone interview with Hugh Halliday, October 3, 2014.

48. Ibid.

49. Letter from E. A. Jurist to Ludwig Kosche, October 5, 1981, Kosche Papers, Canadian War Museum, 58A 3, box 6, folder 17.

50. Pulsifer, "'Hitler's Car' and the Canadian War Museum," 67.

51. Memorandum from Ludwig Kosche to Lee Murray, July 25, 1982, Kosche Papers, Canadian War Museum, 58A 3, box 1, folder 5.

52. It was probably for the best. While Kosche was without question a fine

academic and world-class researcher, his prose style had all the flavor of a radial tire. Kosche's own proposal had stipulated (para. 7, sec. "g") that no pesky book editor be permitted to tinker with his words: "In the event of an editor or other person(s) being appointed to handle this project, my voice must be the deciding one in the event of disputes," he proclaimed. "I know the subject, not the editor." Memorandum to Lee Murray from Ludwig Kosche, August 1, 1982, Kosche Papers, Canadian War Museum, 58A 3, box 1, folder 5.

53. "The CWM is the beneficiary of my efforts," Kosche wrote. "Therefore, it is fair for the Museum to contribute to the expenses which I had." Memorandum to B. Pothier from L. Kosche, October 23, 1983, Kosche Papers, Canadian War Museum, 58A 3, box 1, folder 5.

54. As collections specialist Carol Reid observes, "although he [Kosche] was working at the Canadian War Museum, he wasn't really a War Museum employee." Kosche reported to the National Museums of Canada, not the curator of the war museum. Reid continues, "It was the people in charge of the collections, who are doing research, who should have been doing this [researching the alleged Göring car], not the librarian." Interview with Carol Reid, Canadian War Museum, Ottawa, July 31, 2014.

55. Kosche had also argued, "No curator is expected to pay expenses for the Museum out of his own pocket. . . . Then why am I expected to do so, especially in view of the fact that [as a librarian] I am *de jure* not even part of the CWM staff." Memorandum to Lee Murray from Ludwig Kosche, September 8, 1983, Kosche Papers, Canadian War Museum, 58A 3, box 1, folder 5. Kosche soon hardened his stance, going so far as to suggest that the museum should ask "permission to use my story." It's not clear whether Kosche believed that his permission was required to use the actual article he'd written or if he considered his *findings* to be his own—an assertion, seemingly, that he owned the copyright to facts, which he did not. In any case, Kosche took no action. Notes dated April 29, 1984, Kosche Papers, Canadian War Museum, 58A 3, box 1, folder 5.

56. Untitled typewritten statement by Ludwig Kosche ca. 1986, n.d., Kosche Papers, Canadian War Museum, 58A 3, box 1, folder 5. Kosche received his definitive "no" in a memorandum from the chief curator on March 29, 1984. "I have finally received advice on the matter of some compensation for your research on the [Grosser Mercedes] artifact," Murray wrote. "Unfortunately, the reaction of the NMM [National Museum of Man] Direc-

torate has been negative." Memorandum to Ludwig Kosche from Lee Murray, March 29, 1984, Kosche Papers, Canadian War Museum, 58A 3, box 1, folder 5.

57. "Following up on our recent telephone conversation about how to 'repatriate' . . . the Mercedes 770 captured by the 20th US Armored Division, here are my thoughts," Kosche wrote to Engelstad on May 22, 1984. Kosche advised Engelstad that making a direct offer ("cash on the barrel") to the secretary general of the National Museums of Canada "might cost you more than you are willing to pay." Instead, Kosche suggested that Engelstad acquire a private collection of historic Canadian military vehicles then valued at $200,000 and in turn offer it in trade for the Hitler car. "You see, Ralph, by being able to offer such a collection to the war museum whose primary responsibility is to collect Canadian materiel in exchange for a car bereft of all <u>real</u> Canadian connection, but with genuine American content (to use museums jargon) puts you in a strong moral position." Letter to Ralph Engelstad from Ludwig Kosche, May 22, 1984, Kosche Papers, Canadian War Museum, 58A 3, box 6, folder 16. Kosche's advice was savvy—if also a possible conflict of interest—but Engelstad apparently wasn't interested in acquiring a bunch of old Canadian trucks and tanks, which he might be stuck with if the deal went south. Another problem—again, one that Kosche had counseled Engelstad on—was that a cash offer, if accepted, would have to be returned to the treasury and, hence, did not constitute an inducement for the museum. "This puts us in a very bad position as far as I am concerned," Richie Clyne, the Imperial Palace's Auto Collection administrator, wrote Kosche. Letter to Ludwig Kosche from Richie Clyne, October 31, 1984, Kosche Papers, Canadian War Museum, 58A 3, box 6, folder 16.

58. Letter from Richard Clyne to Leo Dorais, April 25, 1985, Kosche Papers, Canadian War Museum, 58A 3, box 6, folder 16. The author was unable to locate a record of Dorais's response, but whatever it was, Dorais said "*non.*" This letter pretty much concluded the matter.

59. One possible reason that the museum elected not to sell the car in 1985—though it is pure speculation—is among the reasons why it will not sell the car today: "Concern," museum historian Andrew Burtch says, "that it might be purchased by parties that would use it for purposes that were nefarious." Interview with Andrew Burtch, Canadian War Museum, July 31, 2014. Indeed, had the Imperial Palace succeeded in purchasing the

car, a spot in Engelstad's so-called "war room" might well have constituted one of the nefarious purposes that Burtch refers to.

60. "Update on Museum Mercedes," Canadian War Museum press release, September 1986, Kosche Papers, 58A 3, box 1, folder 5. Kosche's response was to nitpick the wording of the release, type out corrections, and then regale the museum with letters and phone calls.

61. Typewritten notes from Ludwig Kosche's photo binder, Kosche Papers, Canadian War Museum, 58A 3, box 2, folder 15. Letter to R. K. Malott from Darrell Williams, January 7, 1987, Kosche Papers, Canadian War Museum, 58A 3, box 7, folder 5. The two-page piece of correspondence does not mention a price, so this was probably ascertained during a subsequent telephone call. Collections curator R. K. Malott wrote Williams back, explaining that while "we would like to acquire this license plate for our vehicle our limited budget for acquisitions . . . preclude[s] us from availing ourselves of your offer." Letter from R. K. Malott to Darrell Williams, February 16, 1987, Kosche Papers, Canadian War Museum, 58A 3, box 1, folder 5.

14. The Cult of a Car

1. Telephone interview with Joseph Andrew Azara and Debra Weidrick (née Azara), March 25, 2015. The quotes herein are based on Azara's recollection.

2. Hitler could well have used the car longer than this, but the only provable period begins with the July 19, 1940, newsreel and ends with the photograph taken on March 15, 1942. Ludwig Kosche, "The Story of a Car," 1.

3. Pulsifer, "'Hitler's Car' and the Canadian War Museum," 67.

4. The placard would be changed to read: OFTEN USED BY ADOLF HITLER, THIS MAGNIFICENT GROSSER MERCEDES 7.7 L[ITER] LIMOSINE WAS "LIBERATED" FROM A SALZBURG RAILWAY SIDING BY AMERICAN TROOPS IN 1945. Canadian War Museum guide booklet (Ottawa: National Museums of Canada, 1987), 14.

5. Pulsifer, "'Hitler's Car' and the Canadian War Museum," 67.

6. Telephone interview with Cameron Pulsifer, September 13, 2014.

7. As Pulsifer phrases it, "It was noticed that there were people over the years . . . people of a certain Nazi ilk would hold it as a place where they could gather." Ibid.

8. Chris Cobb, "Dump Hitler's Car, Museum Boss Says," *Ottawa Citizen*, February 2, 2000, 1.

9. Ibid.

10. All letters to follow quoted from "Hitler's Car Helps Us Learn from History," *Ottawa Citizen*, February 4, 2000, A15.

11. "Hitler's Car to Stay Parked in Ottawa," *Ottawa Citizen*, February 8, 2000, 1. One interesting wrinkle to the story was the issue of who would purchase the car if it actually were put up for sale. From the start, Granatstein acknowledged that "we can't control who buys it," and lamented the possibility that the car would fall into "the wrong hands." Cobb, "Dump Hitler's Car, Museum Boss Says," 1. And indeed, four days into the episode, the *Ottawa Citizen* reported possible interest on the part of Las Vegas mogul Ralph Engelstad, who'd gotten into all that trouble nearly twenty years before over his alleged secret Hitler shrine inside the Imperial Palace hotel. But it's difficult to say whether Engelstad had any real interest in the car at this point—fourteen years and nine months after he'd submitted a formal offer on the car, which had been rejected. The paper said only that Engelstad's name "was mentioned as a potential buyer." Buzz Bourdon, "Hitler Car to Stay, Museum Boss Says," *Ottawa Citizen*, February 8, 2000, A8.

12. Cobb, "Dump Hitler's Car, Museum Boss Says," 1.

13. Telephone interview with Cameron Pulsifer, September 13, 2014.

14. Ibid.

15. The staging for the party rallies at Nuremberg fell to Hitler's chief architect Albert Speer. After the war, Speer composed his memoirs during his twenty-year sentence in Spandau prison. Of his stagecraft, Speer would write, "I dearly loved flags and used them wherever I could. They were a way of introducing a play of color into somber architecture. I found it a boon that the swastika flag Hitler had designed proved more amenable to these uses." Speer, *Inside the Third Reich*, 59.

16. This detail is actually best viewed from the very end of the pathway through Gallery 3, devoted to the homecoming of soldiers from WWII. An inconspicuous window in the corridor wall allows visitors to glance at the limousine's left-hand side (most of which is concealed from view when visitors first enter). Here, a crumpled and filthy swastika flag lies half buried by the fragments of brick and stone—a clear reference not only to the physical collapse of German cities, but to the parallel collapse of the National Socialist ideology. "Most people don't notice this," Carol Reid told me, referring to a curatorial touch that is a kind of reward for those who devote the many hours of attention that a visit to the Canadian War Museum

requires. Interview with Carol Reid, Canadian War Museum, Ottawa, July 30, 2014.

17. On this point, Burtch elaborates: "What we were hoping for was to provide the context without adding to sensationalism." Overuse of Hitler's *Hakenkreuz* (swastika), he added, "could be distressing for people." Interview with Andrew Burtch, Canadian War Museum, Ottawa, July 31, 2014.

18. Ibid.

19. Notes from visit, July 28, 2014, Canadian War Museum, Ottawa.

20. Notes from visit, August 1, 2014, Canadian War Museum, Ottawa.

21. Sara Matthews, "Hitler's Car as Curriculum Text: Reading Adolescents Reading History," *Journal of the Canadian Association for Curriculum Studies,* November 2, 2009, 49.

22. In his own analysis, Pulsifer seemed to conclude much the same thing. The car, he wrote, is "an uncomfortable reminder of the fascination that items associated with Hitler and the Third Reich continue to exert." For as long as the museum keeps it, it will have to manage the fact that it seeks to display the car for the proverbial "right" reasons, even as the fact of the display itself draws visitors on whom history's lessons are lost entirely. As Pulsifer puts it, "The problem for the CWM remains that of reconciling the car's undoubted visual impact and interest to visitors with the equally undoubted interpretative and pedagogical problems that its presence in the museum creates." Pulsifer, "'Hitler's Car' and the Canadian War Museum," 67.

23. It bears noting that not everyone was happy to see the museum retain possession of the Mercedes. As Halliday recalls, an appreciable number were opposed. "The anger that many expressed over its preservation was something that I observed, understood, and disagreed with," he says now. "In view of present 'political correctness,' I would disagree even more strongly today." Hugh Halliday, e-mail message to author, September 27, 2014.

24. Interview with Andrew Burtch, Canadian War Museum, Ottawa, July 31, 2014.

25. Interview with Carol Reid, Canadian War Museum, Ottawa, July 31, 2014.

26. Interview with Andrew Burtch, Canadian War Museum, Ottawa, July 31, 2014.

27. William L. Bird Jr., *Souvenir Nation* (New York: Princeton Architectural Press, 2013) 11.

28. In 1999, the CWM conservation staff photographed the car's ragtop using

an infrared camera and detected the faint outline of a star—the large white star that the 138th Ordnance Battalion had painted on the mohair just before General Daly began using the car in May of 1945. Pulsifer, "'Hitler's Car' and the Canadian War Museum," 67.

29. Interview with Andrew Burtch, Canadian War Museum, Ottawa, July 31, 2014.

15. California

1. Downtown San Diego was slowly climbing out of its doldrums in this period, but the Horton Plaza redevelopment project—a 6½-block outdoor mall rising just east of the old rink—would not open until 1985. And not until 1987 would construction of the San Diego Convention Center, located on eleven acres of unused waterfront land to the south, commence. Following Skateland's closure in 1967, the building at 211 West G Street sat vacant until 1975. It apparently enjoyed one year as the Castle of Cars, an antique automotive business, after which it sat vacant again before opening as a warehouse, doing business as J A A D, Inc. It's unclear whether this concern owned it at the time of the Lyons' visit. E-mail from Samantha Mills, assistant archivist, San Diego History Center, to author, August 31, 2015.

2. Telephone interview with Bill H. Lyon and General William Lyon, January 20, 2015.

3. Today, William Lyon Homes ranks among the biggest homebuilding concerns in the United States, having constructed some 750,000 homes in California, Arizona, Nevada, and Colorado. See "Founder," Lyon Air Museum, www.lyonairmuseum.org/founder, retrieved November 21, 2015.

4. Interview with Gen. William Lyon, Coto de Caza, California, July 14, 2015.

5. This figure, furnished by John Burgess, director of the now-defunct Briggs Cunningham Automotive Museum, is from 1986—two years after General Lyon purchased the 770K—but suffices as a snapshot of the Lyon collection at the time. Doug Brown, "Boy's Dream Becomes $26-Million Collection," *Los Angeles Times*, October 5, 1986, OC-D1.

6. Ibid.

7. Telephone interview with Bill H. Lyon and General William Lyon, January 20, 2015.

8. Ibid.

9. Ibid.

10. It seems possible that Barrett played some role in the sale of the 770K from Frascona to Ward in 1980. The application for the title and registration originated from Maricopa County, Arizona, a jurisdiction that includes Barrett's home base of Scottsdale. Application for Arizona Certificate of Title and Registration, August 19, 1980, furnished courtesy of Bill H. Lyon.

11. Sometime prior to the Lyons entering the picture, it's evident that Ralph Engelstad was interested in acquiring the Mannerheim car for his collection at the Imperial Palace in Las Vegas. Engelstad had recently acquired the 770K limousine that hardware dealers Joe Ogden and Steve Munson had pulled out of the VFW garage in Greeneville, Tennessee, and put it on public display complete with a mannequin of Hitler standing in the front seat. Clearly not sated by this gaudy spectacle, Engelstad appears to have been looking for a mate for the car. Ludwig Kosche was by this time conducting research for Engelstad, who was eager to establish the Nazi provenance of the 770K that Ogden and Munson had discovered. This was the limousine with plate no. IA^{v}148461, a plate that had enabled Kosche to establish a definitive link to Hitler. After realizing the tremendous resource that Kosche was, Engelstad had put the Canadian librarian on the trail for other Grosser limousines. This is apparently how Engelstad became aware of the Mannerheim car. Early in 1984, and probably just before the Lyons entered the picture, Kosche wrote Engelstad a letter that included the line "I hope you'll eventually have success with A. Ward." Letter from Ludwig Kosche to Ralph Engelstad, February 22, 1984, Kosche Papers, Canadian War Museum, 58A 3, box 6, folder 16. Along with an earlier letter, Kosche had also sent Engelstad a copy of the Mannerheim car's original order form. Kosche makes clear to Engelstad that the Mannerheim Mercedes had been "erroneously described as a Hitler car"—meaning that it had been a gift to Mannerheim and not a car that Hitler had used. Kosche Papers, Canadian War Museum, 58A 3, box 6, folder 16. Engelstad disappears from the picture in April of 1984, when Kosche wrote to Richie Clyne, the administrator for Engelstad's collection, "Let's hope your luck holds, and you'll manage to buy the Mannerheim car." Clearly, Engelstad never did. Letter from Ludwig Kosche to Richie Clyne, April 8, 1984, Kosche Papers, Canadian War Museum, 58A 3, box 6, folder 16.

12. Telephone interview with Bill H. Lyon and General William Lyon, January 20, 2015.

13. Richie Clyne of the Imperial Palace got his hands on a number of photo-

graphs of the Mannerheim Mercedes and the other cars inside Ward's abandoned roller rink, and these copies found their way to Ludwig Kosche, who'd been conducting research for Engelstad at the time. The descriptions of the rink and the cars inside come from these photos. Kosche Papers, Canadian War Museum, 58A 3, box 3, folder 1.

14. Kosche's papers contain a number of photographs (color as well as black-and-white) of the 770K at the rink, images that Kosche had obtained from the Imperial Palace, which had probably obtained them originally from Barrett, who was acting as a broker for Ward. The images are poorly lit and grainy, but several cars in the collection can be identified through them. Kosche Papers, Canadian War Museum, 58A 3, box 3, folder 1 and box 1, folder 4.

15. Telephone interview with Bill H. Lyon and General William Lyon, January 20, 2015; interview with Gen. William Lyon, Coto de Caza, California, July 14, 2015.

16. Poshag, "The Spoils of War," 77.

17. Dean, "It's Life in the Fast Lane for a Flamboyant Car Dealer," F1.

18. Telephone interview with Bill H. Lyon and General William Lyon, January 20, 2015.

19. Ibid.

20. "All in all," Melin wrote, "about thirty-five years have been spent researching the information that now, for the first time, is available in book form. What started out as a fascinating hobby for a boy of ten became an all-consuming interest that will last a lifetime." Melin, *Mercedes Benz: The Supercharged 8-Cylinder Cars of the 1930s*, 6.

21. Ibid., 240.

22. Ibid.

23. Ibid.

24. Telephone interview with Bill H. Lyon and General William Lyon, January 20, 2015.

25. Melin, *Mercedes Benz: The Supercharged 8-Cylinder Cars of the 1930s*, 240.

26. Bill Lyon recalls that the limousine's *Führer* Standards (reproductions to start with) were on the car at the time his father purchased it. "Even as a kid I wasn't a big fan of that," he said, and prevailed on his father to take them off—a gesture that was also historically sound, seeing as Field Marshal Mannerheim had never flown Hitler's flags on his car anyway. Telephone interview with Bill H. Lyon and General William Lyon, January 20, 2015.

27. This was the siren that Swedish brewery owner Gösta Sverdrup had transplanted from his 540K to the Mannerheim car's front bumper in 1947. Since the limousine had come to the United States, many had regarded the siren as a sinister relic of the Nazi police state—and, indeed, it looked the part. But it was not. The author is grateful for the existence of this siren, however, since its distinctive shape—and the fact that it was mounted in a slightly crooked position—allowed for the positive identification of the Mannerheim car in newspaper photos and, hence, the reconstruction of the story presented in this book.

28. Martin happily noted that the Grosser's side-mount rims were original, at least. Letter from Richard J. Martin to Jan Melin, June 23, 1994, Kosche Papers, Canadian War Museum, 58A 3, box 4, folder: "To Mr. Jan Melin."

29. The extent to which Martin was in over his head can be seen, in part, because he reached out to none other than Ludwig Kosche—the now-retired Canadian War Museum librarian who'd positively identified Joe Azara's souvenir 770K as having been Hitler's—for help in the restoration. Martin was in search of photos of the Mannerheim car and also of any leads on owners who might have 770K parts for sale. Letter from Richard J. Martin to Ludwig Kosche, May 26, 1994, Kosche Papers, Canadian War Museum, 58A 3, box 4, folder: "To Mr. Jan Melin."

30. Letter from Richard Martin to Ludwig Kosche, April 14, 1997, Kosche Papers, Canadian War Museum, 58A 3, box 7, folder 22.

31. Bill H. Lyon, e-mail to author, December 12, 2014.

32. This is an estimate. A 2000 profile of General Lyon noted that the 770K was in its third year of restoration, but photos show that Martin had had his hands on the car since at least May of 1994. Teryl Zarnow, "Works of Art on Wheels," *Orange County* [CA] *Register,* September 16, 2000, F-06.

33. Telephone interview with Bill H. Lyon and General William Lyon, January 20, 2015.

34. Letter from Richard J. Martin to Jan Melin, June 23, 1994, Kosche Papers, Canadian War Museum, 58A 3, box 4, folder: "To Mr. Jan Melin."

35. George Barris consistently failed to remember his teenage assistant's name and took to calling him "Junior" instead, which is how Conway's nickname stuck.

36. "Five Fast Questions with Hershel Conway," Motorsport online, www.motorsport.com/history/news/fast-five-questions-with-hershel-conway/, retrieved November 29, 2015.

37. "You've got to be a little bit nuts to do business with Junior," one client told *Sports Illustrated* in 1993, "but 'meticulous' is not adequate to describe what he does. There's a depth and quality to the paint; it's like looking into water." Nicholas Dawidoff, "Pssst: Paint Your Car for $75,000?" *Sports Illustrated*, November 29, 1993, 93.

38. The Mercedes took first place in the Mercedes-Benz Prewar category (Class I) at the 2014 Pebble Beach Concours d'Elegance. Kandace Hawkinson, director of Media Relations, Pebble Beach Concours d'Elegance, e-mails to author, December 15, 2015 and July 15, 2016.

39. Interview with Gen. William Lyon, Coto de Caza, California, July 14, 2015.

40. General Lyon notes that the car's previous owners "messed with it, but we brought it back." Ibid.

41. Telephone interview with Bill H. Lyon and General William Lyon, January 20, 2015.

42. Out at the John Wayne Airport in Santa Ana, General Lyon also maintains an air museum that bears his name. The museum is full of bombers and other military aircraft. It welcomes school groups, which in the General's view is the point. "We're trying to teach young people that the war was a huge sacrifice," he told me.

43. Interview with Gen. William Lyon, Coto de Caza, California, July 14, 2015.

44. Sometime before Christopher Janus's purchase of the car in 1948, one of the 770K's Swedish owners decided to keep the medical kit as a souvenir, and it did not accompany the car to the United States. Jan Melin was able to track it down on behalf of the Lyons, which is how it came to be reunited with the car. Bill H. Lyon, e-mail to author, December 12, 2014.

45. In case this point needs further evidence, the Mannerheim Mercedes didn't just carry the world's number-one most despicable man, but the man occupying the number-two slot—Heinrich Himmler, who rode in the 770K several weeks after Hitler did. Photo dated June 19, 1941, of Himmler riding in Mannerheim Mercedes, Kosche Papers, Canadian War Museum, 58A 3, box 3, folder 1.

46. Kandace Hawkinson, director of Media Relations, Pebble Beach Concours d'Elegance, e-mail to author, December 15, 2015.

47. Bill H. Lyon, e-mail to author, December 12, 2014.

48. Telephone interview with Bill H. Lyon and General William Lyon, January 20, 2015.

Epilogue

1. www.theguardian.com/world/2015/sep/13/hitler-car-exerts-grim
   -fascination, retrieved May 7, 2016.
2. John Cheever, *The Stories of John Cheever* (New York: Vintage International, 2000), vii.
3. Richard Hauswald, P.E., director of structural engineering for Burns Engineering, e-mail to author, April 30, 2016. The Department of Sanitation kept its garbage trucks on the pier until a 2005 lawsuit brought by the Friends of Hudson River Park. The trucks finally left in 2011, after which the pier was rebuilt using precast concrete pilings. No visible part of today's Pier 57, then, dates to the days of the Swedish American Line, or to the date of Christopher Janus's visit.
4. "Clinton Cove Park—Hudson River Park: Segment 7," cutsheet, MKW+ Associates, n.d., www.mkwla.com/pdf/Clinton-Cove-Park_cutsheet.pdf, retrieved May 7, 2016.

INDEX

INDEX

INDEX

INDEX

INDEX